TET!

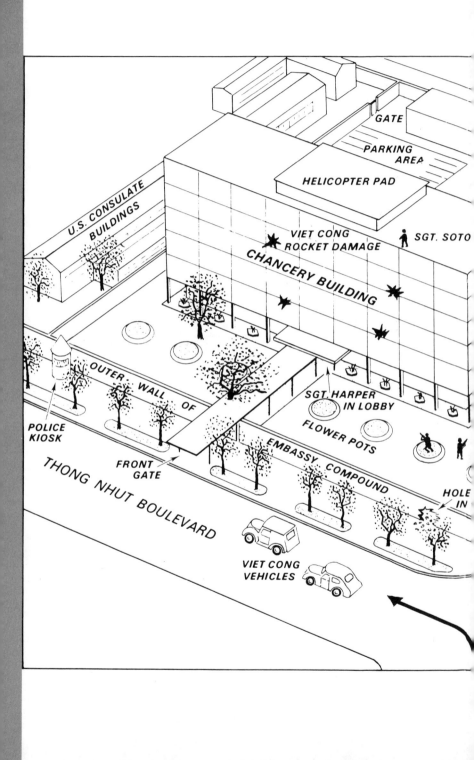

GATE

PARKING AREA

HELICOPTER PAD

U.S. CONSULATE BUILDINGS

VIET CONG ROCKET DAMAGE

SGT. SOTO

CHANCERY BUILDING

OUTER WALL OF

SGT. HARPER IN LOBBY

POLICE KIOSK

FLOWER POTS

FRONT GATE

EMBASSY COMPOUND

HOLE IN

THONG NHUT BOULEVARD

VIET CONG VEHICLES

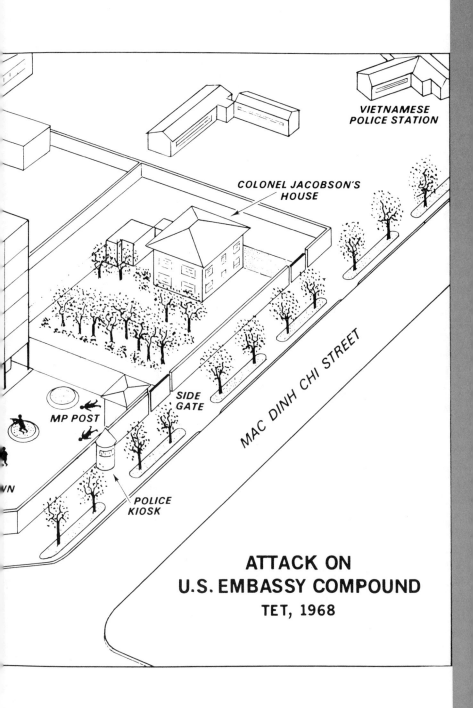

VIETNAMESE
POLICE STATION

COLONEL JACOBSON'S
HOUSE

MAC DINH CHI STREET

SIDE
GATE

MP POST

POLICE
KIOSK

VN

**ATTACK ON
U.S. EMBASSY COMPOUND**
TET, 1968

TET!

by DON OBERDORFER

New Foreword by the Author

A DA CAPO PAPERBACK

Library of Congress Cataloging in Publication Data

Oberdorfer, Don.
  Tet!

  (A Da Capo paperback)
  Reprint. Originally published: Garden City, N.Y.:
Doubleday, 1971.
  Includes bibliographical references.
  1. Tet Offensive, 1965. I. Title.
DS557.8.T4O24   1984   959.7′04′342   83-27161
ISBN 0-306-80210-4 (pbk.)

Maps by Jean Paul Tremblay

This Da Capo Press paperback edition of *Tet!* is an unabridged republication
of the edition published in New York in 1971, here supplemented with a
new foreword by the author. It is reprinted by arrangement with
Doubleday & Co. Inc.

Published by Da Capo Press, Inc.
A Subsidiary of Plenum Publishing Corporation
233 Spring Street, New York, N.Y. 10013

Manufactured in the United States of America

DEDICATION

For Those Who Died
(January 29–March 31, 1968)

3895 officers and men of the United States Army, Air Force, Navy and Marine Corps.

214 officers and men of the Republic of Korea Forces, Vietnam; the Australian Force, Vietnam; the New Zealand Army Force, Vietnam; and the Royal Thai Military Assistance Group, Vietnam.

4954 officers and men of the Republic of Vietnam Armed Forces (South Vietnam).

58,373 officers and men of the Vietnam People's Army (North Vietnam) and the South Vietnam People's Liberation Armed Forces (Viet Cong).

14,300 civilian men, women and children of South Vietnam.

And Those Who Live, and Learn

Official U.S. and South Vietnamese figures

CONTENTS

FOREWORD TO THE DA CAPO EDITION

From the perspective of the 1980s, it seems clearer than ever that the 1968 Tet Offensive was the turning point of the ill-fated U.S. Military effort in Vietnam, and thus a historic juncture in contemporary history. I sensed this at the time of the event, and asserted it in this book, originally published in 1971. What I did not grasp so clearly then was Tet's significance as the first of a series of real life Big Events abroad to be transmitted home via satellite, with powerful impact on American public attitudes and governmental decision-making. In this respect the Tet Offensive is important not only in its own right but also as the precursor of things to come. *Tet!* is an early case study of a new phenomenon of expanding dimensions.

At the time of Tet, the international system of satellite communication had recently been extended across the Pacific, but it was necessary for film to be flown from Vietnam to facilities in Japan for transmission to the United States. Since then the system has become more extensive and sophisticated; film has been supplanted by videotape or live electronic transmissions; satellites and ground stations have proliferated to the point that hardly any spot on earth is beyond their reach. Each year has brought new advances in the ability of human beings to transmit dramatic fragments of reality almost instantly from faraway places to millions of homes, businesses, and government offices. This is something new under the sun, with consequences which press, public, and government alike have been slow to comprehend.

Episodes of political drama which followed Tet include such notable Big Events as Anwar Sadat's journey to Jerusalem in 1977 and the seizure and long captivity of the American diplomatic hostages in Iran during 1979.

As in the case of the Tet Offensive, the greatest media attention and public impact concentrates during the early hours of a Big Event when its novelty is greatest and when its true significance may be unclear. Tet is a lesson that there is a danger in the rush to judgment before important pieces of the puzzle can be identified or put together.

Beyond the significance of this revolution in mass communications, the years since the first publication of *Tet!* have brought forth little that adds to what I reported at the time. The information which has emerged, while sketching in details with new documentation, has not in any major respect changed the story as I told it.

The single most important "unknown" in 1971 was the outcome of the Second Indochina War. The sudden collapse of South Vietnam in 1975 from the weight of attack from the North, the internal weakness of the Southern army, government, and society, and the progressive disengagement of the United States came as a shock, even if, in hindsight, it seems inevitable. I must admit that I did not foresee such a clear-cut ending. Nor did I have an inkling that Vietnam in the late 1970s would become the stage for the Third Indochina War between the victorious communist regimes of the region as stand-ins for the giants of international communism — the Soviet Union and China. All this has postponed the day when the bloodshed will stop and the people of Vietnam can bind up their wounds and live in peace.

—DON OBERDORFER

Washington, D.C.
November 1983

FOREWORD

This is the story of one of the great events of our time and how it came to be. It is the story of a military campaign with political impact, involving military leaders and combatants on both sides, journalists whose words and film marched into a different kind of battle, the people at home who reacted to the events and images, and the political leaders who had to deal with the consequences.

It is the story of a turning point, when people and nations swung around to new opinions and new courses. To depict the military action without its political consequences, or to depict the political action without the moving elements in the field, is to miss half the story. In the history of the Tet Offensive, a sense of relationship, of connection and disconnection in space and time, is as vital as a sense of drama.

The Tet Offensive by the Communist forces in Vietnam in early 1968 was the high point of military action in the Second Indochina War and, in all likelihood, the only battle of the war anyone will long remember. The plan of action—a simultaneous surprise attack on nearly every city, town and major military base throughout South Vietnam—was audacious in its conception and stunning in its implementation. The repercussions were on a scale to match.

On the Communist side, a large portion of the attack force was destroyed, along with a substantial portion of the hard-won prestige and power within South Vietnam of the Communist movement.

Much of the subsequent history of military and political action in the war zone flowed from what happened at Tet.

In the United States the consequences were even graver. The Tet Offensive shocked a citizenry which had been led to believe that success in Vietnam was just around the corner. Tet was the final blow to the sagging credibility of the Johnson administration and to the waning patience of the American people with this remote and inconclusive war. It became increasingly obvious that the American public and its most influential unofficial leaders would not long continue down the seemingly endless road in Asia. In a presidential election year, America had a direct way to enforce its will.

After Tet, the United States Government reexamined and then reversed its military policy, placing new limits on American participation and setting the stage for the withdrawal of American troops. President Nixon chose to continue the battle for South Vietnam, but he was able to buy time and support for his policies only by progressively reducing the level of American troop commitment, casualties and expenditures, and by promising "peace with honor" at the end of the trail.

It would be an exaggeration to maintain that the Tet Offensive alone turned a great nation around, deposed a President and brought sweeping changes in military policy. Tet was the final ingredient in a process involving many other elements—the fortunes of war, tides of public and political opinion, trends in the nature and technology of news gathering and transmission, personalities, errors and accidents of history. It was also a psychological fact, providing the public and it leaders with a rationale for abandoning earlier positions and commitments and changing their minds about the war.

I had been covering the Vietnam story as a Washington correspondent since late in 1965, and from that vantage point observed the erosion of public support for the war, particularly in the last half of 1967. On January 1, 1968, a month before the Tet Offensive, I arrived in Saigon for one of my periodic visits to the war zone, oblivious to the possibility that something spectacular was about to happen. In the weeks following the attack, I had the strong hunch that the hinge of history was turning and that things would never be the same there or in the United States. President Johnson's announcements of March 31, 1968, disclosed the direction of the historic turn and later events confirmed it.

Every political and governmental memoir of 1968 assigned an important place to the Tet Offensive, but none addressed the matter whole. I continued to be fascinated with the human dimension of the story, and I also came to see it as a classic case study in the interaction of war, politics, the press and public opinion. It seemed worthwhile to take a closer look before memories faded and participants disappeared.

Beginning with my original notes and materials from the period, I set out in the summer of 1969 to interview those who might shed additional light on these events and to collect all documents available to me. Late in 1969 the Washington *Post* generously sent me to South Vietnam for a month to report on trends and developments, knowing of my desire to learn more about Tet from sources there. The early drafts of the manuscript were written in Washington during a four-month leave of absence from the *Post* in the summer of 1970.

The list of those to whom I am indebted for information and assistance is almost as large as the scope of this book. They include many of the principal military and civilian officials and semiofficial advisers of the United States Government; junior military and civilian officers; colleagues in the Saigon and Washington press corps; Vietnamese friends and officials; historians, scholars and the invaluable man on the spot who kept his memory clear or his diary intact. Many of these people are named in the narrative and the Chapter Notes at the end. Holding many different points of view about the war and the matters covered in this volume, they contributed much to my knowledge and understanding and asked nothing but candor and fairness. I hope I have been equal to this trust. Without them, this book could not have been written. I am deeply grateful to them all.

I wish to express special gratitude to Robert Shaplen of *The New Yorker*, who made available his extensive files on the Tet Offensive; Bernard-Joseph Cabanes of Agence France-Presse, the only non-Communist correspondent resident in Hanoi during most of the period, who gave access to his dispatches and recollections; David Elliott of Cornell University, whose unexcelled studies and insight on Communist strategy and tactics made a great contribution; Donald Rochlen of the United States Information Agency, for assistance in obtaining and declassifying Viet Cong and North Vietnamese documents; Paul Vogle of *The Vietnam Guardian,* whose deep love for the city of Hue and proficiency in its dialects made possible firsthand interviews there; General William C. Westmoreland and his aide, Major Paul Miles, for assistance in understanding the Tet Offensive as seen from the command level; former Secretary of Defense Clark Clifford, for his insight into Washington decision-making; and my colleague Peter Braestrup of the Washington *Post* for access to the raw data of his Freedom House study on the press reporting of the Tet Offensive.

I also owe special debt to Jan Krause Wentworth, whose enterprise and skill at Washington research contributed so much, and who compiled the Chronology and Index; Hannah Kaiser, for research in Saigon; and John Jay Iselin and Tom Congdon, who believed in the book and brought it alive. I am particularly indebted to the Knight Newspapers, my employers in 1965–68, who sent me three times to Vietnam to cover the story; and the Washington *Post* for the late 1969 trip to Vietnam, my 1970 leave of absence and many other acts of encouragement. The hard work, advice and salami sandwiches of my wife, Laura, and the forbearance of Danny and Karen were essential.

In an effort to make this volume useful to future historians as well as enlightening to readers of today, I have listed my sources and available documentation in the Chapter Notes except for information given to me on a confidential basis. All statements of fact are buttressed by the best evidence available to me at this time.

I begin with an account of the attack on the United States Embassy in Saigon, which, although a minor battle in terms of numbers of men committed, was a shock to the American public. Chapter II describes the theory and planning of the Tet Offensive on the Viet Cong and North Vietnamese side from July 1967 to the eve of battle in late January 1968. Succeeding chapters are arranged in roughly chronological order, moving back and forth from the war front to the home front, until the climax of the narrative on March 31, 1968.

Because the action is viewed from both sides of the battle lines, I have used two sets of terminology for the Communist-directed forces. The Vietnam People's Army is what most of us know as the North Vietnamese Army. The South Vietnam People's Liberation Armed Forces is the force commonly known as the Viet Cong.

The final section of the book, "Afterword," is a statement of personal opinion on the meaning and lessons of the Tet Offensive. The first eight chapters belong to history. The afterthoughts are mine alone.

CHAPTER I

"They're Coming In!"

In Memory of
The brave men who died
January 31, 1968,
defending this embassy against
the Viet Cong

Sp4 Charles L. Daniel MPC
Cpl James C. Marshall USMC
Sp4 Owen E. Mebust MPC
Pfc William E. Sebast MPC
Sgt Jonnie B. Thomas MPC

—Plaque in the lobby of the
United States Embassy, Saigon

W<small>HEN</small> Colonel George D. Jacobson retired from the U. S. Army in 1964 after long service in Europe and Indochina, his friends presented him with a pearl-handled, silver-plated, .45-caliber service pistol. He had no use for it, and gave it away to his brother, a businessman in Minneapolis. "I'm going back to Saigon and be a civilian in the Embassy," the colonel explained. "Nobody shoots at diplomats."

He would mock that blind assurance later, but before the Lunar New Year, or Tet, of 1968, it seemed reasonable and practical. "Jake," as they called him in the Embassy, was an articulate and ebullient man with a touch of show biz in his manner—before his Army career he had been a professional master of ceremonies and a magician—and he was among the few old Indochina hands in the American entourage. He first arrived in Saigon in 1954 as special assistant to Major General John W. ("Iron Mike") O'Daniel, the chief of the first U. S. Military Assistance Advisory Group. There were 342 American military men in Indochina then, advisers and suppliers to the French, and in the months before Dien Bien Phu they labored diligently over periodic rating sheets of "French progress" in the war zone.[1]

Somehow the French defied the official progress reports and lost the war, and Jacobson spent most of the next fourteen years trying to help the United States avoid the same mistakes. He served as assistant to a succession of U.S. commanders in the war zone until his retirement from the Army, and then returned as

[1] The official emphasis on "progress" never flagged. The O'Daniel rating sheets were followed in due time by General Paul D. Harkins' regular "Headway Reports," the CINCPAC (Commander in Chief Pacific) "Measurement of Progress in Southeast Asia" and ultimately by the computerized "Hamlet Evaluation Survey."

civilian assistant to a succession of U.S. ambassadors. The ambassadors gave him the title of Mission Coordinator and set him up in residence in the old French villa at the rear of the site where the new American Embassy began rising in 1965 as if to match the rising American military presence.

The six-story American Embassy Chancery, or office building, was opened in September 1967, and it was one of the most peculiar structures in Saigon. Encased in a masonry rocket shield on all sides and topped by a jutting helicopter pad, the building resembled a giant concrete pillbox rising above the commercial buildings, houses, cathedrals and pagodas of a city almost untouched by physical signs of war. Inside the high-walled Embassy compound, just behind this cyclopean curiosity, was Jacobson's comfortable villa. It was the perfect place for a party.

For Lunar New Year's Eve of 1968, the colonel hired a Vietnamese band, stocked up on whisky, beer and soda pop, and invited 140 Vietnamese and American guests. Everybody came. The weather is pleasant in Saigon in late January, and many people stood on the Embassy lawn, drinking and chatting, the tall Americans towering over the diminutive Vietnamese men in their suits and ties and the slender, quiet women wearing the *ao dai,* the traditional long tunics and pantaloons.

Midway through the evening a loud and continuous burst of explosions erupted in the compound, causing the Americans to wince in spite of themselves and bringing grins to the lips of the Vietnamese, adherents to the Chinese popular superstition that Tet is the time for fireworks loud enough to drive away the evil spirits for another year. A twenty-three-foot string of pyrotechnics had been hung from a tree in the Embassy garden, a present to the Americans from the Vietnamese Prime Minister. If the superstition worked, Jacobson thought, the Year of the Monkey would be a very good year. It had been one of the longest, loudest and fiercest series of explosions that anyone had heard for quite a while at the American Embassy or anywhere else in the secure city of Saigon.

Twenty-four hours later, on New Year's night, fireworks could be heard in every street. For most of the people in Saigon, war itself seemed remote as the moon, though its effects could be felt in the mushrooming growth and congestion of the city, the quickening pace of daily life, the disintegration of the old and honored values. The American presence created an unparalleled affluence among those in position to benefit: businessmen, barkeeps, prostitutes, servants and taxi drivers and so on. Whether affluent or poor, nearly every family felt a powerful urge to spend and celebrate, to prove to one's self and the neighbors that the dizzying pace had not left this family behind. In many cases, wage earners pawned their possessions to celebrate Tet with a bang.

Driving through the streets in his Plymouth sedan on New Year's night, Colonel Jacobson was troubled by something in the air, something unseen, undefined and potentially ugly just beyond his grasp. He was aware of rumors and generalized warnings of Communist action—such forecasts of impending crisis were a familiar feature of the Vietnam scene—but his anxiety that night was unique. For the first time since coming to Saigon many years before, he drove alone without plan or destination through crowded streets thick with people, listening to the fireworks and keeping one ear cocked to the radio transmission on the Embassy security net. After two hours he could find nothing to justify his sense of foreboding, but it would not go away.

At midnight he wheeled up to the Embassy compound and waved to the two American military policemen at the side gate, the only one open at this hour. They raised the heavy steel bar and motioned him past. The colonel drove through the gate and parked his car beside the villa, and went inside to bed.

History was waiting in the wings. At a faded yellow automobile repair shop five blocks away, a tiny band of soldiers of the C-10 Battalion of the South Vietnam People's Liberation Armed Forces, better known as the Viet Cong, was assembling to attack. At the same moment, other men on other missions, organized in commando squads, political committees, military companies, battalions, regiments and divisions, were preparing to strike in other parts of Saigon and more than a hundred other cities and towns throughout the country.

Nationwide, about 67,000 Communist-directed troops were

committed to battle in the initial phases of the Tet Offensive. Of these, less than twenty men gathered in the Saigon auto repair shop that night to prepare to move against the Embassy. This little group, numbering three hundredths of one per cent of the total nationwide attack force, was destined to receive about three quarters of all the attention of the outside world in the first stunning hours of the Tet Offensive. An American officer called the Embassy engagement "a piddling platoon action," and in conventional military terms, it was. But in political and psychological terms, the piddling action was among the most important engagements of the war.

The importance of the Embassy as an installation was more symbolic than real. American diplomacy in Vietnam had long since been subordinated to the demands of the military effort, and the Embassy itself had little to do with the day-to-day direction of the war. At the moment of the attack it was guarded by a handful of men and presided over by a junior Foreign Service officer whose normal daytime duty was investigating the price of rice.

Nevertheless, the Embassy was the place where the Stars and Stripes was officially planted in the soil of Vietnam, and thus it was the symbolic center of the American effort. People who had never heard of Nha Trang, Qui Nhon, Bien Hoa, Ben Tre or those other unpronounceable places knew what it meant—or what they thought it meant—that the Viet Cong were attacking the heart of the American Embassy in the heart of Saigon. For once, they could say the name and summon a mind's-eye picture of the place. For many Americans at home, the Embassy attack was the first understandable battle of the war.

For the American press corps in Saigon, this was also an extraordinary event. Most of the battles erupting throughout the country were unknown to the reporters in the early hours and would have been inaccessible in any case. Word of the struggle at the Embassy, however, spread swiftly among representatives of the wire services, television and radio networks, newspapers and magazines, all of whom maintained residences, offices and transmission facilities within a few blocks of the site of action in downtown Saigon. Since the Viet Cong did not attack power stations or telephone, telegraph or cable facilities, local and international communications continued to operate normally throughout the night. For once, newsmen could observe a celebrated battle while it was still in progress, and send the report around the world without delay. Through the magic of international electronics, the news would travel at 300,000 times the speed of a bullet in flight.

On a Saigon street corner just before midnight, a wiry, muscular man named Nguyen Van Sau kept a rendezvous with an officer of the Viet Cong C-10 Battalion. Sau was a squad leader normally stationed at battalion base headquarters, which was near the Michelin Rubber Plantation only thirty miles north of the capital. He came to the site of battle the day before not as a soldier in formation, but as an ordinary civilian on the back of a commercial truck on a main highway—just one more traveling celebrant of the national festival of Tet.

Like many soldiers of the revolution, Sau had been an illiterate farmer when he was recruited for the cause. Born in a village on the outskirts of Saigon, he attended only one year of school before going to work in the rice fields. He joined the Liberation Army in 1964 during the big drive following the fall of President Diem, and was assigned to a security guard unit protecting VIPs and command posts in a largely "liberated" province between Saigon and the Cambodian border. When the C-10 Battalion was established for sapper and sabotage activities in the Saigon area in late 1965, Sau was assigned to the unit.[2] In 1966 he was promoted to squad leader and in March of 1967 he was permitted to join the People's Revolutionary Party, the Communist Party of South Vietnam.

In November of 1967—three months prior to Tet—Sau's section of the C-10 Battalion began to ship ammunition and explosives to Saigon from a supply cache at headquarters. The first shipment of ammunition and TNT moved in a rented truck piled high with

[2] The term "sapper" originated in Europe, and was traditionally applied to combat engineers. As used by the Viet Cong, the sapper is a commando-raider adept at penetrating allied defenses for sabotage or terrorism. A sapper is often a demolition expert as well as a trained combat soldier.

firewood. Three other shipments were concealed in large baskets of tomatoes which came into the city down Route 1.

Two days before Tet, big and unusually heavy baskets of "tomatoes" and large bamboo containers of "rice" were moved to a house adjoining the small automobile repair shop at 59 Phan Thanh Gian Street.[8] The house and garage were owned by Mrs. Nguyen Thi Phe, who had been working for the Viet Cong in Saigon for thirteen years and had been arrested several times for subversive activities.

Shortly after midnight on Tet night, sapper Sau and the other members of his team assembled at the garage. The shipments of weapons were broken out and distributed, and the soldiers briefed for the first time on their combat mission. It is probable that most of them, including Sau, had barely heard of the United States Embassy and had little understanding of the significance of their mission that night. Sau did not learn what he was supposed to do after penetrating the exterior wall of the Embassy compound. Nothing was said about replacements or an escape route, but there is no indication the soldiers were told this was a suicide raid.

At 2:45 A.M. they were rolling through the streets toward the Embassy in a small Peugeot truck and a taxicab. A Vietnamese policeman a block away from the Embassy saw the vehicles coming down Mac Dinh Chi Street with their lights off. He ducked into the shadows to avoid trouble.

The truck and taxi turned the corner onto Thong Nhut (Reunification) Boulevard, a broad, tree-lined avenue dominated on one side by the eight-foot outer wall of the American Embassy compound. As the taxicab rounded the corner, its passengers opened fire with automatic weapons at the two MPs standing just outside the night gate of the Embassy on the side street. The small truck stopped on the boulevard side of the high compound wall. The men, wearing neckerchiefs and arm bands for identification,

---

[8] This street—like many others in Vietnam—is named for a patriot who fought the foreigners. Phan Thanh Gian (1796–1867) was a mandarin who negotiated a treaty with the French on behalf of Emperor Thu Duc. After the French repudiated the treaty and began seizing Vietnamese territory by force, Phan Thanh Gian committed suicide. His parting command to his sons was never to collaborate with the French.

climbed out and quickly began unloading rockets and explosive charges.

Specialist Fourth Class Charles L. Daniel, twenty-three, of Durham, North Carolina, and Private First Class William E. Sebast, twenty, of Albany, New York, fired back at the taxicab, then moved inside. They slammed the steel gate and locked it with a heavy padlock and chain. At 2:47 A.M. they radioed "Signal 300"—MP brevity code for enemy attack.

A moment later an explosion rocked the compound. With a flash and a blast, a fifteen-pound explosive charge blew a three-foot hole in the high wall of the compound near the corner where the truck had stopped.

Daniel and Sebast wheeled around and began firing at the invaders scrambling through the hole. Daniel shouted into the MP radio: "They're coming in! They're coming in! Help me! Help me!" Then the radio went dead. Daniel's body was found later with bullet wounds in the head; Sebast had been shot through the chest. From the positions of their bodies and the bullet holes in the wall behind them, it appeared they were facing the invaders when they died. It is likely that their first shots killed the two Viet Cong leaders, the first men through the hole in the wall.

A Military Police jeep patrol cruising several blocks away heard the call for help and responded immediately. Sergeant Jonnie B. Thomas, twenty-four, of Detroit, and Specialist Fourth Class Owen E. Mebust, twenty, of Lynwood, California, sped down the boulevard toward the Embassy. They were met by a hail of automatic weapons fire. Thomas and Mebust were the third and fourth Americans to be killed at the Embassy in the first five minutes.

The Defense

When the Viet Cong sappers struck, 492,000 American soldiers, sailors and airmen were stationed in South Vietnam to assist 626,000 Republic of Vietnam government troops and 61,000 South Koreans, Thais and others of the "free world military assistance forces." For months there had been growing signs of highly unusual Viet Cong and North Vietnamese movements and the previous night several cities far to the north of Saigon had been attacked by the Viet Cong in violation of the Tet cease-fire. As a result the Tet truce had been canceled the morning before the Embassy attack and U.S. forces throughout the country placed on "maximum alert" by the Military Assistance Command, Vietnam (MACV), General Westmoreland's headquarters. The alert order directed particular attention to the defense of "headquarters complexes, logistical installations, airfields, population centers and billets." It did not cause great alarm, because alerts had become routine.

Extremely little of the massive American military power was concentrated on the defense of Saigon or the American Embassy near its heart. Six weeks earlier, on December 15, the United States Command had officially turned over full responsibility for the defense of the capital city to the South Vietnamese government armed forces. This was an act of confidence in the Vietnamese military, a sign that it had come of age. Inside the city, U.S. military forces were responsible only for defending themselves and their own installations.

Security for the American Embassy was organized in three separate echelons, or lines of defense.

Outside the outer wall of the large compound, security was in the hands of the host country, in this case the South Vietnamese police. This is the traditional arrangement for the protection of diplomatic posts of all countries throughout the world.

To provide outer-ring defense, four Vietnamese policemen were on duty outside the American Embassy the night of the attack. When the shooting began:

— Officer Number One, stationed near the side gate, hid behind a concrete kiosk and remained there until morning. He was considered mentally unstable, and thus had been given no weapon.

— Officer Number Two, on duty in front of the compound, was asleep. After the action roused him, he fled to the First Precinct station house a block away.

— Officer Number Three, also in the front (where the sappers blew the hole in the wall), melted into the shadows and out of the way. He identified himself to American MPs in a safer moment later in the day.

— Officer Number Four, the chief of the four-man shift, fled to his headquarters, the First Precinct station house.

The next line of defense was the eight-foot-high perimeter wall, easily breached by the Viet Cong sappers with their explosive charge. The two U. S. Army Military Policemen stationed at the only open gate locked it securely just before they were shot by the infiltrators.

The area inside the wall was American diplomatic property, and protected by a U. S. Marine Security Guard detachment under a worldwide agreement between the Department of State and the Department of Defense. In January 1968 the eighty-five-man Marine Security Guard detachment in Saigon was the largest in the world. Supervised by the Embassy security officer, it kept round-the-clock watch on a dozen U.S. diplomatic buildings and official residences throughout the city.

Within the outer perimeter wall were two compounds—the Embassy compound and the separate U.S. consular compound, sealed off by an inner wall and steel gates. The Embassy compound itself, from front to rear, contained a wide lawn, or garden; the six-story Chancery building; a parking lot; Colonel Jacobson's two-story villa; and several small outbuildings of the Embassy motor pool and other facilities. "The American Embassy" is a vague term, a fact which caused considerable difficulty in the news reports of the attack. Sometimes the term was applied to the Chancery building; at other times the term seemed to encompass the entire Embassy compound.

Normally two U. S. Marines were on night duty within the Embassy compound, operating from a guard post in the lobby of the Chancery building. Because of the "maximum alert," the two-man guard had been augmented by an additional man stationed on the roof of the Chancery.

Leo E. Crampsey, the Embassy security officer, had no hard information that anything was about to happen in Saigon, and no hint of an attack on the Embassy itself. Nevertheless, he spent most of the evening visiting the various U.S. diplomatic installations around the city and checking with intelligence officials. About forty-five minutes before the attack, he made a final check with the Central Intelligence Agency duty officer in the CIA headquarters in the Chancery building. Crampsey was told that Saigon was quiet. He went home to bed.

When the sappers opened fire at the MPs on the gate, Marine Sergeant Ronald W. Harper, a twenty-year-old native of Cambridge, Minnesota, was away from the Chancery building. Realizing the compound was under attack, he ran back across the parking lot as fast as his legs could carry him. Inside the rear door of the Chancery building, Harper saw his fellow guard, Corporal George B. Zahuranic, twenty, of Uniontown, Pennsylvania, on the telephone behind the Marine Guard desk calling for help. Harper raced across the lobby to the front door, pulled inside an unarmed and terrified Vietnamese watchman who had been on duty near the front gate and slammed and bolted the great teakwood doors at the lobby entrance. Rifle fire came through the grilled windows beside the door, and bullets ricocheted through the lobby.

Thirty seconds later an anti-tank rocket smashed through the two-inch polished granite slab by the front door bearing the Seal of the United States, penetrated the brick and plaster of the outer wall and exploded near the ceiling over the receptionist's desk. Zahuranic was seriously wounded by fragments in his head, shoulder, arm, chest and leg. The two radio sender-receiver sets for communicating with other Marine posts were demolished. Harper, who was in the armory down the hall getting extra weapons, was knocked to the floor.

Another rocket tore through the front door, traveled across the lobby and exploded against the wall near the rear entrance. A third struck the rocket screen above the armory door. Harper had picked himself up and was trying to administer first aid to Zahuranic when a Viet Cong sapper lobbed a fragmentation grenade into the lobby through the wrecked grill of a window. The grenade blew a hole in the floor and sent up a cloud of dust and fragments.

Harper could hear the voices of the Viet Cong attackers just outside, and he expected them to burst through the door at any moment. With Zahuranic out of action, he was the only defender on the lower floors of the building. He was armed with a .38 pistol, a 12-gauge shotgun and a Beretta, a light Italian submachine gun which was the heaviest armament of the security forces at the time. Harper decided to stay at his post no matter what, certain these would be the last few minutes of his life.

Sergeant Rudy A. Soto, Jr., twenty-five, of Selma, California, the Marine Guard on the roof, saw the sappers coming through the hole in the compound wall. He tried to fire his 12-gauge shotgun, his principal weapon, but it jammed. Six stories up and a good two hundred feet away, Soto fired each of the six bullets in his .38 revolver at the men coming through the hole. Then he watched helplessly as two of the invaders raced across the lawn carrying a rocket launcher and began firing at the front door.

Soto tried to reach Harper and Zahuranic on his two-way radio, but got no response. He assumed they were dead, and that he would be next. He reported by radio on the security net that Viet Cong were probably in the building, and waited to meet his fate.

In addition to the three Marines, two Vietnamese and six Americans were in the building.

The two Vietnamese were the terrified night watchman Harper had brought inside and a Vietnamese employee on night duty in the unclassified communications room. Both spent most of the night on the floor in side rooms on the first floor.

In the Central Intelligence Agency office on an upper floor were the CIA night duty officer, armed with a Beretta, and two CIA communications men. One of the communicators had a snub-nosed .38 pistol.

In the metal-lined secret communications room on the fourth floor was James A. Griffin, an Embassy code clerk. Also on hand was Pfc. Charles M. Fisher, an Army communications man, who had a .38 pistol and a shotgun.

The man officially in charge was E. Allen Wendt, an economics officer who had been in Vietnam four months studying the price and production of rice and who was serving his first stretch as

Embassy night duty officer.[4] When the shooting and explosions began, he rolled out of bed in the duty officer's room on the fourth floor and telephoned the Political Counselor, John Archibald Calhoun. Just then, an explosion rocked the building and Wendt dove under the bed, taking the telephone with him. "Keep calm," advised Calhoun.

Wendt could hear automatic weapons fire just outside the building. He hastily changed from pajamas into clothes, gathered up his toothbrush, the duty officer's .38 pistol and a few personal belongings, and took refuge in the code room next door. It was safer than the duty quarters and there were more telephones for communication with the outside.

One of the first explosions shook Colonel Jacobson's villa just behind the Chancery building. He awoke to find his bed and face covered with glass fragments from the shattered bedroom windows. He heard the crackle of small arms fire outside as he dressed and began searching for a weapon. In the top left drawer of an ornate Chinese desk he found a single M-26 hand grenade. It was the only weapon in the house.

Robert L. Josephson, a retired master sergeant who was a Special Assistant to Ambassador Ellsworth Bunker, shared the villa with Jacobson. After five years in Vietnam, Josephson was spending his last night in the country. He had been guest of honor at Jacobson's party thirty hours before, and was scheduled to leave in the morning for the States. The former sergeant had miraculously escaped death in Saigon twice before, when he arrived at a motion picture theater in 1964 and at a restaurant in 1965 just after Viet Cong terrorists struck. Now he figured the third strike was probably his last. He rushed into Jacobson's room and saw him holding the hand grenade. In desperation he picked up a coat hanger, the closest thing to a weapon he could find.

[4] Until Henry Cabot Lodge became Ambassador, the Embassy duty officer was not required to be present in the building during holidays, nights and weekends. Lodge used to arrive at odd hours and was unhappy to find no Foreign Service officer there. "Nobody tells me that Ho Chi Minh knocks off work at 6 P.M. or on weekends," said Lodge. He insisted that "if Ho Chi Minh is on duty, we ought to be on duty."

Captain Robert J. O'Brien, thirty-six, of Marshfield, Massachusetts, senior officer of the Marine Security Guard detachment, was sleeping fully clothed on a sofa at the Marine Guards' living quarters five blocks away when the attack began. He mobilized his remaining men into reaction teams and headed toward the Embassy. At the Vietnamese police station a block from the Embassy, policemen shouted, "VC . . . VC!" O'Brien and his companions dismounted and moved on foot to the side gate of the Embassy. They found it locked, and the enemy soldiers somehow inside.

Where were the MPs? O'Brien called out softly, hoping they were still alive. At the sound of his voice, five or six Viet Cong on the Embassy lawn whirled around, stared at the Americans for a split second and opened fire. Raymond E. Reed, a big Negro sergeant from New Orleans, poked the nose of his submachine gun between the steel bars of the gate and fired back. Then the Marines retreated and took positions along the side street.

Security officer Crampsey and his deputy, Robert J. Furey, rushed to the Embassy from their home on Pasteur Street. At the side gate, they attempted to shoot off the locks, but failed. They were locked out, and the enemy was within. The security men needed grenades, but had none. Furey dispatched a Military Policeman, who drove to his headquarters several miles away in Cholon, the Chinese section of the city, and returned with the report that all available grenades had been issued and no more could be found anywhere.

Ambassador Ellsworth Bunker, at his official residence several blocks from the Embassy, was roused by security guards and hastily evacuated to a secret hideaway designated in advance—the bedroom of security chief Leo Crampsey's house on Pasteur Street. The Vietnamese maid had been given a holiday for Tet, and Crampsey had not expected company. The impeccable Ambassador found his temporary headquarters littered with dirty shirts and underwear.

Robert Komer, the U.S. pacification chief who had been claiming major gains in security during 1967, heard the gunfire during the night but assumed it was Tet fireworks. A little later he was awakened by his roommates in his villa, Major General George Forsythe and Colonel Robert Montague. With guns in hand, the officers informed Komer that the Embassy was under attack and there was every prospect they would be hit next. Komer asked if there was anything he could do. They said there was nothing, so he went back to sleep.

Gary Lee Bel, assistant to the Saigon bureau chief of NBC News, was awakened by the telephone just after 3 a.m. It was the girl whose family he had visited for Tet dinner earlier in the evening, and she said there was shooting in the streets. Bel told her not to worry. He telephoned Military Police headquarters, identified himself as an official of NBC News and asked what was going on. "Keep it to yourself," a corporal told the newsman, "but Saigon is under a light attack." Bel called the girl back and told her to stay inside.

Peter Braestrup of the Saigon bureau of the Washington *Post* had returned the day before from covering the fighting at Khe Sanh and Da Nang, and was relieved to be back in peaceful Saigon. He was awakened by a telephone call in the night from Lee Lescaze, his bureau colleague.

"They're attacking the city," Lescaze said.

"What city?" asked Braestrup.

"This city," Lescaze said patiently. "Saigon."

"Ridiculous. Just some 'incoming,'" replied Braestrup, an ex-Marine. He went back to sleep, but was awakened by another telephone call later, and headed toward the Embassy.

Barry Zorthian, public relations chief for the U. S. Embassy and the chief American publicist in Saigon for more than three years, heard the explosions in the city and monitored the action on the security radio net. He telephoned Jacobson at the villa to find out what was taking place at the Embassy grounds and then, perhaps on the theory that he would have more influence later if he was helpful now, began alerting wire services, broadcasting networks and newspaper correspondents. He passed along Jacobson's bedroom-window estimate that at least three or four Viet Cong were in the compound.

The Reports

The Associated Press, with 1262 client newspapers and 3221 radio and television subscribers in the United States, and many more in other countries, was first to sound the alarm to the world. At 3:15 A.M., about fifteen minutes after the action began, AP bureau chief Robert Tuckman typed out the first bulletin, based on fragmentary reports by telephone and what he could see and hear from his window.

His sentences were punched on a teletype machine in the AP office at the Eden building six blocks from the Embassy, and transmitted over a direct line to New York, some twelve thousand miles away. The trip took about one fifteenth of a second. In the Associated Press office at Rockefeller Center, a deskman edited Tuckman's report and fed it to a central office teletypist. Within a few seconds, it was clattering across AP teletype machines everywhere:

BULLETIN

VIETNAM (TOPS 17)

SAIGON (AP)—THE VIET CONG SHELLED SAIGON ITSELF EARLY WEDNESDAY IN A STUNNING FOLLOWUP TO ITS ATTACKS ON EIGHT CITIES.

SAIGON—ADD VIETNAM (98)

FIRST REPORTS SAID ROCKET OR MORTAR ATTACKS LANDED NEAR INDEPENDENCE PALACE, SEAT OF THE GOVERNMENT IN THE HEART OF SAIGON, OTHER GOVERNMENT BUILDINGS AND THE U.S. EMBASSY.

SMALL ARMS FIRE WAS HEARD IN THE STREETS.

SAIGON—ADD VIETNAM (99)

THE ATTACK STARTED AROUND 3 A.M. LESS THAN 24 HOURS AFTER THE SERIES OF LUNAR NEW YEAR'S DAY ATTACKS

AGAINST SEVEN LARGE PROVINCIAL CAPITALS AND THE KEY
CITY OF DA NANG, SECOND LARGEST CITY IN SOUTH VIETNAM.

ONE BUILDING NEAR INDEPENDENCE PALACE WAS SET
AFIRE.

ALLIED PLANES TOOK TO THE AIR AND SOME DROPPED
FLARES OVER THE CAPITAL AREA TO ILLUMINATE ENEMY
POSITIONS.[5]

A telephone call from Barry Zorthian provided the first information that the Embassy was under ground attack. Tuckman
quickly inserted this near the top of a new story:

FIRST LEAD ATTACK

SAIGON (AP)—THE VIET CONG SHELLED SAIGON WEDNES-
DAY IN A BOLD FOLLOWUP OF THEIR ATTACKS ON EIGHT MAJOR
CITIES AROUND THE COUNTRY.

SIMULTANEOUSLY, A SUICIDE SQUAD OF GUERRILLA COM-
MANDOS INFILTRATED THE CAPITAL AND AT LEAST THREE
ARE REPORTED TO HAVE ENTERED THE GROUNDS OF THE NEW
U.S. EMBASSY NEAR THE HEART OF THE CITY.

U.S. MARINE GUARDS AT THE EMBASSY, OPENED ONLY
LATE LAST YEAR, ENGAGED THE INFILTRATORS IN AN EX-
CHANGE OF FIRE.

[5] Considering the hundreds of different news outlets with their different
deadlines around the world, the wire services feel intense pressure for
quick action. AP's speedy report that night brought congratulatory telegrams
to the Saigon bureau, which were later mounted in a frame as a trophy of
success:

SAIGON—WE FORTY MINUTES AHEAD UNIPRESS ON FIRST BULLETIN.
NEW YORK.

HERALD-TRIBUNE IN PARIS SAYS [AP] 'FAR, FAR AHEAD' ON SAIGON
EMBASSY DEVELOPMENTS. CHEERS AND KEEP IT COMING.

KYODO PHONED ADVISING SAIGON ASSOCIATED ONE HOUR AHEAD OP-
POSITION ON U.S. EMBASSY ATTACK, AHEAD ON SUBSEQUENT DEVELOP-
MENT AND SUPERIOR IN DETAILS AND PRESENTATION . . . CHEERS,
CONGRATULATIONS AND MANY THANKS. MARTZENBURG. TOKYO.

SAIGON—NEW YORK DAILY NEWS PHONED HIGHEST PRAISE FOR AP
COVERAGE FROM OUTSET. CONGRATULATIONS. NEW YORK.

In the middle of the night in Saigon, it was midafternoon in Washington. Walt W. Rostow, President Johnson's assistant for national security affairs, was playing host to four staff members of the Washington *Post*, a newspaper which had become increasingly skeptical of the progress being claimed in the war. Rostow had promised to show them captured Communist documents proving that the war was going well and the Communists were dreaming of unrealistic "last gasp" schemes to win the war.

Rostow took his guests into the windowless basement chamber known as the White House Situation Room, which is the presidential command center for foreign policy crises. A large photomural of the Khe Sanh Marine base, detailed almost to the last trench, was spread across several desks. Atop the long, slightly curved table in the middle of the room were neat stacks of National Security Council staff memoranda, photocopied for each of the journalists, reporting on recent captured Communist documents, prisoner interrogations and defector reports from the war zone. Rostow excused himself to attend to other business, leaving a briefing officer in charge.

While the journalists were thumbing the memoranda, a door opened from an adjoining communications center and an aide deposited a slip of paper in the briefer's hand. "Get this right up to Walt," instructed the briefer. Another slip of paper arrived and was quickly dispatched to Rostow. "Looks like some trouble in Saigon," said the briefing officer with a thin smile. Another slip of paper arrived. Another. The stream of reports and the rising tension in the room began to be far more fascinating than the documents on the table. "It appears the Viet Cong are attacking the Embassy in Saigon," the official finally explained.

Rostow met the newsmen as they prepared to leave the White House, and referred to the attack on the American Embassy as a "grandstand" play. "Don't you want your copies [of the documents]?" asked the presidential aide. The journalists gathered the stacks of memoranda and took them back to the newspaper, where bulletins from Saigon were coming in on the teletype machines in the wire room.

Back in the White House Situation Room, an assistant felt

"incredible pressure" from upstairs for more information. "Upstairs" is the Oval Office of the President of the United States.

It had been a quiet afternoon in the State Department Operations Center, a communications-monitoring installation created in 1961 to keep American diplomacy abreast of crisis developments. As often happened, the first word of trouble came into the Ops Center via news agency teletypes, in this case the AP bulletin from Saigon.

About a half hour later, watch officer John B. Thompson received a "flash" overseas telephone call from Embassy Political Counselor Calhoun at his home in Saigon. Thompson made notes and passed along the report to Benjamin Read, the executive secretary of the State Department, whose desk was in the private office suite of Secretary of State Dean Rusk.

Read picked up a telephone and placed a priority call to the Saigon Embassy. The voice halfway around the world was that of Allen Wendt, the duty officer on the fourth floor of the beleaguered Embassy.

"There's shooting going on right outside," Wendt reported.

"You mean outside the Embassy compound?" asked Read.

"Inside the compound. It's right outside our building," came the trans-Pacific reply.

Read was shocked. He informed Assistant Secretary of State William P. Bundy, in charge of Far Eastern affairs, who found the news appalling. Read also informed Dean Rusk. The Secretary of State, who was usually briefed in his own office, made a rare trip to the Operations Center during the afternoon to obtain every available scrap of information. The Secretary of State was cool and impassive.

Undersecretary of State Nicholas Katzenbach and Deputy Assistant Secretary of State Philip Habib were making a previously scheduled visit to the new Vietnam Operations Center at Central Intelligence Agency headquarters near Langley, Virginia. Of all the government agencies intimately involved in the war, the CIA was the best insulated from official salesmanship and thus tended to be the least optimistic. In early 1968 CIA officials were increasingly worried about the growing signs of an unprecedented Viet Cong and North Vietnamese offensive just ahead and distressed by what they took to be an attitude of complacency among the U.S. military. The trouble in the air reminded one of the senior CIA men of the atmosphere just before a storm blows up on a sailing trip, when the sun is still shining and the wind still gentle but an uneasy feeling begins in the back of one's neck.

Some CIA officials looked upon Katzenbach as a potential ally in a drive to bring about major changes in U.S. policy in Vietnam, and they viewed the visit that day as a chance to communicate a sense of urgency. Employing maps and charts in the Operations Center, a CIA officer reviewed the latest intelligence reports from the war zone and expressed the view that "we're facing massive attacks, probably at the end of the Tet holiday." About that time a communications officer walked up with a slip of paper in his hand. "There's a report here that the Viet Cong are attacking the Embassy in Saigon and are on the first floor," he said. One of the visitors thought at first this was an elaborate CIA joke, but more information quickly dispelled that notion. "I knew it, I knew it," moaned the official.

The Tet Offensive was to have powerful impact on the emotions, opinions and convictions of millions of Americans and the futures of their political leaders. Coming at a critical time—just before the first presidential primaries in a presidential election year—it caught the American political system at its moment of greatest irresolution and potential for change.

After all else that had recently been said about the war, the news of the attack on the United States Embassy suggested that the Communist forces were far stronger than the United States Government had admitted, and that the war was much further from termination than high officials had implied. Two antithetical lessons could be drawn from this perception: one, that the United States should step up the war massively, because past and present efforts were grossly inadequate; the other, that the United States should give up the war as a hopeless task, because it could not be won at anything like a price that should be paid.

The first political figure to react was a prominent advocate of a more aggressive strategy, Senator Strom Thurmond of South Carolina. In late afternoon he was making a speech against a pending civil rights bill in the nearly empty U. S. Senate chamber when an aide handed him a wire service bulletin. Thurmond stopped and read it. His face flushed and he pounded his hands together in frustration. Addressing President Johnson as if he were in the room, Thurmond implored, "Use your power to bomb them so that they cannot take it—the kind of bombing we did in World War II, if necessary. Whatever is necessary to bring this war to an end should be done to save American lives." He demanded that the President "quit playing around" with the war, allowing American lives to be sacrificed. "How long are we going to wait?" he asked. "How many more Americans have to be killed before we take that firm, decisive action we should have taken several years ago?"

Earlier in the day the Senate had taken action which seemed to increase the likelihood that the plea of the South Carolina senator and others like him would be heeded. With little debate and no dissenting votes, the Senate confirmed the nomination of Clark Clifford to be Secretary of Defense. Clifford was considered a pal of Lyndon Johnson's, a veteran cold warrior and an unswerving defender of the Johnson policy on the war. The common belief in Washington was that he would be more of a hawk on the war than his predecessor, Robert S. McNamara, had turned out to be at the end of his tenure at the Pentagon.

Battle in the Dark

In Saigon another native South Carolinian was having a long night at his villa on Tran Quy Cap Street.[6] General William C. Westmoreland was receiving a stream of telephoned reports telling of strong Communist attacks throughout South Vietnam. Westmoreland had expected a Communist offensive, particularly at Khe Sanh and other areas far to the north, but he had not expected anything so extensive, so well coordinated or—so it seemed to him—

[6] Named for a Vietnamese nationalist and scholar, beheaded by the French in the early twentieth century.

so militarily foolish. Surely they could not take the cities of South Vietnam.

For those first few hours, there was an element of doubt. Nearly every city in South Vietnam was under siege from within and without, and nobody knew how much Communist reserve strength was yet to be committed. Tan Son Nhut Air Base, the site of Westmoreland's headquarters, was under attack by three Communist battalions. Moreover, the situation on the allied side was far from clear. In many places, the actions of the South Vietnamese Army and people were as yet unknown, and reports were only beginning to come in from the United States battalions, regiments and special combat teams which were moving to new battle positions throughout the blazing country.

From this perspective, the commando raid at the American Embassy was more a nuisance than a threat, a minor item blown out of proportion by the concentration of the American press and the concern of the American government. The U. S. Command never doubted how this platoon-sized fight would end. Sooner or later, the commandos would be wiped out.

That pragmatic assurance was good enough for other battles in other wars, but it was woefully insufficient at the moment. The whole world, it seemed, was watching the Embassy, and judging the action as if the whole war somehow turned on the result. With each passing minute of public uncertainty, the clock ticked toward the television evening news shows in the United States and the deadlines of the morning newspapers. The problem of time, which bedeviled the United States throughout its Vietnam intervention, suddenly emerged in its most acute and most absurd form: the civilian authorities not only required victory at the Embassy, but they needed it immediately. In the quickstep of modern mass communications, the measure of military success was not only *what* but *when*.

At 4 A.M. Saigon time Ambassador Ellsworth Bunker, through an aide, requested reinforcements for the Embassy from the Vietnamese police chief, Lieutenant Colonel Nguyen Van Luan. The word came back from the First Precinct station, which was less than a block from the Embassy compound. The commanding officer, a captain, refused to act. He said nobody could tell friend from foe in the dark and his police would be caught in a cross fire. If the Americans would come to the precinct station, escort his men to the Embassy and point out the Viet Cong to them, ah, that would be different. A U. S. Marine and a Military Policeman were dispatched to the precinct house, but the Vietnamese would not let them through the barricades.[7]

At 4:20 A.M. Calhoun, the Embassy Political Counselor, prodded Westmoreland by telephone about a U.S. reaction force and medical evacuation for the Embassy. Westmoreland ordered the 716th Military Police Battalion, the largest U.S. fighting unit inside the city, to clear the Embassy compound as a "first priority effort."

The response at MP headquarters was to request armored vehicles and helicopters for the assault on the commandos in the compound. Such heavy equipment would have had to come from units outside the city. In the meantime, the MPs sent more men to the Embassy. The MP lieutenant in charge there had surveyed the situation and declined to fight his way into the compound in the dark. All the gates were locked and bolted, and the hole in the compound wall was yet to be discovered by the Americans outside. "The VC are inside the compound, they're not going anyplace," reported an MP on the scene over the tactical radio net. "Nobody can get in, nobody can get out. He [apparently the lieutenant] says try to wait here until daylight 'cause we got 'em inside." There was little urgency in his voice or his message.

Inside the compound, men on both sides were doing their jobs as they could understand them and preparing themselves to die.

On the Communist side, the soldiers of the C-10 Battalion were disorganized. The two leaders, known as Bay Tuyen and Ut Nho, had been killed early in the attack, perhaps by the quick action of the American MPs at the side gate. The invaders had

[7] At 5 A.M. the precinct commander called Bunker's aide again to protest that one of his policemen had been hit by a stray bullet from the Embassy battle and probably was going to die. After making the protest, he abruptly hung up the phone.

been armed with over forty pounds of C-4 plastic explosive, more than enough to demolish doors and walls and blast their way from the Embassy garden into the Chancery building. There was no order to do so, however, and the sappers had no way to discover that the Chancery lobby was held by a lone American MP or that only a few other lightly armed Americans were on the upper floors.

In the absence of specific orders or a clear mission, the Viet Cong took positions in or behind the big circular flower tubs on the lawn or elsewhere in the Embassy garden, and fired back at the growing phalanx of Americans shooting at them from rooftops outside the compound walls. Colonel Jacobson, who had seen many men in battle, watched the Viet Cong intermittently throughout the night from the windows of his villa just behind the Chancery building. He was impressed with their extraordinary bravery under fire. None of them gave the slightest hint that surrender ever entered his mind.

Marine Corporal James C. Marshall, twenty-one, of Monroeville, Alabama, climbed the roof of a small building in the consular compound and fired over the wall at the Viet Cong on the lawn. Wounded by a fragment of a rocket fired in reply, he refused to quit. About a half hour later, he was killed, possibly by a stray U.S. bullet from a lot across the street.

The small band inside the Chancery building could hear gunfire outside, but because of the concrete rocket screen around the building and their angle of vision, they could see virtually nothing of the flare-lit battle outside. Their tactical communication with the defense units just outside the compound was non-existent. Sergeant Harper in the lobby, who had a telephone but whose radio was smashed, could not communicate with Sergeant Soto on the roof of the Chancery—he had a radio but no telephone. Pilots in helicopters above the Embassy were on different radio frequencies from the defenders below, and could not make radio contact.

The Americans within the Chancery were strangely cut off from the conflict, except when a rocket slammed into the side of the building or bullets spattered its facing. Their eyes could tell them nothing of the struggle all around them, and their ears could tell them only that the battle still raged. They were nearly helpless. They could only wait in tension and frustration for their hour of trial.

On the other hand, the sound of their voices traveled across the city and around the world through telephone wires, and the telephones were constantly jangling. Wendt and Griffin, in the code room on the fourth floor, received calls throughout the night from the White House Situation Room and the State Department Operations Center in Washington, halfway around the world; from a Marine Corps general in Da Nang, five hundred miles to the north; from U. S. Military Command headquarters at Tan Son Nhut Air Base, the alternate Embassy compound post at the Political Counselor's residence; and even from a foreign aid employee who just called to inquire what was going on. For a while, it was like being in a telephone booth in the *Titanic* while the ship was going down.

The redoubtable Sergeant Harper, who spent much of the night crouched on the floor in the lobby awaiting the Viet Cong invaders, lunged for his telephone whenever it rang lest the bell alert commandos outside. One call in the middle of the night came from Marine Captain Charles W. Sampson, General Westmoreland's aide, who was checking on the situation for the U.S. commander.

"What's the trouble, Sergeant?" asked Captain Sampson, noting the agitated tone in the Marine Guard's voice.

"The VC are right outside the door, I tell you."

"You're not scared or anything, are you, Sergeant?" asked Sampson, who thought Harper was probably exaggerating.

"You bet your ass I am," was the reply.

A U. S. Army helicopter carrying a landing party from the 101st Airborne Division attempted to land on the roof about 5 A.M., but attracted a hail of Viet Cong fire from the ground. Its lights flashing and its massive propellers beating the air, the chopper hovered in the withering fire, hesitated and turned back.

At his command post at Long Binh, fifteen miles outside the city, Lieutenant General Frederick C. Weyand, the commander of U.S. forces in the Saigon area, learned that the helicopter had turned back. Seeing no great need to risk landing men in the darkness, he ordered the assault force to wait until the situation improved.

About 6:15 A.M. a medical evacuation and supply chopper managed to land atop the Embassy. It deposited three cases of M-16 rifle ammunition and took off with Zahuranic (the Marine Guard who had been wounded in the early moments of action), Sergeant Soto and Fisher, the Army communications man.

The defenders inside the building were armed with a motley collection of pistols and other light weapons. Since none of them had an M-16, the helicopter-borne munitions sat uselessly on the roof the rest of the night.

The outside world depended on the newsmen who gathered a block away. The reporters did the best they could with the sources available to them: the action they could see and hear from the compound, talk overheard on the MP radio net, and the comments of confused and excited Military Policemen, some of whom were seeing their first combat action. The reporters did not know that telephones inside the Chancery building were manned and working, even in the lobby of the building itself.

Were the Viet Cong invaders in the Chancery building, or only the garden of the compound? Nobody outside the walls was certain, and the question took on great symbolic importance in a battle where symbolism counted. It would be a greater psychological defeat if the enemy was able to invade the building, roam through offices and kill Americans inside.

Barry Zorthian, the U.S. press spokesman, informed the news agencies early in the fight that so far as he knew no Viet Cong were actually in the Chancery building. He was not certain, nor could anyone be. Even the men on the fourth floor of the Chancery were often uncertain which side held the lobby, and the situation could change quickly. Early in the action, the security radio net had reported that Viet Cong probably *were* in the building—a report which doubtless originated in Sergeant Soto's original alarm from the roof. Moreover, some of the MPs outside the compound walls believed they were being fired upon from the Chancery building (actually, the gunfire was coming from U.S. security men on rooftops beyond the far wall of the compound). One over-weight and overwrought MP sergeant excitedly told the cluster of correspondents down the street, "They're in the building—they're in the building!"

Peter Arnett of the Assoicated Press, a veteran combat correspondent who had won the Pulitzer Prize for his Vietnam reporting, rushed back and forth from the clump of newsmen and MPs outside the compound wall to a telephone a block away. He called the AP office in the Eden building, where his running account was translated into "adds" (additional material), "subs" (substitute material for earlier paragraphs) or "new leads" (material important enough to be the top of a new story).

About 7:25 A.M. Saigon time (6:25 P.M. New York time) the Associated Press bureau transmitted its "fourth lead attack," the fourth new top to the Vietnam story since its original bulletin four hours earlier. Based on Arnett's telephone calls from the scene, it was the first major report that the Viet Cong were *inside* the Embassy building.

BULLETIN

VIETNAM (TOPS 161)

SAIGON (AP)—THE VIETCONG ATTACKED SAIGON WEDNES-DAY AND SEIZED PART OF THE U.S. EMBASSY. AMERICAN MILI-TARY POLICE TRIED TO STORM INTO THE EMBASSY AS DAWN BROKE BUT WERE DRIVEN BACK BY HEAVY OUTBURSTS OF FIRE FROM THE EMBASSY BUILDING.

SAIGON—ADD VIETNAM (169)

DAWN BROKE OVER THE TENSE CAPITAL ABOUT 7 A.M. AND FIGHTING SWELLED UP AROUND THE EMBASSY IN THE HEART OF THE CITY.

U.S. MILITARY POLICE ON THE SCENE SAID IT WAS BE-LIEVED ABOUT 20 VIET CONG SUICIDE COMMANDOS WERE IN THE EMBASSY COMPOUND AND HELD PART OF THE FIRST FLOOR OF THE EMBASSY BUILDING.

THE VIET CONG'S SEIZURE OF PART OF THE EMBASSY FOL-LOWED EXCHANGES OF GUNFIRE WITH THE U.S. MARINE GUARDS POSTED THERE.

At 6:28 P.M. New York time the bulletin was retransmitted from the Associated Press building at 50 Rockefeller Plaza. Nearby, in the National Broadcasting building at 30 Rockefeller Plaza, the NBC-Television *Huntley-Brinkley Report* was preparing to go on the air in two minutes, at 6:30 P.M., live to most parts of the country. The Huntley-Brinkley staff took a quick look at the AP report and revised the script. Chet Huntley read it over hurriedly, and the red light flashed on. Huntley's report had the situation backward—in his version, the Viet Cong were in the building, Americans were in the rest of the compound and Viet Cong were firing at them from outside the walls—but his urgent words conveyed the message of a disastrous event to some fourteen million Americans watching ten million television sets tuned to the show:

> The Vietcong seized part of the U.S. Embassy in Saigon early Wednesday, Vietnam time. Snipers are in the buildings and on roof tops near the Embassy and are firing on American personnel inside the compound.
>
> Twenty suicide commandos are reported to be holding the first floor of the Embassy.
>
> The attack on the Embassy and other key installations in Saigon, at Tan Son Nhut Air Base and Bien Hoa north of Saigon came as the climax of the enemy's biggest and most highly coordinated offensive of the war. There was no report on Allied casualties in Saigon, but they're believed to be high.
>
> The attacks came as thousands of civilians were celebrating the Lunar New Year, and at times it was impossible to distinguish the explosion of mortar shells and small arms fire from those of the firecrackers the celebrants were setting off. . . .

In Washington high government officials sat anxiously in front of television sets watching the evening news shows, which are a prime source of information and attitudes for most Americans. Huntley's one-and-a-half-minute report on the Saigon fighting—and his news that the Viet Cong were holding the first floor of the Embassy building—caused consternation in the government.

At 6:40 P.M. in Washington Philip Habib, the Vietnam co-ordinator for the Department of State, urgently telephoned the alternate Embassy Command post in Saigon. The Embassy's Political Counselor, John Archibald Calhoun, took the call. Two minutes later Calhoun was on the phone with the American Command's Combat Operations Center, which by now was flooded with reports of major battles raging on its perimeter at Tan Son Nhut and throughout the country. Calhoun informed the operations officers, who must have been incredulous at this news, that the "principal concern" in Washington was the clearing of the American Embassy in downtown Saigon. They replied, somewhat defensively, that the high protective wall around the compound was a "serious tactical problem"—since the Viet Cong were inside and the American rescue forces were outside. Nonetheless, Calhoun was informed that a U.S. rescue force was on the way.

Not satisfied with this answer, Calhoun telephoned Westmoreland. Washington was concerned about the Embassy, he emphasized. Westmoreland assured him that troops in helicopters would soon be landing.

As dawn was breaking, security officer Robert Furey stumbled across something on the sidewalk in front of the Embassy. It was rubble from the hole which the sappers had blown in the wall four hours before. For the first time it was clear how the Viet Cong got into the compound—while the American rescuers were locked out.

Furey, a former New York State trooper, crawled cautiously through the hole in the wall. Inside he saw a gravely wounded Viet Cong fighter prop himself up across the lawn and get ready to throw a hand grenade. Furey had the soldier in the sights of his rifle when an orange flash exploded before his eyes, and he was stunned by the shock wave of the explosion. The dying commando had pulled the pin, but was unable to muster the strength to throw the grenade.

There was a tremendous crash at the front gate. After hours of trying, Military Police had shot off the lock of the front gate, and rammed it open with a jeep. They charged into the compound, followed by newsmen and television camera crews. Bodies were strewn around the yard. Nearly all the Viet Cong invaders were dead, dying or in hiding.

About the same time, a helicopter of the U.S. 101st Airborne Division landed on the Embassy roof. Allen Wendt, the duty officer, left the code room on the fourth floor and headed upstairs. As he stepped off the elevator on the sixth floor, he was greeted in the corridor by five U.S. paratroopers in full battle dress, armed with M-16 rifles, M-79 grenade launchers, hand grenade launchers, hand grenades and knives.

Wendt asked for the leader. Major Hillel Schwartz, thirty-three, of Tacoma, Washington, stepped forward and offered him a hand grenade. The Foreign Service officer declined. Wendt told the paratroop commander that so far as he could learn, there were no Viet Cong in the building. As a precautionary measure, Schwartz and his men began to search the building floor by floor as more helicopters landed in rapid succession with additional troops. They found no Viet Cong in the building.

For an hour and twenty minutes the Associated Press had been reporting that Viet Cong held parts of the Embassy. At 9:08 A.M. Saigon time, with the real battle nearly over, United Press International caught up:

> BULLETIN
>
> 4TH NIGHT LD 256A
>
> SAIGON (UPI)—AMERICAN TROOPS WEDNESDAY LAUNCHED A HELICOPTER ASSAULT ON THE U.S. EMBASSY HERE TO ROOT OUT COMMUNIST SUICIDE SQUADS OCCUPYING PART OF THE BUILDING.
>
> 1ST ADD 4TH NIGHT LD VIET SAIGON 276A BUILDING
>
> AS U.S. MILITARY POLICE ATTACKED COMMUNIST POSITIONS IN THE EMBASSY FROM THE STREET LEVEL, HELICOPTERS TOOK TROOPS TO THE ROOF OF THE EIGHT-STORY [sic] BUILDING TO ROOT THEM OUT FLOOR BY FLOOR.
>
> COMMUNIST TROOPS INSIDE THE BUILDING OPENED FIRE ON THE HELICOPTERS AS THEY CAME IN FOR LANDINGS.

This dispatch apparently was written by a UPI deskman in New York. The Saigon bureau had sent a vaguer story saying that Communist suicide squads occupied "portions of the American Embassy" (which could refer to the compound instead of the building) and adding that "it was not known which areas of the Embassy the Viet Cong occupied."

At 9:35 A.M. Saigon time UPI declared that:

> THERE WERE UNCONFIRMED REPORTS THE COMMUNISTS HAD TAKEN OVER THE FIRST FIVE FLOORS OF THE MODERNISTIC WHITE BUILDING.

By 10 A.M. Saigon time (9 P.M. Washington time) UPI erroneously confirmed the earlier "unconfirmed report." In its fifth night lead, "a Viet Cong suicide squad stormed the U. S. Embassy Wednesday and occupied the first five floors for several hours." The dispatch added that nineteen Viet Cong had been killed inside the building. This dispatch was written in part by deskmen in New York City.

At 10:48 A.M. Saigon time UPI reported that for six hours American forces had battled Viet Cong invaders "with small arms and grenades through the carpeted offices" of the Embassy.

At 1:22 P.M. Saigon time (after midnight on the eastern seaboard of the United States) the news agency made its version of a retraction of the earlier battle reports:

> AT LEAST 19 VIET CONG WERE KILLED INSIDE THE EMBASSY COMPOUND. DURING THE HEAT OF THE FIGHTING, U.S. MILITARY MEN SAID THE TERRORISTS HAD OCCUPIED FIVE FLOORS OF THE EMBASSY. LATER, A SPOKESMAN SAID THE COMMUNISTS DID NOT PENETRATE THE MAIN BUILDING AND THE STATE DEPARTMENT IN WASHINGTON CONFIRMED THIS.

George Jacobson spent most of the night in the upstairs hall of his villa, his lone grenade in hand, watching and waiting for the sappers to invade his house from the garden outside, and taking calls on the hall telephone. He could not get through by telephone to the Chancery building a few yards away or to the Americans shooting past his house at the Viet Cong in the compound, but the longer-distance calls were not a problem. Philip Habib called from Washington; Jacobson asked him to telephone his mother in Hutchinson, Minnesota, to let her know he was all right. Ambassador Bunker called twice, and there were at least ten calls from other Embassy officials. Peter Arnett of the Associated Press telephoned at 4:30 A.M. "The Viet Cong sent in a few sapper units to celebrate Tet in their inimitable way," Jacobson told Arnett, who told the world. "They are calculating a big splash all over the world with their activities."

At 6:45 A.M. Jacobson spotted fresh blood and footprints downstairs from his position in the upstairs hallway. He dialed the old Embassy across town and in a low voice asked the Marine Guard on duty to notify the security force at the new Embassy that Viet Cong were on the first floor of his house—and that he was on the second floor. He lay down quietly at the top of the stairs, ready to pull the pin on the grenade and roll it down when the attacker appeared.

Military Police and Marines in the garden outside started a gun battle with the commando in the Jacobson house. An MP tossed in a hand grenade, which blew up the liquor closet downstairs and stunned and deafened the colonel upstairs. It did not kill the Viet Cong soldier. Somebody threw in a tear gas grenade, and the house began to fill with gas.

Jacobson realized that his foe would be forced upstairs by the gas. He rose from the stairway and softly made his way to the back window. He called to security forces for gas masks and weapons for himself and Josephson, who was in a side room. MP Private First Class Paul V. Healey, twenty, of Holbrook, Massachusetts, bravely ran across an exposed stretch of lawn and threw up a .45 pistol and a gas mask. Others followed his lead.

The colonel put on the mask and crouched as low as he could behind the corner of a thin plywood wall. From his combat experience, he knew the lead man would come up shooting.

Almost noiselessly, the Viet Cong climbed the stairs. As he reached the top he fired a continuous burst with his AK-47, moving the weapon in a half circle from left to right, spraying bullets into the walls and through the doors. Jacobson heard the slugs rip through the plywood above his head and saw the snout of the weapon moving past him toward the other wall—and then sprang up shooting at point-blank range with his .45. The man in khaki spun around and sank to the floor.

Jacobson rushed over and seized the AK-47. He took it behind the plywood corner to await the next sapper.

Nobody came. It was all over.

The Aftermath

The Embassy was officially declared secure at 9:15 A.M., six hours and twenty-eight minutes after the first call for help.

At 9:20 A.M. General Westmoreland walked through the smashed front gate to inspect the Embassy. On the little raised terrace under the overhang of the Chancery building were bloody bodies of dead and gravely wounded Viet Cong. The bodies of Daniel and Sebast still lay where they had fallen inside the side gate; some of their buddies were weeping. Reporters and photographers seemed to be everywhere. Kate Webb of UPI, in a memorable description, said the place looked like "a butcher shop in Eden."

The normally garrulous journalists hung back while Westmoreland moved across the littered yard. The six-and-a-half-hour Viet Cong occupation seemed to many of them the most embarrassing defeat the United States had suffered in Vietnam. Even though the scale was small, this was a big story, very big. It seemed to give the lie to the rosy projections and victory claims that Westmoreland and others had been dishing out.

For once the reporters felt sorry for Westmoreland. What could he possibly say of this disaster? They felt certain he would have to say something.

Westmoreland strode into the wreckage of the front lobby and shook hands with Sergeant Harper, who was still at his post. At the general's request, Wendt put in a "flash" priority call to

Philip Habib in Washington. Westmoreland spoke for nearly ten minutes, describing the situation and doing his best to ease the consternation in the U.S. capital.

He put down the telephone, spoke briefly to Barry Zorthian, the public affairs adviser, and walked outside to meet the press. He was wearing starched, pressed fatigues, with his four stars sewn on the lapels.

Facing the half circle of reporters and cameramen, the general gave the military view. "The enemy's well-laid plans went afoul," he said. "Some superficial damage was done to the building. All of the enemy that entered the compound so far as I can determine were killed. Nineteen bodies have been found on the premises—enemy bodies."

Westmoreland said the attacks on populated areas throughout the country were "very deceitfully" calculated to create maximum consternation in Vietnam, and expressed the view that they were "diversionary" to the main enemy effort still to come at Khe Sanh and in the northern part of the country. "The enemy exposed himself by virtue of his strategy and he suffered great casualties. . . . As soon as President Thieu, with our agreement, called off the truce, American troops went on the offensive and pursued the enemy aggressively," the general announced.

The reporters could hardly believe their ears. Westmoreland was standing in the ruins and saying everything was great.

As was often the case in the Vietnam War, the "body count" of Communist troops at the American Embassy turned out to be inflated. Four of those killed were Vietnamese civilians, drivers on late duty that night in the Embassy motor pool. At least three of them were innocent bystanders. A U.S. security man later recalled seeing one of the "enemy" force crouching behind a concrete planter, shouting loudly and frantically waving something just before he was killed. It was his U. S. Embassy employee identification card.

One of the hapless drivers left a wife and seven children; another a wife and six children; the third a wife and a child. Later the Bureau of Economic Compensation of the United States Department of Labor awarded each of the three families a year's salary plus a Tet bonus, a total of a little more than $1000 in each case.

Marines who participated in the battle said they saw the fourth driver, a Vietnamese nicknamed "Satchmo," shooting at them during the fighting. Nguyen Van De had worked continuously for the United States in Saigon since 1950, when the first U.S. minister to Vietnam was appointed. At one time he had been the personal driver for the American Ambassador.

Two of the Viet Cong invaders, both wounded, were captured at the end of the battle. One of them maintained that De was the VC agent who brought him into Saigon. Later the captive retracted parts of this story, but security officials were convinced that De had some role in the attack. An AK-47 was found near his body, and a 9-mm. Browning pistol was found tucked in his belt. A large roll of Vietnamese piasters was in his pocket. Investigators learned later that De kept a "major wife" and six children on the outskirts of the city, and a siesta-hour "minor wife" in the city. He also raised and sold race horses. Everyone at the Embassy knew De, who had a reputation for being the most pro-American of all the Vietnamese employees. "He must be a Viet Cong," the American secretaries used to say in jest, "because he's so much smarter than the other drivers."

Three U. S. Marine Guards raised the Stars and Stripes on the flagpole in front of the scarred Embassy building at 11:45 A.M., nine hours after the attack began. A little later Ambassador Bunker appeared at the Embassy against the advice of his security guards and made a tour of inspection. Bunker was immaculate in twill pants, a white shirt and loafers. He was surrounded by grimy, bloody Marines, MPs, paratroopers and State Department security men who had fought the battle. The Ambassador told correspondents that the Viet Cong had failed in this attack "because they were never able to enter the Chancery building."

The battle at the Embassy dominated the headlines of many American newspapers the following day. The Washington *Daily News,* the afternoon tabloid of the nation's capital, published an unusual front-page editorial titled "Where Were We? Where ARE

We?" Accompanying the editorial was a front-page cartoon depicting Westmoreland colliding head on with a Viet Cong guerrilla at the corner of a structure labeled "U. S. Embassy, Saigon." The general's stars were flying off Westmoreland's uniform, and his gun was dropping to the ground. The Viet Cong had his weapon jammed into the general's belly. The caption read: "'We have turned the corner . . .' —Gen. Westmoreland."

Because Saigon's embattled Tan Son Nhut Air Base was closed to all commercial traffic, the U. S. Air Force agreed to the television networks' requests for emergency transportation of their film footage during the first few days after the Tet attacks. In most cases the film was flown out with the casualties on special medical evacuation flights.

NBC-Television film roll 448, photographer Philip Ross's footage of the Embassy battle, was placed on a medivac flight to Yokota Air Force Base, Japan, where it was met by network personnel. It arrived at NBC's Tokyo studios barely in time to be processed before the *Huntley-Brinkley Report* went on the air in the United States some twenty-four hours after the height of the battle. NBC had purchased time on a communications satellite to make instantaneous transmission possible from Japan. Film roll 448 was threaded into a projector in Tokyo and beamed across the Pacific and into American living rooms without prescreening by NBC.

Many Americans sat up in their chairs as Chet Huntley announced that footage of the Embassy attack was available and would now be viewed via satellite. Jack Perkins, an NBC correspondent in Tokyo, appeared on the home screen and reported that the film had arrived only ten minutes before air time from Saigon. "It is raw. It is unedited. It is just as it happened," Perkins declared.

For the next five minutes, the viewers saw dead Vietnamese bodies, rubble, dazed American GIs and unrecognizable buildings. The high point was a man running with his back to the camera to a house and throwing something up to someone in the window. Perkins had no idea what he was watching, and first identified the house as the Embassy building. In New York

Robert Northshield, the executive producer of the *Huntley-Brinkley Report*, realized this must be Private Healey's run across the lawn to supply weapons for Colonel Jacobson. He quickly told Perkins in Tokyo, via an open telephone line, that the man catching the pistol on the film was Jacobson, that the scene was Jacobson's house and that he needed the pistol to defend himself. In Tokyo Perkins explained this back to the public across the Pacific via satellite:

> This, I'm told, is Colonel Jacobson, who is with the Mission, and this is his house now. It was attacked by VC infiltrators. The Marines were downstairs; he was upstairs, and the Marines fought them off and then tried to throw up—some of the MPs tried to throw up a revolver to him to defend himself in case they got up to him.
>
> Again, I say this is unedited film, just arrived in our Tokyo studios before we went on the air, and we had not seen it before either.

After the film was completed, Chet Huntley in New York asked Perkins in Tokyo—via satellite and on the air—"Jack, would you say they are trying for some sort of psychological Dien Bien Phu?"

"Well, they are certainly trying for a psychological splash and are making it," Perkins replied. "It won't be a Dien Bien Phu, though, and they will not capture Saigon because they cannot. It just can't be done, that's all."

The battle of the Embassy was retold dramatically later that night on news specials over both NBC and CBS.

Hanoi did not place heavy emphasis on the American Embassy battle in its first accounts of the Tet Offensive. Most of its propaganda in the early days was aimed at the South Vietnamese, who were not much interested in the U. S. Embassy skirmish.

A few weeks later, however, the North Vietnamese began circulating a version of the battle at the Embassy titled "Assault on Bunker's Bunker." As subsequently published in *The Vietnam*

Courier, an English-language propaganda organ, it contained some of the most creative writing to grace the whole affair.

The American Embassy was an imposing seven-storeyed building, a fortress of concrete and steel at the corner of Thong Nhut and Mac Dinh Chi avenues. Between the stockade of concrete pipes, sandbags and barbed wire entanglements, and the multicolored glazed porch, was an 80-metre-wide courtyard covered by gunnests all around. Specifically designed elevators would electrocute any users unfamiliar with their function.

The order for the assault was given: the whole detachment rushed forward. It was a fierce lightning attack, a complete surprise for the enemy. The outer ring of defences was breached without any exchanges of fire: perhaps the police and patrols had seen the attackers and had simply shown a clean pair of heels. . . .

The whole of Saigon was aflame. Thunder rumbled over the whole city. Their revolutionary troops' artillery shook doors and windows. Each leading a spearhead, Ba and Ut dashed upstairs. The American bandits had not quite awakened from their sleep. Some bewilderingly opened their doors and were shot dead. Others ran around screaming like madmen. It was too late for them. Our submachine guns crashed. Room after room shook, filled with streaks of fire. The only thing the enemy could do was to cower under the blows. . . .

As floor after floor was captured, the fighting became harder and harder. Entrenched in their rooms, the Americans opposed a desperate resistance. Helicopters skimmed the terraced roof, with blinking red lights under their bellies. Down in the streets, the rumbling of armoured cars was approaching.

Dawn came as they reached the fifth floor. . . . The fight had entered a new phase in which revolutionary troops were at the same time continuing their offensive and countering enemy attacks from two sides. They had suffered practically no losses. . . .

They had killed over 200 enemy personnel, most of

them holding key posts in the American ruling machinery in Saigon; they had captured the lair of Governor General Bunker and, entrenched in it, had beaten back all enemy counter-attacks. They were standing on the highest point in Saigon, red cloth-bands on their arms, holding firm the hot barrels of their guns, ready to defend the Revolution, to protect the lives of their dear ones, to sacrifice their own lives. . . .

Only on the afternoon of the following day, February 1, 1968, did the guns fall silent inside the American Embassy. The detachment had quietly withdrawn, after raining hard blows on the enemy for two days and nights.

Privately, the Communist Command took a different view of the engagement. A few days after the battle was over, General Tran Do of the South Vietnam People's Liberation Armed Forces sent a critical inquiry to the Saigon area tactical command. He reportedly asked why those who planned the assault had failed to take into account the ease with which helicopters bearing airborne troops could land on the roof of the American Embassy. "Was there any error in the planning?" General Do demanded to know.

A number of the most important questions about the battle of the Embassy were not answered clearly at the time, and some of them remain for judgment. What was the objective of the attack force? How much inside assistance did it have? What was the relationship of the American public perception of the battle to the perceptions of the men on the ground? What are the criteria of success in such a battle: The comparative "body count" of those killed on either side? Depth penetration of the attack force? Minutes or hours that an objective is threatened or held? Possession of the objective in the end? Psychological shock or political advantage? In such an engagement, in such a war, do the words "victory" and "defeat" retain their meaning?

As soon as the battle was over, the U. S. Government began making over its Saigon Embassy into the heavily fortified command post which the American public and the Viet Cong propagandists had assumed it was all along. The Army delivered machine guns, M-16 rifles, grenades, gas masks and other arms and equipment to the Marine Guard at the Embassy, and construction began on machine gun emplacements on the roof. Workmen removed the circular flower pots which had made such good firing positions for Viet Cong gunners on the Embassy lawn and relocated them in a downtown park. An elaborate communications system, capable of keeping defenders of the Embassy in constant contact with Army units outside, was installed.

Nguyen Van Sau and Ngo Van Giang, the two captured Viet Cong commandos, were turned over to the South Vietnamese authorities. Embassy security men were able to interrogate them several times in the first weeks after the Embassy attack. Then they vanished into South Vietnamese custody. No one seemed to know where they were or what had happened to them.

Sergeant Harper was awarded the Bronze Star for his solo defense of the Embassy, and later left the Marines to become assistant manager of a service station chain in his native Minnesota. Embassy duty officer Wendt, security officers Crampsey and Furey and code clerk Griffin were all presented with Department of State Awards for Heroism in connection with the attack. Later they moved on to government posts elsewhere in the world.

George Jacobson was given the Award for Heroism by the Department of State. General Westmoreland presented him with the dead Viet Cong soldier's AK-47, handsomely mounted and identified by a small brass plate which said, "A VC fired this weapon and missed / The Colonel fired back—and didn't." Jacobson was still living in the villa in the Embassy compound nearly two years after the attack. By that time, counting the pistols in the night table and desk drawers and the automatic rifles in the closets and behind the bar, there were thirty-seven weapons in the house.

CHAPTER II

Decision in the North

Eyes must look far ahead, and thoughts be deeply pondered.
Be bold and unremitting in attack.
Give the wrong command, and two chariots are rendered useless.
Come the right moment, a pawn can bring you victory.

—Ho Chi Minh, *Prison Diary*

THE BOMBERS high above the clouds could not be heard in the jungle below, and the only warning was the scream of the projectiles, glinting in the sun, on their dive toward earth. For once, the bombs fell not in some deserted rain forest inhabited only by snakes and screeching birds, but in a military headquarters area inhabited by men of great importance. The North Vietnamese four-star general, so the reports said later, was gravely wounded by fragments in the chest.

They carried him overland in haste and secrecy to the airport in Phnom Penh, Cambodia, and from there by chartered airplane to Hanoi. The official announcement, which is widely disbelieved, made no reference to his presence in the South, saying only that he was suddenly stricken by a serious heart attack and died in the 108th Military Hospital, Hanoi, at 9 A.M. on July 6, 1967.

"The life of Comrade Nguyen Chi Thanh was a life of continuous and seething revolutionary activity," proclaimed the announcement. A native of the region around the old imperial city of Hue, he was thirty years a member of the Communist Party and seventeen years in its ruling Politburo. He was imprisoned three times by the French, and became one of only two men—the other was his old rival, Vo Nguyen Giap—to attain the four-star rank of Senior General in the Vietnam People's Army. Since the spring of 1965 he had been Hanoi's senior military representative in South Vietnam, the Communist equivalent of General William C. Westmoreland. He was fifty-three years old when he died.

President Ho Chi Minh appeared at the Hanoi Military Club to lay a wreath beside his casket, and so did the other leaders of the Party, the Army and the government. Two posthumous medals, the Ho Chi Minh Exploit Medal First Class and the Military Exploit Medal First Class, were pinned to his tunic, and high-ranking officers and Army heroes took turns beside the bier throughout the night.

On Friday afternoon, July 7, the assembled political and military High Command of North Vietnam, the Politburo and Military Affairs Committee of the Lao Dong (Communist Party), bore the casket to the hearse between lines of military honor guards. At the burial ground, Le Duc Tho, a veteran member of the Politburo (and later chief North Vietnamese adviser at the Paris talks), delivered the funeral oration.

"Dear Comrade Nguyen Chi Thanh, you have passed away, but you will remain forever in the minds of your comrades in arms and our people as the brilliant example of a genuine communist who has struggled and ·endured sacrifices throughout his life for the fatherland, the people and the great communist idea," the orator declared.

"Please accept the profound regret of the party, government, people and the people's armed forces and of your comrades and dear friends.

"Farewell, comrade. . . ."

It was the end of an era, and the beginning of an era. General Thanh's forces in the South had been pummeled and bloodied by the swiftly growing American expeditionary force, but the Communist troops did not buckle or crack. There was increasing talk in Hanoi that the war was becoming a stalemate. The great question was how to convince the Vietnamese combatants and people that they could thwart the forces of the greatest military power on earth and, even more important, how to demonstrate this lesson convincingly to the United States and sap its strength and will.

In the First Indochina War, the Lao Dong Party brilliantly coordinated military and diplomatic strategy to convince the French it was madness to continue. Now the search was under way in Party circles in Hanoi for America's Dien Bien Phu. Where would it be found, and when could the trap be sprung?

General Thanh, like many other field commanders in this and other wars, was unenthusiastic about the arguments of the armchair generals in the ministries at home. In mid-1966 he spoke out in the Party's theoretical organ, *Hoc Tap*, against those far from the battlefield who lack "realism" about the problems of war. He condemned "mechanically copying one's past experience" and declared that "to repeat exactly what belongs to history in the face of a new reality is adventurism." About the same time, he warned a conference of senior officials in the South against conventional assaults on the forces of the United States. "If we fight the Americans in accordance with modern military tactics, we will be badly battered by them," the general said. ". . . We must fight the enemy as we would fight a tiger as he leaps at his prey. Only by inventing a special way of fighting can we defeat the Americans."

Just before the leaders of the Party and the Army met in mid-1967 to make the great strategic decision, the field commander's voice was stilled. Had he lived, the plans and preparations would probably have been approached with greater caution and the entire design might have been significantly different. It is intriguing to think that some anonymous U. S. Air Force bombardier on a B-52 flight from Guam tripped the trigger that dropped a bomb that caused a death that led in turn, many months later, to the gravest and bloodiest battle of the Second Indochina War.

The Communist Party and government of North Vietnam have compounded the inherent darkness of a closed Communist system with the Vietnamese talent and tendency for clandestine behavior, and the result is one of the most secretive ruling circles in the world. Meetings of the Party Central Committee or its smaller, more important Political Bureau are rarely announced, and even the membership list is secret. Hanoi officials do not leak unauthorized stories to the press, nor do they permit unguarded reminiscences or candid memoirs giving details of decision-making behind the scenes. The ruling group at the top, intact for a generation, has cast little light of any sort on its inner workings.

The mid-1967 decision to launch the Tet Offensive was among the most important ever made by the Vietnamese Communist leadership, but no details of the decision-making sessions have been made public, and none are likely to be available for many years. North Vietnamese leaders do not even formally acknowledge that the decision was theirs, preferring the thin fiction that the war policies are determined in the South. In a rare interview with a Western journalist a year after the battle, General Vo Nguyen Giap, the Minister of Defense, asserted with a straight face that, "We had nothing to do with it. The [National Liberation] Front put it on."

Nevertheless, it is a fact that the Tet Offensive was ordered in the North in July of 1967 and that the ensuing six months of military, political and diplomatic preparations were directed from the North. It is also a fact that, for once, the United States Government was aware at the moment of decision that something big was under discussion at high levels in Hanoi.

The first hint had come to Washington by way of Paris. In the middle of June an informant learned that Mai Van Bo, North Vietnam's senior diplomat in the French capital, had been summoned home to Hanoi. A few days later Washington learned that the North Vietnamese ambassador to Indonesia was preparing a similar trip. Presently, word filtered through the bamboo curtain that the North Vietnamese ambassador in Peking had left. One by one, nearly all the important North Vietnamese diplomats disappeared from their posts around the world and headed home. Some of them were seen making airplane connections in Vientiane, Laos, on the final leg of their journey, and with this news hopes for peace soared in the hearts of some American officials. By making connections through Laos, the ambassadors avoided a stop in China, which had consistently and adamantly opposed any compromise settlement of the Second Indochina War.

In early July the diplomatic correspondent of *The Times* of London heard about the departure of the ambassadors and the speculation that it meant a peace bid was in the making. On

July 13, under the headline "Hanoi Attitude Softening," he reported that Hanoi's diplomats had been summoned home. The British news agency Reuters obtained confirmation of *The Times* dispatch from its sources in the Foreign Office, and sent the news world-wide.

The only resident non-Communist correspondent in Hanoi, Bernard-Joseph Cabanes of Agence France-Presse, asked North Vietnamese official sources about the story. He was told that the recall of the ambassadors was a routine affair. It was, of course, anything but routine.

The General Offensive and General Uprising

To understand what led the Lao Dong Party to stake its forces and, to some extent, its future on a sudden, violent throw of the dice, it is necessary to know something of the history of the Vietnamese Communist movement and of its central strategic concept, the General Offensive and General Uprising.

The General Offensive is borrowed from the Chinese Communist revolutionary theory, but the accompanying stress on an earth-shaking General Uprising is distinctly Vietnamese. This is hardly surprising for a nation whose history has been dominated by rebellions, including ten important uprisings against Chinese rule before A.D. 940, and nearly constant insurrections against French colonial domination, which began about the time of the American Civil War.

Taken together, the General Offensive and General Uprising is the theoretical Sunday punch of the Vietnamese Communist movement, combining conventional military attacks with simultaneous uprisings within the cities. In Western terms, the nearest equivalent would be D day on all fronts combined with simultaneous insurrections in enemy-held areas to collapse the foe from within.

In theory and tradition, it was a General Uprising in August 1945 that brought the Vietnamese Communist movement from obscurity to the forefront of the national resistance against the

French. The facts of history appear to be different, but the myth may be more important.

The French colonial grip on Vietnam was largely shattered in World War II by the military operations of the Axis powers —the German occupation of the French homeland and the Japanese occupation of Indochina. After several years of uneasy tolerance, the Japanese army of occupation in March of 1945 disarmed and interned the colonial French. In August of that year the waning fortunes of the Japanese were shattered in turn by the United States' atomic bomb raids on the Japanese homeland.

The Vietnamese Communist Party had long been preparing itself to oust the French. When Japan began to slip and the direction of the war was plain, the Party laid careful plans to seize the moment between the fall of the Japanese and the return of the French. Three days after Japan sued for peace, the Party called for a General Uprising of the people. Throughout the country, leaflets and posters appeared bearing the name of the Viet Minh Independence League, a popular front movement created by the Party. Viet Minh speakers, who claimed to be the representatives of all nationalists and patriots, led meetings and demonstrations.

Viet Minh guerrillas marched into Hanoi without serious opposition. The Japanese Imperial Delegate fled, Vietnamese Emperor Bao Dai abdicated and the Viet Minh proclaimed itself the government of Vietnam. According to non-Communist accounts, not one person in a thousand knew at the time who Ho Chi Minh was or that the revolution was Communist-led. Hardly anybody cared. The important thing was to rid the country of foreign rule.

When France recovered from her own occupation, she began fighting to regain her colony. The Viet Minh fought back with a combination of diplomatic maneuvers and guerrilla operations. In 1947, at the outset of full-scale war, Party Secretary Truong Chinh set out the three-stage theory of victory, largely borrowed from the Chinese Communist movement, in a tract called *The Resistance Will Win*.

As in the Chinese theory, the revolutionaries would be weak

in the first stage, and withdraw to the countryside to grow stronger. As the enemy pursued into the rural area, dispersing his troops and stretching himself thin, the revolutionaries would begin to nibble at the opposing forces and grow stronger. In the final stage of the war, the General Offensive (sometimes called the General Counteroffensive) would be launched. In the Maoist theory, this stage is a long process, but the Vietnamese speeded it up with a provision for a General Uprising and lightning attacks on cities.

The 1947 blueprint for winning the war against the French, including its apocalyptic vision of the final battle in the cities, remains embedded in Vietnamese Communist theory. Thirteen years later, at the beginning of the intensive phase of the Second Indochina War, *The Resistance Will Win* was reprinted by the Hanoi regime, and it seemed almost as pertinent as before. Substitute the United States for France and change a fact or two, and the 1947 tract is a concise rendition of Communist thinking on the eve of the Tet Offensive:

> . . . as a result of the long war the enemy troops become weary and discouraged, and are tormented by home-sickness. The French economy and finances are exhausted; supplying the army is difficult, the French troops have to put up with privations, the French people do not want the war in Vietnam to go on any longer. The movement against the war and against the diehards in France grows stronger and more fierce. The peoples in the colonies rise up actively against the French rulers. World opinion severely condemns France, which is isolated diplomatically. The world movement for peace and democracy scores great successes, etc. . . .
>
> During this stage, the enemy surrenders many positions and withdraws to entrench himself in the big cities. He will possibly hold false negotiations with us with a view to gaining time, carrying out delaying schemes in order to wait for direct and more active assistance from world reaction. As for us, our consistent aim is that the whole country should rise up and go over to the offensive

on all fronts, completely defeat the enemy and achieve true independence and unification. . . .

Our troops concentrate rapidly and actively launch planned lightning attacks on the cities and enemy positions to encircle and annihilate them. In brief, we throw all our forces throughout the country into the battle to crush the enemy completely and win back the whole of our territory! The machinery of enemy rule temporarily set up in our country is smashed to pieces by our army and people. And at the bottom of the scrap-heap of that machinery lie the rotten corpses of the puppet traitors. This third stage of warfare is relatively the shortest, but it is also the most victorious and valiant.[1]

As it turned out, of course, the First Indochina War did not end this way at all. All three waves of Giap's General Offensive of early 1951 were unsuccessful, and the final wave—an attack in the open in the Red River delta—ran into a newly arrived French weapon known as napalm and became a disaster that nearly cost Giap his command. The Viet Minh did not encircle the cities to win the war, and there was no General Uprising worthy of the name. The Viet Minh won the war—or rather, the French lost it—in a single battle at a place called Dien Bien Phu, not because the military power of France was broken but because the French government and people became convinced they could never win. This was what the Vietnamese have come to call "a decisive victory," one which might be limited militarily but whose psychological and diplomatic consequences would be decisive. The decisive engagement of the First Indochina War left deep marks on Vietnamese Communist thinking and played an important and instructive part in the making of Tet.

In the fall of 1953 the Soviet Union and China, for their own reasons, were unenthusiastic about the struggle in Indochina.

[1] Truong Chinh, *The Resistance Will Win* (Hanoi: Foreign Languages Publishing House, 1960), pp. 76–78. The text was first published as a series of articles in March–August 1947, and republished in this English-language edition. The italics emphasizing the lightning attacks on cities appeared in Hanoi's 1960 translation.

France was weary of the war, and many of her politicians were calling for a negotiated settlement. In this situation, the Lao Dong Party decided to make a massive military push against the French, and at the same time initiate peace talks.

The Politburo met at the end of September 1953 under the chairmanship of Ho Chi Minh to approve General Vo Nguyen Giap's operational plans for a winter-spring offensive, and from November 19 to 23 the senior military committee worked out the details. On November 20, while the military planning was under way, Ho Chi Minh sent a sensational reply to a cable from the Paris correspondent of the Swedish newspaper *Expressen:* a public offer to begin negotiations with the French on a cease-fire and settlement of the war.

The French picked up the peace bid. On March 13, 1954, while diplomatic preparations were under way, the Viet Minh began the assault on Dien Bien Phu. On May 7, the day before the international conference at Geneva was to begin, the Viet Minh broke through the lines at Dien Bien Phu, and ten thousand French defenders surrendered. The French generals and the politicians in charge attempted to minimize the defeat, pointing out that the Viet Minh had suffered a terrible bloodletting. The French people would have none of it. They were tired, and they had little heart for this dirty, far-off war. Dien Bien Phu was the final blow. The fighting continued while the diplomats met, but in reality the First Indochina War was over.

The Americans insisted on salvaging half the country for a nationalist regime, and moved in to replace the departing French. The Second Indochina War was on. For the Vietnamese Communists, the enemy was bigger and tougher, but the theory was the same. From the outset, they knew how they had to win it. "Americans do not like long, inconclusive wars," said Premier Pham Van Dong to Bernard Fall in 1962, "and this is going to be a long, inconclusive war."

In the initial stages, the Communists observed that the United States was engaged in war-by-proxy, supplying advisers, money, matériel and air support while the South Vietnamese government troops did the fighting and dying. The Party theoreticians called this "Special War," and recognized that it was relatively cheap and painless for the United States and that the Americans could keep it up for a very long time.

Late in 1963—following the fall of President Diem in South Vietnam—the Communists mounted a mighty surge against the Army of the Republic of Vietnam (ARVN), the weak fighting element of the Special War. The theorists foresaw that the United States might send its own ground forces to save the day. Nonetheless, the Communists were willing to run this risk of escalation. Deployment of U.S. ground troops in "Limited War" or "Local War" (as they described the next higher stage of battle) would bring sharply rising costs, risks and internal pain to the United States. The North Vietnamese calculated they could endure the added strain longer than the mightier but more impatient U.S.A.

The United States took the bet, and in December 1965 the 12th Plenum of the Lao Dong Party Central Committee met in Hanoi to reassess the situation. The central conclusion, as conveyed to the fighters in the South, was that the Liberation Forces would be able to cope with 800,000 to 1,000,000 American and "puppet" troops and still achieve great victories. The principal conclusion for the future was that planning should begin for a joint military-political-diplomatic push to bring the Limited War to a head on favorable terms. In other words, another "decisive victory."

In the South the Central Office for South Vietnam, the Communist High Command on the ground, adopted a lengthy resolution officially setting forth the Party's decisions. The resolution declared:

> The objective we have in view in the immediate future is to achieve a decisive victory within a relatively short period of time [defined elsewhere as "a few years"]. That objective can only be achieved if we coordinate very closely the armed struggle with the political struggle and the psychological struggle. . . .
> *We have the capability of coordinating the armed struggle with the popular uprising to liberate the cities*

and towns, and of coordinating our offensive with the mass revolt in preparation for a *general attack and uprising which will take place when the opportunity avails itself and the situation ripens.* [Italics in original.]

On the diplomatic issue, the resolution declared that the war could never be settled through negotiations until the "aggressive will" of the Americans is crushed. It added, however:

> At a certain time we can apply the strategy of fighting and negotiating at the same time, in order to support the armed struggle, and thus accelerate the disintegration of the puppet army and regime, and create more conditions favorable for our people to win a decisive victory.

General Nguyen Van Vinh, chairman of the Reunification Department of the Party in the North, instructed the military leadership to begin the groundwork for the big battle of the war. A detailed report of his speech to the 1966 conference of the Communist High Command later fell into American hands. It said:

> With regard to the General Offensive and General Uprising, it was requested that a concrete plan, including the quantity of weapons needed, the number of armed forces needed, etc., be made known in order to carry out the undertaking confidentially. For secrecy's sake, it is not yet necessary to reveal information on these matters.

When to move? How to prove to the Americans they cannot win? How much force to commit? Where? The debate took place at high levels of the Lao Dong Party in late 1966 and early 1967. In the end the logic of events may have dictated the decision as much as the logic of any arguments.

The Communists were well aware that 1968 was a presidential election year in the United States and the time when the American political system was most vulnerable. In view of the slowness of Hanoi's military logistical system and the need for extensive preparation of the political and diplomatic setting, a big engagement in early 1968 would have to be ordered not much later than mid-1967.

Another factor affected both the timing and target of the attacks. Since the U.S. build-up in 1965, 500,000 to 1,000,000 South Vietnamese *per year* had been fleeing their homes in the countryside to seek safety from bombs and bullets in the government-dominated cities. The families leaving Viet Cong areas were no longer available to pay taxes, provide food and shelter and supply soldiers for the Liberation Army. Many Viet Cong soldiers were defecting to join their families in the cities. This massive population shift was hurting the Communist side. As control was eroding, so was its manpower base. Beginning in late 1966, the Viet Cong began shelling urban areas in order to reduce their attractiveness as safe havens and start a flow of people back to the countryside. This was not effective. It was perhaps inevitable that the cities would be the primary target of the next big Communist move.

The strategists recognized explicitly that a general attack was risky business, that just as before the United States might respond by stepping up the war to a more costly and dangerous level. The North Vietnamese were prepared to take the chance. In mid-1967 the Hanoi regime had adequate manpower to carry on the war at existing or even higher levels for a long time. Of the 450,000 men of the Vietnam People's Army (the regular army of North Vietnam), roughly 70,000 were serving in Laos and South Vietnam. Though the losses were substantial, a new crop of about 200,000 young men reached age eighteen each year, and about 100,000 were inducted into the armed forces. In case of crisis, the regime could call on roughly 3,000,000 men in the regional forces, popular forces and self-defense forces in North Vietnam. Its mobilization plan called for expansion of the regular army to 525,000 men within six months of mobilization day and to 625,000 men within a year. No such mobilization order was required for the Tet Offensive.

The invasion of Cambodia, Laos and/or North Vietnam by

United States troops was considered a live possibility by the planners in the North. Large numbers of men were stationed along the seacoast of North Vietnam to guard against amphibious assault, and an alternate capital was established in the mountains in case Hanoi and other vital points should have to be abandoned due to heavy bombing or invasion. Should the United States seriously threaten the existence of the regime, help would be requested from China under long-standing agreements. There seemed little doubt that China would respond.

In this situation, the gamble of the Tet Offensive was substantial but tolerable. If the General Offensive and General Uprising were even partially successful, it would bring the war to a head once more, forcing the United States to take another large step into the quagmire or pull back. If all went well on every front, the results could be even more dramatic—the destruction of the South Vietnamese government and Army, a general uprising of the people and achievement of a decisive victory almost overnight. Whatever the planners in the North estimated the probable result to be, it is not surprising that the optimum version of victory was presented to the fighters in the South.

Five months after the midsummer meeting in Hanoi, a provincial Party committee in South Vietnam summarized for its trusted cadres the meaning of the coming battle as it had been presented from on high. The Binh Dinh Province Committee wrote in a secret report:

> In July 1967 a Resolution for a General Offensive and Uprising was adopted at the Political Bureau Congress. It was adopted after lengthy assessment of the current political and military situation and with the realization that we possessed the capability for successes.
>
> . . . . .
>
> The General Offensive will occur only once every 1,000 years.
> It will decide the fate of the country.
> It will end the war.
> It constitutes the wishes of both the Party and the people.

Military Preparations

The military leaders of the struggle in the South were summoned to a meeting in late July at the headquarters of the
military affairs section of COSVN (the Central Office for South
Vietnam). The headquarters, often referred to by the Communists
as "R," was located in a large huts-and-bunkers complex in the
Fishhook section of Cambodia just across its border with South
Vietnam. Two and sometimes three tiers of jungle trees arched
fifty to a hundred feet above, screening the encampment from
the sight of aircraft and aerial photography. Beneath the shelter-
ing canopy were thatch-roofed buildings—a large outdoor meeting
hall, small huts for living quarters, mess halls and a rough-hewn
club where motion pictures from Hanoi and Peking were shown
and rice wine, Cambodian liquor and soft drinks were available.

Among those called to the meeting from command posts
throughout South Vietnam was Colonel Tran Van Dac, the deputy
political chief for Military Region 4 (the Saigon area) and a
veteran of twenty-two years in the Liberation Army. Dac was
born in Song Cau along the fertile southern coast, the oldest
of seven children of a prosperous farmer, and he was destined
from an early age to be a leader in his land. In 1945, when
the Japanese surrendered and the August revolution broke out,
he was twenty-one years old and a student at the *lycée* in Hue,
and he eagerly answered the call to fight for independence and
defend the homeland against the returning French colonialists.

Tran Van Dac became a member of the Communist Party in
December of 1945, and he rose swiftly through the Viet Minh
ranks, from common soldier to platoon leader, political commissar
for a company, political commissar for a battalion, then for a
military region. In the most glorious days of the anti-French war
he fought in the celebrated 365th Battalion, the "Jackfruit Leaves
Battalion," so named because its members wove their homemade
helmets from the leaves of the jackfruit tree. The unit was very
strong and enthusiastic, and had the trust and support of the
people. It attacked French outposts and convoys nearly every day,
and killed many French officers and men.

After the Geneva agreement which divided the country in 1954, Vietnamese were given their choice of living in the North or South. Roughly 900,000 people, many of them Catholics, chose to leave the Communist-dominated North for the non-Communist South. About 90,000 people, many of them Viet Minh fighters and their families, went from the South to the North. Dac was ordered North by the Party. He left his wife in his home village —her family were large landowners and considered reactionaries —and boarded the last Polish ship for the North. Two days before he left, their first and only child, a son, was born.

In North Vietnam Dac became political officer of the 324th Division, which was composed of ethnic Southerners; they trained to return to the South. In January of 1962 Dac and others marched South through the mountains, along narrow trails and through rain-soaked jungles, to carry on the fight for the revolution. Eventually, he was assigned as one of the ranking political officers for the People's Liberation Armed Forces (the Southern army, or Viet Cong) in the Saigon area.

At the send-off ceremony for Dac and his group just before their return to South Vietnam, Lieutenant General Tran Van Tra, deputy chief of staff of the Vietnam People's Army, had spoken of the hardships and sacrifices which lay ahead and of the victory which would surely come. Now, in mid-1967, almost six years later, the same lean, handsome general stood in the conference hall shed at "R" and told Dac and the other leaders that detailed preparations were to begin at once for the General Offensive and General Uprising. General Tra did not say when the attack would be launched, but all energies were to be put into planning for "N day." (The word "day" in Vietnamese is *ngay*. Borrowing the allied usage of World War II, the Vietnamese Communists refer to "N ngay" or "N day.")

It was to be an ambitious engagement, requiring extensive and coordinated attacks, new cadres and troops, new weapons and frontal attack tactics. It was clear from the discussion that success would depend heavily on popular uprisings in the cities.

Dac was thrilled by the chance to win the war and unify the country, and go back to his village, his wife and his child.

At the same time, he was not certain that the time was right. He was a cautious, methodical and quiet man whose nature and habit in the cause was to ponder everything and prepare carefully before taking action. Could the necessary men and weapons be supplied in a short period of time? What would the Americans do? Most disturbing of all, were the urban masses really ready to rise up as the high commanders said? Dac recalled a trip he had taken along the southern rim of Saigon late in 1965 to check the enthusiastic progress reports of the guerrilla units and political cadres in the area. He had been shocked to find only a small, disorganized group instead of the vigorous movement which had been depicted, and he realized then that the reports of the urban cadres were laced with optimism and even lies. Compared to the fighters in the jungles, these men had soft jobs, and they wanted to keep them. "Progress" reports helped.

Dac took his reservations to his superiors during the mid-1967 meeting at "R." They reproached him for being "overly pessimistic" and told him not to worry. He should go to work and leave the broad strategy and direction to them.

The colonel complied. The days were filled with meetings to discuss the operational and logistical requirements of the General Offensive. At night Dac worked in the thatch-roofed hut assigned to him, writing and dispatching radio messages to his Saigon region headquarters to begin the preparations. Three of his radio directives were particularly important:

— First, the order to begin work on dividing the command. For the purposes of the General Offensive, the generals had decided to divide the Saigon area region into five new subregions. Each one was to begin at the central city and radiate into a sector of the perimeter like a slice of pie.

— Second, a program of preparation for new cadres and troops. Previously, men had been taken from guerrilla squads and local force units to fill out the Viet Cong main force battalions and regiments. Now the flow was to be reversed: replacements from the regular forces, including many from North Vietnam, were to fill gaps in the local units, which were to be the shock wave of the coming attacks on cities and towns.

— Third, a reorganization of the communications and transportation networks from the Cambodian border to Saigon. Relay stations were to be established or improved every four to eight hours' walk along the infiltration routes. Soldiers, liaison men and a chief of station would be posted at each stop. New rockets, small arms, ammunition, men and orders would pour across these routes.

The meeting at "R" concluded in mid-August, and the military leaders made their way through the countryside back to their command posts. Colonel Dac and his three personal aides—a staff aide with the rank of captain, a private secretary and a bodyguard—took nearly two weeks to make the rugged and dangerous journey back to their Military Region 4 headquarters near Ben Cat, north of Saigon.

In September the new subregion organization was completed on paper, though it was not to take effect until several months later. On September 28 the Current Affairs Committee, the ruling body of the military region, dispatched a "flash" message to subordinate headquarters calling for stepped-up political activities in the outer perimeter, suburban areas and inner-city slums of Saigon. Political operatives were instructed to make temporary common cause with all who opposed the government, even though they might not be friendly to the Party and the revolution.

Outstanding fighters of the Liberation Army were called to Binh Long Province near the Cambodian border for the morale-building "Second Congress of Heroes, Emulation Combatants and Valiant Men of the South Vietnam People's Liberation Armed Forces." Ho Chi Minh sent a message extolling the heroes as "flowers of the nation." The honorees included a one-armed guerrilla who had learned to fire a rifle with his elbow and killed two enemy; a boy who, it was claimed, had raised and trained bees to sting the aggressors and a soldier who had planted and detonated mines from ambush positions along busy roads, killing four hundred Americans and receiving the title of Valiant American Killer with the highest record in the entire South. A seventeen-year-old hero declared, "If he has hatred, even a child can kill Americans."

The plan of attack on Saigon was completed in outline in
October. Nearly 100 tons of new weapons were brought into the
Saigon military region for the use of the provincial and district
local forces.[2] (The main force regular units maintained a separate
supply system.) Most of the weapons were transported by bicycle,
oxcart and sampan.

About this time, the briefings for cadres from regimental to
company level began. In the Vietnamese Communist system, it
is essential for everyone who counts—that is to say, the members
of the Party—to be fully briefed on the purpose and significance
of the tasks at hand. *Chinh Huan,* or reorientation indoctrination
sessions, are held at least annually at every level of the Party and
more often whenever the Party doctrine changes. In the late fall a
round of *Chinh Huan* sessions told the fighters in the South of the
"new situation and mission" which would "split the sky and shake
the earth." The news generated tremendous excitement in the Viet
Cong ranks. Some of the combatants burned their miserable
jungle huts when they left for the staging areas to prepare the
big attack. They were certain they would never return; after
the General Offensive and General Uprising they would live in
comfort in Saigon and the other cities.

Lieutenant General Tran Van Tra left his headquarters at
"R" in December, more than a month before Tet, and took up
residence at Colonel Dac's headquarters near Saigon. The presence of this highest-ranking commander of the Liberation Armed
Forces (since the death of General Nguyen Chi Thanh) was evidence to everyone that the attacks on the capital city had a very
high priority.

The commanders of the Saigon attacks took advantage of the
Viet Cong-allied Christmas truce to reconnoiter their assigned
targets. On Christmas Day Colonel Nam Truyen, commander of
the 9th Viet Cong Division, traveled into the capital city disguised

[2] For the Viet Cong this was an unprecedented supply of weapons. However, it was a pittance compared to American supplies. During 1967 U.S.
forces in Southeast Asia consumed more than 1,000,000 tons of ammunition
of all varieties. This is a *daily* average of 2700 tons. During the summer
of 1967 the United States shipped 50 tons *per day* of Post Exchange supplies
to South Vietnam.

as a student returning home for the holiday. He was thirty-five years old, but looked young enough to get away with it. He visited Tan Son Nhut Air Base, which was to be his unit's primary target. One of his regimental commanders paid a call on "the family grave site" in a government military cemetery near the giant air base. All of the visitors were supplied with forged identity papers. None reported any trouble at the police checkpoints on their way into the city or on their way back to their jungle posts.

The visitors reported to the High Command that security in Saigon was lax, and the military portents were favorable. Colonel Tran Van Dac was glad to hear this news, but he was still apprehensive about the plan. The General Offensive might be a glorious day of battle, but would the General Uprising take place? Without the Uprising, could the Liberation forces win?

The Politics of Uprising

While the Party believed (in Mao Tse-tung's phrase) that political power grows out of the barrel of a gun, there was also never any doubt that the gun was to be wielded only for clear and specific political purposes. Thus the Tet Offensive, while largely military in nature, was ordered by the *Political Bureau* of the Lao Dong Party to achieve *political* ends in South Vietnam, the United States and the rest of the world. Without political success, military gains were likely to be fleeting.

The principal Communist political vehicle in South Vietnam was the National Liberation Front, the latest in the long line of popular front organizations which had been created to win the support of the people. As part of the preparation for the Tet Offensive, the Party took measures to strengthen and broaden the appeal of the National Liberation Front.

In mid-August an extraordinary Congress of the NLF was convened in the jungle and on September 1 a broad new 7500-word political program was beamed to the people of South Vietnam by the clandestine Liberation Radio. The new program promised "free general elections . . . freedom of speech, freedom of press and publication, freedom of assembly, trade union freedom, freedom of association, freedom to join political parties, freedom of creed, freedom to demonstrate . . . freedom of residence and lodging, secrecy of correspondence, freedom of movement, freedom to rest and work, and the right to study." Most of these freedoms do not exist in North Vietnam.

An important innovation of the Front program was a section aimed at neutralizing or winning over government troops, police and civilian officials. The Front promised to welcome defecting "puppet" officers and officials. Those who fight against the Americans will be rewarded and promoted to "adequate positions," the program promised. Those who sympathize with the Front or refuse to carry out American or "puppet" orders "will have their merits recorded."

Despite the broadened political program, the National Liberation Front was too well known in the South as a Communist tool to be of great effectiveness, and the Party was well aware of the fact. For more than a year—since the summer of 1966—the Party had been laying the groundwork for a series of new Front groups to make its case at the crucial moment of the war.

The man in charge of preparations in the Saigon area was a slender, bespectacled Party veteran known by the cover name of Ba Tra—in English, Mr. Three Tea. Born Le Ngoc Lan in the Mekong delta area of South Vietnam, he joined the Resistance in 1945 as an undercover police agent and later became a member of the Communist Party and a Viet Minh economic inspector. After the country was divided in 1954, Ba Tra remained in the South to work for the Party in the general elections campaign prescribed by the Geneva Conference. The elections were never held and Ba Tra—by then a high official of Sicovina, one of Vietnam's largest textile firms—remained in place as an underground agent.

When the Party decided to step up the renewed Resistance war in 1960, Ba Tra was ordered to help organize the National Liberation Front. Among those he recruited was his brother-in-law, a Saigon physician named Dr. Phung Van Cung, who moved to the jungle and became vice-chairman of the NLF Central Committee.

In mid-1966 Ba Tra was named deputy chief and operating leader of a new clandestine Intellectual Proselytizing Section for the Saigon area. The job of the new unit was to make discreet connections with anti-government organizations and leading businessmen and intellectuals who would speak up at the right moment for coalition government and peace. Some of the contacts could become ministers or other high officials should the coalition government materialize; ostensibly they would be nationalists and anti-Communists, but actually they would work with the Party.

The last week in March 1967 Ba Tra was summoned to a conference at a base area in the forests of War Zone D northwest of Saigon. There he learned that the fighting-and-negotiating phase of the war would begin at the end of the year, and that intensified efforts must be made to prepare "spontaneous" political support. The conference was told that North Vietnam had notified both the Soviet Union and China that negotiations with the Americans would soon be undertaken, with coalition government the principal demand. The Russians were reported to be pleased, but Chinese Premier Chou En-lai protested vehemently. Any possibility of a deal with the U.S.A. was anathema to the Chinese, who wanted the war to continue.

After the conference in Zone D, Ba Tra began lining up prominent citizens for what would become the Alliance of National and Peace Forces, to be surfaced at Tet as the new pro-coalition group. Before he could get very far, he was arrested by South Vietnamese government police. Among his list of contacts at the time of his arrest in May 1967 were two Saigon magistrates, a high official of the Saigon port authority, the chief of an engineers' association, a prominent bank director, a well-known lawyer and a retired professor.

Rumors of a coming coalition government spread widely through South Vietnam during the late summer and fall of 1967, causing jitters among Saigon government leaders and citizenry, and consternation among American officials. One version of the rumor was that the United States was secretly preparing a coalition arrangement as a convenient way of terminating its costly and increasingly unpopular intervention in Vietnam. Another version was that some South Vietamese government officials were collaborating with the Viet Cong on a coalition plan. Both versions appealed to the Vietnamese fondness for duplicity, and there was just enough truth in reports of secret maneuvering to give credence to the rumors.

The United States Government that fall was in touch with the Viet Cong, exchanging views about a settlement as well as the question of prisoners of war. The top levels of the South Vietnamese government knew of this development, and were very nervous about it. For a time, high officials of the American government— including some at the White House—thought they had made the most important clandestine contact of the war.

In September a Viet Cong agent named Sau Ha was arrested by South Vietnamese police. The agent told his interrogators that he had been instructed by the Communist leadership in July to open a channel of contact to the American Embassy in Saigon. He had a letter to the Embassy suggesting discussions about the exchange of prisoners and other matters of mutual interest, not specified. Sau Ha produced a list of more than a dozen high Viet Cong prisoners being held in government jails whose release was requested.

The South Vietnamese government was skeptical, but dutifully passed the word to the Americans. The report was flashed back to Washington, where it set hopes soaring in high official circles. "Prisoners and other matters" is a classic negotiation-opening gambit. There was speculation that the North Vietnamese might finally be ready to settle, and had chosen the Viet Cong to make the bid. Presidential assistant Walt Rostow was particularly enthusiastic about the affair, which was given the Washington code name of Buttercup.[3]

[3] A budding flower lover in the upper levels of the State Department assigned the names of blossoms to various peace initiatives during the Johnson administration. The most celebrated of the flowers to come to light was Marigold, the code name for extensive peace soundings in Hanoi by Polish and Italian diplomats in late 1966. It was reported in detail by David Kraslow and Stuart H. Loory in *The Secret Search for Peace in Vietnam,* New York: Random House, 1968.

With South Vietnamese government acquiescence, Buttercup was nurtured. The United States sent a letter to the Communist side through the channels opened by Sau Ha. At the same time, the United States began applying pressure on the Saigon government to release some of the prisoners on the Buttercup list as a sign of good faith and in hopes of obtaining some long-held American prisoners from the Viet Cong in exchange.

In mid-October the United States received a lengthy letter of reply. It said there was no possibility of a political settlement so long as the United States did not draw the essential conclusion about the war—that the United States cannot impose its will by military means. The letter suggested as a basis for negotiations the standard five points of the National Liberation Front and four points of the North Vietnamese government, which had been made public long before.

Rostow and some of the others in Washington were crestfallen. Rather than a new breakthrough, this seemed to be a repetition of what the Communist side had been saying all along. Interest in Buttercup wilted.

Finally, Buttercup turned into a snapdragon. Word got around Saigon that the Americans and high Vietnamese officials were negotiating with the Viet Cong and that General Nguyen Ngoc Loan of the National Police was considering releasing some Viet Cong prisoners as part of a deal. An angry speech about the matter was made in the National Assembly in December, and General Loan let it be known he had turned in his resignation in protest against dealing with the Viet Cong and North Vietnamese. (The resignation was not accepted, if indeed it was ever submitted.) A newspaper close to Loan charged that "the Americans and their henchmen" were seeking to sell out the nationalist cause. Rumors about a coming coalition government flew thicker and faster than ever, and were believed by more people.

Some American officials concluded that the Buttercup affair had finally achieved its original purpose—to sow doubt and suspicion in South Vietnam and give credence to the coalition government rumor. Others believed Sau Ha was fake from start to finish, and represented nobody but himself. Still others are convinced that something serious was intended by the Communist side—but they are not certain what.[4]

Readiness in the North

While these military and political preparations were taking place in the South, the leaders of the Party in the North were preparing their own people for the critical stage of the war. Ho Chi Minh himself, now seventy-seven years old and in fading health, would rally the Party and the people of the North to support the coming struggle.

It might seem unnecessary for the monolithic North Vietnamese regime to sell the nation on the wisdom of its policies, but this was not so. According to reports which later trickled out of North Vietnam, the war policies of the regime were under substantial attack at the time within the Party, and both arrests and exhortations were necessary to quiet the dissent.

Beginning in September, more than two hundred officials of the Party and government were taken into custody because of their opposition to the direction of the war, according to a North Vietnamese intelligence officer who later defected. Among those reported arrested were Hoang Minh Chinh, director of the Party's foremost school of theoretical political studies and a leader in the

[4] In late February, well after the Tet Offensive began, the South Vietnamese government secretly turned over three Viet Cong political prisoners to U.S. authorities, who in turn released them to the Front through clandestine channels and without publicity. Two of the three had been on the original Buttercup list. Sau Ha, the agent who started the whole affair, was also released to the Front after Tet.

One of the prisoners the Viet Cong wanted most, a high-ranking Front official named Le Thi Rieng, was mysteriously killed while in custody. According to government police, she was caught in a cross fire of bullets while being moved from the embattled National Police headquarters in Saigon during the Tet fighting. The Viet Cong charged she had been tortured by her captors and executed after she refused to talk.

Nearly a year later, after the whole affair had been pretty much forgotten, someone called one of the telephone numbers designated by the United States as a secret contact point for Viet Cong participants in Buttercup. The caller intimated he might have some important information, setting off a flurry of excitement in Saigon and Washington. The caller never called back.

wave of internal dissent; Colonel Le Trung Nghia, director of Central Intelligence for North Vietnam; Bui Cong Trung, deputy chairman of the State Science Committee and a member of the Party Central Committee; and Nguyen Viet, chief of the finance section of the Ministry of Light Industry.

A few weeks after the arrests began, the Standing Committee of the National Assembly enacted a lengthy decree prescribing death sentences, life prison terms and lesser penalties for a long list of "counterrevolutionary crimes." These included espionage, sabotage, security violations and the crime of opposing or hindering the execution of "national defense plans." The decree was signed by President Ho on November 10, but not made public until four months later—well after the Tet attacks.

Despite growing fatigue and illness and incessant rumors that he was dead or dying, Ho Chi Minh still played an important role in the regime and in the Vietnamese Communist Party, which he had founded in 1930. The old revolutionary was tremendously popular; whenever a major campaign was undertaken, his personal endorsement was extremely important. Just before Christmas 1967 Ho made a public appearance in Hanoi to open the campaign of martial enthusiasm leading to the Tet Offensive. The occasion was a joint celebration of the twenty-first anniversary of the beginning of the war against the French and the twenty-third anniversary of the founding of the Vietnam People's Army. An anti-aircraft gun was mounted on the roof of the National Assembly building where the celebration was held. Every seat was filled for the occasion; bleachers stretching toward the ceiling in the big hall were occupied by colorfully dressed representatives of mountain tribes and other ethnic minorities.

Ho had not appeared in public for four months, and his appearance on the platform that day was greeted with great enthusiasm. He seemed to have put on weight and his once ascetic face had become puffy, but otherwise he appeared vigorous and happy. He was dressed as Commander in Chief in a high-necked tunic and trousers of creamy white. "I feel twenty years younger," he told the crowd, thinking of the days when the war was also young.

Surrounded by his comrades in arms of the Party leadership, he spoke for nine minutes, four of which were taken up by applause. His speech was strong and solemn, the way his oratory had been in the old days. In recent years Ho had addressed his speeches primarily to the people of the North. This time, however, he spoke to both halves of the country. He declared that because the Americans persist in their aggression, "the thirty-one million Vietnamese [seventeen million in the North and fourteen million in the South by Hanoi's official reckoning], young and old, men and women, must be thirty-one million resistance fighters, fearing neither hardships nor sacrifice, going forward in the wake of their victories to accomplish even greater feats of battle." At the climax of his speech, he appealed for new efforts and new victories in the new year.

The Lao Dong Party newspaper, *Nhan Dan,* wrote of Ho's address that "it is an order to advance in our victorious drive, it is a signal for a new wave of attacks. It is the order of the day coming from the supreme command." *Quan Doi Nhan Dan,* the Army newspaper, declared that "the words of Uncle Ho are like a trumpet announcing battle. . . . The solemn appeal of Chairman Ho is the mobilization order to the fatherland passed to one after another of the thirty-one million fighters. . . ." *Ban Tan Viet Hoa,* published for the Chinese minority in Hanoi, printed a poetic dialogue of "war drums pounding, cannons resounding." The dialogue said, "This is the command to advance! This is the call to charge!" Editorials were published in Hanoi appealing to youth, communications troops and logistic troops to heed the President's words.

On Saturday, December 30, government messengers fanned out through Hanoi with individually addressed envelopes for foreign diplomats, high officials and leading citizens. Inside each envelope was a pink New Year's card bearing a poem in Vietnamese:

> This Spring far outshines the previous
>   Springs,
> Of victories throughout the land come
>   happy tidings.

> Let South and North emulate each other
>   in fighting the U.S. aggressors!
> Forward!
> Total victory shall be ours.

The poem was signed simply "Ho Chi Minh." It was broadcast over Hanoi Radio on January 1, and rebroadcast on the eve of Tet.

The final maneuver was ready. As in 1953, the Party would make a bid for negotiations on the eve of the military contest. This time, Foreign Minister Nguyen Duy Trinh of North Vietnam sent up the peace signal. He sprang his surprise on the evening of December 30 in an otherwise routine diplomatic reception for a visiting delegation from the Mongolian People's Republic.

The site was the Hanoi City Hall, the ornate old French building which in colonial times had been the palace of the French Resident-General. On the left side of a grand hallway was a large reception room dominated by an ample buffet of Vietnamese egg rolls, rice salad, fruit and drinks of all kinds. Food being scarce in Hanoi at the time, most of the journalists and many of the dignitaries headed immediately for the buffet table. Across the hall in the right wing of the palace, Foreign Minister Trinh was making a formal speech. Premier Pham Van Dong stood behind him smiling enigmatically, as if he knew a little joke he wasn't telling.

Bernard-Joseph Cabanes, the French news agency reporter, could understand neither the Vietnamese version of the speech nor the translation into Mongolian, but his journalistic eye told him that something interesting was taking place. Official translations in French and English were produced for Cabanes, who soon realized he had a big story. Always before, the Hanoi regime had been vague and conditional in its official statements about the consequences of a United States decision to stop the bombing. Now for the first time Trinh said that after the unconditional cessation of bombing, North Vietnam "will hold talks" with the United States on relevant questions. Cabanes's story made headlines around the world. To ensure that the United States got the point, Hanoi

Radio broadcast the Trinh declaration over its international short-wave facilities—in English.

As the North Vietnamese anticipated, their announcement put Washington on the spot. The American authorities had been saying for many months that they were eagerly awaiting "a signal" from Hanoi of its willingness to go to the conference table. When a newsman had asked President Johnson what steps the North Vietnamese would have to take to gain a suspension of the bombing he had replied, "Just almost any step." Ambassador to the United Nations Arthur Goldberg had asked publicly and pointedly what the Hanoi regime "would" do if the bombing were stopped. And at San Antonio, Texas, in September, President Johnson had publicly offered to stop the bombing "when this will lead promptly to productive discussion."

What did the signal mean? Why now, when American intelligence was reporting increasing signs of a major offensive coming in the South? Was it a trick to get the bombing halted and enmesh the United States in a negotiating trap? Could the United States "assume," as the San Antonio speech also said, that North Vietnam would not take advantage of the bombing cessation to step up the flow of men and supplies to the South?

The Communist government of Romania, which had good relations with the North Vietnamese regime and had tried previously to bring about negotiations, agreed to seek answers to American questions. After receiving a carefully drawn set of inquiries from U. S. Ambassador-at-Large Averell Harriman, Deputy Foreign Minister Gheorghe Macovescu embarked for Hanoi, stopping in Moscow en route to inform the Russians.

When the Romanian emissary reached North Vietnam in the middle of January, the United States placed Hanoi and Haiphong off limits to its bombers as a show of good faith and to protect the go-between. Macovescu was still in Hanoi awaiting final answers to the questions, and the Hanoi-Haiphong bombing was still stopped, when the Tet Offensive broke over South Vietnam.

The Coming of Tet

All the elements of the plan—military, political and diplomatic —were now in place and the clock was ticking toward N day just ahead. The great problem was how to achieve maximum impact through surprise, a problem made more difficult by the magnitude of the undertaking.

The solution was deception. Fortunately, the means were at hand to foster a climate of laxity and false security in the allied camp. Beginning in 1963, the Communist Command had proclaimed annual battlefield cease-fires for Christmas, New Year and Tet, the oriental Lunar New Year. The Saigon government and United States Command followed suit beginning with Christmas 1965. The recurrent holiday truces quickly became accepted and expected in Vietnam as if they were commonplace in wars, which they are not.[5]

On November 17, 1967, the National Liberation Front proclaimed cease-fires of three days each for Christmas and New Year's and a seven-day cease-fire for Tet. The Lunar New Year is by far the most important Vietnamese holiday, universally cherished by every religious group and social class. There is no equivalent holiday in the West. A 1965 pamphlet of the U. S. Military Assistance Command, Vietnam, described Tet to American GIs as "a combination of All Souls' Day, a family celebration, a spring festival, a national holiday and an overall manifestation of a way of life," and acknowledged that this was an incomplete and inadequate description of its importance. The Tet celebration formally lasts a week, of which the first three days are exceptionally important, but the Vietnamese work up to it for weeks in advance. In North Vietnam as well as South Vietnam, Tet is a time for new clothing, new resolutions, new luck and old traditions of family life and ancestor worship.

---

[5] One of the few comparable situations was the Truce of God instituted by the Catholic Church during the Crusades of the eleventh century. The bishops first forbade fighting on Sundays and later extended the cease-fire to cover long weekends as well as Lent, Advent and other holy days. As the Truce of God began seriously to interfere with the warfare of men, it was abandoned.

United States and Vietnamese government officials generally expected light military action by the Communist armies in the South during the Tet truce is 1968, as in the past. Yet very few of the Americans were aware of the numerous precedents for surprise holiday attacks in Vietnam. In 1944 General Giap had sent his tiny Vietnam People's Army, which had been officially formed only two days previously, against French outposts on Christmas Eve. French defenders were caught by surprise and slaughtered. In January 1960 Viet Cong troops had attacked government military headquarters in Tay Ninh, near Saigon, on Tet Eve. The surprise attack was the first large-scale action of the Second Indochina War.

The most illustrious Tet exploit in Vietnamese history was Emperor Quang Trung's surprise attack on Hanoi in 1789, an event with an epic quality similar to that in the United States of George Washington's Christmas Eve crossing of the Delaware in 1776. According to the Vietnamese legends and popular history books, Quang Trung (also known as Nguyen Hue) marched on Hanoi at Tet with several hundred elephants and 100,000 troops. His men had celebrated the holiday early outside of Hanoi so they could attack the unsuspecting and carousing Chinese during the holiday. The Chinese fled in disarray from the city, but Quang Trung wisely made his peace with the Chinese emperor to forestall retribution. The Chinese leader called back his expeditionary force and relations between the two countries were stabilized.[6]

In January 1968 a statuette of Quang Trung was prominently displayed in the Saigon living quarters of the United States expeditionary commander, General William C. Westmoreland, a present to him from a Vietnamese acquaintance. Five days before the 1968 lunar holiday, the General Association of Students of

[6] The Chinese emperor, Ch'ien-lung, was unhappy about the intervention in Vietnam in the first place. He wrote: "Why should we take Chinese troops, horses, money and supplies and waste them in such a hot, desolate and useless place? It is definitely in the class of not being worth it. . . . Even if we chase away Nguyen Hue [Quang Trung] how can we guarantee that there will not be more Nguyen Hues again coming out to cause trouble? . . . The environment of that place is inhospitable. It is not worth any great involvement."

Saigon University celebrated Quang Trung's surprise attack and victory over "foreign aggressors" with a dramatic presentation attended by thousands of people. Many of the songs and speeches carried anti-American overtones.

In Hanoi the Prime Minister's office published a circular urging the people to celebrate the Tet of 1968 "enthusiastically but thriftily, neatly, plainly, wholesomely, in a manner appropriate with wartime." The authorities announced that the Tet slogan for the Year of the Monkey would be "All for complete victory over the U.S. aggressors."

Visitors said Hanoi seemed more cheerful than at any time since the beginning of the bombing of the North in 1965. The capital and the country had become reconciled to the conditions of wartime, and there were hints between the lines of the official propaganda that the end of the war was coming into view.

The harvest had been bountiful, and the authorities had taken pains to prepare for a more abundant Tet than those just passed. On the eve of the holiday, seventeen million dong leaves—the traditional wrapping for the Tet cakes of sticky rice—had been brought into the capital. Chrysanthemums, peonies and gladioli had been shipped into the city in large quantities to decorate homes, offices and the state stores. Extra rations of tea, cigarettes, Chinese noodles, rice wine, candy and other popular items were available at "Tet food centers." Children and old people, who had been evacuated to the countryside to escape the U.S. bombings, were brought home to worship at the family altar and celebrate the holiday. The shouts and games of children were heard in the streets again.

Although the government did not pass along the news that Hanoi had been placed off limits to American bombers because of the visiting diplomat from Romania, everyone was conscious that the usual air raid sirens had not been heard in the city for ten days before Tet. Perhaps to keep the citizenry on its toes, an air raid warning was sounded at three-thirty the afternoon prior to the celebration. No planes could be seen in the sky, but the anti-aircraft batteries fired briefly. People jumped into the bomb shelters in the streets and secured the heavy concrete covers. Soon there was an all clear, and people resumed their preparations for the holiday.

On the eve of Tet, throngs of people strolled through the heart of Hanoi. The electric power authorities diverted current to the downtown area, bathing the city in unaccustomed brilliance and showing off the national flags which had been hung as decorations. Families crowded into photographers' studios to have family pictures taken for the New Year. At the "Little Lake" near the center of the city, the most famous and beloved of the Hanoi landmarks, children took turns in small boats. Gunfire could be heard from shooting galleries which had been set up in parks, with likenesses of grimacing American soldiers as the targets.

At midnight the voice of President Ho greeting the people was heard over the fifty thousand loudspeakers in every quarter of the capital and its suburbs. Rockets and fireworks displays lit up the sky, and firecrackers reverberated through the streets. The cathedral bells pealed to welcome the New Year.

On New Year's Day a strange editorial dominated the front page of *Nhan Dan*, the Party newspaper. Headlined "Onward to Final Victory!" it spoke fervently of Uncle Ho's "combat order" and the moral and historic responsibility of the Vietnamese to defend the nation and build a revolution. The Vietnamese people, it declared, have defeated the Japanese, "the most barbarous fascist aggressors of Asia," and the French, "the shrewdest colonialism of Europe," and are currently crushing "the cruel new colonialism of America, which is playing the role of an international gendarme." The struggles of the Vietnamese people are bringing their nation to the rank of the most advanced nations in the world, the front-page editorial said. "Onward to final victory!" *Nhan Dan* proclaimed. "Let the entire nation move forward to completely defeat the American aggressors!"

The most unusual and, in retrospect, most significant aspect of Hanoi's celebration was virtually unnoticed outside North Vietnam. According to the lunar calendar, the Year of the Monkey was due to arrive on Tuesday, January 30. The government, however, decreed that New Year's Day would be celebrated a day earlier, on Monday, January 29, with New Year's Eve on Sunday night.

Puzzled citizens who inquired about the change were informed that this year the moon, the earth and the sun were in unusual and favorable conjunction a half hour before the beginning of the actual New Year, and thus an early celebration would be more auspicious.

More cogent reasons emerged later. Soon after the news that the General Offensive and General Uprising had been launched in the South, trucks began evacuating the children and old people from the city in anticipation of retaliatory American air raids. Because they began a day ahead, the families of North Vietnam were able to celebrate the most important three days of Tet together.

Almost seven months after the funeral of General Nguyen Chi Thanh and the great decision by the Lao Dong Party, the preparations for the General Offensive and General Uprising were nearly complete. The political and diplomatic initiatives had been taken. The people of the North had been given time to celebrate their holiday. In the South, sappers and propagandists had infiltrated the cities to wait for the signal to act.

The final preparations were those of the men who would assault the cities from the outside. Several days before Tet all leaves were canceled and troops restricted to their posts. The troop movements had taken place in stages, from one jungle base to another, and finally they had arrived in force at the jumping-off points close to the target areas.

During the weeks leading to the holiday, the briefings for officers had become increasingly specific. One Viet Cong division— the 9th—was told to prepare for a march which "entirely differs from combat operations conducted during the last seven or eight years." The movement was to be at night under strict security conditions. The familiar wicker hats of the Viet Cong soldiers were to be concealed in their packs; shirttails were to be tucked inside trousers instead of worn outside in the usual fashion. Only dry rations of roasted rice, canned fish and canned milk were to be eaten during the march, avoiding the need for cooking fires. Nguyen Huu Thu, a North Vietnamese assigned as an artillery leader of the unit, wrote in his notebook that "the march is to be the greatest march in the history of the war against the Americans."

While the Tet firecrackers were exploding in the streets of the cities on the eve of the attack, the soldiers of the Liberation Army were gathered in the stillness of the forests outside. On orders from above, commanders read to every unit an extraordinary document:

ORDER OF THE DAY OF THE HEADQUARTERS, ALL SOUTH VIETNAM LIBERATION ARMED FORCES

To all cadres and combatants,
"Move forward to achieve final victory."

The Tet greeting of Chairman Ho is actually a combat order for our entire Army and population.

And in compliance with the attack order of the Presidium, Central Committee, South Vietnam Liberation Front, all cadres and combatants of all South Vietnam Liberation Armed Forces should move forward to carry out direct attacks on all the headquarters of the enemy, to disrupt the United States imperialists' will for aggression and to smash the Puppet Government and Puppet Army, the lackeys of the United States, restore power to the people, completely liberate the 14,000,000 people of South Vietnam, fulfill our revolutionary task of establishing democracy throughout the country.

It will be the greatest battle ever fought throughout the history of our country. It will bring forth world-wide change but will also require many sacrifices. It will decide the fate and survival of our Fatherland and will shake the world and cause the most bitter failure to the imperialist ringleaders.

Our country has a history of 4,000 years of fighting and defeating foreign aggression, particularly glorious battles such as Bach Dang, Chi Lang, Dong Da and Dien Bien Phu. We defeated the special war and we are defeating the limited war of the Americans. We resolutely move forward to completely defeat the American aggressors in order to restore independence and liberty in our country.

. . . . .

Dear comrades,

It is evident that the American aggressors are losing.

The call for assault to achieve independence and liberty has sounded.

The Truong Son [the Annamite mountains] and the Mekong River are moving.

You, comrades, should act as heroes of Vietnam and with the spirit and pride of combatants of the Liberation Army.

The final victory will be with us.

CHAPTER III

America on the Eve

"We can endure the hardships of a lengthy war,
but they are unable to endure the hardships of such a
war because they are well-to-do people. A poor man can
subsist by spending one piaster a day, but a man who is
accustomed to living in comfort is uncomfortable even
though he spends ten piasters a day."

—Major General Tran Do of the Vietnam People's Army
in a speech to troops in South Vietnam

THE MOST fundamental and the most fluid battle lines during the summer and fall of 1967 were in the theater of American public opinion. From the beginning, the massive United States involvement in Vietnam had been a race between accomplishment and patience, and now patience was running out. Millions of Americans who had tended to leave the war to the President and the generals became increasingly frustrated, unhappy and skeptical about the conflict in Indochina. Many of these people had accepted the war as a desirable anti-Communist venture as long as it appeared to be successful and relatively painless, but success had proved to be debatable and elusive, and the pain was growing.

The government said the war was succeeding, but every few months it dispatched additional troops, and the casualties and the costs went up each time. There was no respite from the daily bulletins of body counts and bombing raids, or the nightly battle scenes on the television evening news. People could see no end to it. Large numbers of practical, down-to-earth Americans in the broad middle ground of public opinion began changing their minds about the war.

The government's response to growing doubts on the home front was to redouble its claims of success on the battle front. Led from the White House, the executive branch waged a campaign of speeches and statistics to demonstrate that the light was dawning at the end of the tunnel. It did not turn out as the government expected. The dawn in Asia would come not softly, but with a lightning bolt.

The action had started in the spring. General William C.

Westmoreland had sent word that once again he needed more troops. Some 400,000 American fighting men were serving in South Vietnam, and the number was scheduled to rise to a ceiling of about 470,000 by the end of the year. On April 27, 1967, Westmoreland presented a two-option plan to the Commander in Chief at the White House: (1) a "minimum essential force" of 80,000 additional troops was required to match the continuing enemy build-up of men and weaponry in and around South Vietnam; (2) an "optimum force" of 118,000 men in addition to that would increase the pressure on the enemy and win the war more quickly.

The question around the coffin-shaped table in the Cabinet Room was, When would this long, frustrating war end? A forecast was difficult, Westmoreland replied, but he guessed it would take at least five years to terminate the war with the minimum additional force. If the optimum force were approved, the war might be cut to three years.

The general's guess was greeted with glumness. Would the American public tolerate the war for five more years, or even three more years? How could the public be shown quick and impressive results to justify the continuing build-up and to prove that the war was no stalemate but a winning proposition?

Walt W. Rostow, the presidential adviser on foreign affairs, suggested one method of dramatic accomplishment—a land penetration of North Vietnam. The idea had been investigated in detail the year before by General Earle Wheeler, chairman of the Joint Chiefs of Staff, and three separate plans were secretly drawn up. Each had envisioned a joint ground-airborne-amphibious invasion, one in the area of Vinh in the southern part of North Vietnam and the other two even closer to the demilitarized zone. The trouble was that any of them would have required about three divisions of troops. Some men were to come directly from the United States (staged through Okinawa), but many others were to be provided by the U. S. Command in South Vietnam. However, Westmoreland had reported to Wheeler that he could not spare the troops to tackle the job.

Troop strength and political will had been at the heart of the problem of taking the war to North Vietnam in 1966. Now the same two problems confronted the men in the Cabinet Room in April 1967. If Westmoreland were granted his maximum request of nearly 200,000 additional men, there would be ample strength for dramatic forays into the southern part of North Vietnam, or even into the Communist supply route and sanctuary areas of Laos and Cambodia. The basic decision was political, and it came down to a question of what the people of the United States would support in a limited war and what the political leadership believed the war was worth in terms of global risk.

Should the decision be made to take the war into North Vietnam, Westmoreland reported, the necessary preparations could not be completed before the spring of 1968 because of weather conditions in the North. The President did not seem to be much interested in the idea. For the moment, the subject was dropped.

Lyndon Johnson decided to get by with as few new troops as possible without breaching his public promise to meet Westmoreland's "needs." Ten weeks after the Washington meeting, Secretary of Defense Robert S. McNamara flew to Saigon to negotiate a minimal version of the field commander's "minimum essential" troop request.[1] In the end, Westmoreland agreed to accept 55,000 additional American troops, considerably less than the 80,000 minimum augmentation he had suggested, with the promise from Washington of additional U.S.-financed troops from Thailand or Korea to come later.

This latest increment of American manpower would raise the United States troop ceiling in Vietnam to 525,000 men, passing both the psychologically important half-million mark and the top United States troop commitment to the Korean War. A practical consequence was even greater: it would require several billion dollars more per year in American military expenditures.

This was the final blow to President Johnson's precarious economic policy of guns and butter, the Vietnam War and the Great Society, all without economic controls or a general tax increase. This "no sacrifice" policy was, in turn, a vital underpinning

---

[1] McNamara and his party arrived in Saigon on July 7, 1967. In Hanoi that day, the North Vietnamese leadership buried General Nguyen Chi Thanh and prepared to move ahead with the General Offensive and General Uprising.

of the fading Johnsonian consensus, but now the economists warned that some sort of sacrifice was imperative. On August 3 the President stood before a blackboard full of budget numbers and proposed a 10 per cent surcharge on all individual and corporate income tax returns.[2] At the same time, he announced he was sending 45,000 to 50,000 additional men to fight in Vietnam in the months ahead.

Until that moment, most Americans had not been asked to do anything or pay anything to support the war. For most of them, the conflict was remote from their personal lives and experience. Of the nation's 13,000,000 young men between eighteen and twenty-six years of age, approximately one in every fifty was drafted in 1965–67. Of those who were inducted, no more than half were assigned to Vietnam even at the peak of the action. Of the group which reached the war zone, one in fifty was killed. For all the talk of coffins coming back, it is likely that the vast majority of 200,000,000 Americans did not know personally any of the 13,000 men who had been killed in action in Vietnam from 1961 to the summer of 1967. More Americans than that died *per year* from accidental falls, twice as many died *per year* of cirrhosis of the liver and four times that many died *per year* in motor vehicle accidents.

In mid-1967 government spending for the war was running at a rate of $20 billion annually, enough to unbalance the national budget and require President Johnson to seek a tax increase. Compared to that of other wars most people could remember, however, the economic drain was modest. World War II at its peak soaked up 48 per cent of the Gross National Product the nation's total production of goods and services. At the peak of the Korean War, 12 per cent of the Gross National Product went for military purposes, the majority of it for the war in Asia. In mid-1967 9 per cent of the Gross National Product was consumed by military spending. Only about one third of this, or roughly 3 per cent of the Gross National Product, was attributed to the Vietnam War.

[2] Johnson had asked Congress in January to enact a 6 per cent surtax, but he took pains not to tie it closely to spending on the war. His proposal got nowhere on Capitol Hill and was not taken seriously in the country.

Though the war did not hurt much or cost much in the usual sense, there was little enthusiasm for it. No significant group was personally and strongly committed to the war—unlike World War II, Jews were not being exterminated, France was not invaded, England was not threatened and, most important of all, Pearl Harbor had not been attacked. Unlike the Korean War, there had been no open invasion across recognized boundaries, and there was no United Nations resolution calling for international action. This time most other nations thought America was wrong.

The United States seemed to have gone to war by inches, and most people could not recall just how or when it happened. Roughly half of those interviewed by the Gallup poll in June of 1967 said they had no clear idea of what the war was all about. Shortly after the Tet Offensive at the highest point of military action of the war, the chairman of the Appropriations Committee of the House of Representatives, who had supervised and approved the provision of nearly all the money which had been spent by the United States forces in Vietnam, asked the Chief of Staff of the U. S. Army to explain the national strategy being followed there and specifically inquired, "Who would you say is our enemy in this conflict?" He was seeking information.

Only a small minority strongly opposed the war as morally wrong, but this group included many of the intellectual and religious leaders of the country. The General Board of the National Council of Churches of Christ in the U.S.A. declared in June 1967 that "it is wrong for the U.S.A. to be the sole judge in the Vietnam conflict" and in September called continued U.S. military action at a high level morally unjustified.

For the first time in the history of the United States, it was considered normal and even fashionable for leading families of government and business not to send their sons abroad to war under the nation's flag. Many of these young men participated in protest marches and others obtained draft deferments and sat it out. The American elite tended increasingly to think it was a bad war which did not merit their participation or support.

At a university commencement where students were seated according to their academic honors, Secretary of Defense McNamara noticed that the higher the level of attainment, the greater was the hostility toward him as a symbol of the war. The incident reflected a fact of life on American campuses. Comparing college graduates' attitudes toward the war with the faculty salaries and academic standing of the institutions they had attended, the Survey Research Center of the University of Michigan discovered stronger than average support for the war among graduates of the less well-known and less exalted institutions. The higher the standing of the school, the stronger was the anti-war sentiment.

For the great majority of Americans, the war was not a moral issue so much as a practical problem. Patriotic, anti-Communist and generally willing to follow presidential leadership in matters of war and peace, most people became distressed only after the war became protracted and doubts grew about military progress toward a tangible victory. Some people wanted to step up the bombing, some favored a negotiated settlement and gradual withdrawal and many people were in favor of nearly anything at all that seemed likely to get it over with. The public was uncertain and unhappy. There was much reality in the joke about a housewife who told the pollster at her front door; "I'm 47 per cent for escalation, 47 per cent for getting out and the rest undecided."

Shortly after the President's surtax announcement, the nation's leading public opinion pollsters, George Gallup and Louis Harris, detected a sharp decline in public approval of President Johnson's handling of the war. Gallup also reported that for the first time in the polling history of the Vietnam conflict more people said the war was "a mistake" (46 per cent of his national sample) than said it was not (44 per cent). As in the Korean experience, only a small minority thought the war a mistake at the beginning, but that number had grown month by month. Gallup calculated that since August of 1965, the first time he had asked whether the Vietnam War was "a mistake," some twenty-five million adults had changed their minds.

Of 205 members of the House of Representatives who responded to a *Christian Science Monitor* survey in September, 43 had recently shifted their positions from support of Administration war policy toward more emphasis on finding a way out. Of 203 representatives, senators and governors responding to a New York *Times* survey in mid-October, 30 high officeholders said they had recently shifted their views toward a stronger peace posture and 10 toward stronger military measures. A much larger number of political leaders said public opinion was shifting against the war.

A fascinating pastime that summer and fall was to watch the dominoes in Congress falling, and to investigate who was changing his position on the war and why. One of the first was Senator Thruston B. Morton of Kentucky, a former Republican National Chairman with a reputation for political sagacity. As an Assistant Secretary of State during the Eisenhower administration, Morton played a small role in establishing the United States commitment to Vietnam and more recently he had been, like most in Congress, a supporter of the United States military moves in that far-off land. Morton had become increasingly disenchanted with the results, and after small-town schoolteachers, taxi drivers and other ordinary citizens in his usually hawkish state had complained long and loud about the war tax, he publicly reversed his posture. "I was an all-out hawk," he said in an interview. "I was all for the bombing; I thought once we started, the war would be over in six months. I was wrong. Our country has been planted into a corner out there. There's going to have to be a change." In a subsequent series of press conferences and speeches, Morton declared the official Vietnam policy to be "bankrupt" and called for a bombing halt, an end to search-and-destroy missions, substantial reduction of American troops in Vietnam and new efforts to seek a negotiated settlement.

Some of the "switchers" on the war in the House were Paul Findley, who represented Abraham Lincoln's old congressional district in Illinois and previously was an outspoken hawk; Claude Pepper of Florida, the old New Dealer and political pro; Al Ullman of Oregon, who had been the only congressman from his state consistently backing President Johnson's Vietnam moves; Morris Udall of Arizona, the brother of Lyndon Johnson's Secretary of Interior; and Thomas P. (Tip) O'Neill of Boston, a Democratic organization pol with the respect and affection of nearly everyone on Capitol Hill and with close ties to the President. All had their own convictions and arguments, and all were hearing from home.

The war had become an issue of intense personal concern as well as public concern to many lawmakers, and they were hearing objections around the family supper table. Representative O'Neill, for example, was bombarded with questions from his twenty-two-year-old son, Tom, and his twenty-year-old daughter, Susan, both students at Boston College. O'Neill brought back the answers from special government briefings, but Tom and Susan shot those official answers full of holes each time. Digging more deeply, the congressman discovered that many of the officials briefing him had their own private doubts about the war, and that these were shared by generals, colonels, Foreign Service and intelligence officers and other pros he knew around Washington. It was also a fact that the electorate was changing, and this included both the academic enclaves of Harvard and MIT and—more important to O'Neill—his bedrock middle-class Irish constituency. O'Neill guessed that the normal 85 per cent Democratic majority in his district was down to 65 per cent and shrinking fast. In September he proposed that the government stop the bombing of North Vietnam, redeploy United States troops to strategic enclaves and take the war to the United Nations for settlement. "After listening to their side of the story for a year and a half, I've decided that Rusk and McNamara and the rest of them are wrong," O'Neill told reporters who came around to inquire. "We are dropping $20,000-bombs every time somebody thinks he sees four Viet Cong in a bush. And it isn't working."

"And it isn't working" was the central justification for the turnabout. Very few of the switchers in Congress objected to the war on moral or legal grounds, and very few of them fit easily under the label of "doves." Some, in fact, represented districts laden with military installations; the office walls of these men and others were adorned with replicas of military weapons and signed photographs of prominent generals. So long as the war appeared to be progressing at an acceptable pace and an acceptable cost, these men did not object. Their quarrel was not with the aims of the war—such as they could perceive—but with failure. It was ob-

vious in the fall of 1967 that these reversals in Congress reflected
inroads into the great middle ground of American opinion, and
that this development was far more serious than peace marches or
anti-war polemics, both of which were rejected by the majority
of citizens. "Hell no, we won't go!" on the lips of youthful protesters was not much of a problem politically for the Johnson administration. "And it isn't working" on the lips of middle-of-the-road
congressmen and their constituents was a serious problem. It could
be far more serious if the battle in Asia did not go well.

The March of Time

The nation's news media was the filter through which the
public received its ideas about the events and portents in Vietnam.
In the beginning of the major U.S. involvement, most of the influential newspapers and magazines supported the war editori-
ally, and the television networks made special efforts to explain it
to the public. As the war continued, the correspondents in Vietnam
became increasingly disillusioned and pessimistic, and so did many
of their editors and news executives at home. As with the general
public, their basic quarrel was with failure.

During the summer of 1967 the Richmond *Times-Dispatch,*
the Cleveland *Plain Dealer,* the Los Angeles *Times* and the Minneapolis *Star and Tribune,* all of them major newspapers of generally conservative editorial bent, shifted their positions. They
expressed increasing editorial doubts about the war and called
for re-examination or change.

A survey of the nation's most influential newspapers, made in
the weeks prior to Tet by the Boston *Globe,* reported a split down
the middle about the conduct of the war. According to the survey,
four papers were calling for an "all-out win policy"; nineteen
papers "support the United States' commitment but oppose further
escalation, favor de-escalation, halt or limitation of bombing and
increased peace efforts"; and sixteen papers "support the Administration's Vietnam policies with no major reservations."

The most consistent and enthusiastic supporter of the war effort among the giants of the news media was Time Incorporated. Week after week, the powerful voices of *Time* and *Life* magazines, with an occasional assist from *Fortune,* told a story of determination, progress and justified sacrifice in Vietnam, and administered editorial punishment to critics and doubters. In the summer and fall of 1967 Time Inc. shifted its position and joined the ranks of the doubters. This was a grievous blow to the government and painful evidence of the seriousness of the crisis in public opinion.

In a sense, the history of conservative attitudes toward the war is epitomized in the story of Time Inc. and its editor in chief, Hedley Donovan, the man who led the Luce publications into the rice paddies in 1965 and began the march out again in 1967. Donovan was in turn detached, urgently concerned, enthusiastic, confident, expectant and then—when his hopes for quick success were not realized—disappointed, skeptical and critical.

Donovan had come out of Naval Intelligence in World War II to the staff of *Fortune,* and had risen swiftly in the Luce empire. In April 1964 he was named by Henry Luce as his editorial heir with the title of editor in chief of Time Inc. Luce, born of missionary parents in China, was a passionate opponent of Chinese Communism, and he had been a strong backer of the fallen President Diem of South Vietnam. Nevertheless, neither Luce nor Donovan was enthusiastic at first about the dispatch of American combat troops to Vietnam. The two men talked about it one day and agreed that South Vietnam might be worth 50,000 to 100,000 American troops but not much more.

Donovan took a trip around the rim of China in early 1965 and returned convinced that Vietnam was more important than he had assumed, and that the danger was grave. When the United States began bombing North Vietnam in February 1965, the *Life* editorial page, which is the official policy voice of the Time Inc. management, declared approvingly that this action "served to commit us deeply in Vietnam, and it is a commitment that must be carried through without hesitation or confusion of purpose." In August *Life* praised President Johnson for dispatching U.S. ground troops in large numbers and declared, "names like Phu Bai, Da-nang, Ban Me Thout [Ban Me Thuot], Kontum, Pleiku . . . may some day be chiseled on monuments in Michigan and Kansas, under those other names, once also thought exotic, like Chateau-Thierry, Anzio, Tarawa, Pusan."

In November 1965 editor Donovan took a ten-day swing through the war zone to inspect the American military build-up and assess its chances for success. His personal report, "Vietnam: The War Is Worth Winning," was the lead story in the February 25, 1966, issue of *Life*, with twelve pages of text, maps and color photographs of helicopters, ports, bases and ships, mostly taken from the air, and not a Viet Cong in sight. The Donovan report was inspirational and optimistic—the Vietnam War may be remembered as "a historic turning point" and is "very possibly as important as any of the previous American wars of this century"—but the article's most breath-taking feature was a daringly precise time schedule. By 1967 or even late in 1966, he forecast, North Vietnamese troops should be heading back up the Ho Chi Minh trail, military action in the South should be declining and the big-unit war should be over.

Donovan said later he did not obtain his timetable for this "first installment of victory" from Westmoreland or other officers who briefed him, but "it was in accord with their thinking." Washington was delighted with the Donovan report; if there was a premonition that it might be a Time bomb, it was not expressed. Henry Luce was enthusiastic. "You've sold me," he told Donovan.

Many *Time-Life* staff members in New York, Washington and, particularly, Saigon had doubts about the grand design, and the doubts grew month by month with greater experience and knowledge of the war. Nearly all those assigned to the Saigon bureau in 1966 and 1967 went out thinking this was pretty good war in a pretty good place, and nearly all of them changed their minds sooner or later. One *Time* correspondent remembers the precise moment—a long conversation late at night with an American major along the seacoast of II Corps. The moon was full and the sky was cloudless, and it was possible to see the rugged mountains of the highlands rising just a few miles beyond the rice paddies where the GIs had slogged that day. "That's triple-canopy jungle out there," the major said. "You could put five divisions there, almost within sight of our camp, and we would never know it."

The correspondent felt it was madness to try to beat guerrillas in that sort of terrain, which is very common in Vietnam, but few such doubts about the war found their way into print in *Time*. Reports from staff correspondents were piked if they were "negative." A New York editor who worked on Vietnam news recalled, "You couldn't print anything negative unless you came in with a lawyer's brief to prove every point." As dissent built up in the nation, it crept slowly up the hierarchy of Time Inc. in New York, beginning with copy boys who might be drafted and spreading to researchers out of Vassar and Smith, and to the staff writers and editors. Managing editor Otto Fuerbringer of *Time*, who had great freedom within the broad bounds of corporate editorial policy, was dedicated to the view that the war was both right and feasible. He would make a refueling trip now and then to Washington or the LBJ Ranch and return with word for the skeptics—"You guys don't know what you're talking about."

Henry Luce died in February 1967. In the spring Donovan returned to the war zone to inspect the reality of the victory he had forecast seventeen months previously. The *Time-Life* correspondents in Saigon told him no victory installment was at hand or in prospect. They had concluded that the war was a stalemate.

Donovan spent several days with his twenty-two-year-old son, Peter, who had been rejected for military service because of bad eyesight and had joined International Voluntary Services, the Vietnam equivalent of the Peace Corps. Peter had learned Vietnamese and was serving in the Mekong delta. He was impressed and distressed by the venality of the local officials and the slow pace of progress in the war. In Saigon Westmoreland and the other generals were as confident as ever, but they declared the war would take more time—and additional troops.

"Vietnam: Slow, Tough but Coming Along," by Hedley Donovan, was the lead story in the June 2, 1967, issue of *Life*, with twelve pages of text and color photographs. This time the pictures were from ground level—the smoke, flame and dust of war, tanks mired in the mud, a dirty, sweaty GI on a steamy search-and-destroy mission, a young blond captain with a crew cut who was killed a week after his photograph was taken. The contrast in the pictures illustrated graphically the dawning of reality, and Donovan's text made the point directly. "Some over-optimistic Americans (this writer included, *Life*, Feb. 25, 1966) had expected to see by now the beginnings of a real momentum in Vietnam, the multiplier point when success in one theater or aspect of a war starts to breed success in many others. It certainly hasn't happened yet," the editor reported.

Two weeks after his report appeared, Donovan delivered a thoughtful commencement address at New York University. The subject was pertinent: "On the Possibility of Being Wrong." He told the graduates that the shape of the final decision in Vietnam should soon come into view—"not in a single thunderclap some Monday morning, but in an accumulation of evidence over several months." He did not predict what the outcome would be, but he appealed to politicians, journalists and the academic world to face the final truth without evasion to avoid a residue of bitterness. If the war should fail, he declared, "I hope that I, as one who has supported the policy, will be prompt to admit that we had attempted something beyond our powers."

After the *Life* article and the NYU speech, the Luce publications began to slip into neutral about the war. Correspondents in the field were emboldened to state their conclusions more strongly. At Donovan's order, a frank assessment of the war from the Saigon bureau was published in the July 14, 1967, issue of *Time*. Under the title "Taking Stock," it reported that Communist forces in Vietnam were as strong or even stronger than a year before.

Developments at home also weighed heavily on the editor's mind. The reports of *Time* correspondents and his own contacts with businessmen and politicians throughout the country revealed the broadening and deepening of domestic opposition to the war. On a stay-at-home vacation that summer in Sands Point, Long Island, Donovan learned that even his conservative Republican neighbors were shifting their views. They didn't like the surtax. They didn't like what they saw of daily bloodletting on television. Many had sons or grandsons of draft age, and they were appalled at the prospect that their young men might have to go to fight. The women were nearly unanimous and many of their husbands agreed that this hateful war did not merit support. They wanted out.

At the end of the summer Donovan decided that Time Inc. would have a new editorial policy about the war. Simply to order such a momentous change would have been destructive to the organization in his view, so he convened a series of meetings in which the senior men went through the motions of reconsidering the Vietnam War. The Washington bureau gave the U. S. Government the courtesy of a final round of interviews to justify continued support. When Lyndon Johnson heard what was in the wind, he offered to send Rusk or anybody else to the Time-Life building in New York to set things straight, but Donovan said no. To sit in judgment on the leaders of the government in their presence would be bad form, particularly since the results were predetermined.

Time announced its change, to those familiar with its editorial methods, in its October 6 cover story on the besieged U. S. Marine base at Con Thien, "a symbol of cumulative frustrations in a complex war." The opening page of the cover story noted that opposition to the war had spread from the intellectuals, the young and the clergy to "apolitical businessmen" and "uneasy politicians." Without taking them to task, the magazine attributed to the citizenry such "pressing reasons for disquiet" as the belief that the bombing of North Vietnam had not succeeded and that the war had divided and disconcerted the United States.

The following week *Life* urged a pause in the bombing of North Vietnam to rally the public at home and abroad, and it made a new statement of its policy toward the war.

> *Life* believes that the U.S. is in Vietnam for honorable and sensible purposes. What the U.S. has undertaken there is obviously harder, longer, more complicated than the U.S. leadership foresaw. . . . We are trying to defend not a fully born nation but a situation and a people from which an independent nation might emerge. We are also trying to maintain a highly important—but

in the last analysis not absolutely imperative—strategic
interest of the U.S. and the free world. This is a tough
combination to ask young Americans to die for.

Four months later, on the eve of the Lunar New Year, the edi-
tors of *Time* scheduled another cover story on Vietnam, and
cabled the Saigon bureau chief, Bill Rademaekers, their prescrip-
tion for this latest assignment: "THE WAR IS NOT GOING WELL
FOR THE ALLIES THESE DAYS, HOWEVER MUCH WE MAY BE 'HURT-
ING THE ENEMY' OR 'HANDING HIM UNACCEPTABLE LOSSES.' WE REALLY
WANT TO EXPLAIN WHAT HAPPENED IN VIETNAM. WHY ARE [WE]
IN SO DEEPLY? WHAT DID WE DO WRONG? AS WELL AS WHAT WE
HAVE DONE RIGHT." The cover subject for the coming issue was
scheduled to be General Creighton W. Abrams, the Deputy U. S.
Commander in Vietnam and chief American overseer of the South
Vietnamese Army. Part way through the week, this plan was al-
tered by dramatic developments. Instead *Time*'s cover subject
turned out to be General Vo Nguyen Giap, and the cover story
was about the Tet Offensive.

Grounded Hawks

Lyndon Johnson had always expected the greatest challenge
to his war policies from the hawk side; the appeal for strong, decisive action was in keeping with the instincts of many Americans.
In the summer and fall of 1967 something happened to the passion
of the hawks. For two years they had been pleading with the government to "win it" in Vietnam. In deep frustration, anger and
despair, they now added a previously unthinkable phrase to their
prescription for the war—"win it, or get out."

From the beginning, there was one method of waging war
they preferred above all others, the way to win quickly, power-
fully, using American industrial might instead of American lives,
the way to win the war from ten thousand feet above the jungles
without getting one's hands dirty or even having to linger to inspect the dead. Bomb.

By late 1967 the United States had dropped 1,630,000 *tons*

of bombs on North and South Vietnam. This was more than the total tonnage the United States dropped on Europe in World War II, twice as much as it dropped during the Korean War, three times as much as it dropped on the Pacific theater in World War II. The Vietnam avalanche came to twelve tons for every square mile of territory in both North and South Vietnam, and about a hundred pounds of explosive for every man, woman and child, many of whom did not weigh a hundred pounds in flesh, blood and bone.

It was not working. The question was, Why?

Representative George Andrews of Alabama, who had been sitting on the Appropriations Committee since 1944, interrogated a very high-ranking military officer about the terrible, frustrating war that seemed to have no end.

"Do you have enough equipment?" asked the congressman.

"Yes sir," the officer responded.

"Do you have enough planes?"

"Yes sir."

"Do you have enough guns and ammunition?"

"Yes sir."

"Well, why can you not whip that little country of North Vietnam? What do you need to do it?" Andrews demanded in exasperation.

"Targets—targets," came the reply.

On June 28, 1967, Senator John Stennis of Mississippi announced that his Preparedness Investigating Subcommittee of the Senate Committee on Armed Services would hold full and complete hearings on the air war against North Vietnam. The subcommittee had been created by Senator Lyndon B. Johnson of Texas in 1950 as his publicity and investigating arm in the military field, and now President Lyndon B. Johnson was the subcommittee's principal object of concern. The purpose of the hearings was to exert pressure on the President to reject a proposed bombing cessation at the 20th parallel of North Vietnam, and to argue for attacks on Haiphong harbor and other sensitive facilities in North Vietnam which had not yet been struck.

On August 4, five days before the hearings were to open, United States aircraft flew 197 bombing missions over North Vietnam in a single day, setting a new record. On August 8, the day before the hearings began, the President released sixteen additional targets requested by the Joint Chiefs of Staff, including some in previously restricted zones. While the hearings were in progress, American bombers struck at rail lines ten miles from the North Vietnamese border with China, less than one minute's flying time from Chinese territory. Planes also hit new targets in Hanoi and Haiphong, but the government refused to bomb Haiphong harbor for fear of hitting Soviet ships.

The subcommittee made its case by hearing first from uniformed military chiefs, all of whom rejected a bombing cessation at the 20th parallel and advocated attacks on additional targets in North Vietnam. The military witnesses, in order of appearance, were Admiral U. S. Grant Sharp, the Commander in Chief, Pacific, who had over-all control of the North Vietnam air war; Admiral Roy Johnson, Commander of the Navy's Pacific Fleet, whose carriers and planes carried out a large share of the raids; General John Ryan, Commanding General of the Pacific Air force, whose land-based bombers were heavily involved; General Earle Wheeler, Chairman of the Joint Chiefs of Staff; Lieutenant General Robert Momyer, Commanding General of the Seventh Air Force in Vietnam; General John P. McConnell, Chief of Staff of the Air Force; and Admiral Thomas H. Moorer, Chief of Naval Operations. A censored version of the military testimony was released to the press each day of the hearings, bringing new headlines each time.

On August 25, after this extensive preparatory barrage, the committee heard from Secretary McNamara. He was very much on the spot. Early in the war, McNamara had been an influential advocate of bombing of the North, the dispatch of American troops to the South and national mobilization at home. More recently, however, he had felt a growing disenchantment. He was distressed by the devastation of Vietnam under the mighty weight of iron and explosives, gravely concerned about losses of pilots and aircraft, unimpressed with the results of the bombing and—most important of all—worried that stepping up the war in the air and on the ground could lead to a wider conflict with China or the Soviet Union. In the spring of 1967 McNamara had recommended cessation of bombing above the 20th parallel. President Johnson had rejected the plan for the time being, but the Defense Secretary had not given up. At the time of the Preparedness Subcommittee hearings, he was among those working on the "San Antonio formula"—an offer to stop the bombing of North Vietnam when this would lead "promptly to productive discussions," assuming that the North Vietnamese would not take military advantage of the cessation.

Unless the case could be made that extensive bombing was not essential, there was no chance of selling the San Antonio formula or any other limitation to Congress or the American people. McNamara was embattled, and he struck back hard, using the weapon of classified statistics and intelligence reports. His testimony was a direct hit on the hopes and dreams of those who were counting on bombing to win the war.

McNamara told the senators that 1900 fixed targets in North Vietnam had been struck, as well as many targets of opportunity which appeared without plan in the sights of U.S. pilots. The specific argument between himself and the Joint Chiefs of Staff was over 57 additional targets which had not been struck.

Of the targets remaining, McNamara said, one was a rubber plant producing 30 tires a day; two were battery plants producing a total of 600 tons a year ("a service station could supply that"); another was a machine shop with 96,000 square feet ("we wouldn't even call it a machine shop in this country"); nine were petroleum targets in heavily defended areas, containing petroleum in excess of North Vietnam's needs; one was a transformer to a power plant that wasn't working; and so on. The most important targets were Haiphong harbor and two other ports. McNamara said that even if these were struck, at great danger to Soviet shipping, supplies could be brought in on lighters along the 400 miles of North Vietnamese beach or overland across the 500 miles of the Chinese border.

Turning to his assessment of the achievements to date, McNamara delivered the most devastating testimony about the value of aerial bombardment ever heard from a ranking Defense official in wartime. He testified:

— 173,000 U.S. bombing sorties had destroyed $320 million in facilities—at a cost of $911 million in American aircraft. (Looking at such disproportionate costs and benefits, McNamara's Office of International Security Affairs had asked in a memorandum, "Can North Vietnam afford a bombing halt?")

— Despite heavy concentration on infiltration routes near the demilitarized zone, only 2 per cent of the North Vietnamese soldiers going South were reported killed by air strikes.

— The bombers claimed to have destroyed 4100 trucks and damaged 4000 others, but North Vietnam was operating more trucks than before the bombing began. Despite intensive bombardment, traffic over the roads South had increased; the whole road network had grown.

— The bombers had destroyed 85 per cent of North Vietnam's central electric generating capacity, but the regime readily substituted 2000 small diesel-driven generating sets to do the job.

McNamara made the point over and over that North Vietnam is not Germany or Japan but a small agricultural country with no real industrial base and only modest requirements for continuing the war. Its leaders remained determined to fight and its people, accustomed to adversity and hardship, continued to respond to the political direction of the regime. He said there was very little reason to think that bombing could force a change. McNamara's conclusion was that the enemy could be defeated only on the ground in South Vietnam.

The senators were quick to see the implications of this testimony on the prospects for a quick and easy victory in the war. Strom Thurmond of South Carolina called it "a statement of appeasing the Communists and of no-win . . . if we follow what you have recommended, we ought to get out of Vietnam at once, because we have no chance to win." Henry M. Jackson of Washington said that unless supplies to the South could be shut off, "I just don't see any end to this conflict." Howard Cannon of Nevada told McNamara that "it seems to me that we are just throwing our hands in the air and we might just as well say, 'Let us get out then because we cannot handle this problem.'" Stuart Symington of Missouri told reporters, "If the position as presented by the Secretary this morning is right, I believe the United States should get out of Vietnam at the earliest possible time, and on the best possible basis; because with his premises, there would appear to be no chance for any true 'success' in this long war."

President Johnson announced the San Antonio formula in a speech to the National Legislative Conference in that Texas city on September 29, a month after the McNamara testimony. The immediate propaganda response from Hanoi was to denounce it, but there were diplomatic rumbles that the North Vietnamese regime was interested.

On November 1 McNamara submitted a final set of recommendations designed to reduce and ultimately terminate American involvement in what had sometimes been known as "McNamara's war." In a lengthy memorandum to the President, he proposed to:
— Halt the bombing of North Vietnam.
— Announce that the United States would send no additional troops to South Vietnam.
— Review American military operations with an eye to reducing casualties, curtailing the destruction of Vietnam and turning over more of the war to the South Vietnamese armed forces.

The President sent McNamara's plan in strictest confidence to eleven of his closest advisers, telling none of them the identity of the author. Secretary of State Rusk and Undersecretary Katzenbach approved some of the ideas, but the others disapproved. One of the strongest critics of a bombing halt was Clark Clifford, then a private lawyer and confidant of the President. Johnson himself did not approve McNamara's recommendations. Later in November he named McNamara to the presidency of the World Bank, and subsequently nominated Clifford to be the new Secretary of Defense.

Its war policies under fire from within and without, the top echelon of the Johnson administration resorted to a time-honored institutional device. It sought reassurance from sympathetic and prestigious outsiders.

This senior seminar of establishment figures and former high officials convened at the State Department on November 2, at the invitation of the President. The idea grew out of a similar private meeting held in July of 1965, just before the announcement of the decision to send American ground combat troops to Vietnam.

The Wise Old Men, as somebody dubbed the senior advisers, were not informed of Secretary McNamara's proposals for a reversal of the policies toward the war. Instead, they were handed a book of government reports to read, given verbal briefings by military, diplomatic and intelligence officials and invited to ask questions and express views.

Not surprisingly, the Wise Old Men concluded with little dissent that the government was on the right track in Vietnam but that American public opinion was a problem. Somebody suggested that the government obtain a weekly block of prime television time for high officials to explain the war and its progress to the American people. (The networks didn't think much of that.) One adviser obtained the distinct impression from the briefings that the end of the war was in sight, and he suggested that this good news be conveyed forcefully to the people to buoy their spirits.

After hearing the comments and recommendations of the Wise Old Men, one of Lyndon Johnson's close White House advisers told him, "The country isn't against you, Mr. President, it's just confused."

"We Are Winning"

To the dwindling band of committed and convinced stalwarts in the government, the state of the war and of American public opinion was a paradox. Month after month, the official reports from Saigon told of slow but steady gains—the rising "body count" of Viet Cong and North Vietnamese dead, the drift of the Vietnamese people into the secure cities, new roads open, new bases built, a government which at least was legitimate and elected, whether or not it was popular—and month after month, Americans were giving up on the war. Support was slipping away. Clearly, U.S. public opinion was becoming a critical battle front.

Lyndon Johnson took it personally. In private, his critics were "simpletons," they were "cut-and-run people" with "no guts." The State Department was "disloyal" and trying for ways to make him look bad. To a visiting historian, Dr. Henry F. Graff of Columbia University, Johnson declared that "It's gotten so that you can't have intercourse with your wife without it being spread around by traitors." As for the press which constantly questioned his policies and the progress in Vietnam, they were out to get him for cheap political purposes. Later he told friends, "The only difference between the Kennedy assassination and mine is that I am alive and it has been more torturous."

At the same time, there was in Johnson an optimistic strain which told him that no man was entirely beyond redemption, that nearly any sinner might somehow see the light. Even during the worst of the criticism, he kept up his personal contact with the dissenters, the opponents, the skeptical newsmen and their publishers, and his associates got the message that they should do the same. Maybe somebody would listen and understand.

Except for McNamara, most of the beleaguered members of Johnson's High Command believed the official reports of progress in the war zone in 1967, and disbelieved the reports of correspondents and the judgments of critics that "it isn't working." All the statistical indices, charts and computer print-outs were flowing upward, ever upward, but the scoffers and doubters didn't see most of them, and if they did, they wouldn't believe them. The Washington High Command did not know that the Hanoi High Command had decided to make its biggest military push of the war, and that part of the reason for soaring statistics of progress was that Communist troops had disengaged to prepare for battle. The absence of Communist pressure was interpreted as Communist weakness. Faced with the erosion of support at home, the White House watchword that fall was, "We are winning—get the message out."

"Nothing is more important than that the public get the facts," Walt Rostow instructed the Psychological Strategy Committee, sometimes known as "the Monday group," which met the first day of each week in the Situation Room of the White House. The group was composed of representatives of the White House Press Office, National Security Council staff, State and Defense Departments, Central Intelligence Agency and U. S. Information Agency. Its job was to win the hearts and minds of the American people.

Rostow was the chairman, and he was a zealot about the war. If he saw a government report indicating progress or refuting an argument of critics, he wanted it released or leaked at once. To *Business Week* magazine went computer data charts of attacks initiated by the Viet Cong and the North Vietnamese (which showed the trend of battle to be down) and the "kill ratio" charts (the other side had suffered four times as many deaths). To the *Christian Science Monitor* went the population control data from the computerized Hamlet Evaluation Survey (despite earlier agreement within government that this tenuous data would not be publicized). The Los Angeles *Times* hit a jackpot of sorts with the leak of "authoritative reports from field commanders" to the President covering junks searched, hamlets secured, population controlled, comparative battle deaths, Communist combat battalions, Communist weapons lost, defectors received and even "overland road haul (in thousands of short tons)." All the numbers rose or fell in the appropriate direction, but the readers—like the President himself—could only guess what they meant or did not mean.

If a government report to the White House reported little or no "progress," Rostow wanted to know what was the problem or —another way of looking at it—*who* was the problem. Convinced that the central military fact in Vietnam was the rapid erosion of the Communist base, he expected reports which buttressed this position. When one official balked at changing reports to suit him, Rostow complained, "I'm sorry you won't support your President."

One of the members of Rostow's National Security Council staff was assigned to keep track of every speech critical of the war which appeared in the Congressional Record. His instructions were to arrange a government rebuttal, and have a report of his plan on the President's desk by the close of business the day the item appeared. The usual effort, of doubtful effectiveness, was a visit, telephone call or a letter from an executive branch official to set the facts straight or a planted counterspeech by an Administration supporter. Thus, when a New England congressman complained of the "stalemate" in the war, and his complaint was published in the Record, he received an unsolicited reply from the State Department citing statistics and indicators of success and asserting that the enemy is "struggling to stave off military defeat."

A four-man Vietnam Information Group was established as part of the Executive Office of the President to provide research for the public relations effort. Thanks to VIG, the output of friendly speeches, counterattack letters and corrective telephone calls soared. The effectiveness was minimal. The critics had their minds made up, and the government lacked dramatic and convincing proof that "we are winning."

The Success Offensive to rally the country went into high gear in mid-November. On Veterans Day weekend the President made a flying whirlwind tour of eight military installations to speak of sacrifice, determination and success. At Fort Benning, Georgia, he read a message he said was written on the side of a box of ham-and-lima bean C rations from a foxhole in Vietnam: "We're going to win this war if it takes our lives to do it." At Camp Pendleton, California, he declared that "Marines are winning in Vietnam." On the flight deck of the U.S.S. *Enterprise,* the largest warship in the world, Johnson offered to meet North Vietnamese negotiators at sea (the offer was promptly rejected) and promised that war would continue "not many more nights . . . not while we stand as one family, and one nation, united in one purpose."

In Saigon the U. S. Command summoned newsmen to a three-hour-and-twenty-minute briefing to claim that the fighting efficiency of the Communists had "progressively declined" in the previous six months. The Command also announced a drop in estimates of Communist military strength for the first time in the war, and made public computerized calculations claiming that 67 per cent of the people of South Vietnam were living in areas under government control. There was bureaucratic controversy about both the substance of these claims and the advisability of publicizing them, but the White House was pushing for action.

The Washington *Evening Star* published the comments of senior U.S. military men in Vietnam, obtained in on-the-record interviews by the paper's Pentagon correspondent in a trip to the war zone. "The war—the military war—in Vietnam is nearly won," reported Orr Kelly on the basis of the generals' assertions. General Bruce Palmer, Deputy Commander of U. S. Army, Vietnam, told Kelly: "The Viet Cong has been defeated from Da Nang all the way down in the populated areas. He can't get food and he can't recruit. He has been forced to change his strategy from trying to control the people on the coast to trying to survive in the mountains." Brigadier General A. R. Brownfield, Deputy Assistant Chief of Staff of the American Command, told Kelly: "We military people are all very optimistic. We see the situation getting steadily better. . . . I know he [the enemy] isn't going to do very well. He just isn't going to make it. . . . By next year this time, he's going to be in bad shape. Personally, I have doubts that he can hang on. He may base some units in Laos and Cambodia and across the DMZ and carry on raids across the border and back again. But inside the country, there will be just small guerrilla bands—harassment and that's all."

Vice-President Hubert H. Humphrey, returning from a trip to the war zone, told the viewers on the NBC-Television *Today* show: "We are beginning to win this struggle. We are on the offensive. Territory is being gained. We are making steady progress." During the Vice-President's trip to Saigon, Independence Palace had been shelled—while Humphrey was there attending a diplomatic reception.

The most important battle order for the Success Offensive came from President Johnson. He summoned Ambassador Ellsworth Bunker, General William C. Westmoreland and Ambassador Robert W. Komer (the pacification chief) to Washington for a "high-level policy review" and a round of speeches, press conferences, television appearances and other public presentations. Bunker, who landed first, reported "steady . . . continual progress."

Westmoreland was the big gun. He was not an Eisenhower or MacArthur in the public mind, not yet, but he was the square-jawed commander of U.S. combat troops in the field, handsome, well-spoken, with a soldier's bearing and four stars on his shoulders. He was the answer to Lyndon Johnson's prayers. He had credibility. He would be believed.

Johnson was ill at ease with many military men, but he felt comfortable with Westmoreland. He had first met him up at West Point in 1961, when Westmoreland was superintendent of the military academy and LBJ—then Vice-President—came to speak to the cadets. He liked Westmoreland's manner and his lingering South Carolina drawl. (Johnson was supersensitive about his own Texas accent and about the clipped cadences of the eastern intellectuals who mocked it.) In early 1964 he picked Westmoreland from a field of four generals to be the new Vietnam commander. He was the only one of the four Johnson knew personally.

Public relations on the home front is not among the ordinary assignments of a field commander, but this was not an ordinary situation. Johnson employed Westmoreland in this role three times during 1967. The general was reluctant at first, fearing that he would get dragged into arguments beyond his realm, but he did as he was told and appeared before the lawmakers, the press and the people.

The first time, in April, Westmoreland was summoned to speak to the annual meeting of the Associated Press and to a Joint Session of Congress. He was properly confident of his men and of the final victory, but he said Vietnam was "a war of attrition" and held out no short cuts or easy answers.

Westmoreland returned in July for his mother's funeral in South Carolina, and he stopped at the White House on his way back to the war zone. Johnson called in reporters and put him on display. Westmoreland declared that "tremendous progress" had been made in the war, and that any report of stalemate was "complete fiction." Despite prompting by both the President and the press, the general would not forecast the future. "I am in no position to speculate on that," he answered with the caution of a lifetime in uniform.

Back in Saigon, Westmoreland was well supplied with news clippings, wire service dispatches and a steady flow of visitors telling of the dwindling support for the war at home. Thus, he was not surprised to be summoned again in November with instructions to be ready for television appearances and at least one major speech. He prepared himself carefully, writing out in advance four single-spaced pages of "Notes for Talk with the President" which would be the basis of his presentations.

Operating without clear and explicit statements of national strategy from Washington, the field commander had undertaken to think it through himself. He had concluded in his own mind that the Communists would never be forced to a negotiated settlement of the war. Barring offensive operations against the North, a classic military victory seemed utterly improbable. Thus, the only practical strategy, it seemed to Westmoreland, was to grind the Viet Cong and North Vietnamese down, build up the friendly Vietnamese and prepare to turn over the war to them. Item 1 of his briefing notes flowed from that conviction: "Our purpose—by military and psychological action to so weaken the enemy and strengthen the GVN [government of Vietnam] that we can progressively reduce the level of our commitment soonest." Item 2 was "Enemy's purpose—seems to be to prolong the war and by psychological and military action to weaken our resolve."

Item 8 of the briefing notes was the touchy and all-important topic of the future. The key sentence said, "In approximately two years or less the Vietnamese Armed Forces should be ready to take over an increasing share of the war thereby permitting us to start phasing down the level of our effort."

Westmoreland alighted from his jet at Andrews Air Force Base on the morning of November 15, and the Washington newsmen were waiting. "I am very, very encouraged," the general declared. "I have never been more encouraged in the four years that I have been in Vietnam. We are making real progress. Everyone is encouraged."

The following day he briefed the House Armed Services Committee in closed session at the Capitol. Afterward, Representative Richard Ichord of Missouri told reporters that Westmoreland's report was "very optimistic." Asked for particulars, he said the general forecast the beginning of the "phaseout" of American troops within two years if present trends continued. The reporters rushed to their telephones. It was the first time that Westmoreland, normally the most skittish of men about predictions, had been known to give a target date when American forces might begin to come home. *FIND FOOTAGE*

Westmoreland delivered his major speech at the National Press Club in Washington November 21. The text was headed, "Progress Report," and the body of the speech was the most detailed blueprint for victory in general circulation since Hedley Donovan's illfated prospectus in *Life* nearly two years before.

The general divided the American participation in the war into four phases. Phase One, the rescue operation from 1965 to mid-1966, had been completed. Phase Two, a build-up and counterattack phase, would soon be completed.

"With 1968, a new phase is now starting," he asserted. Then he uttered fourteen words which the public was longing to hear: "We have reached an important point when the end begins to come into view." *✳ ✳✳ FIND FOOTAGE*

Beginning in 1968, he declared, the United States would provide more training and equipment to the Vietnamese forces, and turn over a major share of the defense of the demilitarized zone. In the last phase, the final mopping-up of the collapsing enemy, the GIs could begin to go home. The transition to the final phase, he promised, "lies within our grasp." In the question period, he repeated that the turnover to the South Vietnamese Army should begin within two years or less.

Westmoreland had finally and officially switched on the light at the end of the tunnel.

The general had chosen his words and his timetable with care to give the people a simple, practical formula for their hopes and expectations. To his staff in Saigon, Westmoreland explained his reasoning:

> I believe the concept and objective planned for our forces as well as those of the Vietnamese is feasible and as such it should serve as an incentive.
> The concept is compatible with the evolution of the

war since our military commitment, and portrays to the American people "some light at the end of the tunnel."

The concept justifies the augmentation of troops I've asked for based on the principle of reinforcing success and also supports an increase in the strength of the Vietnamese forces and their modernization.

The concept straddles the Presidential elections of November '68 implying the election is not a bench mark from a military point of view.

Finally, it puts emphasis on the essential role of the Vietnamese in carrying out a major burden of the war against the Communists but suggests that we must be prepared for a protracted commitment.

One of the ironies of history is that the normally cautious U.S. field commander is likely to be remembered for the only bold prediction he ever made. Though it is likely to be remembered as a blunder psychologically, his forecast turned out to be correct. The first American troop reductions in Vietnam began twenty months after the Press Club address.

The Success Offensive of November 1967 convinced many Americans that their fears and doubts had been erroneous and that the end was indeed in sight. For the moment, the revival of public confidence stemmed the erosion of support for the war.

The price was high. The government had purchased public support in the present with a promissory note on the future. The Vietnamese Communists, in secret, were preparing to match this bet with a long-planned gamble of their own.

The Missing Element

The missing and unknown element in Westmoreland's forecast was the response of the Communist commanders. Would they take defeats and finally quit the field of big-unit action, returning to a guerrilla campaign? Or would they once again double their bet, pour in more men and matériel and escalate the war anew? Westmoreland believed the latter course made no sense militarily.

Each time the Communists had tried a big operation, it had been a military failure in the end.

In the weeks before and during Westmoreland's trip to Washington, large numbers of troops had been committed in ways that were difficult to explain. On October 29 the Viet Cong 273rd Regiment attacked the South Vietnamese district capital of Loc Ninh, ran up a Viet Cong flag and tried to hold it. The United States and South Vietnamese forces responded with massive air and artillery bombardment and reinforcements. Nevertheless, the Viet Cong continued to press the attack on the little rubber plantation town despite heavy losses.

American commanders were puzzled. They had never seen the Viet Cong hang on so tenaciously, and they could not understand the objective. Certainly the Viet Cong could not expect to hold Loc Ninh—and what would they have if they did? The commanders could see nothing to be gained except some fleeting and expensive publicity.[3]

Beginning on November 3 and continuing for twenty-two days, four North Vietnamese regiments fought U.S. and South Vietnamese troops near Dak To, an isolated post in the rugged country of Kontum Province near the Cambodian-Laos-South Vietnam border. The U. S. Command was forced to deploy the equivalent of a full division of troops from the heavily populated coastal lowlands to fight the battle. Again, there were unusual mass attacks and heavy casualties.

And again, American officers were puzzled. The coincidence that Viet Minh forces had launched heavy attacks in the same area in February 1954, a little over a month before the assault on Dien Bien Phu, was largely unnoticed. The only explanation of the 1967 battle was a document captured near Dak To on November 6 containing directives of the B-3 (Highlands) Front Command in its

[3] The theory at the time was that the Loc Ninh engagement was intended to detract from the installation of Generals Thieu and Ky as the elected President and Vice-President of South Vietnam. Months later, a high-level prisoner told Lieutenant General Frederick Weyand, who was still curious, that the Loc Ninh battle had been ordered to test mass formation tactics and previously inexperienced troops in preparation for the Tet Offensive.

1967–68 Winter-Spring Campaign. The document listed four objectives:

— To annihilate a major U.S. element in order to force the enemy to deploy as many additional troops to the Western Highlands as possible and to destroy or disintegrate a large part of the Puppet Army.

— To encourage units to improve, in combat, the technique of concentrated attacks in order to annihilate relatively large enemy units.

— To destroy much of the enemy force, to liberate an important area and strengthen the base area, thus providing support for the political struggle movement.

— To effect close coordination with various battle areas throughout South Vietnam in order to achieve timely unity and stratagems.

The high points of this document were cabled to Westmoreland during his Washington visit, and he read them to a press conference in the Pentagon. The general did not accept the battle or the document as clear indication of a change in strategy.

"Let me clear out one point," said a reporter. "You don't think the battle of Dak To now is the beginning or the end of anything particular for the enemy?"

"I think it's the beginning of a great defeat of the enemy," Westmoreland shot back.

At a cocktail party in Washington over the Christmas holidays, a senior official of the the Department of State met an old friend in the Foreign Service who was home on vacation from his post in the hinterlands of South Vietnam. "Senior Official" was very surprised to learn that support for the South Vietnamese government was very tenuous in the area of Vietnam where "Foreign Service" had been working, and that a recent increase in Communist activity was sharply reducing confidence and safety in government-controlled areas.

"Senior Official" said he thought Dean Rusk and Walt Rostow

should be informed because this view of conditions was very different from the official cable traffic from the Saigon Embassy and the U. S. Command. A few days later "Foreign Service" spent an hour briefing the Secretary of State, who listened attentively, asked questions and made no comment. Following that, he was ushered in to see Rostow at the White House.

It quickly became clear that Rostow was not interested in his report of conditions in the field. The presidential assistant spent most of the time instructing "Foreign Service" on the encouraging situation in the war zone, as seen from Washington, D.C.

At 10:30 P.M. on January 2, a sentry dog at a listening post near the Khe Sanh Combat Base in the far northwest corner of South Vietnam alerted U. S. Marine lookouts that somebody was walking nearby. The Marines could see six people walking outside the defensive wire, not crawling or hiding, but strolling as if they owned the place. A squad from the base was dispatched to investigate.

The six men were dressed in the uniforms of U. S. Marines but since no friendly patrols were reported in the area, Second Lieutenant Nile B. Buffington challenged them in English to be sure. There was no reply. He challenged again. This time the lieutenant saw one man make a quick motion as if reaching for a grenade, and the Marines opened fire.

Five of the six visitors were killed. Intelligence identified three of them later as a North Vietnamese regimental commander and his operations officer and communications officer. The lone survivor managed to get away with a map case the party had been carrying, so the Marines were uncertain about the mission. The fact that North Vietnamese commanders would undertake such a dangerous personal reconnaissance clearly indicated that something was coming.

Two days later an agent reported that two regiments of the 304th North Vietnamese Division had recently moved into the mountains southeast of the Khe Sanh base. The 304th Division, a newcomer to the Khe Sanh area, was an elite home guard unit

from Hanoi which had led the triumphal march into Hanoi in late
1954 with its Dien Bien Phu banners flying.

Before the month was out, this unit had been joined by the
325-C North Vietnamese Division, which had operated in the Khe
Sanh region on previous occasions. On January 20 a second lieutenant from the 325-C Division appeared east of the Khe Sanh base
with an AK-47 assault rifle in one hand and a white flag in the
other. The defector said Khe Sanh was scheduled to be another
Dien Bien Phu. He said the preliminary attacks were to begin that
night, and they did. The main attack was to begin at Tet.

At CIA headquarters in Langley, Virginia, somebody remembered that during the siege of Dien Bien Phu the French had
regularly supplied the United States with aerial photographs and
overlays of their lines and the Viet Minh positions. These were
dug out of the files and copies were flown to Saigon. At U.S.
headquarters, Westmoreland instructed his own staff to analyze
the Dien Bien Phu battle and relate it to Khe Sanh. What can be
learned? he asked.

By mid-January the White House took on the atmosphere and
trappings of a military command post just before a siege. The
Situation Room was dominated by a large aerial photographic
mosaic of the Khe Sanh area showing details of the U. S. Marine
trench line and the latest-reported Communist positions. It was
updated constantly as new information arrived. The White House
had also acquired a large terrain model of the Khe Sanh area for
use by the Commander in Chief. At the President's request, the
Joint Chiefs of Staff prepared a memorandum on the defense of
Khe Sanh, signed by General Wheeler. The President and Rostow
were mentally in the trenches with the boys.

If the battle of Khe Sanh was intended to begin at Tet and
be another Dien Bien Phu, the plan was thwarted. On the weekend
before the Lunar New Year holiday, United States intelligence
pinpointed an area inside Laos believed to be the site of the North
Vietnamese headquarters for the Khe Sanh battle. B-52 bombers
and tactical aircraft assigned to Operation Niagara—a massive
bombing campaign against Communist positions near Khe Sanh—
dropped many tons of explosives on the reported headquarters.

The North Vietnamese Command radio in the Khe Sanh area went off the air and remained silent for almost two weeks. Khe Sanh was one place in Vietnam where there was no big attack at Tet.

On the Eve

January 1968 was not a happy time for the United States. The country was going into the election year more prosperous than ever but somehow sick at heart, empty and worried. The vital rawboned optimism of the American nation was numbed by misfortunes. Its armies were stuck in Vietnam, the promise of success not yet fulfilled, and on the twenty-third the United States intelligence ship *Pueblo* was seized in international waters by the Korean Communists, its helpless crew captured and herded like cattle before television lights.

At home, the country seemed more than ever divided across gulfs of ignorance, mistrust and antipathy—race against race, social class against class, generation against generation. Representative Jonathan B. Bingham wrote home from Washington to the people of the Bronx that "I do not recall a time when Americans seemed so beset, so discouraged, so confused or when there was such profound dissension, distrust and even hatred. Even in the depths of the Great Depression or in the darkest days after Pearl Harbor, when our country was in much deeper trouble than it is now, Americans were held together by a sense of common purpose which seems lacking today."

A federal grand jury in Boston indicted Dr. Benjamin Spock, the household baby authority, and the Reverend William Sloane Coffin, Jr., the chaplain of Yale University, for conspiring with three other opponents of the Vietnam War to counsel violations of the Selective Service Act. Four U. S. Navy enlisted men who deserted because of their opposition to the war were granted political asylum in Sweden. Eartha Kitt, the singer, came to luncheon at the White House and gave Mrs. Lyndon B. Johnson an earful. "There's a war going on, and Americans don't know why," she said. Pointing to the First Lady in front of fifty luncheon guests, the singer said, "You are a mother too, although you have had daughters and not sons. I am a mother and I know the feeling of having a baby come out of my gut. I have a baby and then you send him off to war. No wonder the kids rebel."

In the small town of Abbeville, South Carolina, Tom O'Connor, Jr., a sergeant in the United States Marine Corps, came home from Vietnam in a flag-draped casket. It was a cold, sleety day in Abbeville, and his father remembered how the boy liked to go, booted and wrapped, across the fields into the woods on such a day. He tried to weep but found that he could not. Instead he put some of his thoughts and emotions on paper:

> I cannot accept my son's death as a matter of God's will. I must reject a God who would create so well and then purposely destroy. The God I reverence is the God of creation. My son was destroyed, I am afraid, by me and by you and man's will, denying the will of God. . . .
>
> I see no sense in the present demand that we lay down our arms and thus quit the present war. For to do so would leave us defenseless, at the mercy of rapacious men who have boasted they seek our enslavement and the end of individual liberty.
>
> With all his vaunted achievement, man is still led by savage chiefs. My son's death was decreed in councils of the mighty dominated by vanities against which my God has spoken.

In Jesup, Georgia, a crossroads county seat where piny woods and small cotton and peanut farms stretch toward the sea, the Veterans of Foreign Wars Leon Parris Post No. 4585 petitioned local officials to fly the American flag at half-staff over the courthouse from the time the body of a local serviceman is received from the war zone until he is buried, regardless of race. Jesup is one of those rural Southern towns that have provided more than their share of the common soldiers behind the guns in the nation's wars, and the VFW post has 455 members. On January 18 a quorum declared unanimously in a resolution:

For the sake of Almighty God and those men who have fallen in Vietnam and those that shall fall in Vietnam, let's go ahead and win the war there if we have a justifiable cause to wage war there; if not, let's apologize to the peoples of the world and get out of there. . . .

Who among our number who has a son feels compelled to advise that son to volunteer for service to his country which may lead to combat in Vietnam, as confused as we are about our reasons for being there?

What would you do, you who volunteered for service in World War II and fought the heathen foe on foreign soil, if you were now 18 or 21 years of age? Note the differences now from then!

Early on the morning of Tuesday, January 30, Senator Robert F. Kennedy met a group of Washington newsmen for breakfast in a private dining room at the National Press Club, the site of General Westmoreland's speech two months before. Kennedy had been involved in his brother's presidential decisions to maintain and increase the American advisory effort in South Vietnam, but this seemed to him a far cry from the war which had resulted. In November the senator had made his objections public, saying on nationwide television that the Johnson administration had abandoned his brother's policies in Vietnam and "seriously undermined" the moral position of the United States.

Now Robert Kennedy was feeling increasing pressure to oppose Lyndon Johnson in the presidential primaries, largely on the war issue. Senator Eugene McCarthy was already in the race as an anti-war candidate, but hardly anyone gave him a chance of upsetting the President.

At the breakfast table that morning, Kennedy referred to the Vietnam War as "one of the great disasters of all time for the United States." Much as he would like to lead the opposition, he felt it was not practical at this time. If he were to declare his candidacy for President, he would split the Democratic Party down the middle and bring many good men down. He would have to win every primary to win the nomination, because a President has many assets. Lyndon Johnson could control the news events, he and Ho Chi Minh. The presidential campaign would be in their hands. Kennedy authorized the newsmen to report that he would not oppose Johnson for the presidency "under any foreseeable circumstances."

On the way to the breakfast, Peter Lisagor of the Chicago *Daily News* had stopped by his news bureau office on the twelfth floor of the National Press building and ripped from the teletype machine an early account of a wave of coordinated surprise attacks on seven cities in the northern part of South Vietnam. United Press International was calling the attacks during the Lunar New Year cease-fire the greatest enemy offensive of the war, and reported that American GIs were battling Viet Cong guerrillas in city streets. Lisagor passed the snippet of UPI wire copy to the senator. Kennedy read it with interest, and then spoke with the rich irony which came so easily to his lips. "Yeah, we're winning," he said.

CHAPTER IV

Attack!

"Avoid any display of emotion during Tet and do not discuss subjects with the Vietnamese which breed emotion, arguments or insults."

—Instructions to United States troops in Vietnam, *The MACV Observer*, January 31, 1968

T HE People's Liberation Armed Forces and elements of the Vietnam People's Army had gathered for synchronized assaults on cities, towns and military headquarters throughout the eight-hundred-mile-length of South Vietnam. For years they had been men of the jungle, daring in boast and banner but cautious in the commitment of major military assets. Now they would emerge everywhere.

Planning and moving in secret, carrying supplies on bicycles or on their backs, without a single airplane or helicopter, they had organized the offensive throughout the country and silently moved to attack positions. With one surge, they would strike more than 100 cities and towns—the capital city of Saigon, 39 of the 44 provincial capitals, 71 district capitals. The many hundreds of specific targets would include the United States Embassy, the Presidential Palace and Joint General Staff headquarters in Saigon and headquarters of all four military regions in the hinterland.

In this battle-of-all-battles of the Second Indochina War, the Communist Command was to commit an estimated 67,000 of its 240,000 troops in South Vietnam, one fourth of its force. Ranged against them were 1,100,000 men under arms—492,000 American fighting men; 61,000 South Koreans, Thais and other free world troops; 342,000 South Vietnamese government regulars; and 284,000 men of the regional and popular force militia.

Vietnam was the front line of world conflict between two political and social systems, one backed by the land mass of Asia and the two teeming giants of Communism, the Soviet Union and China; the other backed by the military and economic power of the United States beyond the widest ocean in the world. Both sides in the Vietnam battle were armed with modern small arms and crew-served weapons. The United States expeditionary force, in addition, was armed with 2600 airplanes, 3000 helicopters and 3500 armored vehicles.

The attackers hoped their adversaries would be scattered and stretched thin in the face of sudden assaults on every front, and thus unable to mass and maneuver their powerful weaponry. They also hoped and planned that the government of South Vietnam would be paralyzed, its leaders assassinated, its military officers and men caught off duty and off guard during the Tet holiday, and, in many cases, ready to turn their guns around and join the revolution.

The Intelligence

The plan in its full scope and detail, including the crucial matter of its timing during the Lunar New Year truce, was tightly held in the grip of a few men at the very top of the Communist Command. The broad outline, though, was spread far and wide. Public announcements and newspaper exhortations in North Vietnam had spoken of a historic campaign ahead, and tens of thousands of combatants in the South had been indoctrinated to take part in a great battle to decide the future of the land and its people.

Inevitably, reports of the plan reached the ears of officials of the United States, which employed more than ten thousand American officers and men in military intelligence in Vietnam and many hundreds more in civilian intelligence agencies there. For the first time in history, the attack order for a major offensive was publicized in advance as a press release by the side to be attacked. This unique document was issued twenty-five days before the first of the surprise attacks.

PRESS RELEASE

United States Mission in Vietnam

January 5, 1968

CAPTURED DOCUMENT INDICATES FINAL PHASE
OF REVOLUTION AT HAND

Subordinate level Communist party activists of the National Liberation Front forces are being told that the final phase of the revolutionary war in South Viet-Nam is at hand. According to an enemy document of recent dates, captured by an element of the U.S. 101st Airborne Division in Quang Tin province on November 19, "Central Headquarters concludes that the time has come for a direct revolution and that the opportunity for a general offensive and general uprising is within reach."

The general offensive and uprising has long been heralded overtly as well as internally by the Vietnamese Communist Party (the Workers Party in the North and the People's Revolutionary Party in the South), but hitherto as the final phase of the protracted war. The document released herewith is the first captured document which unequivocally and unambiguously asserts that this phase is "within reach" and that the revolutionary forces are, for the first time, to attempt attacks upon the major towns and cities, including Saigon.

The document is ambiguous, however, as to the time fixed for the all-out revolutionary effort. Also, although it attributed to Ho Chi Minh and Party Headquarters an order for the general offensive and general uprising it states that the troops should be told the order emanates from the Liberation Front and not from the Supreme Command.

Furthermore, the document itself cannot be taken as conclusive evidence that such an order has been given. Obviously, it would only be given by the Central Committee of the Communist Party in Hanoi, since it would stake all the human resources of the revolution upon a general attack against the strongest positions of the Government of Viet-Nam and its allies. The writer was far removed from the highest levels of the party organization. . . . Thus his information may represent, not the actual policy of the Communist Party command but rather an internal propaganda version designed to inspire the fighting troops.

A translation of the full document was attached to the press release. The key paragraph was an order to the People's Army:

> Use very strong military attacks in coordination with the uprisings of the local population to take over towns and cities. Troops should flood the lowlands. They should move toward liberating the capital city [Saigon], take power and try to rally enemy brigades and regiments to our side one by one. Propaganda should be broadly disseminated among the population in general, and leaflets should be used to reach enemy officers and enlisted personnel. The above subject should be fully understood by cadre and troops; however, our brothers should not say that this order comes from the Party and Uncle, but to say it comes from the Front. Also, do not specify times for implementation.

Not many people paid attention to captured documents, and of those who did, very few accepted this one at face value. One reporter picked up a copy of the "final phase" release from the bins of press announcements at the Joint United States Public Affairs Office (JUSPAO), the information—and propaganda—headquarters in Saigon. At the top of the first page he wrote, "How they see war, p. 10-11," referring to the attack order quoted above. Beside the order itself he wrote a single word of comment: "Moonshine."

Nearly everyone considered it moonshine or worse. Why? Why did no one believe? There were abundant signs of coming trouble: the plain language of captured documents; the statements on the lips of prisoners, some of whom reported that the whole country would be 'liberated' by Tet; the precipitous drop in defections from the Communist side (their troops were being promised victory); the strange attacks on Loc Ninh and Dak To; the peculiar incident of forty nearly simultaneous attacks against outposts and towns in Dinh Tuong Province in the Mekong delta, a place where new tactics were often tested by the Viet Cong.

Many of these signs were noted and reported, but few Americans in Vietnam believed that anything truly powerful, extensive and traumatic was ahead. The very boldness of the plan generated antibodies against belief. Militarily, it seemed fantastic. American officers were certain that Communist forces could not seize and hold the cities. Considering the high costs and risks involved, the idea of nationwide urban attacks for political and psychological gains seemed implausible. Outlandish claims of strength and achievement had been made before; perhaps this talk of imminent victory was a desperate attempt by the Communist Command to shore up the sagging morale—or so the theory went.

The inertial force of habit and of bureaucracy overpowered the evidence at hand. Belief in a tremendous impending attack would have required tremendous counterefforts. Personal plans would have to be altered; holdiays and furloughs canceled; daily habits of comfort and convenience in previously safe cities abandoned. If an official reported "progress" last month and the months before that and had been praised for his tidings of success, how did he justify reporting an impending crisis now? Official assessments of Communist weakness would have to be discarded or explained away; public predictions would have to be eaten. It could not be done.

In late November the Saigon station of the Central Intelligence Agency compiled the mounting evidence of a change in Communist strategy. This was not an assessment or prediction, but a collection of scraps, and it was entitled "The Big Gamble." Intelligence officers of the U. S. Military Command protested and dissented. At that moment, the Command was in the process of *reducing* its published estimate of Communist strength in South Vietnam as part of the campaign to show that "we are winning."

As the evidence continued to mount, the Command came around. On December 20 Westmoreland cabled Washington that "the enemy has already made a crucial decision concerning the conduct of the war . . . to undertake an intensified countrywide effort, perhaps a maximum effort, over a relatively short period of time."[1] Even so, the general did not anticipate heavy attacks on cities and towns. At the time of his cable, he was moving troops away from populated areas around Saigon to undertake a series of previously planned operations at the Cambodian border.

On January 15 Westmoreland and his J-2 (Assistant Chief of Staff for Intelligence), Brigadier General Philip B. Davidson, briefed the U. S. Mission Council at the Embassy on the mounting signs of trouble. Westmoreland put the odds at 60–40 for a major attack *before* Tet. Davidson gave his own guess at 40–60 for an attack *after* Tet. Along with most other people, neither of the generals expected the attack during the Lunar New Year holiday itself.

Military intelligence expected a big strike at Khe Sanh and in other border areas, but nationwide attacks against cities and towns were never considered a "likely course of action." A U. S. Army Intelligence officer who played a major role in evaluating the information from the Communist camp said later that "if we'd gotten the whole battle plan, it wouldn't have been believed. It wouldn't have been credible to us."

As it happened, the Communist force itself provided the only sort of advance warning that had much chance to be heeded—simultaneous attacks on seven cities in the northern part of South Vietnam one day ahead of the main assaults on Saigon and most other targets. Why these units jumped the gun has never been fully explained. The most widely held theory is that the nationwide offensive was originally scheduled for the early morning of January 30, the opening hours of the New Year, and that one Communist regional command failed to receive word of a twenty-four-hour postponement. All the cities struck on January 30 were located in Viet Cong Military Region 5.

[1] Based on this and other reports, President Johnson on December 21 told a closed meeting of the Australian Cabinet at Canberra, where he had traveled for the funeral of Prime Minister Harold Holt, that "kamikaze" attacks by the Communists were expected in Vietnam. If the President believed that a truly massive attack was in the wind, he gave no indication of this to many of his close associates or to the American public.

The Opening Gun

A half hour into the Year of the Monkey, a corporal guarding the government radio station in Nha Trang, a city of 119,000 halfway up the coast of South Vietnam, noticed two small motorized carts pull up to a nearby pagoda and discharge passengers. The travelers appeared to be wearing government Army uniforms, but there was something suspicious in their hurried manner. After trying vainly to telephone his headquarters (the line had been cut), Corporal Le Van Thang radioed the news of the arrivals. Headquarters replied that they might be Communist troops in disguise.

Thang alerted his fellow guards at the radio station and then climbed into an elevated bunker just outside. The corporal fired a few rounds with a light machine gun into the open field near the pagoda, and the "government Army" travelers immediately returned the fire.

Five minutes later, at 12:35 A.M., Communist gunners fired six 82-mm. mortar rounds at the Vietnamese Navy Training Center. This first deliberate action of the Tet Offensive was well planned but poorly executed. All the rounds missed the target, and the ground attack on the city of Nha Trang, which should have followed immediately, did not materialize until 2 A.M.

Some eight hundred men of the 18-B North Vietnamese Regiment moved into action. The main body of the attack force ran into a bloody fight on its way into town and never proceeded farther. A "popular demonstration" of two hundred banner-waving people from a suburban hamlet was easily turned back by government troops.

Of the many military targets in the city, infiltrators and underground agents were able to enter only a logistical headquarters and the province administrative headquarters. The province chief, Lieutentant Colonel Le Khanh, asked U.S. officers to launch a ground attack to recapture the administrative headquarters. The Americans responded instead with an air strike which caused extensive damage and set the headquarters afire. The bodies of four invaders were found inside.

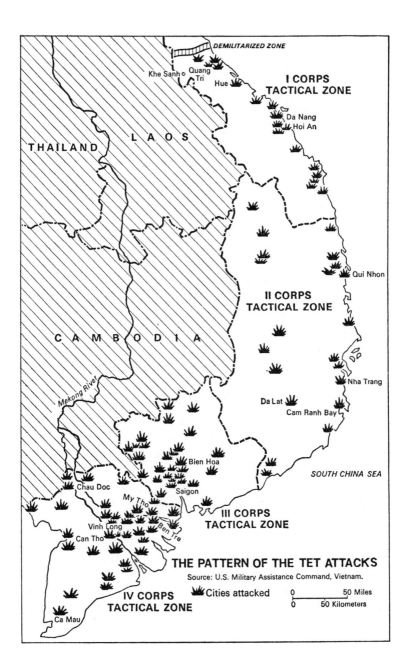

DEMILITARIZED ZONE

Khe Sanh ○ ☀ Quang
Tri
Hue ☀

I CORPS
TACTICAL ZONE

☀ Da Nang
Hoi An

LAOS

THAILAND

C A M B O D I A

☀ Qui Nhon

II CORPS
TACTICAL ZONE

☀ Nha Trang

Mekong River

Da Lat ☀
Cam Ranh Bay

Bien Hoa

SOUTH CHINA SEA

Chau Doc

My Tho

Saigon

III CORPS
TACTICAL ZONE

Vinh Long

Ben Tre

Can Tho

THE PATTERN OF THE TET ATTACKS

Source: U.S. Military Assistance Command, Vietnam.

☀ Cities attacked

IV CORPS
TACTICAL ZONE

Ca Mau

0   50 Miles

0   50 Kilometers

Fourteen hours after the attack, government troops controlled the entire city, and after another fourteen hours Nha Trang was declared "clear" of the attack force. According to the Vietnamese government Command, the outcome of the battle was 377 enemy killed, 77 captured and one surrendered; 88 friendly troops killed and 220 wounded in action; 32 civilians killed, 187 wounded, 600 houses destroyed and 3192 people homeless.

Huynh Tuong, the Communist Party political officer, and most of the Nha Trang city apparatus was captured. Tuong told his captors he had protested in advance that a force of 800 men could not hope to take over a military and administrative center of 119,000 people. Higher-ups assured him that a rocket company and two more battalions of infantry had been assigned to join the battle. This appears to have been pure fiction, intended to reinforce the zeal of the local organization and convince its leaders to fight.

The opening gun, at Nha Trang, was recorded at 12:35 A.M., Tuesday, January 30. The other attacks erupted in the night like a string of firecrackers:

1:35 A.M.—Ban Me Thuot in the central highlands

2:00 A.M.—Kontum, another mountain city

2:55 A.M.—Hoi An, a province capital on the coast

3:30 A.M.—Da Nang, the country's second largest city, on the coast

4:10 A.M.—Qui Nhon, a major coastal city

4:40 A.M.—Pleiku, a mountain city

Five of the cities struck were covered by a truce proclaimed by both sides. In Hoi An and Da Nang, part of I Corps Tactical Zone, the United States and South Vietnamese government Commands had canceled the truce the previous afternoon. In the case of Da Nang, Hanoi Radio announced that the attack had been carried out "to punish the U.S. aggressors . . . who insolently slighted the traditional Lunar New Year festival of the Vietnamese people."

For military control purposes, South Vietnam was divided into four corps tactical zones from north to south.[2] One of the early attacks was at the headquarters city of I Corps, a very old port called Tourane by the French and renamed Da Nang after Vietnamese independence. In 1858 it had been the first city invaded and occupied by the French in their conquest of Indochina. A century later, in 1965, U. S. Marines landing nearby became the first American ground combat troops sent to fight in Indochina.

The French admiral in the first invasion was led to expect a "popular uprising" to greet his men, and the Viet Cong troops of 1968 expected something of the same. It didn't happen either time. Just prior to the Tet Offensive a police agent in the local Viet Cong organization gave warning that the city was to be attacked. There was no uprising, and very little penetration of the city proper by the attack forces.

I Corps headquarters on the outskirts came under mortar and ground attack by a company of Viet Cong infiltrators, and a dozen men penetrated the compound briefly. When the corps commander, Lieutenant General Hoang Xuan Lam, arrived from home at dawn, the headquarters was still under fire by small arms and anti-tank

[2] I Corps Tactical Zone began at the demilitarized zone in the extreme north and extended over the five nearest provinces. Being contiguous to North Vietnam, I Corps was very exposed. I Corps headquarters (Vietnamese) was at Da Nang. The counterpart American command with jurisdiction over this area was the III Marine Amphibious Force (III MAF), also at Da Nang.

II Corps Tactical Zone ranged over the next twelve provinces to the south. It was by far the largest corps zone in terms of area but the smallest in population. The sparsely populated mountains of the central highlands dominated II Corps, which also contained a fertile and populous strip of coastal lowlands. II Corps headquarters (Vietnamese) was at Pleiku in the highlands. The counterpart American command, the U. S. I Field Force, Vietnam (I FFV), maintained its headquarters at Nha Trang.

III Corps Tactical Zone encompassed Saigon and eleven surrounding provinces, containing the capital city, 38 per cent of the country's population and 90 per cent of its industry. III Corps headquarters (Vietnamese) was at Bien Hoa northeast of Saigon. Close by at Long Binh was the counterpart American headquarters, the U. S. II Field Force (II FFV).

IV Corps Tactical Zone encompassed the Mekong delta south of Saigon, rich in rice, people and a history of insurgency. IV Corps headquarters (Vietnamese) was at Can Tho. The United States Command was represented by a senior adviser to the corps commander.

The Viet Cong Command was also organized in military regions, which did not coincide with those of the allies.

rockets. Lam looked over the situation, then turned to the U.S. adviser on duty at the Tactical Operations Center, Major P. S. Milantoni.

"Milantoni, bomb here. Use big bombs," said Lam, tapping the map with his ebony swagger stick.

"General, that's pretty close," replied the major skeptically.

"Bomb," repeated Lam.

Milantoni called the air support center in another room of the I Corps headquarters building. "That's too close, you'll never get a clearance for it," said the surprised watch officer.

"General Lam just gave it," Milantoni announced.

The bombs fell two hundred yards away, shaking the building and causing defenders to hit the dirt. The Viet Cong rifle fire slackened and the general smiled. He called in more air strikes, and as the Viet Cong began to disengage, he sent helicopter gunships to pursue from the air. U.S. and South Vietnamese troops took chase on the ground. Lam smiled again, tapped his swagger stick against his leg and walked out.

The headquarters of II Corps Tactical Zone, the mountain city of Pleiku, had three weeks' advance notice that it would be hit by a surprise attack. On January 5 the United States 4th Infantry Division captured "Urgent Combat Order Number One," a five-page plan of movement and attack for Pleiku Province. The plan listed specific assignments for the local force units, including roads to be cut, outposts to be attacked and "popular demonstrations" to be staged on signal. One section of the plan specified action to be taken "before the Tet holidays."

On January 24 American units at Pleiku were placed on alert and a platoon of U.S. tanks assigned to the city as a reaction force against the invaders. On January 26 Major General Charles P. Stone, commander of the 4th Infantry Division, convened American advisers and commanders in Pleiku Province for a briefing on the enemy plans. Stone also briefed Lieutenant General Vinh Loc, the Vietnamese II Corps commander, and his senior staff officers.

II Corps received additional hard evidence of what was

planned from the coastal city of Qui Nhon. There on Sunday, January 28—two days before the Tet holiday—South Vietnamese Army security men raided a house in the suburbs and captured eleven Viet Cong agents, a tape recorder and two tapes. Under questioning, the Viet Cong captives said their forces would probably raid Qui Nhon and other cities during the holiday, and they said the tapes had been prepared for broadcast on the local government radio station after its seizure. One of the tapes announced (falsely) that the government military commander in the city had joined the uprising. The other tape said:

To all people in the province and all people in the city of Qui Nhon. To all officers and men, officials and policemen in the city of Qui Nhon. Pay attention. We will read an appeal from the action committee of the People's Forces Struggling for Peace and Sovereignty for Vietnam in the province of Binh Dinh.

Officers and men of the ARVN [South Vietnamese Army], security forces, popular forces and fighting youths. The sound of gunfire of national salvation of the people is resounding throughout the South. The people are arising like a storm. Their uprising is now smashing the dictatorial, fascist regime of Thieu and Ky.

The people and the dissident regiments and divisions of the People's Forces Struggling for Peace and Sovereignty for Vietnam have occupied and now control the cities of Saigon, Hue, Da Nang, etc. Many units of the armed forces of the Republic of Vietnam of the Thieu-Ky puppet regime have joined the people and the dissident troops in an uprising throughout the South.

The government in Binh Dinh [Province] is perplexed and wavering, and is rapidly falling apart. Many ARVN units have changed sides and fought hard to save the nation. Many district and provincial capitals have been liberated. In these critical times, the time has come when you cannot use American weapons to fight the people, who are your kith-and-kin. You must act urgently:

1) Join the people and the dissident forces and turn your guns to overthrow the Thieu-Ky regime, thus

taking over the entire government for the People's Forces Struggling for Peace and Sovereignty for Vietnam.

2) Immediately cease all armed acts against demonstrations and meetings of the people, students, other groups, etc.

3) The units and soldiers guarding warehouses must open the doors and let the people obtain weapons and attack the enemy, while also destroying all the enemy's ammo dumps and fortified posts.

4) You must resolutely punish the obstinate criminals and take their weapons, which are to be given to the people to fight the enemy.

5) All families of enemy soldiers must persuade their husbands and sons to defect and do meritorious deeds to save the nation.

During these times, anyone who hesitates one day will have committed a crime against the Fatherland. All officers, NCO's and men should bravely arise and, together with the People's Forces Struggling for Peace and Sovereignty for Vietnam, overthrow the Thieu-Ky regime and demand that the Americans not intervene in the internal affairs of Vietnam.

After playing the tapes, Lieutenant Colonel Pham Minh Tho, the province chief, placed security forces of the city on alert and ordered increased surveillance of vehicles and visitors entering the city. He played the tapes on the telephone for officers of the Joint General Staff in Saigon.

In Pleiku the II Corps Chief of Staff, Colonel Le Trung Tuong, received word of the tapes on Monday morning, January 29. During the day he sent warning to all the provinces in II Corps that the Viet Cong might not honor the Tet truce. As more suspicious signs were seen around his headquarters city of Pleiku, Tuong ordered four additional tanks into the downtown area that night—"Tet or no Tet," he told the reluctant tank commander.

A little after two o'clock Tuesday morning Tuong summoned his intelligence officer to an urgent meeting at corps headquarters. As the officer left his home in town, three "ARVN soldiers" saluted him smartly. The three men were among the first killed when

1. December 1967: In a rare public appearance sometime after the Tet Offensive was conceived, the ailing Ho Chi Minh came before a rally in Hanoi to rouse support for it. Sharing the platform were (from left): National Assembly chairman Truong Chinh, Vice-President Ton Duc Thang, President Ho, Le Duan, the first secretary of the Lao Dong Party, and Premier Pham Van Dong.

2, 3, 4. Viet Cong field commanders: Four-star general Nguyen Chi Thanh, shown above in his jungle headquarters, was believed to be dubious about the Tet plan; he was killed by American bombers shortly before the plan was finally approved. Lt. Gen. Tran Van Tra (center) carried the Tet Offensive plans from Hanoi down to the fighters in the south. Maj. Gen. Tran Do (right) was responsible for the attack on Saigon.

5. In mid-1967 President Johnson called for more troops and higher taxes for the war, prompting widespread public dismay.

6. Gen. William Westmoreland, summoned home from Vietnam in November of 1967, told Americans that success "lies within our grasp."

PRESS RELEASE

141. NGUYEN-HUE SAIGON
Tel: 92.026 - 92.031

United States Mission in Vietnam

January 5, 1968

CAPTURED DOCUMENT INDICATES FINAL PHASE OF REVOLUTION AT HAND

Subordinate level Communist party activists of the National Liberation

Front forces are being told that the final phase of the revolutionary war in

- 11 -

Action to be taken: Use very strong military attacks in coordination
with the uprisings of the local population to take over towns and cities.
Troops should flood the lowlands. They should move toward liberating the
capital city / Saigon 7, take power and try to rally enemy brigades and
regiments to our side one by one. Propaganda should be broadly disseminated
among the population in general, and leaflets should be used to reach enemy
officers and enlisted personnel. The above subject should be fully understood
by cadre and troops; however, our brothers should not say that this order
comes from the Party and Uncle / Ho Chi Minh 7, but to say it comes from the
/ Liberation 7 Front. Also, do not specify times for implementation.

Emulation: From 1 December on, all units should take the initiative to

7. Twenty-five days before Tet, the U. S. Embassy issued this
translation of a captured Viet Cong document—the order for "very
strong attacks" on Saigon and other cities. Yet not even the
Embassy took it seriously.

8. After the Viet Cong's assault on the American Embassy, MPs rushed a prisoner from the scene.

9. The Great Seal of the United States, blasted from the Embassy wall, lay amid the wreckage.

10. In the wake of the battle, Westmoreland and Embassy officials discussed what they should tell the press.

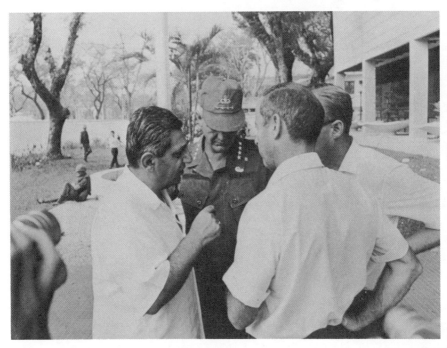

11. Ambassador Ellsworth Bunker, absent during the attack, returned to view his damaged Embassy. On his right, Capt. Robert J. O'Brien, chief of the Marine Guards. On his left, Maj. Hillel Schwartz, whose troops had landed on the roof, and security man Robert Furey.

12. Col. George Jacobson (left), who killed a Viet Cong invader in his Embassy quarters, with reporters afterward.

13. From *The Herblock Gallery* (Simon & Schuster, 1968).

14, 15, 16. Life went on almost as usual in downtown Saigon (above) during the Tet attacks, despite Viet Cong corpses in the street. Lt. Gen. Vinh Loc (upper right) directed the mop-up around his mansion in Pleiku—but became enraged when American officers suggested that he show up at his command post. At lower right, government soldiers watch a flame thrower in action in Pleiku.

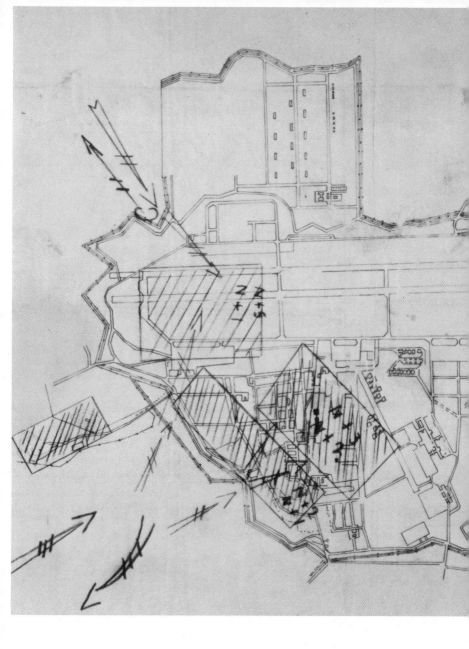

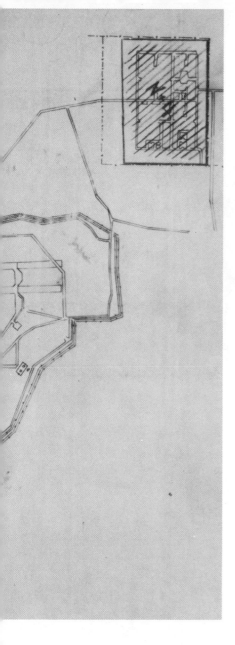

17, 18. An original Viet Cong battle map, taken from a prisoner, shows the plan of assault on Bien Hoa Air Base. The arrows mark the lines of attack on designated objectives (striped boxes). Below, Lt. Gen. Frederick Weyand, U. S. commander in the Saigon-Bien Hoa area, whose troops stopped the attackers.

19, 20. The young Vietnamese above, recruited as terrorists by the Viet Cong, were captured during Tet at Nha Trang. At right, Huynh Tuong and Duong Van Hien, leaders of the assault on Nha Trang.

21. Pictures of devastation such as this, in Vinh Long, shocked the American public.

22, 23. January 31, 1968: As Vietnam blazed, Gen. Earle Wheeler briefed congressional leaders and high officials in the family dining room at the White House. Listening to Wheeler, the President showed grave concern.

the attack began, and were later identified as members of the Viet Cong H-15 Battalion.

The Vietnamese civilians had been firing firecrackers all evening in Ban Me Thuot, a town of 65,000 people on a plateau amid the forest and jungle of the central highlands. At midnight the government soldiers began shooting off their rifles in celebration of the New Year, sending tracer bullets streaking into the mountain air. An American MP, Specialist Fourth Class Ron McCollar, began clearing GIs out of town and closing down the five bars which catered to the Americans. With all the firecrackers going off, it would be a perfect time for the Communists to hit, he thought.

A barrage of mortars and rockets slammed into the town at 1:35 A.M., followed by a ground assault of more than two thousand men. Some had infiltrated the city with the merrymakers, and others attacked from staging points on the northwestern and southeastern fringes of the city. Gunfire broke out everywhere. Communist troops roamed through tree-lined streets, attacking nearly every military installation and invading the provincial headquarters, the treasury building and the police station at the market place. The city was a horror of blood, bullets, death and destruction.

Government forces counterattacked during the night, led by a squadron of tanks and armored personnel carriers spewing fire from cannon and machine guns. Townspeople streamed into their pagodas and the Catholic church, past the dead and dying soldiers and civilians in the embattled streets. In the light of day propaganda agents began organizing civilians, particularly Rhade mountain tribesmen, to stage anti-government demonstrations. The crowds were dispersed by police.

Southwest of town near a Rhade tribal village, the American missionaries of the Christian Missionary Alliance took refuge in a garbage pit they had converted to a makeshift bunker. When North Vietnamese troops swarmed into their compound, missionary Robert Ziemer climbed out and ran toward them with his hands in the air. He was cut down by bullets in the head and chest and collapsed over a low clothesline.

The soldiers advanced on the pit. Ed Thompson, a six-foot-three missionary, nicknamed "the Giant" by the diminutive tribesmen, cried, "Mercy! Mercy!" The reply was gunfire. Thompson fell across his wife, Ruth, in an unsuccessful effort to shield her from death. A missionary nurse, Ruth Wilting, died with them.

Marie Ziemer, badly wounded, was ordered out of the hole by North Vietnamese soldiers. They dressed her wounds, walked her to a house containing other American captives and later released her. Five missionaries were killed at Ban Me Thuot, and a sixth died of wounds. Two more were led away and have never returned.

In Cleveland, Ohio, Ruth Wilting's mother turned in her Bible to Paul's epistle from a Roman prison: "I have fought a good fight, I have finished my course, I have kept the faith." Beside it, in the margin, she wrote, "sweet will of God." Ruth had served in Vietnam since before the defeat of the French in 1954.

At dawn on Tuesday the battle raged in each of the cities which had been assaulted during the night. Three battalions were attacking Kontum. Two battalions pressed against the outskirts of Qui Nhon. Despite the warning and precautions, Viet Cong commandos had infiltrated that city and held the government radio station—though they were unable to broadcast any tapes. Ban Me Thuot, which had never been hit hard before, was aflame for six days before the last of the invaders were driven out. U. S. Army officers said later that in the II Corps area the Communist forces lost 5405 killed and 704 captured, and that the allies lost 427 killed. The toll of civilian death and destruction was very high.

Despite the warnings of trouble ahead, the II Corps commander, Lieutenant General Vinh Loc, left his post before Tet to celebrate the holiday in splendor in Saigon. A graduate of the French cavalry school at Saumur as well as the U. S. Command and General Staff College, Loc was among the last of the old-style "war lord" corps commanders, and he was known for his high living. He came naturally by his aristocratic tastes and bearing. His father was a cousin of Bao Dai, Vietnam's last emperor,

ATTACK! 131

and had been a minister of the imperial court at Hue. He was executed by the Communists in 1946.

Shortly after 9 A.M. on Tuesday, January 30, the corps commander flew back to Pleiku from Saigon in his personal airplane, a converted DC-3 with an executive interior design including a bed. He went immediately to the center of the flaming, bleeding city and began directing a platoon action to clear Communist troops from the area of his official mansion. After a while Colonel J. W. Barnes, the chief U.S. liaison officer at II Corps headquarters, sent word that the problems of battle throughout the II Corps Tactical Zone required Loc's attention at the command post. Loc turned on the American emissary who brought him this message, shouting in English that President Thieu had personally ordered him to hold Pleiku City at all costs, and that he would not be ordered about by Americans.

A little later Loc rode up the hill to his headquarters, preceded by a jeep of security guards. He entered the building pale with anger and encountered Colonel Barnes. "I am not an American corporal, I am the II Corps general in command!" he cried. He slammed his fist through a fiberboard partition and ran up the stairs to his office, than ran back downstairs and chewed out Barnes again. After that, he refused to speak to Barnes and turned his back if the colonel came into his presence. Despite the problems this posed during the period of greatest military action of the war, the U. S. Command stuck by Barnes, refusing to transfer him to another post and insisting that he had only been doing his job in summoning the corps commander to headquarters. A month after Tet, Loc was removed as corps commander and reassigned as commandant of the National Defense College.

End of a Truce

Early Tuesday morning the first reports of fighting in the cities of I and II Corps began pouring into General Westmoreland's concrete-and-steel Pentagon East at Tan Son Nhut Air Base near Saigon. The intelligence chief, General Davidson, came in early to read the news from the stricken cities. "This is going to happen in the rest of the country tonight or tomorrow morning," he told Westmoreland, and the field commander agreed.

From nearly the beginning of the planning of the 1968 Tet truce, Westmoreland had been edgy about it. At first he agreed in principle to a forty-eight-hour Tet cease-fire but thought better of it as the military pressure mounted and after Communist violations of the January 1 truce. Westmoreland urged President Thieu to have no Tet truce at all, but Thieu insisted, saying this would hurt morale in the Army and play into the hands of Communist propagandists. Thieu did agree to shorten the cease-fire to thirty-six hours, and promised that while 50 per cent of the Vietnamese armed forces would be allowed to celebrate the holiday on leave, the other 50 per cent would be on alert.

By late January Westmoreland was more certain of the Communist build-up and apprehensive that the foe would use the cease-fire to move men and weapons. On the twenty-fourth he confided his fears to Ambassador Bunker, and the two men recommended to Washington through diplomatic and military channels that the allied truce be canceled in I Corps and U.S. planes be permitted to bomb as usual in the supply-and-infiltration area in the southern part of North Vietnam. Their justification for this request was a massive and overt invasion by North Vietnamese regulars in the northern sector of South Vietnam.

Washington agreed, and Westmoreland took the plan to Thieu. The Vietnamese President approved the cancellation of the truce in the northern part of the country (I Corps), but it was agreed that the Vietnamese government would withhold the announcement until the day before the cease-fire was to take effect.

The American Command went ahead with its plans, thinking that the matter had been settled. The appointed hour came and passed, but there was no cancellation announcement from the Vietnamese. Two hours before the cease-fire was to take effect throughout the country, the Americans realized there had been no official change in I Corps. The government press office, which should have made the announcement, was closed tight for Tet. To the Americans, this was a telling indication of Vietnamese priorities: between the holiday and the war, Tet won easily.

The United States authorities did the only thing possible. Without waiting for the Vietnamese, they hastily announced Monday afternoon that the truce in I Corps had been canceled.

At 9:45 A.M. on Tuesday, January 30, after the night attacks in I and II Corps, the U.S. and South Vietnamese governments officially canceled the truce throughout all of South Vietnam. At Pentagon East, this set off a chain of orders and directives, the most important of which was a "flash" priority message signed at 11:25 A.M. by Major General Walter T. Kerwin, the American chief of staff:

> 1. The GVN [Government of Vietnam] has cancelled the 36-hour ceasefire for TET. Accordingly, the TET ceasefire for U.S. forces is hereby cancelled.
> 2. Effective immediately all forces will resume intensified operations and troops will be placed on maximum alert with particular attention to the defense of headquarters complexes, logistical installations, airfields, population centers, and billets. All units will be particularly alert to deception measures by the enemy and be poised to aggressively pursue and destroy any enemy force which attacks.

At this point in the war, a grand total of ninety-two U.S. generals and admirals were assigned to duty in Vietnam, and many of them worked at Pentagon East. These and other high-ranking officers at U.S. headquarters were warned to be careful during the night. As the place cleared out at 5 P.M. the brass could be seen lugging a motley collection of assault rifles, carbines, pistols and grenades to their staff cars and jeeps.

The U. S. Armed Forces Radio told the GIs of the cancellation of the truce, declaring that "for allied forces across the Republic it will be business as usual." This was closer to what happened than the stern imperatives of the official "maximum alert" order which had been issued. President Thieu, whose name was signed to the order canceling the truce, was celebrating at the comfortable home he had built in his wife's home town of My Tho in the Mekong delta; he did not return to Saigon. There is no evidence of a widespread attempt by the Vietnamese government to recall its officers and men to duty.

On the American side, attack warnings had become routine. A senior U.S. officer estimated later that since the summer of 1967, American forces had been on some kind of heightened state of alert about half the time. Usually nothing happened.

By the time of Tet, "maximum alert" orders and predictions of attack were widely viewed in the field as "cover your ass" papers for the protection of headquarters officers. When President Johnson and military officials made much of the "maximum alert" orders in the wake of the surprise attacks, junior officers in Vietnam were reminded of one of Westmoreland's favorite stories. Visiting a unit which had been badly battered in a surprise Viet Cong attack, the four-star general had demanded to know why there had been no warning. The unit's intelligence officer responded quickly that he had predicted the attack the day before. "Yeah, he's right," interjected the weary unit commander, "but he also predicted an attack for ninety-nine straight days before—and nothing happened."

The Saigon Circle

Saigon was not ready for war. During twenty-one years of revolutionary conflict, it had been spared the trauma of major battle. The countryside was the battlefield and Saigon was the seat of government, the center of commerce and luxury in the piaster culture of the rich, the haven of the foreigners on the broad tree-lined boulevards and the dwelling place of poverty-stricken squatters in the back alleys and slum districts. Saigon heard little about the war and seemed to care less.

In 1954, when the Viet Minh defeated the French at Dien Bien Phu, Saigon was a city of 550,000. In 1961, when the war resumed in earnest, the population was approaching 1,000,000. In 1964, just before the Americans arrived en masse, the population was estimated at 1,300,000. At the end of 1967, American officials estimated that 2,200,000 people were crowded into the city and 1,000,000 more had come to live in the swollen suburban

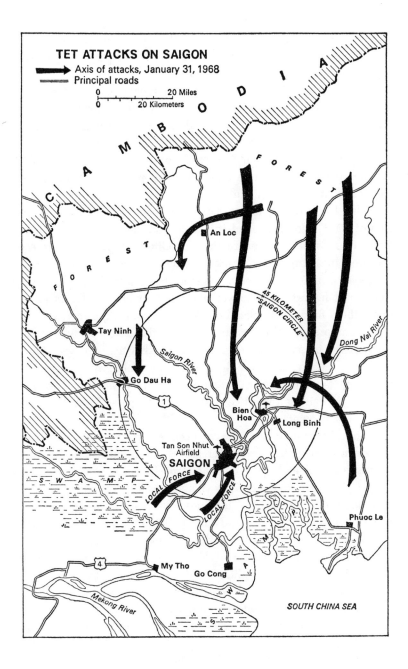

TET ATTACKS ON SAIGON

➤ Axis of attacks, January 31, 1968
══ Principal roads

0   20 Miles
0   20 Kilometers

CAMBODIA

FOREST

An Loc

FOREST

Tay Ninh

45 KILOMETER "SAIGON CIRCLE"

Saigon River

Dong Nai River

Go Dau Ha

1

Bien Hoa

Long Binh

Tan Son Nhut Airfield

SAIGON

LOCAL FORCE

LOCAL FORCE

S W A M P

Phuoc Le

My Tho

4

Go Cong

Mekong River

SOUTH CHINA SEA

perimeter of Gia Dinh Province. By this reckoning, roughly one fifth of all the people of South Vietnam were squeezed into the capital city and its immediate environs.

Saigon is within easy march of the jungle to the north and west, and only thirty-five miles from the jutting Parrot's Beak of Cambodia to the west. About half the perimeter is accessible to sampans through the serpentine Saigon River and hundreds of tiny inlets and waterways. Thousands of trucks, buses and small vehicles pour into the city daily bringing pigs, rice, fruit and a constant flow of human traffic.

This big, inviting target had never been defended in depth against the Communists, and it had never been seriously attacked. Early in 1967, a year before the Tet Offensive, American forces captured the plan of an attack on Saigon by the 5th Viet Cong Division, a unit long active on the perimeter. The plan was considered fantastic and unworkable, and American officers joked that "they fired that planner." At one point, the mayor and police proposed a tight security screen for the city, including physical barriers in many places. American authorities believed, however, that a Great Wall of Saigon would be prohibitively expensive in money and manpower, of doubtful military value and mainly effective in raising the price and extent of pay-offs at the controlled entry points.

The Vietnamese had always been extremely sensitive about American participation in the defense of cities, particularly Saigon. It was all well and good for the Americans to fight the Communists in the hinterland; if a village was in the way, that was regrettable but acceptable. The cities were another matter. Money, power, influence—the personal and political stakes of the ruling group—were involved there. In the case of Saigon, the chief military worry of the Vietnamese leaders was the possibility of a coup, and they wanted military and police power firmly in their own hands. If the United States forces were deeply involved, that was a potential danger. There was always the possibility that the Americans someday might decide to use this power against the ruling regime.

On December 15, 1967, the United States Command turned

over full responsibility for the close-in defense of Saigon to the South Vietnamese Command. The realignment in the Saigon area was a reflection of diminishing Communist activity near the capital and a gesture of confidence in the Vietnamese. It also released U.S. combat forces for planned offensives against Communist base camps in the Cambodian border region early in 1968.

A forty-five-kilometer (twenty-nine-mile) circle anchored on Saigon contained three fourths of the people of III Corps Tactical Zone and nearly all the important military and governmental headquarters. According to the U.S. plan, only fourteen United States and free world combat maneuver battalions were to remain inside this Saigon circle by Tet. The other thirty-nine battalions in III Corps were to be in remote areas guarding against infiltration or searching for bases and troop concentrations. Thus, one quarter of the available U.S. force would be in the circle with three quarters of the people.

Just about the time American units were moving to the border areas, Communist units were moving closer to Saigon. Around the turn of the year, U.S. probes into usual Communist base areas failed to stir the usual resistance. Presently the sensitive ear of communications intercept began picking up transmissions from more stations than before, some of them closer to Saigon than the weight of U.S. forces.

Lieutenant General Frederick C. Weyand, commander of U.S. field forces in III Corps, had long been unenthusiastic about the strategy of pursuing the Communists in remote jungle and border areas, and in early January the signs of Communist interest in the Saigon area raised his doubts to the level of alarm. On January 9 he telephoned Westmoreland for an appointment, and the following afternoon at Pentagon East he presented his superior officer with the latest intelligence gleanings and a recommendation that American forces be shifted back from border assignments toward the populated area. Westmoreland, who had also become aware of strange stirrings, gave the order to redeploy U.S. troops. Westmoreland has since called this decision one of the most critical of the Vietnam War.

Several American newsmen called on General Weyand at his

headquarters northeast of the capital on January 11. The lanky, slow-talking Californian, a former chief of U. S. Army Intelligence, discussed the "marked changes" in Communist tactics, including mass attacks against district and provincial towns. "Militarily, these attacks don't hurt us at all," he told the reporters. "Psychologically, though, I don't think we should kid ourselves—they have a considerable impact on the people."

The people were the prize and the object of the war, he emphasized, and the enemy seemed to be sniffing up to the populated areas. Three or four battalions had been detected within twenty miles of Saigon. Vice-President Ky had told Weyand that the capital would probably be attacked, perhaps by rockets or mortars, to make an impression on the people. "You could make a case for putting companies in eighty or so critical spots around the city," Weyand said. Some of the journalists began to wonder about their own security in supposedly safe Saigon.

By the eve of Tet, twenty-seven of the U.S. maneuver battalions were back inside the Saigon circle, and twenty-two battalions were still outside. Four battalions had been sent north as reinforcements for Khe Sanh and the DMZ.

On Tuesday, January 30, an ominous quiet descended upon the III Corps area. Some American units near Saigon were searching for Communist units, and others were positioned northwest, northeast, southeast and south of the city. The only significant Communist force spotted in III Corps that day was a convoy of oxcarts and Viet Cong south of Tay Ninh, well outside the Saigon circle.

At 9:15 P.M. Tuesday, South Vietnamese troops captured a Viet Cong soldier on the outskirts of the city carrying three AK-47 assault rifles in a burlap sack. He said attacks were planned that night against Tan Son Nhut Air Base and the government radio station downtown.

Weyand spoke to each of his three U.S. division commanders during the evening. He told each of them to earmark forces to be alert for quick movement during the night ahead.

"Direct Hit!"

Colonel Marvin D. Fuller, Weyand's operations officer, set the alarm clock in his trailer for 3 A.M. on the basis of intelligence that this would be the time of attack. The alarm went off as planned, and the drowsy officer telephoned his Tactical Operations Center a few yards away on the grounds of II Field Force headquarters.

"What's going on?" Fuller asked the officer on duty. Before he could get an answer, a flash lit the trailer, followed by a blast which knocked the telephone off the crate next to the bed and caved in part of the trailer.

Fuller scrambled around in the dark and found the telephone. "What happened?" he barked into the mouthpiece.

There was a short pause, and then he heard the voice of the duty officer. "We've had a direct hit!" he cried.

Fuller realized that if this were true, the major on the other end would be dead instead of talking. He told the man to calm down and look around. The shock wave of a mammoth explosion in the nearby U.S. ammunition dump had sent the furniture in the Tactical Operations Center flying and jolted the fluorescent light bulbs from their fixtures. They had crashed down in the big and vulnerable Quonset hut, plunging it into darkness.

"No, we're all right," the duty officer replied.

Within two or three minutes Fuller was in the TOC. A half-dozen radios and fifteen telephones came alive with news of attacks throughout the Saigon area.

— Long Binh Post, where Weyand's headquarters and the TOC were located, was under rocket and ground attack.

— Bien Hoa Air Base down the road, the busiest airport in Vietnam and the entire world, was under rocket attack, and a ground assault was developing on its perimeter.[3]

---

[3] In 1968 Bien Hoa Air Base recorded 857,000 takeoffs and landings, mostly bombing and supply runs. Da Nang Air Base recorded 846,000 aircraft movements. Tan Son Nhut Air Base was third with 804,000. The next busiest airport in the world, O'Hare International Airport in Chicago, recorded 690,000 aircraft movements for the year. The Vietnam aircraft movements do not include helicopter traffic, which is also heavy.

— The III Corps headquarters compound at Bien Hoa was under attack.

— Tan Son Nhut Air Base was under a heavy ground attack, threatening the hundreds of airplanes and helicopters, the communications hub of the Vietnam War effort and the headquarters of the U. S. Command and the Vietnamese Joint General Staff.

— Fighting was reported in downtown Saigon at the American Embassy, the Presidential Palace, the government radio station and other points.

Lanterns in the TOC cast eerie shadows as a dozen officers and ten enlisted men hustled back and forth to maps plotting the continuous reports. Charges set by Viet Cong sappers blew up four pallets of ammunition at the Long Binh ammunition dump, shaking the Operations Center with earthquake force. Weyand, wearing his flak jacket and a steel helmet, moved from map to map, issuing laconic orders for the movement of U.S. forces.

Except for the 199th Light Infantry Brigade north and east of Long Binh, none of Weyand's forces had intercepted major Communist attack units on their way into the Saigon area. Now the map of the Saigon circle reminded the general of a pinball machine, one light after another going on as it was hit by the steel ball until all the lights were lit. As each attack was reported and evaluated, he moved troops to counter it. Between 3 A.M. and 5 A.M. he ordered nearly five thousand mechanized and airborne troops into battle at new locations—mostly to defend United States installations at Long Binh, Bien Hoa Air Base and Tan Son Nhut Air Base. The least of the problems militarily but one of the greatest in terms of command pressure was the platoon action at the United States Embassy. Weyand dispatched thirty-six men of the 101st Airborne Division to land on the Embassy roof and join the fight.

In Saigon flashes, flares and tracer bullets lit up the sky as far as the eye could see. A Vietnamese senator, Truong Tien Dat, watched Viet Cong soldiers moving into the city over a prominent bridge—and thought at first they were government troops sent to stage a coup. Near the City Hall, citizens stumbled onto a young

Viet Cong recruit sitting on the curbstone and weeping profusely;
he had become separated from his unit and was scared. (They took
his rifle and turned him over to police.) A Viet Cong propagandist
sent into Cholon stopped cars and trucks to hand out leaflets announcing the uprising; one of the vehicles was a police jeep which
put the young man in the back seat and took him along to headquarters.

Toward dawn General Weyand rechecked the action in his
command post at Long Binh. He hoped that no more big attacks
were coming, because he had run out of forces which could be
quickly moved. When the G-2 informed him that elements of every
major enemy unit known to be in the III Corps Tactical Zone had
been identified in action, Weyand was sure that the worst was over
and that the defenders would be able to repulse the attacks within
a few hours or a few days. Still there was a nagging worry: what
if another major unit or units had infiltrated from North Vietnam
for the attack without being detected?

The Communist Command committed thirty-five battalions to
the assault on the Saigon area. Of these, eleven battalions—perhaps four thousand men in all—were launched into the Capital
Military District, the most heavily populated area of the city and
its environs. Most of them were local force units with the shortest
distances to travel and the best knowledge of the geography and
people of Saigon. Major attacks were launched against the city
from the north, the west and the south.

On the outskirts, the 5th Viet Cong Division was responsible
for the attacks on the big U.S. and Vietnamese bases at Long Binh
and Bien Hoa, northeast of the city. The 7th North Vietnamese
Division was assigned to keep U.S. forces busy in the peripheral
areas to the north and northwest and to block U.S. reinforcements
over the roads. Some elements of the 9th Viet Cong Division attacked Tan Son Nhut Air Base; others interdicted roads and prepared to reinforce if the attacks inside the city were successful.

When Weyand analyzed the battle later, he saw that the assault on Saigon was actually a large number of relatively small in-

dependent actions, with each unit assigned to its own job and its own area of operation. Despite the large number of Communist troops committed, insufficient force was applied in any one area to take and hold the objective. Some of the attacks were intended to divert U.S. troops from more important actions, and other attacks seemed peripheral to the main battles. The assault had been launched piecemeal, and it was repulsed piecemeal in a series of relatively small battles.

The attacks inside the central city against the Presidential Palace and the Vietnamese Navy headquarters were the work of the C-10 Battalion, and they closely followed the pattern of the commando unit's assault on the United States Embassy. In each case, the soldiers had infiltrated into the city beforehand on public buses, trucks and other civilian vehicles and assembled at "safe houses" where weapons and explosives were distributed and final instructions issued.

The Presidential Palace, which is probably the most heavily defended installation in the downtown area, was attacked by a team of thirteen men and a woman, nearly all of them under twenty years of age. In view of the odds against them, this was clearly a low-cost attempt at political impact. The sapper team, which arrived in three vehicles, including a truck loaded with TNT, was repelled at the side gate of the palace within a few minutes. The Viet Cong took refuge in an unfinished apartment building across the street and held out for more than fifteen hours in a running gun battle until nearly all of the small unit was killed.

The intermittent gun battle in daylight provided a live-action bonanza for American television crews, who were able to reach the site with no difficulty. Barrages of automatic weapons fire, scenes of men running for cover behind trees and the bodies of two dead MPs—it was a "shoot-'em-up" in the Hollywood tradition with the added impact of true-life news. On the network evening news show of February 1, CBS-Television (Walter Cronkite) presented one minute of the Presidential Palace gun battle. NBC-Television (Huntley-Brinkley) presented two minutes. ABC-Television (Bob Young), whose Vietnamese sound man was wounded on-camera by a stray bullet, presented three minutes. Each network bought time on the commercial communications satellite to transmit the footage instantly from Tokyo, where it was received from Air Force medical evacuation planes flying out of Saigon. In early 1968 the minimum charge to hire the trans-Pacific satellite was $4031. An American official calculated later that the total value of the weapons, ammunition and explosives carried by the fourteen-member Viet Cong team was $3980.

A twelve-man unit of the C-10 Battalion arrived at the main gate of the Vietnamese Navy headquarters at 3 A.M. in two civilian cars. According to a surviving member of the team, the sappers were told to take the headquarters and await the arrival of two battalions of Viet Cong troops moving in from positions across the Saigon River. The attackers blew a hole in the wall of a sentry post, but were quickly stopped inside. All but two of them were killed in the first five minutes. The enemy battalions just across the river apparently were a myth. There was no trace of them.

The 716th Military Police Battalion, the only major American combat unit inside the city when the fighting began, logged these calls in the first hour:

0300: BOQ [Bachelor Officers' Quarters] *No. 3 reports enemy action*

0315: U.S. Embassy under attack.

0316: Explosion at Phoenix City BOQ

0317: Explosion at Townhouse BOQ

0318: BOQ No. 1 under attack

0319: MacArthur BOQ under attack

0321: Report of hostile attack at Rex BOQ

0325: Explosion at BOQ No. 2

0340: Automatic weapons fire and attack at BOQ No. 3

0341: MPs at U.S. Embassy request urgent ammo resupply

0342: Heavy sniper fire at Metropole BEQ [Bachelor Enlisted Quarters]

0350: Incoming mortars at Montana BOQ
0358: Saigon port area reports small-arms and automatic weapons fire
0359: Mortars and rockets fired at U.S. Embassy; reinforcements requested

Some of the reported attacks were actually stray bullets or nearby explosions; others were fire fights which developed on the spur of the moment. With the exception of the assault on the American Embassy and a few much smaller incidents, American installations were not deliberate targets of the Viet Cong that night.

The most serious and best-organized downtown attack was directed against the government radio station, an extremely valuable asset in any coup or insurrection. Here the Communist planning had been thorough, but the government had done a little planning too.

Just before 3 A.M. a convoy of jeeps and civilian automobiles rolled up to the gate of the radio station and armed men dressed as South Vietnamese QCs (Riot Police) piled out. A "government lieutenant" jumped out of the lead jeep and briskly informed the guard that the reinforcements for the station had arrived. "I haven't heard anything about it," the guard was heard to say just before he was shot with a .45 pistol.

The station had been reinforced during the night by a government airborne platoon, most of whose members were asleep on the roof. Viet Cong machine gunners in the window of an apartment building overlooking the roof annihilated them with a few surprise bursts. Meanwhile, ground level attackers blasted their way into the compound, accompanied by a North Vietnamese radio technician qualified to operate the station. He was equipped with detailed diagrams of the studios and offices and a duplicate set of keys, all provided by a sympathizer on the station's staff. The invaders carried tapes to be played on the air proclaiming the General Uprising and announcing the liberation of Saigon.

The afternoon before, Lieutenant Colonel Vu Duc Vinh, the director-general of the station, had arranged to take the station off the air at a prearranged signal in case of attack, and at the first gunshots, a technician in the studio gave the signal. At the transmitter site fourteen miles away, the night crew got the message and shut off the lines to the downtown studio. The Viet Cong held the station for six hours, but they were never able to broadcast the tapes.

When it became clear that the downtown studio was off the air, the invaders began destroying the main control room, which had just been equipped with the most modern gadgets by the United States at a cost of $1 million. After the Viet Cong were driven out in violent and destructive fighting, government soldiers looted the place of most of the equipment that was still intact.

Colonel Vinh had thought of almost everything for his alternate site except program material. In the first hours of the attack Saigon Radio beamed an incongruous mixture of Viennese waltzes, the Beatles, the Rolling Stones and Vietnamese martial music—which was all that was on hand at the transmitter site. At the same time Hanoi Radio and Liberation Radio (Viet Cong) were on the air with hopped-up "reports" of the nationwide attacks and fervent appeals to the people to join the uprising.

The 6th Battalion of the 165-A Viet Cong Regiment was assigned to occupy "Chi Hoa Reeducation Center," the main Saigon prison, and liberate its five thousand inmates, many of whom had been jailed on political charges. The battalion's guides were killed in a brush with police on their way into the city, and the unit became engaged in a battle in a cemetery nearly a mile away from the prison. It never reached its objective.

Two battalions of the 101st Viet Cong Regiment attacked and occupied the South Vietnamese Armored Command headquarters and the Artillery Command headquarters on the northern edge of the city. The units planned to use captured tanks and howitzers from the installations in their drive against Tan Son Nhut and other targets. Trained Viet Cong tank operators accompanied the troops into the Phu Dong Armored headquarters, only to discover that the tanks had been removed to another base several months earlier. At the Co Lao Artillery headquarters, defenders removed the breechblocks from the howitzers before abandoning the compound, thus rendering them useless.

A City Lane

Nguyen Thi Do, as we shall call her, was awakened in the night by gunfire near her house in one of the little back alleys off the main street in Cholon, the predominantly Chinese section of the capital. About 10 A.M. twenty-six armed Viet Cong entered the lane, led by two barbers from the neighborhood and a tall, attractive man of Chinese descent wearing white undershorts and a white tee shirt, the Cantonese-style early-morning apparel. The barbers and the man in shorts appeared to be at ease with the Viet Cong.

Most of the soldiers wore olive-drab uniforms with red arm bands, though two of the visitors wore civilian clothes with red cross arm bands. All were barefoot. The leader carried an automatic rifle. She had bobbed hair and was about seventeen years old, the only female in the group.

In a Northern accent, the leader called upon the people to take down the orange-and-yellow Republic of Vietnam flag, which she called the "sell-out-your-country flag," and announced that tomorrow or the next day there would be a new flag. "Saigon is liberated," she shouted. After a few minutes the group moved on through the back alleys, leaving a pock-marked soldier with a submachine gun in charge. He disappeared after about twenty minutes.

The reaction in the neighborhood was fear, but nobody lowered the national flag.

During the next several days the lane was alternately occupied and searched by American GIs looking for Viet Cong and by Viet Cong looking for Americans, government soldiers or anyone who worked for them. Nguyen Thi Do gave the GIs a cold drink, but she was severely criticized by her neighbors for this gesture of partiality.

The home of a government Army veteran caught fire in the confusion and nearby shooting, and the man attempted to drag some of his belongings to the main street. American GIs called to him to stop, and when he failed to heed them, they shot him.

His body lay in the alley until sanitation crews took it away three days later.

Nguyen Thi Do saw two government officer candidates with their arms tied behind their backs. They were being led away by the Viet Cong. A neighbor was carrying six AK-47s and some grenades into the street. He explained that six Viet Cong had hidden in his house during an American search, and afterward they changed into civilian clothes, hid their weapons and departed. The neighbor and his wife decided it was essential to get rid of the weapons lest the family be implicated with the Viet Cong.

As Nguyen Thi Do was fleeing after a Viet Cong search, a VC soldier stopped her. "Where are you going? It is safer for you at home. The South is liberated already." The soldiers refused to be addressed as "sir" (*Ong*). "Let's call each other brother and sister," one of them said.

After a night in the market place with many deeply frightened neighbors, Nguyen Thi Do returned to the lane. Two houses were burning, and she fainted. "Don't be afraid," said a Viet Cong soldier who came to her aid, "this harm has been done by the Americans." Nguyen Thi Do, who worked for Americans and whose sister was married to an American, did not know whether or not he was telling the truth.

Tan Son Nhut Air Base came under attack during the night from the west, north and east. The most serious assault was from the west, where the advance party of two Viet Cong battalions moved across a supposedly mined field, blasted a Vietnamese guard bunker with B-40 anti-tank rockets and sent the occupants of another bunker fleeing into the night. Viet Cong troops began to swarm into the giant installation, which had been expanded many times since the French established it in 1935 as the first air base in Indochina.

An American security force clashed with the invading troops and two companies of government airborne troops counterattacked on the ground. They suffered heavy casualties but temporarily halted the invasion. At 6 A.M. the U. S. Cavalry—armored variety

—arrived to save the day. An armored cavalry troop from the 25th Infantry Division had raced across country toward Tan Son Nhut during the night, guided by flares dropped from the tank commander's control helicopter. As it approached the base, the cav unit attacked the Viet Cong force sharply from the rear.

In broad daylight, the Viet Cong battalions were pounded by dive bombers, armed helicopters, tanks and ground troops. Many of the Viet Cong retreated to the Vinatexco cotton mill, South Vietnam's largest and newest, located just outside the air base. The Vietnamese High Command authorized helicopter gunships to attack. A total of 162 bodies were found inside the wrecked textile mill. It was restored later with the help of $3 million in U.S. aid.

The Headquarters Area

BOQ No. 3 was down the road from Joint General Staff headquarters, the command post and control center of the Vietnamese government Army and a prime target of the Viet Cong assault. On the way to its attack position, a company-sized element of Communist troops became embroiled in a gunfight with the American guards and residents of the bachelor officers' quarters.

A little after 4 A.M., twenty-five men of the 716th Military Police Battalion, most of them riding in a two-and-a-half-ton truck, headed down a narrow alley toward the BOQ to answer the call for reinforcements. Suddenly there were two loud explosions and bright flashes of light, and fusillades of automatic weapons fire raked the truck and the two escort jeeps. Some of the MPs were killed instantly; others were badly wounded or trapped in the alley. A few MPs managed to reach the BOQ and radio for help:

—Waco Six Zero [MP headquarters], that alert force is laying down there in the alleyway. They're pitched up against the wall if any of them is still alive. . . .

—What are the chances of getting an ambulance in there or near there and taking out injured by foot?

—We can try it. . . .

— Number One, I've got an ambulance here, could you use him up there?

— We need him bad. I don't know how you're going to get him in here. We need him at the main gate of BOQ 3, but I don't know how you're going to get him in here without being hit.

— OK, I'm taking him up. . . . We'll see how far we can get without being fired upon. He's willing to go. Over.

— Be extremely careful. . . .

— Duty Officer Number Two, this is Number One. . . . We need that ambulance bad.

— This is Number Two (*sighs*). . . . We'll try to get her into you.

— 10-24 [acknowledged], Tango Yankee [thank you].

— Have that ambulance still, we'll cover it.

— 10-24, baby. . . .

— I'll start 'em moving out. Make sure you cover this man now. . . .

[A little later]:

— Number One, this is Number Two (*puffing*). We tried to go down the alley (*catching his breath*). They blew up a claymore [mine] on us. We're going to hold tight right here. It's about the best we can do. Over.

— 10-24 (*the MP is near tears*). I know you can't help it. Just keep trying. Do the best you can. . . .

Sixteen American Military Policemen were killed in the alley outside of BOQ 3, and twenty-one wounded. Some were in two rescue teams which fought their way into the alley in twelve hours of combat.

General Cao Van Vien, chief of the Joint General Staff (JGS), drove to work from his home in Cholon through back streets of the embattled capital. Just after daylight he arrived at JGS headquarters, a big yellow masonry building with a circular driveway which was constructed by the French decades ago to house their military staffs. The headquarters is at the southern edge of Tan Son

Nhut, and sounds of battle—from the air base, from BOQ 3 nearby and from the gates of the JGS compound—could be heard on every side. At 7 A.M. the headquarters compound commander reported to Vien that the Viet Cong had taken Gate 4 of the air base, threatening the headquarters itself.

Vien was down to two battalions of general reserve troops. The day before, he had promised them to the embattled cities of I and II Corps, but at the end of the day the men had still been camped at the airport in battle dress, waiting to depart. During the evening one battalion had been diverted to the radio station, the prison and other obvious city targets. Two companies of the remaining battalion had counterattacked and stopped the Viet Cong during the night at the western edge of Tan Son Nhut.

Now Vien picked up the telephone and ordered the final two companies of the last battalion of reserves to join the battle at Gate 4 near his own headquarters. There was nothing left.

The Viet Cong easily turned aside the first platoon sent against them. As more troops arrived, the Viet Cong hesitated and finally moved to positions around the Armed Forces Language School.

By the end of the morning, two fresh battalions of Vietnamese Marines were flown by helicopter from the Mekong delta to the parade field at JGS headquarters. The battle near the gate raged intermittently for twenty-four hours, but the invaders were repulsed.

President Thieu was picked up by a United States helicopter at his vacation home in My Tho in the Mekong delta and flown to JGS headquarters. Vice-President Ky arrived from his residence close by. By Wednesday noon most of the highest-ranking generals and cabinet ministers had gathered in Vien's large office on the second floor of the old French headquarters building. Thieu, Ky and many of the other officials stayed there for several days, sleeping at night on cots, sofas or the big rug in the middle of General Vien's office.

Agents of the Viet Cong Saigon-Cholon Security Section had orders to kill Thieu, Ambassador Bunker, the chief of South Vietnamese Central Intelligence (General Linh Quang Vien), the chief of National Police (Brigadier General Nguyen Ngoc Loan) and the chief of Saigon Police (Lieutenant Colonel Nguyen Van Luan). One of the assassination squads got lost, another became separated from its cache of weapons. All the assassination attempts failed.

Despite these setbacks, the Viet Cong might have killed the senior echelon of South Vietnam's military and political leadership with a single accurate or lucky rocket round at JGS headquarters. Three rockets hit the compound. The closest one was fifty yards from the yellow masonry building loaded with VIPs.

The story of a battle is a story of "ifs."

If Viet Cong Military Region 5 had not attacked seven cities twenty-four hours ahead of time and thus sounded an alarm . . .

If General Weyand had not moved American battalions back to quick-reaction positions inside the Saigon circle . . .

If Vien's two battalions of general reserves had immediately responded to orders and flown north the day before . . .

If the Long Binh Tactical Operations Center had been hit by a rocket or overrun . . .

If the Viet Cong had been able to broadcast their tapes on Saigon Radio, declaring that the government and city had fallen and the General Uprising had begun . . .

If the attacking troops had taken over government tanks and artillery as planned for use against Tan Son Nhut or JGS . . .

If JGS headquarters had been hit by a rocket or overrun . . .

If any or all of these things had happened, the Tet Offensive in Saigon would have been a much closer thing. Conceivably, the Communist Command might have demolished the Vietnamese government and its military forces. That might have been the end of the Second Indochina War.

The Mekong Delta

One vital area remained to be heard from: the populous Mekong delta to the south, where the mighty Mekong River ends its 2600-mile course from the mountains of Tibet through China and Southeast Asia on its way to the sea. The great green flatness of the delta is the rice basket of South Vietnam, growing enough of this

Asian staff of life in a good year to meet the needs of the country and several other countries besides. This heartland of South Vietnam was also rich in pigs, bananas, coconuts—and insurgency.

The delta was the real world to the Vietnamese. Almost by definition that meant it was unreal to the Americans, who operated on different premises and were in too much of a hurry to learn or to change. The delta was a uniquely South Vietnamese theater of action. There the insurgents were the local people, generally landless peasants recruited and directed by leaders of greater sophistication and operating in keeping with the canons of guerrilla war. Until Tet, no North Vietnamese soldiers were assigned there. At Saigon's edict, the United States was limited to sixteen hundred military advisers, several aircraft and helicopter companies and two battalions of ground combat troops which the Vietnamese reluctantly permitted to operate in the upper reaches of the delta from a base dredged out of Mekong River silt. When not a sea of mud, the place was as dusty and arid as the craters of the moon. The Americans named it Dong Tam ("United Hearts and Minds").

Three weeks before the Tet Offensive, Brigadier General William R. Desobry held a farewell news conference after eighteen months as U.S. military advisory chief in the delta. Desobry said the Viet Cong forces were "poorly motivated, poorly trained" and that the South Vietnamese Army "has the upper hand completely." At the time he spoke, Viet Cong units were closing their grip on important roads, canals and routes of approach to provincial and district capitals throughout the region.

Hundreds, perhaps thousands, of ordinary citizens in the Mekong delta knew that Viet Cong troops were about to attack the cities. Supposedly friendly hamlets on the outskirts of Can Tho and Vinh Long had been invaded by the assault troops four days before Tet and the people had fled to town. Simple people in the cities were building bunkers in previously secure neighborhoods. Wealthy folk were quietly leaving town.

The American advisers knew nothing. If the government officers knew anything, they did not report it.

In the opening hours of the Tet Offensive, Viet Cong troops attacked thirteen of the sixteen provincial capitals of the Mekong delta and many of the district capitals. There was no alarm, in many cases, until enemy troops began firing in the middle of town.

Especially in the Mekong delta, the Tet Offensive was a flash of lightning which was not blinding but revealing. For a fleeting instant, some of the hidden realities of Vietnam were illuminated in sharp and dramatic relief. These included the determination and fanaticism—heroism, one might say—of the Viet Cong officers and men, and the failure of will and nerve of a number of South Vietnamese government officers. In the moment of crisis, many U.S. "advisers" became the commanders.

Major General Nguyen Van Manh, the IV Corps commander, was in his mansion at Can Tho behind tanks, armored personnel carriers, troops and acres of barbed wire. He did not come out. A few blocks away, American military advisers manned their side of the IV Corps Tactical Operations Center, feverishly fielding requests for air strikes, emergency resupply and reinforcements from all over the region. On the Vietnamese side of the room were a few junior officers with no authority to do anything. When General Manh did come out days later, he seemed primarily concerned with the defense of the headquarters city. He was relieved of his command in late February and reassigned as Inspector General of the Vietnamese Armed Forces.

One of the three government division commanders in IV Corps went to pieces during the Tet attack; his U.S. adviser virtually took command. In another delta province, the American adviser discovered the province chief was wearing a set of civilian clothes under his military uniform in case he needed to disappear in a hurry.

At the moment of attack in Vinh Long, the American duty officer at the Tactical Operation Center received urgent radio requests over the U. S. Command's advisory radio net. Lieutenant John Lippincott and his interpreter walked across the room to the Vietnamese colonel in charge.

"Helicopter pilots are receiving intense fire from these coordinates, sir. Should they return fire?"

No answer. No permission. No sign of recognition at all.

Lippincott walked back to the radio. The senior American adviser, whose headquarters was under attack, wanted to know if the government's 43rd Ranger Battalion, quartered just outside of the city, had yet been committed to the battle.

Lippincott and his interpreter walked across the room again. "Excuse me, Colonel. Are the Rangers committed yet?"

No answer. No sign of recognition. Only a glassy stare. And so it went through the night.

In Can Tho government commanders refused to make a ground assault against Viet Cong holed up in the gleaming Faculty of Science building at the new university, the pride of the city. Instead, government artillerymen in sight of the building pumped high-explosive shells into their howitzers and fired away at close range, giggling with nervousness and a macabre humor as they did so. Then Vietnamese Air Force planes dropped five hundred-pound bombs. The building was demolished (later to be reconstructed with U.S. funds). Only a few Viet Cong bodies were found inside.

In time, the Communist forces were driven out of the delta cities, mainly by the staggering firepower of American weaponry. According to the official reports, 2400 civilians were killed, 5000 wounded and 211,000 made homeless in the battles of the Mekong delta. This probably underestimates the death and destruction, and in any case, the figures do not begin to suggest the nightmare of the cities.

A total of 5200 Viet Cong are reported to have been killed in the Mekong delta and 560 captured. Whatever the accuracy of this estimate, it is clear that large numbers of the most dedicated and most experienced guerrillas and local force troops met their death inside the unfamiliar cities.

In the Balance

The fog of war hung over the burning, weeping, suffering country and the battered, bloody armies on both sides. It would take weeks to find out what had happened and a longer period to analyze and assess what had taken place. Some things, though, soon became evident.

The Communist Command had suddenly changed its strategy

and tactics, speeding up the tempo and timetable of the war and lavishly expending in the cities resources which had been husbanded for years in the forests and jungle.

In most parts of the country, North Vietnamese main force units were held in reserve or given peripheral missions while the guerrillas, local force battalions and commando units led the attack and suffered the heaviest losses. This appears to have been dictated for reasons of state policy in North Vietnam—perhaps as part of a political compromise in the Politburo when the attack was ordered. Losses were very high. The North Vietnamese troops would have been easier to replace than veteran Southern fighters, many of whom were irreplaceable.

There had been no General Uprising and nothing resembling the beginning of one. Except in the city of Hue (Chapter VI), the period of occupation was far too brief for Communist cadres to stimulate major political movements. The Vietnamese people had bent like bamboo in the wind, but they did not break in any direction. The stoicism and caution of the people had rejected the Communist political commanders just as it rejected the American efforts to rouse the country behind the Saigon goverment.

On the Communist side, the battle had shattered the illusion of the General Uprising and set back the dreams of a quick and easy victory. Moreover, it raised grave doubts in the minds of those who had seen their comrades sent into battle with false assurances and little chances of survival.

Among the Vietnamese people, the battles had created doubts about Communist military power. The Liberation Army had attacked in the middle of the Tet truce when the South Vietnamese Army was on leave, and even so it had been able to achieve only temporary inroads. If the Communists were unable to take the cities with a surprise attack in such circumstances, they would probably be unable to do better at any other time. Many people had little faith in the South Vietnamese Army from the beginning. Now the Viet Cong were whittled down to the same level.

Among Americans in Vietnam, there was a sense of shock and the realization that many basic questions had been raised. How could a failing enemy organize and carry off such a powerful, well-coordinated and nationwide offensive? Why did nobody cry alarm? How were the Communists able to move into position and even infiltrate the cities without warning from the government Army or the people?

The most urgent questions concerned the immediate future. Could this happen again? What was coming next? And perhaps more important in a fundamental sense, What would be the reaction of the American people and their government nearly halfway around the world? How would *they* see it? What would *they* do?

CHAPTER V

The Shock Wave

LITTLE BIG HORN, Dakota, June 27, 1876—Gen. George Armstrong Custer said today in an exclusive interview with this correspondent that the battle of Little Big Horn had just turned the corner and he could now see the light at the end of the tunnel.

"We have the Sioux on the run," Gen. Custer told me. "Of course, we still have some cleaning up to do, but the Redskins are hurting badly and it will only be a matter of time before they give in."

—Art Buchwald in the Washington *Post*
February 6, 1968

IN THE *CBS Evening News* room on West Fifty-seventh Street in New York City, the story from Saigon came clattering across the teletypes, and this time Walter Cronkite did not puff his pipe in quiet detachment. "What the hell is going on?" he cried out to nobody in particular, slapping a swatch of press association copy on the newsroom table. "I thought we were winning the war!"

Jason McManus, who edited the Vietnam news for *Time*, got the word on the radio at his Manhattan apartment. He decided immediately that this would be fatal to those who had been selling "success" and suggesting that peace was around the corner. "That's the end of the war," McManus said to himself. He was certain that Johnson, Westmoreland and some of the steadfast hawks on his own magazine would never recover.

Consternation and anger flashed across the land with the high-voltage leap of modern mass communications. The public at large had paid little or no attention to the rumbles of impending trouble in Vietnam which had cropped up since November. It had not been warned in any serious way by officials of the government. Most people were unprepared for this stunning evidence of Communist resourcefulness, determination and power.

It is hard to tell whether the public initially was more furious at the Communists in Asia or at the government of the United States. The trend records of the public opinion polls, which are fever charts of the body politic, show a blip just after the Tet Offensive—a sudden jump in public hawkishness followed by a fall. The immediate feeling was, "They hit us, by God let's hit them back." The same charts show a steep drop in public approval of President Johnson's handling of the war. This was not expected. The usual public reaction to a foreign crisis is to rally round the President, at least at first.

The full dimension of the crisis in the living rooms was not immediately grasped in official Washington. The leaders there were attuned at first to action in Asia rather than reaction at home, and they assumed that favorable developments on the battle front would automatically dissipate the anger and dismay in the United States.

The cables from Saigon presented a reassuring and bloodless picture snapped from the lofty perspective of high headquarters. They emphasized Communist shortcomings and losses rather than Communist achievements and said little or nothing of the "negative" aspects. Washington did not seek the darker side. It wanted desperately to hear that all was well.

The cables were thus doubly welcome. The leaders in Washington took heart and believed the country would take heart as well. The leaders were mistaken. While they were receiving, reading and disseminating after-the-fact official summaries of what had happened, the public was *experiencing* the worst of the bloodshed through the new technology of television. The summaries were not believed. The projected experience was.

Vietnam was America's first television war and the Tet Offensive was America's first television superbattle.

At the time of Pearl Harbor, only ten thousand television sets were in use in the United States. When the Korean War broke out, ten million sets were in use. By January of 1968, nearly a hundred million sets were distributed across the land, reaching sixteen of every seventeen homes and a potential audience of 96 per cent of the population. In midwinter, when days are short in the United States, the early-evening television news programs reach their highest audiences. According to national Nielsen surveys, the *CBS Evening News* with Walter Cronkite and

the NBC *Huntley-Brinkley Report each* were seen in more than
ten million homes nightly during the first weeks of the Tet Offensive.

The Vietnam War was an important television story beginning
in 1963 with the revolt against Diem and the growing U.S. involvement, and it became the most important story beginning
with the bombing of the North and the dispatch of U.S. ground
troops in 1965. Even so, this big story was rarely a great story
for the television medium. Though there had been several in-
tensively covered sieges and battles, the live action was difficult
to capture and the significance of the action seemed to run counter
to the pictures. There would be a fight for a hill or a valley,
bullets flying and helicopters swarming, the Communists would
fall back and the United States would "win." Then the prize
would be abandoned and the area returned to Communist control. The other fruit of "victory" was the body count chart behind the TV anchor man, and the Communists never seemed
to run out of numbers to join the digits of the dead.

Tet was a far better story. The action was plentiful and
easily accessible: correspondents and camera crews in Saigon could
leave their homes or hotels in the morning, drive to the "war"
in their own automobiles, drive back to the office with the film
and their reports and then return home to turn on the hi-fi,
have a drink and cook a steak. "Covering the war was easy,"
observed Ron Steinman, chief of the thirty-two man NBC News
bureau in Saigon. "It was like springtime with buds of fire popping
out wherever you chanced to turn your head." When the battle
of Saigon diminished after several weeks, there was the battle
of Hue and the siege of Khe Sanh, both of which were great pic-
torial episodes.

The Tet story had suspense, high drama and enormous public
interest. The United States and its allies were not the inevitable
winners in every battle; the Communists had taken the initiative.
The plans and purposes of the United States hung in the balance;
political and military reputations were at stake; there was an
enveloping aura of controversy at home and in the field. And for
once, the pictures tended to agree with the dominant opinion of

the correspondents and their editors at home—that the war was a
stalemate and a mistake.

The Flight of a Single Bullet

*On a street corner in Saigon on February 1, a Vietnamese
in a military uniform fired a bullet into the head of another
Vietnamese in a checked shirt and black shorts. A human being
was destroyed, his soul was gone, his body shattered. Neither he
nor his death could ever be called back—and yet they were.
The final moment was recorded on plastic emulsion backed with
silver salts, developed in chemicals in a darkroom and distributed
in literally hundreds of millions of copies throughout the world
via electronic scanning devices, space satellites and a ganglion of
cables and magnetic circuits.*

*As this photographic record hurtled across the globe, the
political and military leaders of the United States sought to im-
print a quite different set of images upon the minds of men.
At every turn, the governmental leaders lost the contest for
attention to the elemental power of one man's moment of death,
face to face with his killer.*

The President rose early Wednesday morning, January 31, to
read the cables from the war zone. He had telephoned the
Situation Room for news several times during the night. After
reading the 6 A.M. report, he called for another summary prior
to his breakfast with congressional leaders.

The breakfast was a very somber session which dealt with
two dangerous, embarrassing developments—the seizure of the
Pueblo off Korea and the Tet Offensive in Vietnam. Like many
other foreign policy meetings during the Johnson presidency,
it took place in the family dining room of the White House,
where the antique wallpaper depicted scenes from an earlier revolutionary war. Between the old-fashioned fireplace and a tall
window of thick, green-tinted bulletproof glass was a scene of the
British expeditionary force surrendering to the American revolutionaries at Yorktown.

The President sat at the head of the long table, between Representative Mendel Rivers of South Carolina on his left and Senator Margaret Chase Smith of Maine on his right. He looked tired and worried. There were deep circles under his eyes.

General Earle Wheeler, chairman of the Joint Chiefs, stood at an easel and briefed the lawmakers and the President from a map. The Communists still seriously threatened Westmoreland's headquarters at Tan Son Nhut, and Communist troops were still entrenched in parts of Saigon, Ban Me Thuot, Kontum, Hue, Qui Nhon and several cities in the Mekong delta. Still, Westmoreland thought the attacks had produced no significant military results, and he considered them diversionary efforts in preparation for an assault at Khe Sanh or the DMZ. An even bigger battle might be ahead.

Despite his private concern, the President gave a public impression of unruffled confidence. In midafternoon he invited several White House reporters to join him for coffee while he ate his customary late lunch in the family dining room. On the way from the Oval Office to the White House living quarters, he bounded along as if he had not a problem in the world, joking and chatting with the reporters. He denied being upset at the turn of events and said he was getting plenty of sleep, an assertion which was belied by his haggard appearance. Over soup, a sandwich and milk, he read aloud excerpts of cables from Saigon saying that the Communists were being resoundingly defeated and that the offensive had gained them nothing militarily. Johnson made a practice of reading selected portions of secret cables to reporters whenever it suited his purposes, but the press corps took this with more than a grain of salt. There were even rumors in the press room that the President had two sets of Saigon secret cables, one set to read to visitors and another and more balanced set for his own information. On this Wednesday afternoon, the reporters in the off-the-record session with the President thought the cables he read them were incredibly optimistic, even euphoric. They did not believe them.

Privately, the President was seeking reassurance to quiet his own fears and doubts. The same afternoon, General Wheeler telephoned Westmoreland in Saigon on a secure line and asked six questions which were to be answered immediately and directly to the White House. What were the casualty figures, the number of towns in enemy hands, the probable duration of the current battles? What about the impact of the offensive on the South Vietnamese government and people? The French press was already saying Tet proved the war was at an impasse. How could that be answered? Finally, there was the worrisome possibility that the seizure of the *Pueblo* and other threatening moves of the Korean Communists might be connected somehow with the Tet Offensive by the Vietnamese Communists. What did Saigon think?

It was before dawn in Saigon but Westmoreland roused Bunker by telephone and the two men composed a joint reply, reflecting the confidence with which both were imbued. The allies were gaining and the Communists losing an unprecedented number of men. The battles in the cities should soon be over, leaving the government in the good position to show strong leadership and strengthen itself with the people. As for coordination with Korea, that seemed likely—though nobody in Saigon had a way to be certain.[1]

While the reassuring views of Westmoreland and Bunker were distributed to a few officials in the top rank of government, a quite different and much more sobering version was broadcast to the American people on the Wednesday evening television news shows. This was the first chance for the networks to show film of the battles which had erupted in Saigon. *Huntley-Brinkley* presented NBC's unedited "just as it happened" film of the battle at the American Embassy. Later that night the footage was repeated on the thirty-minute NBC-Television News special, *Vietcong Terror: A Guerrilla Offensive*. The same shocking events were covered by CBS that night in a thirty-minute television special report, *Saigon Under Fire*.

[1] There is still no hard evidence one way or the other. A North Vietnamese military aid delegation visited North Korea in August 1967, after the planning for the General Offensive and General Uprising had begun. Whether the Vietnamese told the Koreans their plan and its timing is yet unknown in the West.

There was frustration and worry in the high ranks of government. The Viet Cong were being decisively beaten in the Saigon cables, but they were scoring great feats on television and in the press. The cables were seen by only a few, and the news reports were seen by nearly everyone. Even when cables were made available in cautious fashion, reporters were unconvinced. Their papers and networks continued the heavy coverage from Vietnam emphasizing the surprise and power of the Tet Offensive and the continuing battles in many cities.

The best place to disseminate the official view was in Saigon, where the war reporting that caught public attention originated. If only Westmoreland and Bunker would tell the world in public what they were telling the President in secret. The White House sent the message to them that public reassurance was urgent and they could help by appearing before the newsmen and cameras right away. In view of the uncertainty of the situation and the scarcity of solid information, Bunker limited himself to a background briefing in which he could not be quoted directly. It received little attention. Westmoreland, despite contrary advice from his staff, agreed to make a personal report to assembled newsmen.

As the White House request for public relations assistance was being processed, Brigadier General Nguyen Ngoc Loan, chief of South Vietnam's National Police, arrived at the street corner near the An Quang Pagoda. Vietnamese Marines had a Viet Cong suspect in tow. The man had been armed with a pistol, usually the mark of an officer, but wore no military insignia or garb, helmet or body armor—just a checked shirt and black shorts. His hands had been tied behind him, and he had been beaten.

As the prisoner was marched down the street toward Loan, the general drew his own revolver and waved away the soldiers and bystanders. The man was standing three or four feet away, his eyes downcast. He heard no death sentence—indeed, Loan had said not a word to him—but he knew what was about to happen.

The general's right arm stretched out straight and his index finger squeezed the trigger. There was the crack of a shot. The

*man's legs folded beneath him and he sat down backward in
the street, then fell flat, blood spurting from his head. Loan returned the gun to its holster and walked away.*

Westmoreland strode into the late-afternoon news briefing for
correspondents at the Joint United States Public Affairs Office
(JUSPAO), the daily event known as "the Five O'Clock Follies."
The auditorium was unusually crowded, and the klieg lights
and cameras were ready.

"Gentlemen, I thought I would try to put into perspective
the events of the last several months and those of the last several
days in particular," he began. The enemy campaign plan was
drafted in Hanoi, he reported, and consisted of three phases:
(1) the early attacks in Dak To, along the Cambodian border
and in the Mekong delta, to inflict heavy casualties and to force
the allies to deploy men from the populated urban areas; (2)
the Tet Offensive in cities and towns throughout the country; and
(3) the main effort in Khe Sanh and northern I Corps, still to
come.

He ran down a long list of cities which had been heavily
attacked, and summarized the status of each one. The general
credited the Communists with the ability to continue the current
urban attack phase for "several more days," though some evidence
suggested they were about to run out of steam. Westmoreland
announced that 5800 enemy troops had been killed, compared to
530 friendly troops. "In summary, gentlemen, this second phase of
the campaign was a bold one. It was characterized by treachery
and deceitfulness. It showed a callous disregard for human life,"
he said.

*Directly across Nguyen Hue Street² from where Westmore-
land was speaking, a strip of 35-mm. still photograph film was
being processed in the Associated Press darkroom.*

*Photographer Eddie Adams had joined forces that morning
with an NBC-Television crew, and they rode across town together
to the An Quang Pagoda. Adams spotted the Vietnamese Marines*

_____

² Named for the hero of Tet 1789, also known as Quang Trung.

with a man in custody. He followed them down the street, snapping pictures as he went.

Suddenly Loan appeared. Adams watched Loan draw his gun, and instinctively followed the action in the viewfinder of his Leica. As Loan fired, Adams tripped the shutter.

When the AP bureau developed the film, there was jubilation. The camera had captured the whole scene at the split second of impact—the general's straightened arm, his finger on the trigger and inches away (it seemed in the distorted distance of the wide-angle lens) the grimace on the suspect's face as the bullet slammed into his head.

The picture was prepared for transmission via photographic scanning devices and radiophoto circuits to New York, and from there throughout the world. Everyone knew it was a prizewinner, one of the great pictures of the Vietnam War.[3]

Lyndon Johnson picked up the morning newspapers looking for the report of the Westmoreland press conference. It was there all right, but it was upstaged by spectacular front-page display of Eddie Adams' picture of an execution.

The main headline in the Washington *Post* said,

CLASHES PERSIST IN VIET CITIES;
GENERAL WARNS OF DMZ PUSH

Under the headline, the *Post* splashed the Loan picture across five of its eight columns, four inches deep.

The New York *Times* printed the Westmoreland story in column eight of page 1, the most prestigious spot in the paper. Just above it, four columns wide and five inches deep, was the dramatic photograph from Saigon. In a gesture extremely rare for the *Times*, the Loan photograph was printed twice in the same

[3] The photograph subsequently won for Adams the Pulitzer Prize for Spot News Photography; the Grand Prize and First Prize for Spot News of the World Press Photo Contest, The Hague; the Picture of the Year Award and First Prize for Spot News of the National Press Photographers Association; the Sigma Delta Chi Award for Distinguished Service in Journalism; the George Polk Award for Outstanding News Photography; the Associated Press Managing Editors Award and the Overseas Press Club Award for Best Photographic Reporting from Abroad.

edition. Besides appearing on the front page, it was also printed on page 12, three columns wide, along with Adams' pictures of the prelude and aftermath of the killing.

At noon the President called the White House press corps to the Cabinet Room for his first news conference since the battle began. He opened with a carefully written statement prepared by Rostow, reporting that the attacks were no surprise—"We have detailed information on Ho Chi Minh's order governing that offensive"—and that "the biggest fact is that the stated purposes of the general uprising have failed." Rostow was warned that a presidential posture of "no surprise, great victory" was unbelievable and would backfire, but this objection was ignored.

After reading the statement, Johnson paced back and forth on one long side of the Cabinet table, answering questions of the reporters jammed in behind the other side. Militarily, he declared, the Tet Offensive "has been a complete failure."[4] The enemy was now trying for a psychological victory. "I do not believe when the American people know the facts, when the world knows the facts, and when the results are laid out for them to examine, I do not believe that they will achieve a psychological victory," he said.

Robert Northshield, the executive producer of the NBC-Television Huntley-Brinkley Report, *arrived in late morning at his office at 30 Rockefeller Plaza to find an exciting cable from Saigon. It concerned the Loan shooting, which Northshield had already seen on the front pages of the New York* Times *and New York* Daily News.

The cable, which arrived during the night, said that NBC cameraman Vo Suu had filmed the execution in color with a 16 mm. Auricon sound-on-film camera. Correspondent Howard Tuckner,

---

[4] In the beleaguered city of Can Tho in the Mekong delta, an American officer heard the President's remarks and wrote a letter to a friend. "We have set up an old Browning automatic rifle in my room with a clear field of fire into the Vietnamese military hospital next door. I also have a grenade launcher and 100 grenades. . . . I just heard the President on Armed Forces Radio saying, in that awful drawl, 'My fella Americans, the Viet Cong attack has bin broken—and they have bin defeated.' I wonder who's going to tell him about the thousand of them on our doorstep?"

*who was on the scene, had supplied a narration for the story. The
film was being shipped to Tokyo for developing and transmission
via satellite to the U.S.A.*

"FILM NUMBER 456 IS TUCKNER'S PAGODA FIGHTING [said
the cable]. TROOPS WENT INTO THE AN QUANG PAGODA,
SEAT OF BUDDHIST MILITANCE, AND TRIED TO CLEAN OUT
THE VIET CONG WHO HAD TAKEN IT OVER. THIS STORY IS COM-
PETITIVE. CBS AND ABC WERE THERE BUT WE ARE THE ONLY
ONES WHO HAVE FILM OF THE EXECUTION. . . .

". . . VIET CONG OPEN UP ON MARINES. THEN THE LOAN
SEGMENT. THIS IS SUU'S SOUNDROLL AND HE THINKS HE GOT
MOST OF IT. HIS CAPTIONS IN BRIEF READ AS FOLLOWS:
A VC OFFICER WAS CAPTURED, THE TROOPS BEAT HIM, THEY
BRING HIM TO LOAN WHO IS HEAD OF SOUTH VIETNAMESE
NATIONAL POLICE, LOAN PULLS OUT HIS PISTOL, FIRES AT
THE HEAD OF THE VC, THE VC FALLS, ZOOM ON HIS HEAD,
BLOOD SPRAYING OUT. IF HE HAS IT ALL IT'S STARTLING
STUFF. IF HE HAS PART OF IT IT'S STILL MORE THAN ANYONE
ELSE HAS."

*Northshield telephoned Tokyo and discovered that the film
had arrived from Saigon via a military plane, and was being
processed. About 3 P.M. New York time he talked to the Tokyo
bureau again. Producer William Wordham reported that the footage
was "quite remarkable."*

*As received in Tokyo, the action around the An Quang Pagoda
was recorded on 1080 feet of film, about 30 minutes' worth. This was
edited to a 3-minute, 55-second version of the most dramatic
sound and pictures, ending with the Loan shooting. Five other
Vietnam film stories were received by NBC Tokyo that day.
Two of them, showing action in Hue and Ban Me Thuot, were
edited for the* Huntley-Brinkley Report. *The others, including film
of the Westmoreland press conference in Saigon, did not go on
the air.*

At 4:15 P.M. that day, Lyndon Johnson went back to the
family dining room to do some more "convincin'." This time he

played off-the-record host to ten reporters from major newspapers, newsmagazines and television networks. Rostow and Deputy White House Press Secretary Tom Johnson were also there.

Over coffee, the President tried to convince the reporters, with limited success, that American forces had been ready and waiting for the big attack. There may have been a sergeant asleep with a beer in his hand and his zipper open, or a man in a jeep with a woman in his lap, Johnson said, but overall he was satisfied that the precautions were adequate. He praised the South Vietnamese Army for its part in the battle.

Johnson told the newsmen that even he was staggered at first by the skyrocketing Communist death toll reported by Westmoreland. It had reached nearly ten thousand and was still going up, and was now a major point in the Administration's campaign to convince the public that the Communists had failed.

At one point in the lengthy discussion, the President expressed concern about the television reporting of the Tet Offensive and the *Pueblo* affair. The networks ought to make time available for Rusk and McNamara to give the facts to the American people. A TV newsman asked if the Cabinet members would be available. Johnson answered that if a network wanted them, they would be. After the late-afternoon coffee session ended, it was arranged that Rusk and McNamara would be on a special hour-long edition of NBC's *Meet the Press* that Sunday, February 4, to put forward the Administration view.

NBC Tokyo completed its editing of the Loan film and fed the finished product into a projector. At the touch of a button, the sounds and full-color photographic images of the Saigon street corner execution—now some forty-five hours old—were relayed from the Tokyo studio to the Ibaraki, Japan, ground station 90 miles north, beamed to a communications satellite in orbit 22,300 miles above the Pacific Ocean, retransmitted to the Jamesburg earth station in the Carmel Valley of California and relayed via cables to New York City. The whole process took about one fourth of a second for each frame of film.

It was 6:20 P.M. in New York, ten minutes before the Hunt-

ley-Brinkley Report *was to go on the air. Executive producer Northshield and correspondent John Chancellor sat in the NBC control room and watched the scene from Tokyo roll in. Northshield was a combat veteran of World War II and Chancellor, former director of the Voice of America, had seen the blood and gore of revolutionary warfare in Algeria. Nonetheless, both men were stunned by the brutal impact of the Loan execution footage. There was never any question about running it—it was an important and powerful statement of the reality of war—but Chancellor urged that the film should stop as soon as possible after the gunshot. This way the viewers at home would be spared the blood spurting from the head of the man whose death they witnessed. Northshield had already instructed Tokyo to trim the final close-up, and now he trimmed seventeen seconds more. He instructed the technicians to "go to black" as soon as the dead man hit the ground, and leave the screen empty for three seconds before the Huntley-Brinkley slide came on. The purpose was to provide an additional buffer before the commercial which followed.*

Roughly twenty million people watched the *Huntley-Brinkley Report* that night. They heard that fighting was still heavy from Hue to the Mekong delta, and they *experienced* a gun battle in Hue, the burning city of Ban Me Thuot and then the action at the An Quang Pagoda in Saigon. The final fifty-two seconds of the An Quang report was the Loan shooting, which seemed to many people to confirm the suspicion that this was a "wrong war" on the "wrong side."

Secretary of State Rusk was watching in Washington, and he was "teed off" at the execution. It was obvious to him that this would give critics a *cause célèbre* and further impede the government effort to shore up public opinion. Before a week was out, Rusk would vent his anger about reporting of the war in a "background" session with twenty-nine newsmen at the State Department. "Whose side are you on?" the usually imperturbable Rusk demanded of the newsmen. "None of your papers or your broadcasting apparatuses are worth a damn unless the United States succeeds. . . . I don't know why, to win a Pulitzer Prize, people have to go probing for the things that one can bitch about when there are two thousand stories on the same day about things that are more constructive in character."

Assistant Secretary of State William P. Bundy also watched the Loan television shooting with horror and dismay. He felt it cost the government side an "unnecessary roughing" penalty at a time when it could least afford it. One of Bundy's deputies watched the segment in color on a big-screen set at the State Department. After it was over, he sat silent in front of the television, looking off into space for a long time.

Only later, under close examination of the film, did anyone realize that this most shocking piece of television footage was an optical trick of sorts. At the split second when the executioner's bullet slammed into the prisoner's brain, someone had stepped in front of Vo Suu's Auricon camera. In fact, the murder itself was never shown on television, but the motion before and after left the impression that it was. In the world of transplantable time and chemical reality, the final illusion was unnoticed.

Gloom in Washington

A wintry gloom as bleak as February settled in on official Washington. For the record, all was well, the Communists had suffered a resounding defeat. Our Vietnamese had "pulled up their socks," Walt Rostow kept saying, to the amusement of those who knew that most of them did not wear socks. Unofficially, off-the-record and between-us-over-the-back-fence, which is how the mood of the American capital is set and transmitted, the U. S. Government had been shaken by the Communist offensive and was worried sick about what was coming next.

Westmoreland was saying this was act two of a three-act play and while much of Washington had come to doubt most everything else the general said, it believed him in this. The greatest worry was the fate of the Marines at Khe Sanh. Before Tet, Lyndon Johnson had insisted on a formal paper from the Joint Chiefs, "signed in blood," as he put it, that Khe Sanh could be held. The Commander in Chief was haunted by the vision of a military debacle for which he would be held responsible. He kept telling Wheeler to ask Westmoreland if more troops and support were needed. "I don't want anybody coming back and saying if we had had this and that we would not have suffered so many losses," the President confided to visitors. On instructions from Washington, Westmoreland began making special daily reports on the situation at Khe Sanh, some of them including such minute detail as the condition of the airstrip and the supply of lubricating oil. Largely because of Khe Sanh, Westmoreland was sleeping every night just outside the Combat Operations Center at his headquarters, a practice he continued until late March.

Lyndon Johnson was tugged at the heart as well as the head. He went to church with his daughter Lynda and her husband, Marine Captain Charles Robb, who was preparing to leave for battle duty. While they were together, the President read a cable from the war zone and he could tell by Lynda's expression just what she was thinking. She did not know whether Chuck would ever come back. Her father awoke that night at 4 A.M. thinking about that, and about the other Marines in the Asian hills so far away.

If only he could find an answer to this thing—but none was in sight. "Nearly every option open to us is worse than what we are doing," he told a group of college students who came to call. Retired General Matthew B. Ridgway, U.S. troop commander during most of the Korean War and former chairman of the Joint Chiefs of Staff, was summoned for a private talk about the crises in Vietnam and Korea. Ridgway went home to Pittsburgh and told his wife, "The President is a distraught man, a tired man, a very worried man, a very sincere man."

The American urge was to hit 'em back, to get it over with, win it and then get out, and the idea had considerable appeal. Johnson asked Ridgway, among others, what he thought of a ground invasion of North Vietnam. (The retired general was against it.) At the moment, a major invasion was impractical. American troops were stretched thin defending the cities in Vietnam, the U.S.

strategic reserve was dangerously depleted to the point of being non-existent, more trouble seemed to be looming in Korea. The forces were not available.

A more serious question was a smaller-scale diversionary amphibious operation in the eastern portion of the DMZ just inside North Vietnamese territory. The purpose would be to divert Communist troops and thus ease the pressure on Khe Sanh and the southern part of the DMZ. This was seriously discussed at the White House, but no decision was made. A White House official dropped hints in private that something might be coming, that the Communists may have bitten off more than they could chew. "People had better hold onto their hats," he said.

A diplomatic settlement seemed out of the question. The President had made a bid in September in the San Antonio speech, the North Vietnamese had answered in December with a public peace feeler, the U.S. dispatched a Communist emissary from Romania in January and stopped bombing Hanoi and Haiphong as a show of good faith—and the answer was the Tet Offensive. It was galling. "We have been suckers and we are going to quit being suckers," Clark Clifford, soon to take over as Secretary of Defense, told a visitor. "There is no point in this kind of negotiation. The next time, they come to us, and they had better mean it! San Antonio is the final formula—the furthest we can go."

The President told reporters he was certain that Ho Chi Minh did not intend to negotiate anytime soon. Johnson guessed that Ho was thinking he'd do better after the U.S. election. Johnson told the newsmen, without explaining what he had in mind, that Ho was wrong in this belief.

The Challengers

The war in Vietnam was far and away the President's single greatest political problem, his most conspicuous failure and the one for which the public was most likely to hold him politically accountable. If he were to be beaten in 1968 the war would be the lethal weapon, but like any deadly instrument, it was also dangerous to those who chose to wield it.

Blood and the flag were involved, as well as possible imputations of disloyalty, cut-and-run and "soft on Communism" on the one side, and charges of warmongering, blow-up-the-world potentialities on the other. Though his longer-range options were very limited, the President retained considerable control in the short run. He could suddenly step up the war and generate martial fervor and hopes for victory in the country, or he could make a grand public bid for peace, generating hopes and outflanking his challengers on that side. It was, in short, a very tricky political issue.

The Tet Offensive made two immediate and important contributions toward legitimatizing the war as a political issue. First, it provided dramatic evidence that the Johnson administration had been misleading the public. This was an increasingly important line of attack, and it was a relatively safe one politically—both hawks and doves could agree they were being lied to without having to agree on the remedy to the true condition. Second, Tet liberated politicians, journalists and ordinary citizens from the restraining influence of their earlier positions on the war. It constituted a dramatic change in the situation sufficient to justify a dramatic change in opinion.

By the weekend after Tet, the challengers were speaking up. The day after Lyndon Johnson's news conference claim that the offensive had been a "complete failure" militarily, Eugene McCarthy issued a strong and sarcastic reply. "If taking over a section of the American Embassy, a good part of Hue, Dalat and major cities of the Fourth Corps area constitutes complete failure, I suppose by this logic that if the Viet Cong captured the entire country, the Administration would be claiming their total collapse," he said. Recalling the claims that "we are winning," McCarthy declared that "the Administration's reports of progress are the products of their own self-deception. . . . Their [the Communists'] attacks on the cities of South Vietnam show that we don't have the country under any kind of control and that we are in a much worse position than we were in two years ago."

Governor George Romney of Michigan had begun as a supporter of the war and moved increasingly against it in the course of his quest for the Republican presidential nomination. In August of 1967 his candidacy was seriously damaged by an offhand, but on-camera, remark in explanation of his change of heart about the war—that he had had "the greatest brainwashing that anybody could get" during an earlier trip to Vietnam. Now, after Tet, he too zeroed in on the Administration's false optimism. "If what we have seen in the past week is a Viet Cong failure, then I hope they never have a victory," Romney said at a meeting with newspaper editors in New York State. In his view, the conflict in Vietnam was more political than military. He asserted that the Tet Offensive showed that "the people of South Vietnam are supporting the enemy."

Richard Nixon, whose timing was incredibly lucky in 1968, was announcing his formal candidacy for President when the Viet Cong struck in Asia. Nixon's instincts and natural constituency were hawkish, and his first reaction was down the Administration line. He described the Tet Offensive as a "desperate" and perhaps "last-ditch" effort by the Viet Cong, directed primarily against public opinion in the United States, and declared the Communists could not count on such a division among the American people. One of his advisers with good contacts among the younger military men in the Pentagon sent word to "get off it," saying that the situation in Vietnam was actually much more serious than the Administration was admitting.

Nixon began modifying his position. He attacked the Johnson administration for issuing "these glowing reports that the war is going so well, that peace is just around the corner," and at the same time suggested that the Administration exert stronger and firmer pressure on North Vietnam. When his hawkishness began to stir mixed reactions in his target audience, Nixon shifted emphasis again, stressing the notion that the South Vietnamese should do more of the fighting—and thus implying that the United States should do less.

Robert Kennedy, whose timing was tragic in every respect, had declared himself out of the presidential race "under any foreseeable circumstances" at the National Press Club breakfast just as the Tet Offensive was breaking out in Asia.[5] In the first days after that, Kennedy agonized about his blunder, pacing the floor in his office, refusing to answer his telephone or read his mail. Kennedy thought of the millions of people now in recoil —as he was—against the Johnson administration and the war, and with only Eugene McCarthy to lead them. Even more important, according to close advisers of the time, he recognized Tet as a climactic event of sufficient power and persuasiveness to justify a change in his own public position about the war.

Robert Kennedy had always been a passionate anti-Communist and in the early 1960s he had seen Vietnam as the proving ground for the theories and tactics of counterinsurgency which fascinated him. He was a leading sponsor of the Special Forces, the Green Berets, who were supposed to wage unconventional war to defeat the Communists. In February 1962 he went to Asia to inspect the situation. "The solution there [in Vietnam] lies in our winning it; this is what the President [his brother] intends to do," he said in a Hong Kong stopover. In Saigon he declared, "We will win in Vietnam and we shall remain here until we do."

After his brother's assassination, Robert Kennedy no longer had any working responsibility for the direction of the Vietnam effort and as the months and years went by, he became increasingly convinced that it was a mistake. He was always more forceful about this in private than in public, and he took pains to minimize the gap between himself and Lyndon Johnson on the war. Until Tet, he avoided a clean, definitive break with either the President or his policy.

A week after Tet he was not yet ready to go all the way in his quest for the presidency, but he did decide to go all the way against the war. Richard Goodwin and Adam Walinsky prepared a strong speech on the meaning of Tet, and Kennedy delivered it February 8 at a book-and-author luncheon in Chicago.

"Our enemy, savagely striking at will across all of South Vietnam, has finally shattered the mask of official illusion from which we have concealed our true circumstances even from ourselves," Ken-

[5] See Chapter IV, p. 117.

nedy declared. He ridiculed the idea that Tet was some kind of allied victory and Communist defeat—"it is as if James Madison were able to claim a great victory in 1812 because the British only burned Washington instead of annexing it to the British Empire."

For twenty years, he said, first the French and then Americans had been predicting victory in Vietnam—and he cited his own 1962 prediction. "But for twenty years we have been wrong. The history of conflict among nations does not record another such lengthy and consistent chronicle of error. It is time to discard so proven a fallacy and face the reality that a military victory is not in sight, and that it probably will never come," he said.

This being so, a political compromise including the participation of the Viet Cong was the only path to peace, risky and unpalatable as it might be. Kennedy declared that "if we proceed on our present course, it promises only years and decades of further draining conflict on the mainland of Asia—conflict which, as our finest military leaders have always warned, could lead us only to national tragedy."

Saigon at Bay

In Saigon the silence was deafening.

The first group of correspondents to enter South Vietnam since Tet broke flew into Tan Son Nhut Air Base on Saturday, February 3, courtesy of the U. S. Air Force—because commercial airlines would not permit their planes to land in the suddenly blazing war zone. The din of fireworks had died; the merrymaking was over. Suddenly Saigon was a city at war.

There was no pretty stewardess to lead the way to the passenger terminal at Tan Son Nhut, no immigration and customs formalities, no exorbitant taxi ride through the traffic-choked streets to the middle of town. This time it was different. A military bus pulled up to the C-130 on the runway and an Air Force MP wearing a steel helmet and flak jacket and carrying an M-16 rifle told the correspondents to step aboard.

"Keep your bags in the aisle in case we have to get out of here fast," said the somewhat overdramatic MP. "There are still snipers around. Anybody on the streets after 5 P.M. gets shot."

"Except correspondents," somebody piped up brightly.

"That's your privilege, sir," the MP replied.

They passed a tank and a newly constructed machine gun nest next to the main gate of Tan Son Nhut, and more new fortifications outside the entrance to the Joint General Staff headquarters. The late-afternoon trip to town took only fifteen minutes (instead of the usual thirty to forty-five minutes) through empty streets, past closed and barred stores and honky-tonks, past the locked and barricaded French-style grand post office. The people of the city had vanished from sight. They were sitting behind shuttered windows, listening to their radios, eating their rice and Tet candy and thinking God knows what.

The bus pulled up in front of the Caravelle Hotel, the air-conditioned luxury palace for foreign journalists and others on lavish expense accounts. A withered Tet bush lay forlornly in the entranceway, and the East Indian doorman had been temporarily supplanted by a group of well-armed Vietnamese soldiers. Inside the lobby, a dozen Americans lounging on the sofas and easy chairs provided immediate evidence that not all that was "normal" in Saigon had disappeared. The Americans were watching a replay of the Cotton Bowl game on U. S. Armed Forces television. "Who's playing?" asked Keyes Beech of the Chicago *Daily News*, an old Vietnam hand who was one of the correspondents on the incoming flight. "Alabama and Texas A&M," replied a spectator, never taking his eyes off the television screen.

Some of the reporters dropped their bags and walked through the deserted streets to the Public Affairs Office, where the "Five O'Clock Follies" was already in progress. An Army general was standing on the stage of the auditorium with a black pointer and a large map of Saigon, recounting to correspondents how the cavalry had saved Tan Son Nhut and declaring with pride that the enemy force had failed to take and hold the capital city. The mind reeled. If that had happened, men in black pajamas would be running Saigon, the yellow-starred flag of the NLF would be waving in the streets, the general would be imprisoned or dead, most of the reporters might be locked up and there would be no Five O'Clock Follies any more. The United States of America would have lost the war to the Vietnamese revolutionaries.

There was nothing of the smell of victory about the city but rather the odor of rotting garbage and, here and there, the stench of the dead. A few sanitation trucks were back at work, picking up unclaimed corpses in badly damaged sections of the city and dumping them in common graves on the edge of town. In the southwest section, whole blocks had been riddled by bullets and crumbled by heavy weapons from the ground and the air. More than 125,000 Saigonese were reported homeless. In the country as a whole, 821,000 people had become refugees from military action in addition to 904,000 refugees prior to Tet. The final total of 1,725,000 refugees was 10 per cent of the national population.

Around the corner from a ruined block, life would go on almost normally. War or peace, comfort or privation, daily routine or devastation had been and to some extent still was a function of where one happened to be standing at the moment. There were scattered fire fights and some huge fires in Cholon and action on the edge of the city, but most of Saigon was quiet. The main problem was sniper incidents, which were reported all over town. The U. S. Command's intelligence estimated later that most of them involved no Viet Cong at all, merely jumpy sentries and accidental shots.

The American Command's headquarters was often reported under fire, but the only projectile to hit the building turned out to be a U.S. 81 mm. mortar shell. Colonels could be seen in the office building halls with drawn guns as if they had just entered no man's land or were bound for the stagecoach at Laramie. The most truly dangerous emergency developed when a nearby U.S. security unit fired an accidental burst of bullets in the direction of Pentagon East and staff officers began firing back. The battle ended when the U.S. security detachment chief worked his way over to the headquarters. "If you guys don't stop shooting at us, we're coming over here and clean you out," he told the staff officers.

And what of the Vietnamese people, in whose name and for whose future the war, in theory, was being waged?

The American grip on Vietnamese reality was extremely slim in the best of times, and now it was more tenuous than ever. Vietnamese acquaintances were holed up wherever they had gone to celebrate the Tet holiday. Transportation and communication were difficult. Vietnamese interpreters and other English-speaking staff members were busy with their private problems, and did not appear for work. The Vietnamese newspapers had suspended publication for Tet, and did not resume for several weeks.

When news and gossip began to flow, Americans were dumfounded by what they heard. One of the principal reactions of the Vietnamese to the Tet Offensive was—the Americans are secretly behind it! Incredible as this seemed to beleaguered U.S. officials and newsmen, the theory had a certain logic from the Vietnamese view. Here was the mighty United States, the greatest power in the world, rich beyond belief, full of energy at work and play. Did "Nguyen" think the Viet Cong could have attacked every city without the Americans knowing and approving in advance? Certainly not.[6] If Americans were not part of this plan, then why were not American installations hit harder? Many of them were bypassed by the attack forces on their way to strike South Vietnamese government targets.

The motive for this collusion between Uncle Sam and Uncle Ho? Ah, the Americans are very clever. They will force a coalition government on the South, so Johnson can placate the Senate doves, bring the U.S. troops home and still retain influence over Vietnam through the new coalition government. Another theory was that the United States invited the Viet Cong to take the cities in a swap for countryside military bases such as Cam Ranh Bay, which the U.S. would retain under the Communist-controlled coalition government.

[6] Even President Thieu shared this suspicion. Late in February he received a visit in Saigon from an important Washington functionary. According to the visitor, the conversation went like this:

"Now that it's all over," said Thieu, "you really knew it was coming, didn't you?"

"No, we didn't," was the answer.

"Don't kid me, you had to know," said Thieu, suggesting collusion with the Viet Cong.

"We didn't know, Mr. President."

"Well, you're just not willing to level with me. Why don't you tell me the truth?"

The rumors were so widespread that Ambassador Ellsworth Bunker went on Saigon television to deny "this ridiculous claim" of American-Viet Cong collusion. For many Vietnamese, that was conclusive confirmation that the rumors were true.

Throughout the war, the internal political weakness of the Saigon government was the Achilles' heel of the United States and allied effort. Whatever the defects and outrages of Ngo Dinh Diem—and there were many—he was respected. He was a known patriot and the leader of the Ngos, a prominent family at the court in Hue. Whether he was loved or hated, he was always "Ong Diem," Mr. Diem. This was not true of the leaders who followed—Nguyen Khanh, the goateed son of a Dalat barkeep; Nguyen Cao Ky, the Air Force cowboy married to a stewardess; Nguyen Van Thieu, the most acceptable of the lot among the Vietnamese, but still nobody much. These leaders were not referred to as "Ong" but as "Thang" —that fellow. The United States was forever trying to think of ways to transform them into popular leaders.

The Tet Offensive was both the great test and the great opportunity for the Saigon government. Immediately after the early attacks on seven cities in I Corps and II Corps, a high official of the U. S. Embassy drew up a plan for Thieu to assert his leadership, American-style. Thieu was to go live on American-provided national television to rouse the people and call the National Assembly into emergency session. Just before the TV show he would summon Vice-President Ky, Prime Minister Nguyen Van Loc, Chief of Staff Vien and the Cabinet for a briefing and have them present behind him when he "faced the nation." Thieu, who was in My Tho celebrating Tet with his wife and mother, did nothing of the sort.

"It is time for a leader to talk staunchly to his people in plain language they can understand so they can take heart and rally to the effort now needed," declared the American official. "FDR did this right after Pearl Harbor. Churchill did this as the Battle of Britain began." Lyndon Johnson, however, was unable to do the same in the United States after Tet or at any other time during the Vietnam War, and Thieu was even less a dynamo. Inspirational leadership was not his way.

At American instigation, a National Recovery Committee was

formed to spearhead the job of burying the dead, caring for the wounded, feeding the refugees and rebuilding the many devastated areas. The committee was headed by Vice-President Ky, with General Nguyen Duc Thang, the energetic former pacification chief, as staff director. Each official of the committee had an American "counterpart" adviser to suggest what he should do. The Americans provided or paid for most of the resources—transportation, medicine, supplies, construction materials.

Because of the Recovery Committee, Ky emerged as "the man of the hour," claimed a CIA report to Washington made available to Washington newsmen by Walt Rostow. When the news stories extolling Ky came to Thieu's attention, a reaction was inevitable. Thieu's allies began privately charging that Ky was usurping power, and they began applying none too subtle pressure on Ky and Thang to give up this new activity. Thereupon Ky and Thang resigned from the Recovery Committee, much to American dismay.

Washington was furious that the regime did not seem to be rising to meet the crisis. Moreover, nothing was being done about lagging land reform, corruption and the other problems underlying its political weakness. If the Saigon government did nothing now, surely it never would.

In a meeting in Undersecretary Katzenbach's office at the State Department, a plan was put forward. Since only strong leadership and basic reforms could save South Vietnam in the long run, and since both were lacking, the United States would issue an ultimatum. The Saigon government was to be given three months to make certain reforms, and if that failed, the United States would "reconsider its stance toward the war." The implication was that the United States would withdraw its support from the regime and/or the war.

When Dean Rusk heard about Operation Shock, as it was dubbed, he put his foot down. That was not the way to handle an ally. More fundamentally, Rusk was strongly opposed to bluffs. If the United States implied it might pull out, it would have to be prepared to do so. And that, in his mind, was unthinkable.

The Tet Offensive had become the big story in the United States and throughout the world, and correspondents, photographers and film crews were pouring into Saigon to report it. During the month of February, 52 additional American correspondents arrived, and 86 additional correspondents from other foreign countries (many of these Frenchmen who smelled the comeuppance of the U.S.). By the end of the month, 119 Vietnamese (mostly interpreters and technicians), 248 Americans and 260 "third-country nationals" were accredited as war correspondents, making a grand total of 627, the highest number recorded in Saigon at any time.

The influx of newsmen, some of whom had never set foot in Vietnam before, put a further strain on the already overcrowded luxury hotels, the cable and telephone facilities and the press agents and other officials. Most of the new arrivals were frustrated for a simple but important reason. They were having trouble finding the Tet Offensive or the war.

Just about the best view was the roof of the Caravelle Hotel at night, looking across the city to the great fires in Cholon, the flares over Tan Son Nhut and the tracer bullets spewing down from airplanes into the woods across the Saigon River to the northeast. Watching the war became a nightly social event. The Caravelle, always alert to money-making opportunities, began sending waiters in white coats to the roof with brandy and cigars on silver trays.

Covering the war at closer range was more of a problem. After the first few days there was little action in the city during daylight. Movement on the streets at night was forbidden by a tight curfew and made dangerous by trigger-happy government soldiers and National Police. This situation created a serious problem for the American officials trying to convince the press that Tet was a disaster for the Viet Cong. The generals came down to the Five O'Clock Follies to proclaim the war was being won and the enemy on the run; they would be followed by a civilian official warning the press that anyone who ventured out at night in the center of Saigon without an armed MP escort was in gravest peril. If the Viet Cong are on the run, the correspondents wondered, why is it so dangerous to go out at night?

Getting out of Saigon was difficult at first because the crush of military action created a shortage of air transportation, and most of the roads were insecure. After a few days the military public relations men pleaded with the Command for transportation to get the correspondents out of Saigon so they could substitute reality for rumor. Many went to areas of continuing action, primarily Hue and Khe Sanh, and others began making rounds of smoldering cities where the action had died. The reality was not a pretty sight.

Unless the action was still hot, most cities were rated as one-day stories. Correspondents and camera crews wanted to fly into a town, obtain their interviews and pictures and fly back to Saigon to file their stores, ship their film and call it a night. In response to the demand, the U. S. Command organized a series of day trips using Army aircraft to take a large group of the press corps to a single town at once.

Much to the dismay of the military, each trip produced a new wave of stories of surprise attack, inadequate defense and death, destruction and discontent in the city visited. The story of each stricken city was news because it had not been told before, and it was competitive because everyone had his chance simultaneously. Thus, the military action of the first few days was recounted over several weeks of stories on television and in the papers at home.

The day trip of February 7 was to the shattered Mekong delta city of Ben Tre. There U.S. advisers and emergency reinforcements bombarded Viet Cong troops in built-up areas with artillery and helicopter fire to save themselves from being overrun. The battle produced a high toll of civilian casualties and—during the press tour—one of the most famous and damning quotations of the war: "It became necessary to destroy the town to save it."

Of the planeload of newsmen on the trip, Peter Arnett of the Associated Press was the only one to report the quote, which he attributed to an otherwise unidentified U.S. major, and apparently Arnett was the only one to hear it. The AP Pulitzer Prize-winner built his story around the exclusive quote, which was an ironic capsule summary of a basic contradiction in the American position. The United States claimed to be fighting to build a nation and protect the freedom of a people, but the immense weight of its modern weaponry was destroying Vietnam in the process. The Viet Cong, whose military means were more closely tailored to political ends, placed strict limitations on the use of their firepower. They killed for a purpose, and put a high value on the good will of the people—for example, their orders in the Mekong delta at Tet were that "in attacking the enemy, we are required to respect the lives and property of the people, not to fire freely, and not to exploit the people's goodness in any way." The United States and South Vietnamese government forces, on the other hand, were indiscriminate in their use of firepower, and seemed to value their own safety far beyond the political purpose (if any) for which they fought.

The newsmen and critics zeroed in on this moral and strategic blot. The Ben Tre quotation, which summed it up nearly in a single sentence, gained great currency in the United States and abroad and was repeated in almost every argument against the war. The embarrassed U. S. Command ordered an investigation in Ben Tre—not to learn what happened to the town or whether the quotation was true, but to discover who had said it.

The Military View

Of all the United States officials who were deeply affected by the Tet Offensive, General William C. Westmoreland was probably the least worried and the most invigorated by the turn of events. For four years he had been building and managing a vast force of men and machines with airports, seaports, posts and stations to support them, but the little man on the other side obstinately refused to stand and fight. In the absence of a great change in Communist strategy—the very sort of change which came at Tet—this powerful Westmoreland war machine would have been slowly and gradually dismantled and shipped back home without ever having been used to full effect.

COMUSMACV (Commander, U. S. Military Assistance Command, Vietnam) had been a corporate manager with stars on his shoulders, called to duty at the home office from time to time as a public relations man and wet nurse for the press. Now at last he had the chance to be the commanding general of a great army in a real fight. He had been yearning for the day, and now it had come. His impulse and attitude was "Let's go."

His early reports to Washington and to the public—there was very little deviation—reflected his optimism and exhilaration. In his view, the Communists were employing desperation tactics in a "go for broke" drive reminiscent of Hitler's last fling in the Battle of the Bulge. U.S. and South Vietnamese government forces were giving the Viet Cong and North Vietnamese a terrible pounding. The body count was mounting. The cities attacks were ebbing, and doomed.

Westmoreland's principal concern was far to the north at Khe Sanh, and here he was certain that the North Vietnamese would be defeated by the heavy weight of bombs and artillery, and the U.S. ability to reinforce and resupply the garrison from the air. He had granted the Marines at Khe Sanh the capability and authority to use COFRAM, newly arrived anti-personnel shells which fragmented into murderous slivers of metal, and thus he did not see the need, unless the situation should change dramatically, to consider tactical nuclear weapons or chemical agents. Let Giap try him at Khe Sanh; Westmoreland was ready.

While Westmoreland was confident, Washington was shaken to its roots. In an earlier day before instantaneous worldwide communications, a field commander might not have known for weeks about tremors at home and by then it might not have mattered. No such felicitous ignorance was possible for Westmoreland. He talked by telephone to General Wheeler at least once a day and sometimes several times a day, and the chairman of the Joint Chiefs told him of the gloom and doom on the banks of the Potomac. It reminded Wheeler of historical descriptions of the federal city just after the rout of the Union army at Bull Run, when all seemed lost and recriminations filled the air. Wheeler was doing his best to quell the nervousness, but on behalf of the Commander in Chief he had one question for Westmoreland day after day: "Is there any reinforcement we can give you?"

The question was intriguing and the prospect alluring, but there was a worm in the apple. Throughout the war, discussion of additional resources placed the field commander in an ambiguous position. To keep up morale at home and in the field, Westmoreland was required to demonstrate and report success. But to obtain additional forces and authority from Washington, it was necessary to demonstrate *need*. Need implied lack of success.

Shortly after the first suggestions that more troops might be obtained, The U. S. Command's situation reports developed a cautious on-the-other-hand dimension. Continued news of Communist setbacks began to be balanced by mention of Communist achievements and of the dangers, difficulties and uncertainties on the government side. By February 4, after five days of battle, new dimensions of the situation were beginning to emerge in the reports to Washington. The Communists had dealt the Saigon government a severe blow by bringing war to the cities. Communist forces had shown great discipline and determination and impressive ability to infiltrate populated areas. The enemy had failed in his military objectives, as Westmoreland had said earlier, but he had inflicted psychological damage and posed a tremendous challenge to the government.

The field commander continued to anticipate the big attack in the Khe Sanh-DMZ area, perhaps coordinated with another round of battle in the cities. A test was soon to come.

A few minutes after midnight on the morning of February 7, five Soviet-built PT-76 medium tanks clanked slowly up a narrow trail toward the Special Forces camp at Lang Vei, five miles west of the Khe Sanh Combat Base. Behind the tanks, wearing green uniforms and steel helmets, two platoons of North Vietnamese infantrymen followed, their weapons at the ready.

As the first two tanks reached the barbed wire barrier around the camp, a trip flare ignited, bathing the green metal tanks and the dust-covered soldiers in a flickering light. From an observation tower inside the camp, Sergeant Nikolas Fragos, a twenty-four-year-old medic, stared in bewilderment at this sight. Just then, both the attackers and defenders of the camp began firing furiously.

Fragos radioed Captain Frank C. Willoughby, the Green Beret

detachment commander, in the operations bunker. "We have tanks on our wire!" he reported.

The twenty-four Americans and five hundred native troops at the Lang Vei camp had been expecting an attack, but nothing like this. While there had been rumors and fragmentary reports of Communist tanks in action across the border in nearby Laos, armor had not been used previously by the Communist Command in Vietnam. Now five tanks were attacking Lang Vei from the south, four from the east and two from the west, plodding forward through the barbed wire and across the trenches, turrets swinging slowly from side to side, raking the camp with bursts of machine gun fire and high-explosive cannon rounds. The North Vietnamese troops crept behind them, firing at any target they could see.

In the operations bunker, Captain Willoughby called for Marine reinforcements from Khe Sanh in compliance with a prearranged reinforcement plan, but the Marines refused. They felt that any relief force along the highway would be ambushed en route, and they declined to try a helicopter assault against Communist armor in the dark. Artillery whistled in from Khe Sanh, and flights of U. S. Air Force jets roared over dropping bombs. Small groups of North Vietnamese troops were all over the camp.

By 4:30 A.M. North Vietnamese soldiers were dropping grenades down the stairwells of the bunker, and Willoughby and the other defenders could hear scraping and digging noises just outside one of the walls. Around 6 A.M. a thermite grenade rolled into the bunker and exploded with a bright orange flash, followed by a flurry of fragmentation grenades and tear gas wielded by the enemy. A voice called down the stairway in Vietnamese: "We are going to blow up the bunker, so give up now."

The South Vietnamese camp commander and his fifteen men in the bunker decided to comply. They marched up the stairwell and there was excited chatter in Vietnamese outside. Then a voice in English—possibly that of one of the South Vietnamese interpreters—floated down the stairwell.

"We want to speak to your captain. Is he still here?"

"Yes!" shouted Sergeant Fragos, the medic.

"Have you got a weapon?"

"Yep!"

"Do you have ammo?"

"I've got plenty for you!" the sergeant shouted defiantly, firing his M-16 up the stairwell. A barrage of grenades rolled down in reply.

A few minutes later the talking between the North Vietnamese troops and the South Vietnamese captives ceased, and automatic weapons fire broke out. The Americans heard screams and yells amid the shooting—then silence.

When the dawn was about to break, the North Vietnamese blew a hole in the side of the bunker with an explosive charge placed in the tunnel they had dug. The invaders had direct access to the bunker, but the final assault never came.

Westmoreland was awakened twice in the night by Brigadier General John Chaisson, U. S. Marine Corps, the director of the U. S. Command's Combat Operations Center. Colonel Jonathan Ladd, commander of the Army Special Forces, had telephoned to report the assault on the Lang Vei camp and to request an emergency rescue operation from Khe Sanh. By now the Khe Sanh commander had twice refused to send reinforcements on the hazardous mission, and Ladd wanted Westmoreland to order the Marines to change their mind.

Westmoreland declined to issue such an extraordinary order from high headquarters about a tactical situation in the field. Early the next morning he and Chaisson flew to Da Nang to meet with U. S. Marine and Army commanders in the I Corps area. The battle of Lang Vei sounded like the beginning of the long-expected move against Khe Sanh and other bastions of the far north.

For nearly three hours, the unruffled and unhurried Westmoreland heard his generals report on their areas of operation, beginning with a report on Quang Ngai by Major General Samuel W. Koster of the Americal Division and moving slowly up the line to the big threats in the north. After each general reported, Westmoreland gave emphatic orders: "Get the roads open"—"Get troops between the enemy and Da Nang Air Base; time is of the essence; get a task force from Koster; get at it; we've got to take some risks"—"The Qua Viet [River] *must* be kept open; this is a *must*"—and so on.

Item 25 on the list was Lang Vei, which was being pounded with new air strikes and artillery in daylight and where small groups of defenders, including Americans in the operations bunker, still hid out from the North Vietnamese invaders. The orders were crisp: assault the camp, extract the survivors, use CBUs (cluster bomb units, anti-personnel fragmentation bombs similar to COF-RAM)—"Go."

Chaisson wrote in his pocket diary: "One of Westy's best days."

On the return trip from Da Nang, Westmoreland's mind turned to the future. He instructed Chaisson to make a study of the additional resources which might be needed in the coming year, without regard to the previously established ceiling of 525,000 American troops. Westmoreland would ask for what he needed and could use. It would be up to Washington to decide what he would get.

The following day Westmoreland informed Wheeler that his staff had begun a requirements study in depth emphasizing problem areas in the current force structure, and based on the assumption that the 525,000-man ceiling would be lifted. The general areas to be addressed included modernization of the South Vietnamese government forces, the deployment of the long-promised South Korean division (or a U.S. substitute, if the Koreans would not provide more troops) and the requirement for still another division of U.S. troops by the fall, "particularly if operations in Laos are authorized." Chaisson ordered the study right away. The result, several weeks later, laid the groundwork for an eventual request for 206,000 more American fighting men.

Westmoreland had decided at the Da Nang meeting to transfer a brigade of the 101st Airborne Division from the Saigon area to northern I Corps to reinforce the troops around Hue, beef up the reserve and be ready for the expected new Communist assault. The withdrawal of this unit meant a thinning-out of U.S. forces near Saigon, despite the fact that the fight in that area was not over. Indeed, the very next day—February 8—Westmoreland instructed General Weyand to send some of his thinned-out U.S. force into Saigon itself to speed the clearing of the city.

The field commander was robbing Peter to protect Paul because he had no uncommitted reserve he could move around. When Wheeler asked again, "Do you need reinforcements?" Westmoreland was interested. Wheeler pointed out that U.S. capabilities at the moment were limited, but he mentioned two units which could quickly be provided—the 82nd Airborne Division at Fort Bragg, North Carolina, and about half of a U. S. Marine brigade at Camp Pendleton, California. Westmoreland replied that it was only prudent to plan for the worst, in which case he would definitely need more men. Specifically, he urged that plans be made to send him the two units mentioned—perhaps in an amphibious landing when the weather cleared near the DMZ in April.

Then began a military minuet between Saigon and Washington. Wheeler would have a suggestion about Westmoreland's possible requirements—for example, Wheeler wondered if the additional men might not be needed before April—and Westmoreland would tailor his request to the Washington thinking. Westmoreland's first cabled justification for more troops was not quite formal and explicit enough to suit the White House; Westmoreland came back with a more strongly worded cable. After a flurry of telephoned and cabled messages, Westmoreland stated on February 12 that his immediate requirement for more troops was firm—"not because I fear defeat if I am not reinforced but because I do not feel I can fully grasp the initiative from the recently reinforced enemy without them."

At 3 P.M. the same day—Lincoln's Birthday—Westmoreland's request was approved. By 6 P.M. the Pentagon ordered a brigade of the 82nd Airborne Division and the 27th Marine Regiment to immediate duty in South Vietnam. Within a few hours the first of 10,500 additional American fighting men were en route direct to I Corps from the United States.

Hail and Farewell

The country was restive and the situation uncertain. The Commander in Chief decided to leave the White House and see his men off to war.

On Saturday morning, February 19, the President decided on short notice to fly to Fort Bragg and Camp Pendleton to say farewell to the troops, and then to spend the night on a U.S. aircraft carrier at sea as he had done during his November tour of military forces. Secret Service men, White House communications personnel and others who travel with a President were called in from their homes, the golf course and shopping expeditions. Calls went out to the correspondents, cameramen and sound men who regularly cover the White House, instructing them to be at Andrews Air Force Base within ninety minutes for a trip of undisclosed duration to an undisclosed place. They had no idea that by midnight they would be landing on the flight deck of the USS *Constellation* in the Pacific—and neither did the officers and men of the ship. It was tied up for repairs in San Diego, many of its boiler room steam pipes disassembled and half its crew on shore leave. As many sailors as could be found were rounded up in bars, hotels and other places of recreation, and the big ship hastily steamed out of port to be at sea by the time the presidential party arrived.

At 12:25 P.M., Saturday, Washington time, it was 1:25 A.M., Sunday, in Saigon. Correspondent Ed White of the Associated Press was writing a routine roundup story, and he had just written that "Saigon itself appeared relatively quiet. . . . The rumble of artillery could be—" Before he could finish the sentence, a blast shook the building and literally blew open the door of the AP bureau. White made a quick telephone call and began writing:

BULLETIN

ATTACK

SAIGON (AP)—A SERIES OF EXPLOSIONS ROCKED SAIGON EARLY SUNDAY AND U.S. MILITARY OFFICERS SAID TAN SON

NHUT AIR BASE IN THE CITY'S OUTSKIRTS "APPARENTLY IS
UNDER ATTACK."

SAIGON—ADD ATTACK

ONE OFFICER AT U.S. HEADQUARTERS INSIDE THE AIR BASE
SAID:

"IT SOUNDS LIKE ROCKETS AND MORTARS AND IT'S MIGHTY
DAMN CLOSE. I'M LEAVING."

FLARES LIGHTED UP THE SKY OVER THE BASE AND HELI-
COPTERS SWIRLED OVERHEAD.

At the White House, aides in the Situation Room began
scrambling for additional information. Before the hour was out, it
was learned that at least five other cities and installations had been
hit, and reports were still coming in. Before the night was over,
Communist forces had sent rockets or mortars against more than
forty-five cities and major installations throughout the country. A
few places were hit by ground attacks, but this simultaneous nationwide demonstration was a weak thrust compared to the Lunar
New Year strike.

Air Force One landed just before 4 P.M. at Pope Air Force Base
adjoining Fort Bragg, North Carolina. Some thirteen hundred men
of the 82nd Airborne Division, in combat fatigues and steel helmets,
stood on the concrete runway waiting to board big windowless jet
planes which would carry them to war. Many of the men had seen
service in Vietnam before, and quite a few of them were theoretically ineligible for battle assignment so soon again except in an
emergency.

At a signal from an officer, ninety-four men left the formation
in front of the President and marched off to the hatch of one of
the big jets. They were led by a first sergeant carrying a sawed-off
pool cue as his swagger stick. The wind was whipping the colors
and snapping the little company flags, and the President's words
probably did not carry as far as the men standing by the airplane,
their backs to the ceremony.

"I come here today as your President to tell you that on your
journey the hearts of this nation and the hopes of men in many

nations fly with you and will follow you until this duty is done," Johnson said. He told the men that it is not easy to leave home, but that the duties of freedom are not easy. "Those duties may become more demanding, the trials may become more difficult, the tests more challenging, before we or the world shall know again that peace on this planet is once more secure," he said.

Turning to Vietnam, he spoke of the "pillage" of the sudden offensive, and said its objective was to shake the foundations of the Vietnamese government and people, and to destroy the will of the American people to see the struggle through. The first attempt —three weeks before, at Tet—had failed.

"And now he has struck again. At this very hour, a second wave of terrorists is striking the cities. Our forces are ready. I know they will acquit themselves, as they always have, however tough the battle becomes and wherever it comes. . . .

"God bless you and keep you," the President said.

The tall Texan was wearing neither a topcoat nor a hat in the February wind, but he headed for the big jet across the field and stood by the hatch as the men climbed inside. As each soldier approached, the President shook his hand and said a few words. His manner was solemn. One of the White House newsmen thought his eyes looked misty.

When the last man was inside, Major General Richard J. Seitz, the division commander, signaled the pilot to start the engines. "Wait!" cried the Commander in Chief, disappearing into the hatch for a final visit with the men inside as if he wanted to say goodbye again. The last thing they heard in their native land was the voice of the President who was sending them to war.

Johnson and his retinue of aides, security guards and press flew on to El Toro, California, on the shores of the Pacific, to say goodbye to five hundred men of the 27th Marine Regiment who were going to war, and then the presidential party flew in helicopters to the flight deck of the *Constellation,* now thirteen miles at sea. The carrier and its fighter-bombers had recently returned from Yankee Station in the waters off North Vietnam, and some of the White House aides asked to talk to pilots who had participated in U.S. bombing raids. The President did not participate—his presence might have been intimidating to young officers—but the discussion took place in a wardroom just outside the President's quarters, and one of his aides thought he might have been listening.

The senior men, the commanders, spoke first and said the missions were being accomplished and the bombing was going well. After they finished, there was an awkward silence. Finally, a young lieutenant j.g., an Irish kid from the Northeast, spoke up. He said the bombing was crazy, absolutely insane. "We are going through the worst fucking flak in the history of man, and for what—to knock out some twelve-foot wooden bridge they can build back a couple hours later. We can't hit the docks [at Haiphong] where they unload the war matériel because we might hit the ships, and we can't hit the ships because some of them might be Russian. . . . We've got a great big country with sophisticated equipment, trained pilots, expensive aircraft and it's not worth a damn, it's not worth the loss of planes or the loss of a single pilot —and plenty are being lost, believe me. . . ." The other junior officers spoke up and said much the same thing. None of them objected to the purposes of the bombing, but all of them said it was not worth the cost, the risk and the sacrifice that was going into it.

The last stop was the winter home of former President Dwight D. Eisenhower beside the golf course at Palm Desert, California. In a big living room with glass doors overlooking the golf course on one side and the California hills on the other, Walt Rostow and General Lewis W. Walt of the U. S. Marine Corps briefed Eisenhower on the Tet Offensive and its implications abroad and at home. Rostow said the Communists in Vietnam had been badly hurt but added that "we are in the middle of a battle which is unresolved."

Eisenhower asked some penetrating military questions, but offered no advice. He said he never believed in substituting his judgment for that of the military men who direct a battle on the ground. General Westmoreland, he continued, had "the greatest responsibility of any general I have ever known in history."

President Johnson was surprised by that statement. Could Westmoreland's responsibilities for a half-million American men at war be greater than Eisenhower's own responsibility for five mil-

CHAPTER VI

Death in Hue

The bodies of the dead float on the river
They lie exposed in the fields
On the housetops of the city
And in the winding streets.

The bodies of the dead lie lonely
Under the roofs of the pagodas
In the aisles of the churches
On the floors of the deserted houses.

Oh Spring!
These bodies nourish and perfume the furrows in the fields
Oh Vietnam!
These bodies breathe life into the land for the future
The road to the future, though it be difficult,
Will be made easier by these bodies.

The bodies of the dead lying all around, in these cold rains
Alongside the bodies of the old and the weak
Lie the bodies of the young and innocent.
Which body is the body of my little sister?
Under this shell hole, or in that burned-out area?
Or alongside the furrows of corn and potatoes?

—Ballad to the Dead
Hue 1968
by Trinh Cong Son

THE BARRAGE began at 3:30 A.M., shaking the city and lighting the sky with violent flashes. Then came the flares fluttering down from above, casting a metallic glow upon the villas and gardens, old palaces, temples and ramparts. Automatic weapons fire could be heard in the streets.

Two North Vietnamese battalions, the 800th and 802nd, stormed across lightly defended bridges and lotus-choked moats, past rotten wooden gates, through the great stone entrances of the Citadel and into the heart of the Imperial City. Heavy fighting broke out around the military airstrip; an ammunition warehouse exploded; blazing fuel sent flames high into the air.

In the Gia Hoi suburb at the eastern edge of the city, the men of an armed security unit crossed the river in small boats at the Strawberry Patch and headed down Vo Thanh Street to make contact with the district Party committee. Along the way they stopped four men on Hondas fleeing the scene, one a policeman and another a third lieutenant from the government infantry school at Thu Duc. Comrade Van gave the order to open fire; the four were mowed down in a burst of bullets in the street. The unit proceeded to the Gia Hoi police substation and called to the defenders to surrender and live. There was a pitched battle instead.

South of the River of Perfumes, American officers and men inside the high-walled U.S. advisers' compound scrambled into bunkers and gun positions, many dressed only in the undershirts and skivvies they were wearing when awakened in the night. North Vietnamese troops of the 804th Battalion poured in machine

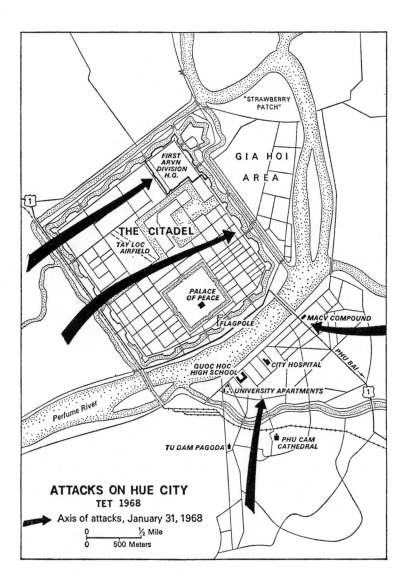

"STRAWBERRY
PATCH"

GIA HOI

AREA

FIRST
ARVN
DIVISION
H.Q.

THE CITADEL

TAY LOC
AIRFIELD

PALACE
OF PEACE

FLAGPOLE

MACV COMPOUND

PHU BAI

QUOC HOC
HIGH SCHOOL

CITY HOSPITAL

UNIVERSITY APARTMENTS

Perfume River

TU DAM PAGODA

PHU CAM
CATHEDRAL

ATTACKS ON HUE CITY
TET 1968

Axis of attacks, January 31, 1968

0   ½ Mile

0   500 Meters

gun and small arms fire from positions they had seized in the Jesuit school across the way. Mortars and rocket shells began exploding all around; some of the mortar positions were so close the Americans could hear the projectiles dropping into the mortar tubes. A young radio operator, a draftee with only a few more days of Vietnam duty, fired at attackers from an exposed position in an unfinished tower. They finally blasted him down with a B-40 rocket round. It took five hours for him to die.

By dawn the mixed North Vietnamese-Viet Cong force had the run of the city except for the U.S. advisory (MACV) compound and the camp of the 1st South Vietnamese (ARVN) Division in a corner of the Citadel. Captured jeeps patrolled the boulevards, along with squads of men on foot. The battle had diminished and the din had stopped. The city had no electricity. The government radio was silent. The shutters of homes were closed and doors were locked. Most of the streets were deserted.

Mr. Tran, the leading son of a well-known family, awoke to an eerie silence broken only by the sounds of distant battle and the twitter of the songbirds in the fruit trees of his walled garden. The traffic, the noisy neighbors and the rest of the city seemed to have vanished, leaving him alone and puzzled. Mr. Bui, living inside the Citadel walls and thus closer to combat, got into his ancient Citroën and headed down the road to visit his aged parents. Near the Citadel gate he saw two dead government soldiers lying in the grass, another slumped over in his bullet-ridden jeep and Viet Cong soldiers on guard a few hundred yards away. He wheeled his car around and headed home. Mr. Pham, a former teacher living in the Gia Hoi section, could see nothing in the street through the crack in the shutters at first light. He quickly dressed, cautiously unlocked the front door and slipped outside. At the nearby street corner were armed men in black pajamas and conical hats. He jumped back inside and bolted the door.

At midmorning a man with a megaphone came down a main street in Gia Hoi instructing everyone to keep their shutters closed and stay inside, and then handcarts with wooden wheels clattered past. There were corpses on the carts. A little later, "the people with their hair in buns," rough peasants from the countryside, began appearing in the streets. They were armed and seemed to have authority. Behind the shuttered windows, people were afraid.

The proud and lovely city of Hue had entered a different world with a different set of ruling personalities and principles from those it had known. From dawn on January 31 until 5 A.M. on the morning of February 24, the yellow-starred flag of the National Liberation Front flew from the flagpole atop the fortress gate of the Citadel, and a People's Army command post occupied the restored throne room of the Nguyen emperors in the Palace of Perfect Peace. During all of that time large sections of the city, containing many thousands of homes and inhabitants, were under Communist control.

The twenty-five-day struggle for Hue was the longest and bloodiest ground action of the Tet Offensive and, quite possibly, the longest and bloodiest single action of the Second Indochina War. Because of the commitment to battle of large numbers of U. S. Marines, the picturesque setting and the extensive destruction of the historic city, the military action was well publicized in the United States and made a substantial impact on public opinion at the time.

The story of what happened on the other side of the occupation lines was more important in the long run than the battle, but it came to light slowly and received far less attention. At first this story was mere rumor and assertion; and then, little by little, the rumor began to be substantiated. Residents gradually began to speak more freely of what they had seen and heard. Over weeks, months and even years, the earth yielded up the evidence from schoolyards and parks, coastal salt flats and jungle creek beds—the bodies of 2800 victims of the occupation, shot to death, bludgeoned or buried alive in the most extensive political slaughter of the war.

Hardly anyone took the trouble to investigate the full details of what had happened; after Tet, America and most of the world was interested in proofs and prophecies, not in history. The President of the United States and others cited the killings in Hue as an object lesson in Communist immorality and a foretaste of the bloodbath ahead should the Communists triumph in South Vietnam. Opponents of the President's policies treated the killings as an aberration of war or denied that any purposeful large-scale slaughter had taken place. In time, the ghastly slaughter of something over a hundred civilians by United States troops at My Lai 4 in Quang Ngai Province seized the attention of the world. The picture faded; Hue and its people dropped out of sight.

In the Buddhist imagery so important there, Hue was a lotus flower growing from the mud and slime. It was a paradox and an illusion: in a region of insecurity and terror, a city of peace. More than any other city in the land, Hue embodied the tradition and values of the past and a clear sense of time remembered. Its bittersweet charm and faded glory were deeply affecting to almost every visitor. The city radiated a haunting attraction difficult to define or fully explain.

For a Western visitor, one part of its charm was the nostalgic and familiar: the boulevards and parks beside the River of Perfumes; the Cercle-Sportif, with its comfortable riverside veranda and 1930s furnishings; the ancient French automobiles; the tile-roofed houses inside the Citadel with their small gardens, inhabited by cultured people expressing in English and French a sophisticated view of the world and the war. Beyond this was the fascination of the exotic: the slanting decorated roofs of the old palaces and shrines; the monumental tombs of the Nguyen monarchs; the sampans floating lazily on the river; the aged mandarins with wispy beards and porcelain teacups and a commission from the emperor on the wall; the echoing gongs of the pagodas, filled with gray-robed monks and nuns and youthful novices, chanting singsong prayers before a golden Buddha. One of the most beautiful sights in all Vietnam could be seen in the mornings along the riverside street: great swallow-flights of slender schoolgirls, their long black hair and clean white *ao dai* billowing behind them, pedaling their bicycles on their way to school.

Central Vietnam, where the mountain range called the Annamite Cordillera swings eastward toward the sea, is a region of stubborn soil, cold and wet winters, hot and arid summers and hard, determined people. It has produced a large proportion of the leaders of the nation for many centuries. The Nguyen war lords who ruled in south Vietnam established their capital at Hue in 1687 and built two great walls between the mountains and the sea, near the present DMZ, to protect themselves from the Trinh war lords who ruled in the north. Both rival families and their armies were vanquished by a third group headed by Quang Trung (Nguyen Hue), the patriot and military genius who drove the Chinese from Hanoi in the surprise Tet attack of 1789. Quang Trung unified the country, exterminated his defeated enemies and proclaimed himself emperor over all.

A sixteen-year-old nephew of the deposed Nguyen rulers escaped the massacre, and he returned to the battle a decade later with the help of French weapons and advisers. Starting from Saigon, he reconquered Hue and took Hanoi in 1802 and re-established the Nguyen dynasty. To frighten potential enemies and avenge the deaths of his family, Gia Long (as he called himself) executed the surviving members of the previous royal family and the defeated generals and their families. The fallen ruler, Quang Toan, was forced to watch while soldiers exhumed the bones of his father, the illustrious Quang Trung, and urinated on them. Then the king's hands and feet were bound to four elephants and the beasts were driven in different directions, tearing him apart.

To make his capital impregnable and impressive, Gia Long built a gigantic fortress city, adapted by French advisers from the Imperial City at Peking, complete with towers and ramparts, moats and high stone walls on every side. Its three-square-mile interior, which encompasses roughly half of the modern city of Hue, contained a series of inner walled cities with royal palaces and temples at the heart. Gia Long's chosen successor, the son of his first concubine, expelled the French from the court and began to seal the country against the West—but the French returned in 1883, bombarded the Citadel from warships and took control of the court. From that day on, the emperors ruled from the throne at Hue under the guiding hand of the French—until the last of the line, Emperor Bao Dai, presented his gold seal and sword to the Viet

Minh revolutionaries during the August revolution of 1945 and renounced the throne forever.

After World War II the French returned once more, and many of the people fled to the countryside. The foreigners held the city in a tenuous grip, fending off attacks and terrorist incidents. After the First Indochina War, the line between the north and the south was drawn again near the ancient walls and Hue became a part of South Vietnam. The leader of an old court family, Ngo Dinh Diem, the son of the grand chamberlain and minister of rites of the Emperor Thanh Thai, returned from self-imposed exile in the West to become the President of South Vietnam. Diem was a Catholic, and he built a political following based on Catholicism. A Buddhist reaction was inevitable, and an uprising led by monks in Hue in 1963 was the beginning of the end for Diem. Three years later a Buddhist-led rebellion centered in Hue threatened to bring down the Saigon military junta, until the rebellion was crushed with the assistance of the United States.

Still the independent spirit of Hue survived. Here the old ways and the old families remained more important than money or military power. The life of the city had been damaged but not destroyed. Imperious and formerly imperial Hue remained aloof from the money-grubbing Saigon generals, the power-hungry Hanoi commissars and the rich and ignorant Americans. Hue viewed them all with disdain.

The city seemed peaceful and secure, so much so that government army officers paid large bribes to be assigned to duty there, but in fact it was among the most poorly defended and most vulnerable in South Vietnam. Just a mile or two to the west were the foothills of the rugged mountains, dotted with Viet Cong campsites and rarely penetrated by either Saigon government forces or the Americans. Less than forty miles south was the Ashau Valley, the durable infiltration-and-base area of the Communist forces. Because of the political sensitivity of the city, anti-foreign sentiment and a few early incidents of "grave-whacking" by GIs among the royal tombs, Hue and its immediate suburbs were off limits to American military forces except a small group of U.S. advisers. The defense of the city, such as it was, rested in the hands of a reserve battalion of the 1st South Vietnamese Division with headquarters in a corner of the Citadel.

The Plan

In September of 1967 an important meeting was held in a pagoda at Tay Ho hamlet, four miles east of the city. The man in charge was Hoang Van Vien, known as "Ba," secretary of the Hue City Committee of the Communist Party. Ba explained to his coworkers that the revolution against the Americans and their Saigon puppets was developing very fast, that conditions were ripe for the General Offensive and General Uprising and that preparations must be undertaken immediately to prepare for the liberation of Hue.

Comrade Son Lam, thirty-five years old and a native of the Hue area, was assigned the task of organizing the uprising for the Right Bank, the section of the city south of the Perfume River. He had joined the anti-French Resistance while attending high school in Hue in 1948, became a member of a Viet Minh secret intelligence cell in 1950, was ejected from the intelligence service in 1952 when his well-to-do parents were denounced as "oppressors of the people," regrouped to North Vietnam after the country was divided in 1954 and infiltrated south in 1962 as the head of a nine-man group of Hue-area natives working for the Party. Despite the fact that his older sister was married to a government policeman, Lam lived safely in his native hamlet just east of the city.

After receiving his instructions, Lam selected as aides the men who could work best within the city and sent them to prepare the way. One night in mid-October, he walked to Hue accompanied by a squad of bodyguards and took up residence in a rented house at the edge of town. He was an ideal organizer: he knew the city and the people, he understood them and they understood him. He began making the rounds of old friends and acquaintances and, with the aid of letters of introduction, called on Hue citizens whose relatives were working for the Party.

Within a week or two he had organized five cells of residents in the Right Bank district—two cells of small-business men and three cells of youths, including the framework of a "Young People's Democratic Group" to be unveiled at the proper moment. He went back to the countryside, where his recruits joined him in small groups for a week's instruction on the aims and organizing principles of the Party. Lam did not tell them when the General Uprising would erupt; he himself had been led to believe that N day would be sometime in March.

On January 26 the leadership committee of the Party completed an eight-page plan for the offensive and uprising in the Right Bank district, specifying general missions as well as targets, the jobs of particular leaders, headquarters locations and policy guidelines. The plan suggests that the leadership did not expect to be able to hold Hue for very long, for it emphasized destruction of "the enemy" over establishment and consolidation of the new order. As set forth in the Party plan, the general missions were:

1. Destroy and disorganize the enemy's restrictive administrative machinery from the province and district levels to city wards, streets and wharves. To pursue until the end spies, reactionaries, and reactionaries who exploit Catholics in and outside the country. To prevent them from escaping and to punish scoundrels, hoodlums, and robbers who kill the people and disturb peace and honor.

2. Motivate the people to take up arms, to pursue the enemy and to seize power and establish a revolutionary government.

3. Make every effort to establish strength in the military, political and economic fields in order to conserve the government. Our immediate mission is to pay particular attention to armed and security forces.

4. Make positive efforts to develop [our forces] in the city wards, streets and wharves in order to expand the guerrilla war.

5. Encircle the reactionaries who exploit Catholics and isolate them. Pay special attention to the Phu Cam area, Thien Huu and Binh Linh schools and at the same time try to gain the support of the Buddhist sects of Tu Dam and Bao Quoc pagodas.

6. Promptly motivate the people to participate in

combat, transportation and supply activities and to serve
the wounded soldiers, etc.

7. Maintain order and security in the city and sta-
bilize the people's living conditions.

The plan divided the Right Bank into four tactical areas, each
with its own priority targets and special missions, its own organization and assigned leaders. The forces were given an activity schedule for their first three days of occupation and specific instructions
for handling prisoners in different categories. Important prisoners
of war were to be closely guarded and evacuated from the city at
the first opportunity; they were to be killed on the spot only if
evacuation were impossible. "Cruel tyrants and reactionary elements" were to be imprisoned separately and moved outside the
city for "punishment," a euphemism for execution. As for foreign
civilians such as teachers, newsmen and artists, the attack force
was instructed to "gain the sympathy" of the French residents
but to arrest Americans, Germans and Filipinos.

Viet Cong agents had prepared a profusion of reports on the
defenses and defenders of the city, the deployment and habits of
military and police patrols at night, the identity and activities of
political opponents, government officials and foreigners and even
the schedule of doctors on duty at the Central Hospital. Working
from this mass of information, Viet Cong intelligence prepared two
documents for security forces moving into the city. One was a
target list for each area of the city of United States and "puppet"
civil and military installations. The other list, more detailed and
important, included 196 targets in the city to be given priority
attention, arranged by street location. For example, these were the
items for Duy Tan Street on the Right Bank:

> The Garrison Town Office is located on Duy Tan
> Street at the corner and adjacent to Truong Dinh Street.
> U.S. personnel live at No. 4 Duy Tan Street.
> Thua Thien [Province] Sector Headquarters is lo-
> cated at Phan Sao Nam Camp, No. 3 Duy Tan Street.
> Pham Tra Dang, native of Quang Nam, teacher at

the high school, long-standing Vietnamese Nationalist
Party member, an extremely anti-revolutionary element,
lives at No. 34 Duy Tan Street.

U.S. personnel live at Thuan Hoa Hotel, No. 5 Duy
Tan Street.

A house used by U.S. personnel is at No. 21 Duy
Tan Street.

No. 52 Duy Tan Street is the house of the concubine
of Captain Pham Lien, Phu Thu District Chief. He was
formerly Duc Hoa District Chief and was active against
us. He usually sleeps at his concubine's house at night.

No. 71 Duy Tan Street is the home of Nguyen Giang,
father of Nguyen Vi Hoc. Hoc is chief of the Psywar office
of the Province Rural Development Group. Hoc is also a
member of the Dai Viet Party. He usually comes and
stays at his father's house.

No. 59 Duy Tan Street is the home of Nam, a member of the National Police Service, Nam Hoa District.

Comrade Son Lam, who moved back to the city from the
countryside in early January, was awakened by a messenger in the
night at 2 A.M. on January 30, the first day of Tet. His presence
was required immediately outside of town. At a meeting in a
family chapel north of the city he was informed for the first time
that the General Offensive and General Uprising would coincide
with the Lunar New Year. The troops were moving, the hour of
attack was close at hand. In order to maintain security, no one was
permitted to leave the meeting.

The main force units began arriving shortly after dark. Lam
was assigned as liaison officer between the troop units which would
occupy the Right Bank and the political organization he had built.
The provisional battalion, composed half of North Vietnamese regulars and half of South Vietnamese Liberation Army forces, began
its march a little after 10 P.M., crossing rice fields, highways and
streams and arriving at the jumping-off point after midnight. There
in darkness and in silence the soldiers waited at the edge of a rice
paddy only a few blocks from the headquarters of the American
advisers. Son Lam was excited and anxious, but he was not fearful.

He had waited twenty years for this day. His ears were eager for the "signal from above," the mortar and rocket barrage which was to be the call to battle.

United States and South Vietnamese government intelligence, charged with keeping up with threats to the city, was confused, uncoordinated and ineffective. The government police, headed by a former sports announcer who kept a bottle of Johnnie Walker Black Label on his desk, did not customarily exchange intelligence —if indeed it had any—with the 1st South Vietnamese Division. The small CIA station in the city, which advised the police, rarely exchanged information with the U.S. military advisory team which worked with the provincial troops. The forces within the city rarely received any intelligence of value from the U.S. air, logistical and ground installation at Phu Bai, just eight miles southeast of the city along Route 1.

On January 22 the U. S. Command in Saigon informed the Pentagon in Washington of good evidence in hand that the enemy would attempt a multibattalion attack on Hue. Whatever the good evidence was, it did not reach the people most immediately endangered. Both United States and Vietamese government forces in Hue were unprepared for a major attack.

About January 28 a U.S. military adviser in Huong Thuy district just east of the city reported signs that three North Vietnamese/Viet Cong battalions had recently left their mountain base camp and were now located in his lowland district. The officer was known at U.S. advisory headquarters in Hue as a habitual worrier and, in the absence of corroborating information, his report was discounted. The following night many of the American and Vietnamese military intelligence officials celebrated New Year's Eve at a party in the back room of the best Chinese restaurant in the city. There was plenty of food and drink, and not a whisper of impending disaster.

On January 30, New Year's morning, Brigadier General Ngo Quang Truong, commander of the 1st South Vietnamese Division, attended the flag-raising ceremony near the Emperor's Gate of the Citadel to mark the coming Year of the Monkey. Shortly after the ceremony he received reports of the attacks on Da Nang, Nha Trang and other cities during the night just past. Many of Truong's men were on Tet holiday, but he placed his remaining forces on alert and called his division staff officers to their posts at division headquarters for the night. This precautionary action preserved the command structure of the division and saved the lives of many staff officers whose residences were in unprotected areas of the city.

At this point, strong evidence of Communist troop movements converging on Hue was in U.S. hands at nearby Phu Bai, but neither Truong nor the U.S. advisory team in Hue was aware of it. The evidence consisted of telltale signals from radio transmissions, picked up by the U.S. radio intercept field station at Phu Bai on January 30. Under Army procedures of the time, this information was not forwarded directly to Hue but was sent back to Da Nang regional headquarters for posting and analysis before being relayed from there to Hue via teletype. The usual bureaucratic delays at headquarters were compounded by the attack on Da Nang itself. By the time the radio intercept reports arrived in Hue, the "signal from above" had already been fired, the Communist units had attacked from all sides and nearly the entire city had been taken over.

Marked Men

The first travail was of those who had been named as targets on the Viet Cong intelligence lists: Vietnamese officials, military officers, political figures and functionaries and Americans and foreigners other than the French. Most of them tried to hide and some of them managed to flee, but many were caught in their homes. They were marched down the nearly empty streets, their arms bound behind their backs, to prisoner collection points in the city.

Lieutenant Colonel Pham Van Khoa, the province chief, fled from his house and made his way in the darkness to Central Hospital six blocks away. There he hid for a week in an attic while a Viet Cong unit conducted the business of a command post on the floor below. Khoa, who had risen to high authority from a lowly position as a personal retainer of the Diem family, was badly shaken by the experience. He was relieved of his post a few weeks later and ultimately assigned to a less important military job in Da Nang.

The senior American adviser in Hue, Philip W. Manhard, radioed the U. S. Command in Saigon on the first morning that his house was surrounded and that he and two assistants were going into a hiding place within the residence. Manhard, a veteran Foreign Service officer, was captured and taken away. As this is written, he has not been heard from since.

Stephen H. Miller, a twenty-eight-year-old Foreign Service officer assigned to Hue as a United States Information Agency representative, had dinner the night before with James R. Bullington, a Foreign Service classmate who had previously served in Hue and was engaged to marry a Hue girl. The girl's uncle, the son of an old mandarin, had heard rumors that the night would be very dangerous, but the two young Americans had heard such talk before and they were unconcerned. They stayed up late drinking and singing college songs before Miller went home to his house on Phan Dinh Phung Street.

All hell broke loose during the night and in the morning a neighbor boy reported to Miller that many, many Viet Cong were about, including more than thirty at the very next corner. Miller was invited by Vietnamese friends to flee with them to the big Catholic cathedral nearby, but he decided to remain in his house. When his friends returned, the house was occupied by a platoon of Viet Cong who said they had discovered the Foreign Service officer and another American hiding in a closet. Miller's body was found a few days later in a field behind a Catholic seminary which had been used as a prisoner collection point. His arms had been tied and he had been shot to death.

Bullington was luckier. Since he was not regularly assigned to Hue at the time, he was staying in the guesthouse of a friend, who hid him, in turn, with Vietnamese neighbors who had no connection with the government or the Americans. For eight days he watched North Vietnamese troops in khaki patrol the neighborhood and once saw men in black pajamas rumbling down the street in a captured American tank. On the ninth day the North Vietnamese fled and U. S. Marines liberated the house where he was hidden.

Courtney Niles, an NBC International official serving under contract as a radio-television technical adviser, was staying with a U. S. Army communications crew in a house in the Right Bank area. For two days nothing happened. On the third day a Viet Cong team marched up to the house and pounded on the front door. One of the Americans opened fire, a Viet Cong soldier fell dead and the rest of the team withdrew. The Americans gathered their weapons and steeled themselves for a last stand—but again, nothing happened. The invaders were all over the area, walking back and forth through the streets with leafy camouflage hanging from their shoulder packs, carrying mortar tubes and projectiles, machine guns and other weapons, but they simply ignored the Americans in the marked house.

Two or three nights later the attack on the house came, beginning with dynamite charges which blew out a wall without warning. Niles and several others fled. The NBC official was hit in the legs but made it nearly to the church where he had decided to seek refuge. A friend saw him fall in the street. His body was found after the area was cleared. Some of the other Americans in the house surrendered; they were bound and marched off to the Ashau Valley and have never been heard from since.

Father Elizalde, a Spanish Jesuit who lived two blocks from the U.S. advisory compound, was awakened by the barrage in the night and then by a message from the invading troops—delivered by his cook—to open all the doors or suffer the consequences. The troops swarmed in, setting up machine gun posts and mortar pits. The Spaniard and his superior, a Belgian, retreated to the little villa behind their garden while the war erupted around them.

During a pause in the fighting on the third day, a Viet Cong patrol shot off the lock on their door and a political officer summoned them, in broken English, to come outside with their hands in the air. The leader wore khaki shorts and shirt with a green and red arm band and a Ho Chi Minh medal, and he carried a clipboard full of papers describing inhabitants of the area. Copies of identity card pictures were pasted on many of the sheets. He handed the Jesuits a pamphlet printed in English containing the Communist version of American activities all over the world and of the cries of people that "Americans go home."

The priests protested that they were not Americans and that the school had nothing to do with politics or the war, but their arms were bound and they were marched across a field and through a nearby seminary, crowded with North Vietnamese soldiers, to the residence of the senior American adviser. Manhard was nowhere to be seen but five other Americans were crowded into temporary confinement in the shower stall, their arms bound behind them. The priests were searched and then interrogated. The Spaniard said he was from "south of France" and the Belgian from "north of France" and both repeated the humanitarian and non-political nature of their mission. They were vouched for by Vietnamese university students of their acquaintance who seemed to be working with the invading troops. After a while the senior Viet Cong commander on the scene wrote out a safe-conduct pass and let them go. The Americans were later marched away, except for one badly wounded civilian who was left behind.

Dr. Horst Gunther Krainick, a German pediatrician and professor of internal medicine, had come from the University of Freiburg in December of 1960 to help establish a medical school at Hue University. With the assistance of the German and Vietnamese governments, teams of German doctors—mostly from Freiburg—had labored under increasing difficulties to bring first-class medical education to a region and nation woefully short of physicians. Dr. Krainick and his wife, Elisabeth, were torn between their love of Hue and the memories of the happy early years and the growing hostility and bureaucratic difficulties at the university. They were planning to return to Germany as soon as the school year ended and the small class of senior medical students had graduated.

During the Buddhist uprising of 1966, the Germans had been left alone and as non-combatants and medical workers they felt certain they would be left alone at Tet. They placed their German identification on their door in the university faculty apartments and watched the Viet Cong from the windows. They had no way to know that the Viet Cong order was to pick up Germans and that they were listed—though not by name—in Item 65 of the Right Bank target list.

On Sunday morning, the fifth day of the occupation, a well-armed squad wearing red arm bands, neat uniforms and boots arrived in a jeep and a cream-colored Volkswagon bus and began searching the building. The Krainicks stayed put and the Viet Cong went away. Three hours later they returned and entered the Krainicks' apartment. Elisabeth Krainick screamed and when she and her husband were led away she was heard to shout in English, "Keep your hands off my husband." The couple and the two other German doctors in residence, Dr. Raimund Discher and Dr. Alois Altekoester, were taken away in the Volkswagen bus. The four bodies were found later in a shallow grave in a potato field a half mile away, all victims of executioner's bullets. Vietnamese nuns who knew them gently washed the bodies and wrapped them in black cloth and then white cloth in traditional fashion for the long trip home to Germany.

Father Urbain and Father Guy, two French Benedictine priests at the Thien An Mission in the tall pines on a bluff south of the city, had been able to coexist with the local Viet Cong who dominated the area. When the fighting began, several thousand local peasants flocked to the monastery seeking refuge, and they were followed by Communist troops. Father Urbain's body was found in a common grave with ten other victims near the monumental tomb of the Emperor Dong Khanh (1883–89), who was installed on the throne by the French and whose reign was marked by a bloody Vietnamese attack on the French at Hue. Father Urbain had been bound hand and foot and buried alive. Father Guy's body was found nearby. His cassock had been removed and he had been allowed to kneel before being shot in the back of the head.

Three fourths of Hue's Roman Catholics lived in the Phu Cam area of the Right Bank, and the Right Bank plan contained special instructions to "destroy the power and influence of reactionary ring leaders" there. On the fifth day troops came in force to Phu Cam Cathedral and ordered out about four hundred men and boys, some by name and others apparently because they were of military age or prosperous appearance. When the group was assembled, the Viet Cong leader told everyone not to fear, they were merely being taken a half mile away to Tu Dam Pagoda, headquarters of their Buddhist adversaries, for political reorientation. They marched away to Tu Dam and two days later troops returned to the cathedral to ask the women to prepare packages of food and clothing for their loved ones. After this was done, the group disappeared, marching south, and was not heard of for a long time.

Nineteen months later three Viet Cong defectors led the U. S. 101st Airborne Brigade through the royal tombs area, across a river and through some of the most rugged country of central Vietnam to a creek bed deep in double-canopy jungle ten miles from Hue. There spread out for nearly a hundred yards in the ravine were the skulls, skeletons and shards of bone of the men of Phu Cam, washed clean and white by the running brook. The skulls showed they had been shot or brained with blunt instruments. Hue authorities later released a list of 428 victims. About 100 were South Vietnamese servicemen, including two officers; about 100 were students; the rest were civil servants, village and hamlet officials, government workers and ordinary citizens.

Of all instances of Catholic leaders singled out for slaughter, none was more poignant than that of Father Buu Dong, the radiant and popular parish priest of a village east of the city. The area was inhabited by many Viet Cong, and Father Dong worked hard to stay on good terms with both sides in the war. In 1967 he invited Viet Cong and government soldiers to sit down together for Christmas dinner and, according to local legend, he carried it off. He kept a picture of Ho Chi Minh in his room and told his parishioners that he prayed for Ho because "he is our friend too." At the same time, he accepted sewing machines for the people from the American AID program.

On the first day Viet Cong troops led Father Dong to a nearby pagoda for questioning but released him after a passionate appeal by the elders of the parish. Five days later the troops returned. They searched the rectory, seized his binoculars, camera,

typewriter and his picture of Ho Chi Minh and led Father Dong
and two seminarians away.

The remains of his body were found twenty-two months later
in a shallow grave in the coastal sand flats along with the remnants
of three hundred other victims. In the priest's eyeglass case were
three letters. One was to his aged parents, another to his brothers,
sisters and cousins. The third, to his parishioners, said:

> My dearly beloved children,
> This is my last chance to write to you my children
> and remind you of the lesson of St. Peter on the boat in
> the storm (three illegible words) the faith.
> My words of greeting at this beginning of Spring are
> a hope that my works in the faith among you will make
> you remember (two illegible words) as my life is about
> to end by the will of God.
> Love one another and forgive my wrongs, thanking
> God with me. Ask God to forgive all my sins and re-
> member to love and pray for me that I will live in belief
> and patience during difficulties to bring about the peace
> of Christ and serve the spirit of God and the interests of
> everyone in Mother Mary.
> Please pray that I will be serene and clear-headed
> and brave in every adversity of the spirit and of the
> body and will send my life to God through the hands of
> the Blessed Mother.
> With a promise to meet again in Heaven,
> I hope for grace for all of you, my children.

From the position of his body and the lack of visible wounds,
it is believed that Buu Dong was buried alive and left to die.

Battle Report

At 8:30 A.M. on January 31, five hours after the Communist
assault, the U. S. Marine command at Phu Bai dispatched reinforcements down the road to Hue. The state of U.S. information
about the attack, which had been executed by at least eight and
probably eleven Communist battalions, roughly a division-sized

force overall, is illustrated by the size of the initial reinforcements: a single U. S. Marine company.[1] On the way to the city, Company A, 1st Battalion, 1st Marines, fortuitously met and joined four U.S. tanks which had been headed for the landing craft ramp in Hue for a scheduled trip up the Perfume River and beyond to the DMZ where action had been expected. This column of trucks and tanks soon was hit hard south of town and called for help. At this point, a second company of Marines, together with a small command group and two self-propelled 40-mm. guns, was dispatched from Phu Bai. This motley column fought its way into the U.S. advisory compound at 3:15 P.M. Two platoons of Marines were sent on across the Perfume River bridge toward the Citadel, but they were

[1] Throughout the first days of the battle, an amazing amount of misinformation was given the Marine command, the U. S. High Command and ultimately the American public.

At 5 P.M. on January 31, thirteen and one half hours after the attack, Lieutenant General Hoang Xuan Lam, the I Corps commander, announced that Communist troops had been ejected from all cities in the corps except for Hue, where "a platoon" was still holding positions near the Citadel airport.

On February 1 the U.S. advisory team at I Corps headquarters (Da Nang) declared that friendly forces "were pushing VC out of Hue this morning." According to the news release, forces of the 1st South Vietnamese Division, their U.S. advisers and a force of U. S. Marine reinforcements "were in firm control of the Division headquarters, the Thua Thien sector headquarters and the Hue MACV [U.S. advisers'] Compound." The release failed to add that this was about all of Hue they did control.

In Washington General Earle Wheeler reported to the Senate Armed Services Committee on February 1 that the Communists still had "some troops" in the Citadel and "a remnant of a battalion" on the south side of the Perfume River. On February 2 Wheeler quoted Westmoreland as saying it would take "several days" to clean up Hue.

On February 3 Brigadier General John Chaisson, the U. S. Command's Operations Center director, told newsmen in Saigon that the clearing of Hue was "just a matter of time" and should be completed "in the next day or so." General Truong, the embattled commander of the 1st South Vietnamese Division within the Citadel, was astounded to hear this statement on the radio and sent word to Chaisson that the situation was much more serious.

On February 5 the U. S. Command said "small pockets of enemy forces" were still present in the Citadel and "mopping up continues." On February 7 it declared that "at 1100 this morning it was reported that a small pocket of enemy resistance still existed along the wall in the extreme southwest corner of the Citadel" and is being "mopped up."

By then newsmen were on the scene, braving fire, living with the troops and reporting the battle at great hazard to themselves. Their accurate reports completely contradicted the rosy official statements. When members of Congress and the Washington press pointed out the contradiction, ranking officials in the American capital said the press was wrong.

stopped by intense fire after a block and withdrew to the U.S. compound.

Meanwhile, General Truong had ordered outlying armored, airborne and infantry troops of the 1st South Vietnamese Division to move to headquarters in the Citadel, where the situation was serious. The units were stopped by Communist blocking forces before they could reach the city, and were delayed twenty-four hours. By late on February 1, the equivalent of three South Vietnamese battalions were within the Citadel and less than one battalion of U. S. Marines had reached the U.S. advisory compound across the river. Before the fight was over, elements of eleven South Vietnamese battalions and three U. S. Marine battalions would be committed to battle.

The original plan was for the Marines to clear the area of the city south of the Perfume River (the Right Bank) and the government soldiers to clear the north side, including the Citadel, the inner Forbidden City of the Nguyen emperors and the repository of most of the symbolic and important relics of the past. It proved to be a tough, bloody business on both sides of the river—house-to-house fighting under heavy fire in the chill rain of the northeast monsoon. It took the Marines until February 6 to fight their way west from the advisers' compound to the province hospital four blocks away. Inside the Citadel, little progress was made against occupation troops, who were freely reinforced and resupplied each night through the western gates of the old fortress. In order to minimize the damage to Hue, a policy was initially established that the city was not to be bombed or shelled. As the battle continued, that policy was abandoned.

By February 13, the city was a shambles—nearly every building in the populous area shattered by rockets, mortars or bombs and pocked by bullets; trees and power lines down across streets and yards; bodies of Communist soldiers sprawled wherever they had fallen. The cold and rain had created a natural mausoleum but this day the sun came out for two hours—for the first and only time during the siege of the city—and the putrid smell of rotting flesh was in the air.

The Right Bank section had been cleared after bloody fighting three days before, but it was a tenuous security. There were constant reports of sniper incidents and frequent shelling from Communist units on the other side of the river. Le Loi Street, the riverside boulevard, was a litter of shell holes, bodies and battered buildings which the Marines had paid a heavy price to take. To two reporters who had just arrived in Hue, a Marine pointed out "Building 221," used by the invaders as a barracks and armory, which had been the center of a fierce battle. Few if any of the Marines were aware that it was Quoc Hoc High School, one of the most illustrious in the country. It had been founded at the turn of the century by Ngo Dinh Kha and attended by his son, Ngo Dinh Diem, and many of his eventual allies and adversaries—among the latter, Ho Chi Minh, Vo Nguyen Giap and Pham Van Dong.

Next door at the Dong Khanh Girls' High School, where the beautiful schoolgirls used to flock on their bicycles every morning, the halls and classrooms were crowded with refugees living on the floor. It was a potpourri of Hue: cyclo-rickshaw drivers and their families, charwomen, servants, grand ladies who once dined at the governor-delegate's palace and men who used to meet for tennis at the Cercle-Sportif.

The university apartments, where Mrs. Krainick used to serve little glasses of Goldwasser, the German liquor flecked with bits of gold leaf, was now being used as a U. S. Marine command post and mortar position. A kindly American chaplain was horrified to see the two reporters walking around without flak jackets or steel helmets, which were scarce during the battle, and he stepped back of a building and returned with equipment taken from the bodies of the dead. A flak jacket he got was stained with the blood of the last owner. One of the steel helmets in the discard pile had been badly dented by a bullet or shrapnel. Written on the back of the muddy helmet cover was a motto in sturdy black letters: "The Lord Is on My Side."

The heavy action now was across the Perfume River in the walled Citadel. The 1st Battalion, 5th Marines, had moved across the river a day or two before when it became clear that the government troops could not clear the area alone. The Truong Tien (formerly Clemenceau) bridge had been blasted by a Viet Cong demolition team and nearby parts of the Citadel were in enemy hands, so the two reporters made their way in a slow, flatbottom landing craft, loaded with reinforcements and ammunition, around the Communist-held Gia Hoi area and into the back corner of the Citadel. A tattered U.S. flag was flying from the bow. Along the narrowest part of the passage, a Viet Cong gunner fired his recoilless rifle at the craft and missed. The Marines responded with a hail of bullets.

Inside the Citadel the reporters met their press colleagues who had been covering the battle day by day, dodging bullets and shrapnel and watching young men fight and die. The Marine command post was a typical Citadel residence with masonry walls, a tile roof, bookshelves full of Jean-Paul Sartre and other works in French, a family ancestor portrait (the old man bearded, with the black mandarin robe) and half-burned joss sticks on the family altar. Major Robert Thompson, the commanding officer of the 1st of the 5th, was weary and discouraged. His men had been taking heavy casualties and making little progress. The government forces were moving even slower. Of all the crazy places to fight an enemy with rockets and machine guns, this was the worst—a medieval-type castle with a moat around it. Thompson's men had been pounding a strategic stone tower; despite 155-mm. howitzers, 8-inch naval gunfire from off shore, 40-mm. self-propelled guns, napalm and tear gas, snipers were still dug in there and the tower was still standing. The Nguyens had built their fortress for the ages.

The view from the other side of the lines was far from rosy.

On the Right Bank, Comrade Son Lam's force had run into immediate difficulty. One of the attack companies was hit by one of their own side's rockets, causing many casualties. One of the two battalion officers, a major, was killed almost immediately by machine gun fire from a government militia squad. In retaliation, sappers blew holes in the militia strong point and annihilated everyone inside.

The attack force on the Right Bank was told to occupy the area at least seven days. By the third day, Son Lam's provisional battalion had suffered heavy casualties and was being pushed out of the area near U.S. headquarters; a member of the Hue City Committee gave the order to the unit to withdraw. Two days later the order was given to return. The remnants of the battalion marched back into the city, fought a day and a night, and then retreated under the pressure of the advancing Marines. The other battalions on the Right Bank also made a slow withdrawal. As the Americans approached, the soldiers fought to make every step costly and dangerous. When the final assault was made on their positions, the Communist troops scampered back to repeat the battle at the next line of defense.

On the Left Bank, the North Vietnamese commander within the Citadel was killed by artillery on February 16, and his replacement requested permission to withdraw. Higher headquarters refused. It instructed him to defend his position until further orders.

The Vinh Family

In the southern part of the Citadel, not far from the stubborn watchtower which would not crumble under fire, was the sturdy five-room house of the Vinh family. Mr. Vinh, a cultured and learned man, had lived there most of his life and in the Vietnamese tradition had gathered many relatives to his hearth—his daughter and her husband and their small children; an unmarried younger daughter who was a student; a distant cousin and her husband who had no other place to live.

For several weeks Mr. Vinh had heard rumors of a coming attack on Hue and he had seen Viet Cong leaflets in the market place by the river. He considered this just talk, as in the past, and did not expect much action. A few days before Tet, a woman came to the house ostensibly selling fruit but actually delivering a letter from an old acquantance who had served many years in the Resistance, first against the French and then against the Americans. The friend sent word that he would come to visit at Tet. This had never happened before and Mr. Vinh did not know what to make of it.

Several hours after the barrage and gunfire began, there was a rattle at the gate and his old acquaintance appeared. He said total victory was near. A few days later two men came by in the early evening delivering letters to people in the area, one of them for Mr. Vinh from some of his relatives in North Vietnam. When the men left, the whole family sat around a candle while the younger daughter read the letter aloud. It said there was plenty of food and work for everyone in the North, and expressed the hope that the family in Hue would do its best to resist Yankee imperialism. It was dated in August—more than five months before Tet.

Another evening two young political workers came to call, one a schoolteacher in town and the other a former medical student at the university who had joined the Viet Cong after the Buddhist movement was crushed by Saigon troops in 1966. Over tea, they said the Liberation Army hoped to hold the cities of Hue and Quang Tri in order to bring about negotiations and an end to the war. Still other Viet Cong callers spoke of the formation of a new political front, the Alliance of National, Democratic and Peace Forces of Hue City. They said it was led by Professor Le Van Hao of Hue University and Mme. Nguyen Dinh Chi, former principal of Dong Khanh Girls' High School, and that it was designed to be acceptable to the Americans in the coming negotiations. The alliance broadcast an appeal over Liberation Radio, the NLF station, for all the patriotic organizations and people of Hue to rise up against the Americans and their treacherous henchmen. Like many families, the Vinhs had ties on both sides and stayed out of the battle as best they could, hoping it all would go away.

Instead, the battle was all around, and it was often difficult to tell who was winning or what was happening. A mortar blasted a hole in the side of the house; shrapnel shattered the front door and sprayed into the front room; more shrapnel pierced the roof. Automatic weapons and small arms fire was heard nearby on several occasions. American helicopter gunships strafed the area and later in the battle two rockets hit part of the house. Vietnamese skyraiders and American Phantom jets circled the area, screamed into a dive and released their bomb loads, ever closer to the house. The ground shook, shrapnel and debris landed on the roof and a strong smell of gunpowder rolled under the door. Finally an older cousin who had been kneeling in prayer at an altar outside was killed when a mortar shell exploded. They buried him amid the fruit trees behind the house; Mr. Vinh placed a message in Chinese in his grave so he would do well in his after-life.

During periods of bombing, the Vinhs lay on the floor in a bedroom, enduring the situation together and repressing conscious-ness of the present in daydreams or dozing. Occasionally they would come to life with uproarious laughter at one another, finding humor in the children and the talkative aunt who was always making none too bright remarks. They could hear the jets over-head and the artillery shells exploding in the middle distance, and the sounds of gunfire and shelling helped locate the direction and the distance of the danger. For this reason, the Vinhs found the silences to be the most frightening times of all.

Radio broadcasts and loudspeaker announcements from the two sides were contradictory and confusing. At first the government radio was silent but a loudspeaker plane came over saying allied troops would soon arrive to destroy the enemy. A few minutes later Liberation Radio said all Hue had been taken by the Liberation forces. A government loudspeaker in a truck or airplane (the family couldn't tell which) called on all Viet Cong to surrender in the streets with their hands up, and promised to give them each two cans of dried food and a Tet cake. A Viet Cong announce-ment about the same time called for police, government military officers and students to report in.

The Viet Cong moved with complete freedom through the streets of the quarter, on foot, bicycles, in cars or on Hondas or Suzukis. Besides the soldiers and political officers who had come out of the hills, there were local country girls in black pajamas who tied their hair back in buns, did not smile or shake hands and said little. Some were city boys, recently recruited to the cause, with long hair and American-style blue jeans. One Viet Cong soldier was the girl elected queen of her senior class at a local high school. She wore a revolver on each hip.

The Vinhs heard rumors of assassinations—the village chief of the quarter, a local police station chief, a government Army colonel and others. The political officers who came to call denied these stories. They said officers of the government Army were summoned every day for indoctrination but allowed to return home at night.

On the seventeenth of February the Vinhs heard movements near the house and cries of "Stick 'em up" in broken French. It was the U. S. Marines. The Viet Cong had vanished from this block in the Citadel almost as swiftly and mysteriously as they had come.

Gia Hoi

The section of the city most securely occupied for the longest period was Gia Hoi, a large triangle of land lying east of the walled Citadel on the northern banks of the Perfume River. Beginning with a popular market place and several heavily populated commercial streets near the main river bridge, it broadens out to pleasant residential suburbs and rich farmland in its northern reaches. Lacking the presence of foreigners, governmental headquarters or the symbolic importance of the Citadel and some areas across the river, Gia Hoi was accorded lowest priority in the effort to recapture the city. Early in the battle, the 1st South Vietnamese Division decided to leave Gia Hoi to last, believing that once the invasion force inside the Citadel was defeated the adjacent Gia Hoi triangle could be easily surrounded and won with a minimum of difficulty.

This judgment saved South Vietnamese and American manpower, which was fully committed to the other areas during the lengthy fight, and it spared Gia Hoi from the extensive physical destruction visited upon the Citadel and the Right Bank in house-to-house fighting. On the other hand, the decision left the Viet Cong in virtually unchallenged control of Gia Hoi for nearly the entire period of the battle of Hue. For more than three weeks it was a small Communist-dominated city in which the occupation force could do whatever it wished.

The first move was to order down or rip down all South Vietnamese government flags and call for the flag of the National Liberation Front to be put up in its place. Virtually nobody had an NLF flag—possession of one would have been grounds for severe punishment during government rule—and so the political organizers went through the streets calling for the Buddhist flag to be flown instead. Many Vietnamese have such standards to be brought out on Buddha's birthday and other religious occasions, and a substantial number were hung from houses and stores.

On the second day announcements in the streets called on civil servants, military personnel and police to report to an office near the Gia Hoi High School. "Whoever works for the Americans should go immediately," the men with the megaphones said. The Viet Cong spread the word that if a person reported as instructed and if his attitude was good, nothing would happen to him.

Most of the functionaries did not believe this, and were afraid. Many of them stayed out of sight and when anyone approached they hid in the family bunker, the side closet, the attic or whatever place seemed safest. There were many family discussions about whether it was best to remain hidden or to report. At first there was a strong feeling among the people that government troops would arrive at any minute and oust the occupation force, but as the days went by and nothing happened, that began to fade. The announcements gradually became tougher. Houses would be searched, they warned, and anyone discovered hiding would be shot on the spot. Underground cadre and newly recruited informants began making the rounds pointing out the homes of officers and officials who had been left off the original Viet Cong target list.

On the fourth day the Viet Cong "suggested" that at least one adult member of every family should attend a meeting to be held in the yard of Gia Hoi High School. A political leader dressed in civilian clothes traced the history of the revolution in the old three-stage pattern: in the first stage, the NLF had been weak and small and limited to the forests and mountains; in the second stage, it had grown stronger and arrived at the deltas and plains; now, in the third stage, it had invaded the cities, ousting the Americans and their mercenaries in the action that would bring the victory to the people. The leader appealed to everyone to participate. At the end of the meeting, a group of local youths were presented with weapons and designated as the uprising troops for the Gia Hoi area. There was an air of excitement and revolutionary change.

A political cadre set to work organizing separate groups of youths, workers and teachers to act as arms of the revolutionary administration. The cadre used a show of force, a whiff of fear, appeals to patriotism, anti-foreign sentiment and the mass psychology that "we are winning" and "everybody is doing it."

Nguyen Thanh, a nineteen-year-old Saigon University law student who had returned home for Tet, was visited on the ninth day by three North Vietnamese soldiers, two local Viet Cong soldiers and a political officer named Ngoc, a man in his late twenties. The student was given a lengthy questionnaire to complete about his life, his family and his political ideas. His political aim, he wrote, was a peace acceptable to all Vietnam. The following day the soldiers returned and summoned him to a meeting with fifteen other young men. Ngoc convened the meeting and declared that "the revolution has triumphed in Hue for ten days now—you are all young men, you must work for your country." The student's ideas about a universally accepted peace were ridiculed. He was assigned a practical job—chief of a propaganda unit in the city.

Each night Nguyen and two other students listened to radio broadcasts, made notes and prepared a newscast with the "positive viewpoint" suitable for dissemination to the people. After the broadcast was checked by a former Hue University student acting as a political supervisor, Nguyen and his friends recorded the "news" on a Japanese-made tape recorder supplied by the political officer and took it house-to-house to play for the people. The broadcasts emphasized Liberation Army victories and American and government defeats.

On the twelfth day Nguyen and about forty other young men were called to Phu Hoa Pagoda, which doubles in normal times as a community center, and told to form themselves into a permanent organization to carry out tasks for the revolution. They stalled for time, saying they would have to work it out, but the following day they were summoned again. Nguyen was nominated and elected president of the new organization, Students and Young Men of Zone Two. The other officers were a Catholic student who attended a French-sponsored college in Da Nang, a Hue high school student and a Hue University medical student. The chief political officer, Ngoc, declared this was "a historic act for the revolution" and a cultural drama team from North Vietnam performed an anti-American, anti-government show for the occasion. Before Nguyen was faced with either the opportunity or necessity of doing anything more, he fled with his family across the river. Several weeks later he was arrested by government police for his activities during the occupation.

The functionaries had slowly begun reporting to the occupation headquarters, the home of a former Hue mandarin near the high school. Tran Van Tam, who worked in an American office in the Right Bank area, decided to report because he saw a neighbor shot down in the street. The Viet Cong spread the word that the man had been discovered hiding and that he would have been left alone had he done as he was told.

With a great deal of trepidation, Tran left his house and headed on foot toward the high school. Along the way he saw for the first time regular troops in khaki uniforms and conical hats of jungle leaf. Near the check-in place he saw several high school students he knew, armed with Chinese rifles. He spotted a coolie laborer he'd known for many years going house-to-house on errands for the occupation forces.

At the check-in station in the house of the mandarin, Tran was greeted warmly by officials who took his name and address and told him to go home and return the following day. The next day he was required to complete a declaration of his life, work and political ideas and then was allowed to return home. The more Tran thought about what was happening, the more nervous he became. Before anyone could summon him again, he fled to the house of his daughter's fiancé on another street and hid in the attic for the rest of the occupation.

Le Van Rot, the owner of Hue's most celebrated Chinese soup

shop, was visited by four armed men—two from Hue and two from North Vietnam—who called for him by name at his shop and took him to the high school for questioning. They returned with Rot that afternoon and began questioning neighbors about him. Back of his house, the soldiers found some weapons hidden away but they said everything was all right, they understood why he would want them, and they went away.

The men returned at 4 P.M. the same day and had some Chinese soup. When the bowls were drained, they turned to Rot and said, "We found out you sold soup here as a cover for spying." They bound his arms behind his back with wire and began to tug him toward the door. When he resisted, one of the visitors put a bullet through his head. Rot was the government block chief of his area (which may have been the real reason for his execution) and well-known throughout Hue. The Viet Cong spread the word that he was a CIA agent who had been caught spying. Others said that the fate of Rot proved what happened when a person failed to report.

Duong Chang Vinh, a former government chief of an outlying district, decided he had better report before a search party could find him and punish both himself and his family. He walked out the door of his large house, down the driveway and through the gate into the lane outside. When a group of soldiers saw him, they immediately tied his arms and began to tug at him. He resisted, and was shot down in the street outside his house. Vinh and his oldest daughter, who was later killed by a mortar shell, were buried in two large circular graves in the side yard of the house.

Le Van Phu, whose name was on the Viet Cong target list as a government police official, was in his family bunker when a squad of soldiers surrounded the yard and called for him to come out. His wife and children began weeping and protesting but the man in charge told them, "Don't worry. We're just taking him to a meeting. We'll be back." His twenty-one-year-old daughter hastily gathered a bundle of food and clothing and ran down the street after the soldiers to give it to her father. The men threatened her with the butt of a rifle and said her father didn't need the package

—he was going to a meeting and would be back the next day. He was executed that night and found later in a grave at the Strawberry Patch, a fertile patch of land in the northeast corner of Gia Hoi.

Pham Van Tuong, who worked as a part-time janitor at the government information office, lived in a small house under a big tree on a small lane off the beaten track. He and his family—his wife, eight children and three nephews—spent much of their time tucked away in a bunker beside the house. One day four or five men in black pajamas came to the door of the bunker. "Mr. Pham, Mr. Pham the information office cadre, come here!" they called. He climbed out of the bunker with his five-year-old son, three-year-old daughter and two of his nephews. There was a burst of gunfire. When the rest of the family came out, they found all five of them dead.

Mrs. Nguyen Thi Lao, a forty-eight-year-old widow who supported her family by selling cigarettes from a stand in the street, simply disappeared without explanation one afternoon. A day or two later two men wearing shorts and black shirts and carrying weapons came to the house, questioned the five children, searched the house and went away. The body of the cigarette seller was found later in a common grave at Gia Hoi High School. Her arms had been bound and she apparently had been buried alive. No one could explain why she was marked for death, unless she had been mistaken for her sister, a clerk at the government information office.

After three weeks of occupation it became clear that the U. S. Marines and South Vietnamese troops were closing in on the last Communist unit within the Citadel and that Gia Hoi would be next. At this point, the Viet Cong security units began going house-to-house in a final series of visits to some of those who had reported in and some of those who remained unchecked on the original list.

A leader in civilian clothes with a Hue dialect led a group of North Vietnamese soldiers to a house just off Vo Thanh Street. They asked the old man and the old woman if any young men were there. The couple said no, but the leader began to call a list of names in a loud voice and the team began to search. A South

Vietnamese Army captain, two lieutenants, two sergeants and a civil servant from the local treasury office surrendered without a fight, coming from their hiding places in a side room after their names were called. Their arms were bound and they were marched away, but the man in charge said, "They're only going to a meeting—don't worry."

The old woman found them later under the spreading arms of a fruit tree in the playground of the high school. Two of them had wires twisted around their necks, and all their hands were tied. Each had been shot in the head. The two sergeants, ages twenty-two and twenty-three, were her sons; the civil servant was her son-in-law; the officers were close relatives. She and her husband laid the young men to rest in the long, narrow yard where they had played as children, in six circular burial mounds, Vietnamese-fashion, each with a headstone bearing the name of the one who lies beneath. Each stone bears the date 2-22-68.

On February 24 the 1st South Vietnamese Division's elite Black Panther Company seized the flag tower at the south wall of the Citadel and ripped down the National Liberation Front flag which had flown there since January 31. The soldiers raised the yellow and red banner of the Republic of Vietnam, and moved into the inner courtyard of the Nguyen palace. The Communist troops had vanished.

As the soldiers in the Citadel were making their final assault, a South Vietnamese Ranger task force under Captain Pham Van Phuoc, a native of Gia Hoi, landed at the Strawberry Patch at the northern end of the Gia Hoi triangle and began fighting its way southward. On February 25 Captain Phuoc's task force took the last enemy holdout in Gia Hoi, the Cambodian pagoda across the street from the high school. Gia Hoi was declared cleared. The battle of Hue was over, twenty-five days after it began.

The Aftermath

The Hue City Committee of the Communist Party met in mid-March at its headquarters in the mountain fastness of the Nam Hoa district south of town. Hue is part of the Tri-Thien Military District, composed of the two northernmost provinces of Quang Tri and Thua Thien (the latter including Hue City), under direct command and control from North Vietnam instead of indirect control through the Central Office for South Vietnam (COSVN). Thus, a team from higher headquarters brought word direct from General Vo Nguyen Giap that the battle of Hue was "an unprecedented victory of scientific quality." A message attributed to Pham Van Dong said the battle was the greatest success in the people's revolution in South Vietnam, an assertion which was echoed later by official South Vietnamese Army historians, who called it "the most spectacular enemy action in the war."

A written Communist report on "the victory of our armed forces in Hue" declared that "the most outstanding feature was that we won an overall success, militarily and politically. This was a typical example of our tactic on how to occupy and defend a city. . . . The most significant fact was that we were masters for an extended period of time and completely reversed the economic and political balance in our favor, rendering the enemy helpless." The report added that "Hue was the place where reactionary spirit had existed for over ten years. However, it took us only a short time to drain it to its root."

United States military officers described it as a victory for the allies. Colonel G. O. Adkisson, the commanding officer of the U.S. advisory team in Hue, signed a citation for every American who participated under his command "as a combatant in the historic battle of the City of Hue, Thua Thien Province, Republic of Viet Nam, from 31 January 1968 through 25 February 1968, when the Viet Cong and North Vietnamese invaders were driven from the ancient imperial city during the longest battle in Viet Nam since the conflict began in 1960."

The U. S. Marine Corps added Hue to its battle streamers and received a presidential unit citation. "By their effective teamwork, aggressive fighting spirit and individual acts of heroism and daring, the men of the First Marines . . . soundly defeated a numerically superior enemy force and achieved an illustrious record of courage and skill which was in keeping with the highest traditions of the Marine Corps and the United States Naval Service," the citation read.

The Marines listed their own losses as 142 men killed in action and 857 seriously wounded. They listed South Vietnamese Army losses as 384 killed and 1800 wounded, and Communist losses as 5113 killed and 89 captured. *Leatherneck* magazine, an official publication of the Marine Corps, declared that in the end the Communists had given their lives for "nothing more than the dream of obtaining a propaganda victory." *Leatherneck* added that while the foe had fought well in a hopeless cause, "the Marines had defeated the enemy in the place he had chosen to fight. It was the Marine, with his rifle in his hand and, perhaps, a tight knot in the pit of his stomach, who had routed the invader from Hue. . . ."

The Viet Cong had used the battle of Hue to destroy as much as they could find of the government administrative machinery and personnel, in keeping with the general missions of the attack. No one has yet compiled a complete list of the roughly 2800 bodies found in mass grave sites or made a thorough analysis of the occupations, governmental connections or political leanings of those killed. Nonetheless, it is clear from the overwhelming weight of evidence that this was for the most part a deliberate slaughter, ordered from on high for plain and specific purposes. Among those executed were a senator; political party officials; city officials; civil servants; village, hamlet and block leaders; Army and militia officers and enlisted men; policemen; priests and other religious people; and teachers—all Vietnamese—in addition to Americans, Germans, Filipinos, Koreans and other foreigners.

In the last stages of the occupation and thereafter, the scales began to tip the other way. It was reliably reported that a South Vienamese government intelligence unit employed the confusion to send out "black teams" of assassins to eliminate some of those believed to have aided the enemy. Some of the North Vietnamese and Viet Cong suspects who were brought into Hue during those days mysteriously disappeared, with no record available of what had happened to them.

On March 14 more than twenty prisoners, including three women and some schoolboys, were brought into provincial military headquarters in the devastated city with burlap bags covering their heads and hands tightly wired behind their backs. Guards began beating some of the captives with sticks and fists. After one man confessed he had been an economic and finance cadre for the Viet Cong, two guards beat him senseless, one kicking him brutally and the other standing on his face. An American who was present was affected particularly by one of the prisoners, who under the burlap bag was a very pretty girl with long, silky black hair and clear complexion. She was described as a Viet Cong nurse.

The prisoners were taken into a stone building which served as a temporary house of detention and, according to general belief, a place of execution. There was no trace of them in the morning.

On November 3, 1969, twenty months after the battle and occupation, President Richard Nixon cited events in Hue as a justification for his policy of slow and gradual withdrawal from Vietnam rather than the swift withdrawal which many Americans had been demanding. Precipitate withdrawal of United States forces from Vietnam would be a disaster, the President said in a televised address to the American people.

> We saw a prelude of what would happen in South Vietnam when the Communists entered the city of Hue last year. During their brief rule there, there was a bloody reign of terror in which some 3,000 civilians were clubbed and shot to death. With the sudden collapse of our support, these atrocities of Hue would become the nightmare of the entire nation—and particularly for the million-and-a-half Catholic refugees who fled to South Vietnam when the Communists took over the North in 1954.

After the President spoke, American journalists and politicians began to debate about what happened in Hue and to argue about the legitimacy and probable accuracy of Nixon's prediction of a bloodbath should the Communists win South Vietnam. Two American graduate students, one of whom had previously lived in Hue and visited there after the battle, wrote in *The Christian Century* that the killings in the Gia Hoi area "were not the result of a policy on the part of a victorious [Viet Cong] government but rather the revenge of an army in retreat." Their report was cited by those who objected to the bloodbath theory. The White House responded with copies of reports of the Hue massacre and other such Communist-directed killings, compiled by the Vietnam Information Group and presented to the U. S. Senate by a willing Republican lawmaker. By then the American massacre at My Lai had been uncovered, and interest in Hue was minimal.[2]

It was officially estimated immediately after the battle that 80 per cent of the houses and buildings in Hue were destroyed or damaged in the battle. This estimate was probably high but it did justice to the visual impression of the devastated city. Twenty-one months later a reporter returned to Hue to find that much of the damage had been cleared, houses had been razed, rebuilt or patched, the shell craters and foxholes had been filled in, the collapsed bridges had been restored. The holes in the roof of the throne room of the Nguyen emperors had been patched with American tin. The Chinese red throne, with its gold leaf and inlaid mirrors, had not been damaged by the Communist forces who used the place for a command post or by the shells which struck the building in the fighting. In a low building in the courtyard outside, six young boys with reedy instruments were practicing the music of the Long Nhan, the Contemplation of the Dragon, under the instruction of an aged tutor. The music had been traditionally played on festival occasions to signal the approach of the emperor.

The spirit of the city, however, seemed to have been sadly affected by the events of the Tet Offensive. There were graves everywhere—in parks, front yards, alongside streets and lanes. Almost two years after the battle and the occupation, many survivors wept when asked to tell what they had seen and heard, and virtually everyone seemed still worried that the war would come again.

[2] The My Lai killings took place on March 16, 1968, about a hundred miles south of Hue in Quang Ngai Province. They did not come to public attention until November of 1969, twenty months later. They too are part of the story of the Tet Offensive, and they have been chronicled in detail elsewhere, notably Seymour M. Hersh's book, *My Lai 4* (New York, Random House, 1970) and in the records of the court-martial of Lieutenant William L. Calley, Jr.

The most pathetic grave sites were in Gia Hoi near the big fruit tree in the high school playground, where twenty-three permanent burial circles and nineteen small grassy mounds marked the location of the dead, and in the rich earth of the Gia Hoi Community Cemetery at the Strawberry Patch, where the bodies of civil servants, businessmen and community leaders were found. Four Viet Cong soldiers killed in the battle were also buried there, but people had strewn garbage and trash atop the unmarked mounds where they lie.

Trinh Cong Son, a slender young man who is South Vietnam's most celebrated song writer of the present day and a hero to the youth of the country, was living in Hue in late 1969. He is a native of the city and was there during and after the Tet fighting, when the bodies from the battle were being buried and bodies from the Viet Cong executions were being unearthed. Twenty-one months after the ordeal of Hue, Son wrote out for a visitor a ballad he had written in March of 1968 to express his feelings. Translated into English, it says:

When I went up a high hill of an afternoon
I sang on top of corpses
I saw, I saw, I saw beside a garden hedge
A mother hugging her child's corpse.

Mothers, clap for joy over your children's corpses
Mothers, clap in cheer for peace
Everyone clap to add another beat
Everyone clap to welcome hardship.

When I went to the Strawberry Patch
I sang on top of corpses
I saw, I saw, I saw on the road
An old father hugging the corpse of his frost-cold child.
When I went to the Strawberry Patch of an afternoon
I saw, I saw, I saw holes and trenches
Full of corpses of my brothers and sisters.

Mothers, clap for joy over war
Sisters, clap in cheer for peace
Everyone clap for more vengeance
Everyone clap instead of repenting.

CHAPTER VII

America the Vincible

U.S. Is Losing War in Vietnam, NBC Declares

—Headline in the New York *Times*
March 12, 1968

IN THE United States, the shock and anger of the first days after Tet gave way to frustration and that in turn to a sense of futility and despair. With the intense and bloody fighting continuing and dramatic allied victories not in sight, many Americans began to reject the whole affair, to turn off and give up on the war. The fragile confidence of November had been shattered by the first shock wave and now even hope seemed to be fading. The oracles of American society, the commentators, editorial writers and leaders of private America, many of whom had been uneasy and uncertain before, now became convinced that the war was being lost or, at the very best, could not be won. Those who had reached the same conclusion earlier now found the final proof that their information and their hunches had been right and that the government had been disastrously wrong. Their attitude was "I told you so."

The government in Washington and the U. S. Command in Saigon declared that the Communists had been defeated, suffering unprecedented losses for which there was nothing to show but propaganda. The officials, however, had nothing much of their own to show to prove their case. No Communist-dominated cities had been taken, territory seized or captive peoples "liberated"— except for cities, territory and people that had been counted in the government camp before the Tet Offensive had begun. American and Vietnamese troops were fighting to reclaim what they had lost, nothing more. The American government had previously relied on statistical indicators of population and territorial security to prove "success," while the dissenters had relied largely on intuition and intangibles: the attitudes of the Vietnamese people, the determination of the Viet Cong, the limited effectiveness of American power

in a civil war in a faraway place. Now the tables were turned. The
facts on the ground argued that the Communists had achieved
success, and the indices of security showed a sharp deterioration
in the Saigon government's position. The U. S. Government argued
that all this was fleeting, but the argument rested on prediction,
deduction and intangibles. Beyond the claimed "body count" of
the dead—numbers which seemed then, as now, fantastic and unreasonable—there was little hard evidence for the government's
case.

The assertions of the President, his senior aides and the American military chiefs were more suspect than ever before. They had
sold success before, and Tet had proved the product faulty; the
public was not inclined to buy again. Communiqués and claims
had been devalued, words had lost their ability to persuade. It
seemed more than ever true that a picture was worth more than
ten thousand words, and a profusion of pictures with sound were
beamed into the nation's living rooms each evening. The twenty-
one-inch version was of the horror of a hotter war: battle action
throughout the country in early and mid-February; the house-to-
house fighting in Hue, which continued nearly all of February; the
shelling, ground probes and forever "imminent" annihilation of the
surrounded Marines at Khe Sanh, which went on through March;
the ruined and smoking cities, visited one by one via the camera
eye, revealing different nuances of destitution and destruction
every time.

There is much dispute about the effect of such war footage on
the opinions of Americans, one school holding that it deadens
public sensitivity to slaughter and another that it heightens public
revulsion and strips away the false glory of war. Some believe that
television battle tends to deepen whatever tendencies and convictions are brought to the set by the viewer—that he selects those
facets which reinforce his opinions and rejects or reinterprets those
which refute his initial views. Still another theory is in vogue
among interpreters of audience reaction in the research staffs of
television networks—that the impact of war reporting is less than
meets the eye because most of the public does not associate television news with real life. The mass public, in this view, watches

television for escape and accepts Hollywood drama and comedy as a heightened version of reality—but considers news programs, which are remote from daily experience, to be a fiction staged for the viewers' benefit. The extraordinary thing, in view of the importance of the topic, is that there has been so little serious, disinterested study of what the newscast viewers perceive and what they believe, how much they consider reel and how much real, and what conclusions they draw from their impressions.

In the case of the Tet Offensive, a few facts about the television coverage are known and something of the impact can be reasonably inferred.

First, it is known that the audience of the network evening news programs was very high during this period. According to the Nielsen rating service, whose nationwide samples are the accepted standard for audience measurement, the *CBS Evening News* with Walter Cronkite was seen in 20.3 per cent of the television homes in early February, and the NBC *Huntley-Brinkley Report* in 18.8 per cent of the television homes, on the average, in late January and early February. Applied to the estimated 56 million television homes in the nation at that time, the Nielsen ratings indicate that television sets in 11.2 million homes were tuned to Walter Cronkite and 10.5 million to Huntley-Brinkley. This was close to the record peak of viewership for both programs. The ratings slowly dwindled through late February and March.

Second, it has been established that film reports from Vietnam were a daily staple of the evening news shows during the two-month period. In addition to the large Saigon bureaus—each with a staff of twenty to thirty people, about half American and half Vietnamese—the networks sent extra correspondents and camera crews to cover the big story, and used communications satellites from Japan to transmit filmed reports. ABC News employed the Pacific satellite three times in the first few days, NBC News six times, and CBS News ten times. Most of the film reports portrayed battle action or devastation and many of them showed the military or political position of the United States in grave danger. Roughly one fourth of all the film reports on the evening news programs during the two-month period were devoted to portraying the plight of the U. S. Marines at Khe Sanh. Because most correspondents and camera crews did not remain at Khe Sanh for more than a day or two—there was a waiting list of journalists requesting visits to the combat base—a sense of continuity about the battle was difficult and the sense of danger and impending disaster was more intense among the newsmen than among the Marines who were accustomed to living under the enemy's guns.

Public opinion polls taken at the time registered wide swings in public attitudes about the war. The initial hawkishness of early February was followed by a wave of pessimism about the military position of the United States in late February. In mid-March the pollsters detected a decline in hawkishness to a level below that of any previous time and an upsurge in the number of Americans favoring a reduction in the U.S. military effort in Vietnam. For the first time, self-professed hawks in the public at large were outnumbered by self-professed doves. Gallup poll data suggests that nearly one person in every five switched from the hawk to the dove position between early February and the middle of March. It can be reasonably inferred that the television reflection of events was an important factor in the swing of public sentiment.

PETER KALISHER, CBS NEWS (at Khe Sanh): What do you think of the chances of this place getting overrun?

CORPORAL CHARLES MARTIN: I would not say, sir. I know every night we stand a 100 per cent watch all night long and try to get sleep during the day time and working parties also when the fog comes in. Everybody is supposed to be in their bunkers up there [at an outpost] just like they do here, filling sandbags and digging trenches deeper. That's about all there is to it.

KALISHER: Well, thanks, and I hope you have a good R & R.

MARTIN: I'd like to say Hi to Mom back there at home. I know she's worried about me and [we've] had no mail or resupplies, so to Momma back there in Greenfield, Tennessee, hello Momma.

CBS Evening News, February 15, 1968

For those with a personal tie to Vietnam, the selective reality of the television film reports was more depressing than living in the war zone would have been. In Vietnam, most places were quiet most of the time, a fact which tended to be obscured in the reporting of dramatic conflict. Televison recorded the high points of drama and tension, compressed them into two-minute or three-minute stories containing the most electrifying moments, transmitted them around the world and broadcast them nationwide to the American public. It is probable that a regular viewer of the Cronkite or Huntley-Brinkley shows saw more infantry action over a longer span of days than most of the American troops who were in Vietnam during the Tet Offensive.

Some viewers were reported to have turned off the set when confronted with episodes of battle action, and it is probable that some tuned out mentally and emotionally. There is no evidence that most of the public tuned out, however, and it is clear that those who were particularly troubled about the war reacted strongly to the scenes unrolling on their home screens. An American Foreign Service officer who had served in Hue watched from his living room as the bombers pounded the houses and old walls of the town he'd known and loved. Tears began welling up in his eyes and before long he noticed they were streaming down his cheeks. Similar films made a great impression on Tran Ngoc Chau, a Vietnamese national assemblyman and former province chief, who was on a visit to Washington and staying at the home of an American government official. Chau found the twenty-one-inch reality "horrifying, cruel and tragic" beyond anything in his long and rich experience in the war. He wrote in his diary: "Over more than 20 years, I had seen many bodies with fresh blood of Asians, whites, blacks, by the dozens, the hundreds. Sometimes I hated it, sometimes I was moved, but never before was I so moved, did I hate it so much, was I so fed up as at this time, even though the scene was only brought by television." Because of what he saw on the television screen, he was unable to sleep at night.

"I feel we are just getting to the real agony, like going through psychoanalysis we are now entering the darkness of ourselves," wrote Joseph B. Cumming, the Atlanta bureau chief of *Newsweek*, a native Georgian who had mixed emotions about the war. "We could have done no less than be where we are today in Vietnam. Remember the thunder of the right in the early '60's that a third of the world is Commie and nothing could be won back for freedom. So we had no choice (fate would say) than to fight, to show that we had guts, and step by step we arrived at today when the question of guts is too literally, revoltingly displayed in the bloody entrails on TV, in magazines. We have proven in ourselves the old epic values of courage and fortitude.

"But now war has become obscene. Every man's death does now diminish me, I think people are beginning to realize. I don't believe anyone feels a glow about casualty figures of the enemy as we did in World War II. 'War isn't fun any more,' said my son as we began to discuss the above notion last night. Every bullet hurts us on television; we suffer too realistically. My wife, hesitant up to now between 'get out' and 'stick it out' views, was prompted by the bombing of the village [Ben Tre] to write to Senator Russell. She has never done that before and felt afterwards that it was a stupid letter." Cumming reported that a majority of his acquaintances seemed to avoid the topic of the war. He himself was still persuaded intellectually of the strategic and international justification for continuing the fight. "Yet I feel a pounding deep in the marrow that we are all facing an even greater facing of ourselves," he wrote.

Deeply impressed by the evidence of Communist military power and projecting what the Communists might do next, some sophisticated and articulate Americans began to speak of the possibility of defeat. An official working on Secretary McNamara's secret Pentagon history of the war, writing from long experience in Vietnam and with a high opinion of Communist capabilities, predicted in memoranda to his superiors that a "red tide" of Viet Cong influence would flow through the countryside right up to the edges of the province and district towns and over the edges of some of them. He predicted that by April the South Vietnamese armed forces would be experiencing mass desertions, total apathy, deals with the Viet Cong and high-level or group defections, and that among the civilian populace there would be chaotic demonstrations, new NLF-inspired "fronts," a soaring black market and widespread attempts to leave the country. The only way to stave this off, he said, was dramatic United States action demonstrating a total commitment to hurt the Viet Cong badly. Perhaps 400,000 additional American troops would be needed to reverse the tide.

Professor John Kenneth Galbraith, the national chairman of Americans for Democratic Action and a former Ambassador to India, had declared prior to Tet that the United States was involved in a nearly hopeless struggle with indigenous nationalism in Vietnam, and urged American withdrawal. In mid-February he predicted, "Anything that can effectively be called a government" in South Vietnam would disappear within a few weeks, and he forecast "the effective dissolution of the South Vietnamese Army" in the same brief span. In Saigon Ambassador Ellsworth Bunker, Galbraith's Vermont neighbor, read the predictions and sent word to his old friend that he was wrong. It wouldn't happen, Bunker said, and invited Galbraith to come and see.

Joseph Evans, chief editorial writer for *The Wall Street Journal,* a quiet, conservative, reticent man who works in a book-lined office down the street from the New York Stock Exchange, had long been dubious about the war. Evans and the *Journal* had taken a hardheaded approach befitting the financial capital—approval of the purposes of the war, skepticism about its practicality and the progress being claimed, and strong opposition to both the sweeping pretensions of global purpose by the Johnson administration and the sweeping condemnation on moral grounds by some of the critics. Now, in the wake of Tet, the influential paper began speaking out more strongly in a series of editorials raising the "fundamental question" of South Vietnam's determination and the "insistent question" of whether the war was worth its tremendous cost to the United States.

In keeping with his accustomed practice of fifteen years as editorial writer for the *Journal,* Evans had no special briefings or inside sources to tell him what to think about the events in Asia, and there were no editorial board meetings to debate the problems and their solutions. His was the time-honored editorial tradition—one man thinking and reacting, on the basis of a scholarly background and the information available to any reasonably diligent citizen. Evans read the papers and listened to the radio and television reports, and he sat in his office, put a sheet of paper in the typewriter and wrote. This process of one man thinking about the turn in the war and the prospects for the future resulted on February 23 in a gloomy editorial titled "The Logic of the Battlefield," which bluntly expressed what many other people were also thinking.

"We think the American people should be getting ready to accept, if they haven't already, the prospect that the whole Vietnam effort may be doomed, that it may be falling apart beneath our feet," the editorial began. The *Journal* reasoned that North Vietnam's manpower and its allies' weapons could keep the war going indefinitely, while the South Vietnamese government appeared ineffective even in the heart of its own cities. The fault was not U.S. will or valor, but something lacking in Vietnam itself, the editorial said. Furthermore, the American military effort seemed to be destroying the country in order to "save" it.

"We believe the Administration is duty-bound to recognize that no battle and no war is worth any price, no matter how ruinous, and that in the case of Vietnam it may be failing for the simple reason that the whole place and cause is collapsing from within.

"Conceivably all this is wrong; conceivably the Communists are on the brink of defeat and genuine peace talks are about to begin. It doesn't look that way, and as long as it doesn't everyone had better be prepared for the bitter taste of a defeat beyond America's power to prevent," the *Journal* declared.

After the North Vietnamese peace maneuvers early in January, the stock market had jumped to new highs, but the collapse of those hopes and the Tet Offensive sent stock prices sliding. Against that background, Evans' editorial in the influential financial daily was accepted as a clear sign by many people that Wall Street had turned against the war.

One of the many newspapers to reprint the editorial was the daily in Salina, Kansas, just west of Abilene in the flat and fertile land in the center of the nation. Editor Austin Whitley of the Salina *Journal* agreed completely, and he added a comment of his own. "It is hard for a proud nation such as this to admit defeat and error. But if we are a moral, honorable nation with a sense of duty and destiny, we cannot go on killing and destroying to perpetuate an error and deepen it. . . . The only honorable and wise course is to de-escalate the war and prepare to withdraw from Vietnam in the best order and with the fewest casualties possible. If President Johnson finds his personal pride too stubborn, the weight of defeat too grievous, then Congress should reassert its Constitutional authority, if necessary remove him from office, and put this nation back on the paths of peace." The editorial was placed in the Congressional Record, along with a tribute to its author, by Bob Dole of Kansas, whose withered arm was evidence of battle wounds in World War II and who later would become Richard Nixon's Republican National Chairman.

During the Success Offensive the previous November, Gallup poll interviewers had asked the public, "Just your impression, do you think the U.S. and its allies are losing ground in Vietnam, standing still, or making progress?" The last week in February Gallup asked the same question again. The results:

	NOV. 1967	FEB. 1968
Losing	8%	23%
Standing still	33	38
Making progress	50	33
No opinion	9	6

The Passage of Walter Cronkite

The government might lie and the generals exaggerate, the news might be unreal, the pictures posed or the sound dubbed in, but the kindly, businesslike man with the modest mustache was a person to be trusted. Five nights a week at 6:30 P.M. Walter Cronkite put his well-worn pipe aside, picked up his script and recounted the day's events to a nation of viewers. Whenever there was a national crisis or a superstory, when a presidential candidate was nominated, a President elected or a President killed, when astronauts hurtled into space or returned to earth, Cronkite was there on the home screen, presiding over the telling of it all.

The *CBS Evening News* with Walter Cronkite was the first and most consistently popular half-hour nightly news program. President John F. Kennedy inaugurated the first edition on September 2, 1963, with an exclusive interview which expressed his displeasure at President Diem of South Vietnam, and played a role in triggering Diem's fall from power. Then and thereafter the Cronkite show was a coveted forum for politicians and statesmen and others seeking the eye and ear of the country. Pollster John Kraft, hired by the AFL-CIO Committee on Political Education to investigate the opinions of rank-and-file union members in January 1967, reported that 47 per cent of those polled said television was their most reliable source of information, and by far the most popular television newsman was Walter Cronkite. Chairman John Bailey of the Democratic National Committee took a close look at labor's findings, and told a Democratic Party conference, "What I'm afraid this means is that by a mere inflection of his deep baritone voice or by a lifting of his well-known bushy eyebrows, Cronkite might well change the vote of thousands of people around the country. . . . With the vast power he obviously holds over the nationwide audience, I hope he never becomes too unhappy with my candidate."

In early 1968 Cronkite became mightily unhappy with Chairman Bailey's candidate, Lyndon B. Johnson, and with the candidate's war. After Tet, Cronkite went to Vietnam to see what was going on and returned with a judgment against the war. Coming from a man who rarely expressed strong opinions on any controversial subject, the impact of this conversion was substantial. Presidential Press Secretary George Christian said later that when Walter Cronkite announced his post-Tet stand, "the shock waves rolled through the government." They rolled through the American body politic as well.

Cronkite had been an illustrious United Press correspondent in World War II, landing with the Allied troops in North Africa and at Normandy beachhead, dropping from the skies with the 101st Airborne Division into Holland, participating in the first B-17 mission over Germany, breaking out of the German encirclement at Bastogne with the Third Army in the Battle of the Bulge. He was anything but a pacifist and like most Americans he was inclined to approve the purposes and policies of the United States in its postwar struggle with the Communist world.

Cronkite is one of the few television news stars with long experience as a newspaper or wire service reporter, and he thinks of himself as a reporter rather than a pundit. When the Vietnam War began to heat up in mid-1965, he went out to take a look and was impressed with the extent and purpose of the American undertaking. He was told that for the first time, the United States was trying to build a nation while fighting a war on foreign soil, instead of fighting and destroying and rebuilding later as in World War II. In view of the positive objective, Cronkite could understand and accept the limits on the use of American military power, and he had no doubt that this was a long-term engagement. After returning from Vietnam he praised "the courageous decision that Communism's advance must be stopped in Asia and that guerrilla war as a means to a political end must be finally discouraged." In the introduction to a book of CBS broadcasts about the nature of the war, Cronkite declared, "this is the meaning of our commitment in Southeast Asia—a commitment not for this year or next year but, more likely, for a generation. This is the way it must be if we are to fulfill our pledge to ourselves and to others to stop Communist aggression wherever it raises its head."

In 1966 and 1967 he was troubled by reports from the war zone and by the growing opposition to the war among colleagues he respected. He was reassured by government officials, who said the reporters were wrong. He was called to Washington three times by President Johnson for private meetings and briefed by senior officials. "They kept saying there was light at the end of the tunnel," he recalled later—but somehow it never dawned. Cronkite was shocked by the first news of the Tet Offensive and fed up with the contradiction between the official reports and the news reports from the war zone. He decided he owed it to the people who watched him every night to find out what was going on and let

Index is on Page 3
Classified advertising starts on Page 41

The WASHINGTON DAILY News

CITY EDITION

WEDNESDAY, JANUARY 31, 1968

Second Class Postage at Washington, D. C.
Published Daily Except Sunday

Weather
Consider-ably cloudy, high 58. Tonite, cloudy, upper 30s. Tomor-row, cloudy, high mid 50s, chance of rain.

7¢

WAR HITS SAIGON

Parts of Embattled City Evacuated to Permit Bombing VC Strongholds; GI Clerks, Patients Join the Fight

(Pages 2 and 3)

An Editorial

Where Were We? Where ARE We?

THE bold, massive communist attacks yesterday on Saigon, eight provincial capitals and 30 or 40 lesser towns were a shocker.

American Military Police having to land on the roof of the U.S. Embassy in Saigon under fire to recapture the supposedly "guerilla-proof" building from communists who held it six hours: That scene alone is enough to force the Johnson Administration to stamp invalid its optimistic assessment the war is showing "continual and steady progress."

The half-dozen jets destroyed at Da-Nang, the sacking of part of Pleiku, the seizure of the radio station and railroad terminal at Qui Nhon, the street fighting in Nha Trang, Bao Me Thout, Tuy Hoa, Kontum, Hoi An and Saigon itself are all evidence of the vulnerability of those supposedly "secure" areas to Viet Cong assaults, when and where our foes want to strike.

There is small consolation in the fact that the communists took advantage of the relaxation and revelry of the lunar New Year's "truce" to strike. The sneak attack and the broken word are the rule in this war, not the exception. The fact is intelligence and defense were both wretched, and the responsibility rests primarily with the South Vietnamese charged with security.

Once again American hopes and ex-

pectations in Vietnam have been blacked by our costly bad habit of underestimating our enemy and overestimating our ally.

The success of the co-ordinated communist attacks becomes all the more stunning in the light of Gen. Westmoreland's Jan. 17 prediction of stepped-up communist activity around Tet "Tet is an emotional time when family and friends gather. Any display of strength by the Viet Cong would benefit the enemy both psychologically and politically."

Particularly, the communists' New Year's Day triumph gives them a tremendous boost on the eve of the coming key battle of Khe Sanh. Doubtless their success y e s t e r d a y especially in the Highlands and Central Coast cities, was due in part to the thinning out of U.S. troops in preparation for that battle.

If this kind of Viet Cong attack had occurred as the war's opener — a sort of Pearl Harbor — it would be easier to understand, and more forgivable. But the war has now been raging five years, and the U.S. has been on the scene in strength for nearly three years. Is this the sort of defeat we should be suffering when we have a half-million men on the ground, and our top officials, flown back from Saigon six months ago, tell us things are going well?

"We have turned the corner..."
—Gen. Westmoreland

BASSET

U.S. EMBASSY SAIGON

24.

25, 26. The pictures that shocked the world: South Vietnamese police chief Nguyen Ngoc Loan executing a Viet Cong suspect on the street in Saigon. The Associated Press photo above was blazoned across America's front pages. The NBC-Television film footage at right, originally in color, brought the cruelty of the war into the nation's living rooms.

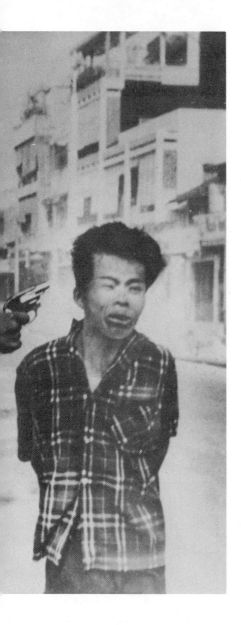

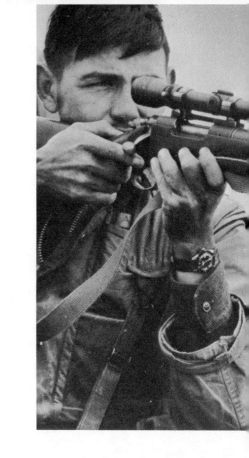

27, 28. American commanders doggedly believed the Tet attacks were a feint, intended to draw attention from a massive impending assault on the Khe Sanh Combat Base. Above, a Marine sniper team at Khe Sanh. Left, a photo from the other side of the lines shows North Vietnamese troops storming an American position.

29. In a classic photo of the war, U. S. Marines emerge from the battle of Hue.

30, 31. Young men at war in Hue: a North Vietnamese trooper (above) and a U. S. Marine.

32. The battle took its toll on Hue's gracious streets and the monumental towers of its Citadel.

33. This American gun position in Hue guarded the shattered Quoc Hoc High School, the alma mater of such illustrious Vietnamese as Ho Chi Minh, Ngo Dinh Diem, Pham Van Dong and Vo Nguyen Giap.

34, 35. Among the victims of the massacre at Hue were Father Buu Dong, whose funeral is shown above, and Dr. and Mrs. Horst Gunther Krainick, shown at a Tet party just before the attack.

36, 37. An elder lights incense for 428 men and boys of Hue. Their skulls and bones were discovered in the jungle creek bed where Communists had killed them. Below, a wife weeps for her husband, whose body was found in a mass grave.

The Gallup Report

— THE MOST ACCURATE POLLING RECORD IN AMERICA —

Down 7 Points Since January

Johnson's Popularity Rating

By George Gallup

PRINCETON, N. J., Feb. 17 — The percentage of Americans who approve of President Johnson's performance in office has declined sharply following the recent Vietcong offensive in South Vietnam.

In the latest survey conducted Feb. 5 through 7, 41 per cent of the nation's adults say they approve of the way the President is handling his overall job, down 7 points from an early January survey.

This marks one of the sharpest declines over a period of three to four weeks yet recorded for President Johnson, and ends a three-month upward trend in his popularity rating.

Approval of the President's handling of his job climbed from 38 per cent in October (his low point) to 48 per cent in January. Increased optimism over the course of the war was an important factor in this rise.

LBJ Job Rating: 1966-1968

38.

39. Thumbs up in Vietnam. By the time he returned from his inspection tour, Walter Cronkite had turned thumbs down on the war.

Shows Sharp Decline

Equal proportions of "hawks" and "doves," for example, support a plan to turn the Vietnam problem over to the UN and to abide by its decision, as well as a plan to encourage the South Vietnamese to take the major role in the fighting with a phased withdrawal of American troops.

Over 300 Localities
Covered in Survey

To determine the public's rating of the President's performance, the following question was asked of 1503 adults in more than 300 sampling points across the nation:

ed (who have been found to be more "hawkish" than those with less formal education) and among men (who are more "hawkish" than women).

Popularity Decline
Often Temporary

Evidence collected over the last three decades shows that sudden drops in the President's popularity are often temporary. These findings also reveal that a Chief Executive is frequently the victim of circumstances.

President Truman's popularity dipped sharply after widespread labor strikes (12 points over a two-month period) in the fall of 1946.

A recession in the spring of 1958

40. Sen. Eugene McCarthy's unexpectedly strong showing against President Johnson in the New Hampshire primary was attributed to an antiwar surge after Tet.

ork Times

LATE CITY EDITION

SECTION ONE

40 CENTS

WESTMORELAND REQUESTS 206,000 MORE MEN, STIRRING DEBATE IN ADMINISTRATION

Enemy Hammers 7 Sites On the Outskirts of Saigon

FORCE NOW 510,000

Some in Defense and State Departments Oppose Increase

Warsaw Students Battle Policemen 2d Day in a Row

Saigon General Says Foe Has Replaced His Losses

41, 42, 43. When the New York *Times* disclosed that the military wanted an immense troop increase in Vietnam, there was consternation in government and among the American people. President Johnson's closest advisers, shown above in a January photo, told him the nation would not support a wider war. One of the "Wise Old Men," former Secretary of State Dean Acheson (right), gave his unvarnished opinion that the war was a failure.

44. The decision makers: Lyndon Johnson, William Westmoreland, Clark Clifford, Dean Rusk.

45. The end of the line: backed to the wall by public opinion, the President prepared the speech that would halt the bombing—and his own political career.

them know point-blank in a personal report. After consulting the CBS front office, he flew to Vietnam. An hour-long CBS News special was planned for his return.

He arrived in Saigon February 11 and saw the deserted streets and smelled the stench of garbage, which reminded him of home—in New York, a garbage strike was under way. After dinner, somebody took him to the Caravelle roof to watch the war five or six miles away. After a tour of Saigon and interviews with the U.S. generals, he reported in a filmed summary from the Caravelle roof that "the Viet Cong suffered a military defeat" but that on the other hand, "the Tet Offensive has widened a credibility gap which exists here too between what the people are told and what they see about them."

The veteran war reporter toured the country to inspect the damage, and was astounded to hear military officers and pacification advisers claim victory for the government side. Cronkite flew to Hue while the battle there still raged. He donned a steel helmet and a flak jacket, slept on the floor of a Vietnamese doctor's house commandeered as a press center, ate C rations, sucked his pipe and took a close look at the Marines at war. The more he looked, the more it reminded him of Europe in World War II, and the less relevant it seemed to the original conception of a struggle to build a nation.

He spent an evening at nearby Phu Bai, where General Creighton Abrams, the U.S. deputy commander, had established a forward headquarters. Cronkite had known him as Colonel Abrams of the 4th Armored Division at the Battle of the Bulge, and the two men were at ease with one another. In the commentator's presence, Abrams and other senior officers sat around a fireplace in the general's quarters at Phu Bai mulling the deployment of task forces and separate battalions, speaking of pincers movements, blocking forces and air strikes and drawing blue arrows on the battle maps. "It was sickening to me," Cronkite recalled later. "They were talking strategy and tactics with no consideration of the bigger job of pacifying and restoring the country. This had come to be total war, not a counterinsurgency or an effort to get the North Vietnamese out so we could support the indigenous effort. This was a World War II battlefield. The ideas I had talked about in 1965 were gone."

On the long plane ride home Cronkite and his producer, Ernest Leiser, worked on the details of their news special, reviewing the footage which had been shot and the conclusions which had been reached. After arriving in New York, they were disturbed to learn that the planned one-hour show had been shaved to thirty minutes. Cronkite and Leiser argued in vain for more time. When they were unsuccessful, they decided to use the best of their leftover footage for a series of short, hard-hitting reports on the regular 6:30 P.M. *Evening News.*

The half-hour CBS News special, *Report from Vietnam by Walter Cronkite,* went on the air at 10 P.M. on February 27, and according to the Nielsen rating service, some nine million Americans were watching. Beginning with an introductory statement amid the rubble of a blasted street in Saigon, Cronkite showed films of the action and its aftermath and alternating interviews with optimistic and pessimistic Vietnamese and Americans. After the final station break, he confronted the camera from behind a desk in New York to deliver his personal assessment, labeled as such.

Who won and who lost in the great Tet Offensive against the cities? I'm not sure. The Viet Cong did not win by a knockout, but neither did we. The referees of history may make it a draw. Another standoff may be coming in the big battle expected south of the Demilitarized Zone. Khe Sanh could well fall with a terrible loss of American lives, prestige and morale, and this is a tragedy of our stubbornness there: but the bastion is no longer a key to the rest of the northern regions and it is doubtful that the American forces can be defeated across the breadth of the DMZ with any substantial loss of ground. Another standoff. On the political front, past performance gives no confidence that the Vietnamese government can cope with its problems, now compounded by the attack on the cities. It may not fall, it may hold on, but probably won't show the dynamic qualities demanded of this young nation. Another standoff.

. . . It seems now more certain than ever that the bloody experience of Vietnam is to end in a stalemate. This summer's almost certain standoff will either end in real give-and-take negotiations or terrible escalation; and for every means we have to escalate, the enemy can match us, and that applies to invasion of the North, the use of nuclear weapons, or the mere commitment of one hundred or two hundred or three hundred thousand more American troops to the battle. And with each escalation, the world comes close to the brink of cosmic disaster.

To say that we are closer to victory today is to believe, in the face of the evidence, the optimists who have been wrong in the past. To suggest we are on the edge of defeat is to yield to unreasonable pessimism. To say that we are mired in stalemate seems the only realistic, yet unsatisfactory, conclusion.

On the off chance that military and political analysts are right, in the next months we must test the enemy's intentions in case this is indeed his last big gasp before negotiations. But it is increasingly clear to this reporter that the only rational way out then will be to negotiate, not as victors but as an honorable people who lived up to their pledge to defend democracy, and did the best they could.

This is Walter Cronkite. Good night.

The Viet Cong Camp

Across the battle lines, a parallel wave of dismay was sweeping the Communist camp. The "once-in-a-thousand-years opportunity" had come, the trumpet had sounded, the troops had rushed forward into the cities and—after fierce and bloody fighting, the survivors pulled back, the battle continued and the war went on.

Where was the glorious victory? What happened to the seething revolutionary masses, rising up against the foreigners and lackeys who enslaved them? Where were the legions of puppet troops who were ready to turn their guns around and join the revolution? What happened to Commander Tran and Comrade Van and all the others who marched forward into battle and did not come back? Where was the light at the end of the tunnel?

Battle-scarred survivors slowly made their way back to jungle bases they hoped they would never see again. Whispered conversations spread the news of what had been seen and heard in the cities, the names of well-known fighters and commanders who had been killed and those who were missing. There was a pervasive air of sorrow and disappointment, rivaling in intensity the elation and expectation of a few weeks before.

A message arrived from Uncle Ho arguing that "the more we are approaching victory, the more we have to undergo hardships and difficulties." Like the commanders on the American side, Ho argued that the enemy was making a violent last-gasp effort, "writhing madly" like a wounded beast before the moment of death. The leaders reiterated Ho's seven "musts":

> The will must be very resolute.
> Plans must be very meticulous.
> Control must be very careful.
> Actions must be very well coordinated.
> Execution must be very thorough.
> Cadres must be very exemplary.
> Secrecy must be strictly safeguarded.

Reading between the lines, Liberation soldiers decided that even in the North, the Tet Offensive had not been considered a success. Instead of victory, they had been presented with the requirement for greater efforts.

Colonel Tran Van Dac, whose enthusiasm had been laced with misgivings ever since he learned of the plan in the July 1967 meeting at "R," summoned political officers from the Saigon suburbs to a post-mortem in a civilian house near the city. He confronted them one at a time with searching questions: What went wrong inside the city? Had the Liberation soldiers fought badly, or had the situation been falsely reported ahead of time? Why did the people not provide food and supplies and voluntary labor as expected? Why were the inner-city units incapable of evacuating the wounded soldiers as planned?

The lower-ranking Party officials said many problems had arisen: military forces did not penetrate the city in sufficient numbers; they lacked effective coordination; the people wanted to cooperate, but were afraid the revolution would not last and they would be left to suffer for their sympathies when government troops returned. Colonel Dac was not satisfied with these answers. The lack of popular support, the heavy casualties, the failure to make greater gains despite extensive preparation raised grave doubt in his mind about the movement and its future. He wired "R" that the people's attitudes should be reevaluated, and he began reevaluating his own convictions. A few weeks later he slipped away from the bodyguards and defected to the government side.

No hard information is available on the state of mind of the senior political and military leaders of the Vietnamese Communist movement. In view of their sophistication and experience, it seems unlikely that they expected to seize and hold the cities with the force expended, though it is likely they had hoped for greater gains. Whatever their private thoughts, their immediate tasks were to assess the impact, shore up morale and keep up the pressure against the Americans and puppets.

On the night of January 31, less than twenty-four hours after the main attacks in Saigon, Hue and other major cities, the Current Affairs Committee of the Central Office for South Vietnam (COSVN) and the Military Affairs Committee of the People's Liberation Armed Forces met in a jungle headquarters to assess the first returns. Their estimate was completed the following day and issued to subordinate commands as a COSVN circular. Allowing for Communist jargon and morale-building rhetoric, the verdict was sober and realistic:

> We have launched simultaneous and timely attacks on almost all towns and cities, district seats, sectors and military bases as planned. Generally speaking, achievements were scored at the first step. . . . Within a short period of time we succeeded in paralyzing the puppet

government administration from central to local echelons, and confusing the U.S. command channels. . . .

It enables us to make greater efforts to continue to attack and to be resolute to attain the final victory. We have beaten the enemy accurately and successfully. The Current Affairs Committee and Military Affairs Committee warmly cite and commend all cadre, party and group members of all echelons, within and outside the Army, and all cadre and troops within the armed forces.

However, we still have the following shortcomings and weaknesses:

We failed to seize a number of primary objectives and to completely destroy mobile and defensive units of the enemy. We also failed to hold the occupied areas.

In the political field we failed to motivate the people to stage uprisings and break the enemy's oppressive control. . . .

Since we did not succeed in completely destroying many of his mobile and defensive units at the very start, nor did we closely coordinate offensive with uprising and troop proselyting, the enemy still resisted and his units were not disrupted into pieces.

If in the coming days we fail to quickly motivate a large and powerful force of the masses to stand up against the enemy in time and if we fail to concentrate our armed forces to attack them continuously, they will certainly recover their strength and counterattack us more strongly. Not only will it limit our victories, it will create new difficulties for us.

Having said this, the High Command addressed the ticklish problem of success around the corner. They had waved the banner of victory to instill fighting spirit on the eve of the battle, and now they had to tuck it away without conceding that the colors were faded or false.

To this end, the February 1 COSVN circular began a redefinition of the General Offensive and General Uprising. No longer was it the short, sweet, violent phase that would end the war. "It is imperative to be fully aware of the fact that the General

Offensive and General Uprising, which are directed against an enemy with an army of more than 1,200,000 stubborn, reactionary and well-equipped soldiers, is a strategic offensive phase covering many military campaigns and uprisings," COSVN announced. There had been errors and shortcomings and "we cannot yet, therefore, achieve total victory in a short period." The preparations for a total victory must be made during a three- or four-month period, the Command declared.

The regional and provincial Party committees dutifully passed the bad news down. "It is of primary importance to realize that this phase of the General Offensive is not a battle that lasts some two or three days," said the February 6 resolution of the Party committee in Can Tho in the Mekong delta. "We must thoroughly realize that this phase of attacks may last three or four months in the big cities and towns."

Like the mechanical rabbit at the dog races, the final phase of the General Offensive and General Uprising continued to stay just beyond the grasp of the Liberation troops, no matter how hard they tried to race ahead to reach it. Over the months to come, official circulars and other documents would refer to "the second offensive phase" of the General Offensive, then "the third phase of the General Offensive" and the "General Offensive and Uprising Campaigns." Ultimately COSVN would speak of "the erroneous conception of the transitional nature of the General Offensive and Uprising" and attack the idea of unnamed people that it was "a one-blow affair." Instead of a mighty battle which would shake the earth and win the war, the General Offensive and General Uprising had slowly become a long-term project with an unlimited number of phases and campaigns and a terminal date nowhere in sight.

The most pressing problem for the Communist Command immediately after the Tet Offensive began was the question of new orders to the attack forces in or near the cities. Many of the units had been unable to reach their designated objectives, others had held them briefly but were forced to let them go. In nearly every case, elements of the initial attack forces remained engaged in battle in the cities or on the outskirts in the first few days.

Moreover, most of the North Vietnamese main force units had never been committed. They remained poised for the order to follow the initial assaults.

The first directive was the circular which emerged from the January 31–February 1 meeting of the political and military commands in the South. Translated from the Communist verbiage, the order added up to this: First, any strong points which have been seized should be defended against counterattack. Second, units already committed in "disputed areas" should attack again, three or four times if necessary, in an attempt to carry out original orders. Third, in regard to American troops, rely primarily on artillery, mortars and sappers for continuing harassment and attack only if there is a well-prepared attack plan. "We must not use main force units to attack them in order to avoid casualties."

On February 18 the Communist Command launched "second wave" attacks throughout the country, employing artillery and mortars and only a few ground attacks. This kept up the war of nerves at low cost and low risk and made new headlines around the world. The action quickly subsided, however, without making any basic change in the situation. By now, most of the units which were initially committed had suffered heavy losses; new elements sent to the Saigon outskirts had met strong resistance; in Hue, the Right Bank had been lost to the U. S. Marines and the hard-pressed units in the Citadel had asked permission to withdraw. The time had come to commit new forces or roll back.

The Standing Committee of COSVN and the Military Affairs Committee of the People's Liberation Armed Forces met again on February 21. The decision was to disengage from advanced and risky positions near the cities and reduce the level of attack to small unit encounters or harassment by fire. "In regard to cities and towns, it is advisable not to conduct large-scale attacks in the immediate future because the enemy defense therein has been strengthened recently," the COSVN order said. Instead, "special action teams, sapper/guerrilla units and artillery shellings [should] harass the enemy every night to keep him under constant stress." The political cadres within the cities should sharpen the political struggles through "appropriate means," but major risks were not recommended. "Large-scale demonstrations are not necessary."

The decision recognized the realities and amounted to a lowering of the sights. The forces relieved of major efforts in and around the cities were to concentrate now on the countryside, to "liberate" rural areas, interdict food supplies going to the urban centers and ambush rescue teams if they should be dispatched. The withdrawal to the countryside also permitted the troops to recuperate, regroup and refit.

All the COSVN orders and Party resolutions were secret; neither the specifics nor the drift of the orders was publicly announced on the Communist side. The United States Command did not learn of these decisions until later.

Even if the U. S. Command had obtained the orders as they were issued, it might have chosen to ignore them. On February 21, when the Communist Command was lowering its sights, the American Command was engaged in preparing a request for a massive increase in U.S. military power in South Vietnam. One of the principal justifications for the troop request was the stated need to stop Communist onslaughts believed to be looming just ahead.

The Wheeler Mission

General Earle Wheeler, Chairman of the Joint Chiefs of Staff, had sent word to Saigon on February 18 that he would arrive on a visit five days later to assess the Tet Offensive and discuss the future of the war. In a message to Westmoreland, Wheeler said the U. S. Government faced hard questions in the near future. As was common in the dialogue between Washington and its Vietnam field commander, the questions raised in Wheeler's cable gave a broad hint of the desired answer—a request for large numbers of new troops for the war.

Westmoreland was not surprised at the impending visit or the drift of Wheeler's thinking. In the negotiations earlier in the month, Washington—not the field commander—had taken the initiative in suggesting that more troops might be needed, and after Westmoreland took the hint, Washington had supplied 10,500 additional men faster than the field commander dared to hope. By the middle of February it was evident to Westmoreland and others in Saigon that official Washington as well as the American public had been shaken to an unprecedented degree by the Tet Offensive—to a far greater degree, in fact, than most Americans in Vietnam. It seemed likely even from afar that time was running out on the previous war policies. It might be true, as Lyndon Johnson had said, that nearly every option open to the government was worse than the course being followed—but the course being followed had reached a dead end with the American public. Change was essential.

Westmoreland was informed that discussions of a change in United States strategy had been taking place at the White House, and there were hints in both public speeches and private communications from home that some people were inclined to strike back hard. This would require additional resources and new orders, and Westmoreland was quick to make a bid for them. "This has been a limited war with limited objectives, fought with limited means and programmed for the utilization of limited resources," he argued. "This was a feasible position on the assumption that the enemy was to fight a protracted war. We are now in a new ball game where we face a determined, highly disciplined enemy, fully mobilized to achieve a quick victory." From the vantage point of U.S. headquarters, this seemed a golden opportunity to meet force with force, boldness with boldness, and thus break out of the long war of attrition and its unpalatable restrictions imposed from above.

Since the very beginning of large-scale American involvement in 1965, the American military had lacked the full resources and authority that it desired to do the job in Indochina. The Joint Chiefs wanted a larger expeditionary force than President Johnson and Secretary of Defense McNamara would allow (the standard estimate of the requirement was 750,000 men). They wanted to extend the war on the ground into Laos in order to cut the Communist supply and infiltration routes, and to cross the border of Cambodia in order to attack Communist base areas and cut off the supply flow from the port of Sihanoukville. They wanted to bomb and/or mine the port of Haiphong in North Vietnam to attack military supplies at their source. Some of them wanted to invade Vietnam across the demilitarized zone in the area of Vinh—to put the Communists on the defensive and relieve the pressure on South Vietnam. All these proposals, except the last, had been formally and repeatedly urged by the Joint Chiefs and all had been rejected by higher authority. Now, in the wake of the Tet attacks, the leaders of the American military effort sensed that the final moment of decision was at hand. Out of the disorder, confusion and destruction in South Vietnam, the public anger and dismay in the United States, the potential dangers and crises abroad and at home, the replacement of Robert McNamara by Clark Clifford as Secretary of Defense—out of all this might come a determination to push ahead with strength and daring and a commitment to the war as a conflict to be won.

Except for the intensified air strikes against the North, all the initiatives favored by the Joint Chiefs would require large numbers of additional U.S. ground troops, and any substantial troop augmentation would require national mobilization—a reserve call-up, war taxes, nearly inevitable price and wage restraints and other public sacrifices. National mobilization was the critical underlying issue, even more important in the military view than the additional resources it would provide. Once accepted, mobilization could generate a "win the war" psychology at home under which nearly any military initiative would be possible, instead of a "tolerate the war" psychology under which nearly anything was difficult.

In the summer of 1965 the Joint Chiefs of Staff, in this case joined by McNamara, had recommended national mobilization at the beginning of the U.S. troop build-up—but the President rejected the idea. Such a national emergency would have meant the end of the Great Society legislative program, which was just beginning to roll through Congress, and the other domestic advances nearest Lyndon Johnson's heart. He chose to take the country to war ever so slowly, to slip in the needle an inch at a time so the patient would never jump. This came close to the nub of the American difficulty in a limited war: Johnson, the U. S. Government and the bulk of the U.S. public wanted to win the war in Vietnam, but they did not want it all that much. Success in

Vietnam was a desirable goal among many other goals at home and abroad. It was not an overriding goal, but one to pursue at limited cost and limited risk. By 1968 resources committed had become too great to be sustained in a long war but not large enough to bring the war to a swift conclusion. The Joint Chiefs believed the war effort should become the major national goal through mobilization and then it could be won. Many of the civilian leaders, on the other hand, thought just the opposite—that the war had grown too large and too long, that it was not worth the existing cost to the nation and that the proper course was to turn it down, not turn it up.

In the Joint Chiefs' view, a new decision about national resources was imperative. On the eve of Tet, 40 per cent of the Army's combat-ready divisions, 50 per cent of the Marine Corps divisions, 50 per cent of the Air Forces' attack aircraft and 30 per cent of the Navy's ships were tied down in fighting or supporting the war. Much of the rest of America's non-nuclear might was assigned to semipermanent missions elsewhere, leaving a thin margin of uncommitted "strategic reserve" force available in case of trouble. Of the Army's five strategic reserve divisions, only one—the 82nd Airborne Division—was considered combat-ready on short notice, and Westmoreland's post-Tet reinforcement had taken one of its three brigades. "We are down to two thirds of one division for the defense of this country," complained a member of the Senate Armed Services Committee.

Coincident with the planning toward a large Vietnam troop increase, the Joint Chiefs began considering the need for large numbers of additional forces elsewhere. After the Blue House raid and the *Pueblo* incident in Korea, the North Koreans were speaking publicly of a general war and the South Koreans were speaking publicly of withdrawing their forces from Vietnam unless they received more United States aid to protect their homeland. The Joint Chiefs discussed the possibility that more Americans might be needed in General Charles Bonesteel's Korean Command. There were rumbles of trouble in Berlin—General Lyman Lemnitzer's European Command might need more troops. The Middle East war on the previous June had stoked passions in that region. All this added to the Joint Chiefs' case that national mobilization, so often rejected by the civilian leaders in the past, was now urgent. General Wheeler, presenting the view of the Joint Chiefs, informed the President that if a serious emergency arose in the existing circumstances, he might not be able to act.

Lyndon Johnson was impressed and concerned about both Vietnam and the broader picture. Shortly after ordering the dispatch of the 10,500 additional troops as reinforcements for Westmoreland on Lincoln's Birthday, he authorized Wheeler to travel to Saigon to survey and evalute Westmoreland's needs for the future. The question Johnson sent to Westmoreland, "What do you want?" was an open invitation to put anything and everything on the table. Decisions about mobilization and a new strategy in the war would await Wheeler's return.

General Wheeler and his party, including Deputy Assistant Secretary of State Philip Habib and Major General William E. DePuy, Special Assistant to the Joint Chief of Staff for Counterinsurgency, arrived in Saigon on February 23. The military men immediately plunged into a round of talks with Westmoreland and his staff on two overlapping subjects—the current war situation and plans for the future.

In the formal briefing at Westmoreland's headquarters, the familiar dichotomy between success and need quickly arose. The U. S. Command's briefing reported that the Communists had lost more than 40,000 men killed, that at least 3000 had been captured and perhaps 5000 had been disabled or had died of wounds since the Tet campaign began three weeks before. This reported toll was both enormous and satisfying, but it left an obvious problem: if it were accurate, the Communist attack force of 67,000 had been two thirds destroyed, thus leaving little justification for the dispatch of additional American troops. Obviously, something had to be done —either the body count estimate would have to be reduced, a step which would be highly embarrassing in view of press charges that the estimates were padded, or somehow the total strength of the attack force would have to be raised.

The solution was ingenious. U. S. Command intelligence was

asked, What was the magnitude of the attack force, including forces committed which were not in the Communist order of battle? It took the hint. In addition to the known Communist maneuver force estimated at 67,000, there were also guerrillas, combat support, infrastructure support and newly impressed recruits. Nobody had any idea how many of these people were involved in the battle, but all the "unknowns" together might possibly increase the attack force by as much as 10 to 25 per cent, the U. S. Command guessed. Wheeler's staff took the highest guess —25 per cent—and applied it to the previous estimate of 67,000. Thus, the total attack force was raised to 84,000, and under this reasoning the enemy had nearly half of it left.

In truth, this guess was probably as good or as bad as any. Though Westmoreland's headquarters at one point actually listed the attack force as 67,305—as if they had all filed through a turnstile someplace—nobody on the U.S. side had any more than a guess about total North Vietnamese and Viet Cong strength and losses in the Tet Offensive. It is probable that even the Communist Command had no precise figures.[1]

The next problem was whether to base the troop request on the needs of the present or the plans for the future. Given the initial optimism of Westmoreland and the U. S. Government about the Tet Offensive, it was inconsistent now to claim that many more American soldiers were needed to ward off the foe. On the other hand, given the political objections at home to widening the war, the need for security in planning any future operations into Laos, Cambodia or North Vietnam and the fact that war critics in government were leaking damaging information to the press in

[1] The practice of assigning definite numbers to pure guesses—such as Communist strength figures, Communist casualty estimates and hamlet security evaluations—has been among the greatest absurdities of a peculiar war. Originally intended to place the conduct of the war on a "scientific" and thus manageable basis and to enhance public confidence, the practice ultimately consumed vast amounts of time and energy, led to misconceptions and erroneous conclusions about the war and was a major factor in the erosion of public confidence. Nevertheless, the "numbers game" may be now so deeply imbedded in military, press and public thinking that it will persist in future military conflicts.

Washington, it seemed even riskier to base a troop request on plans for a dramatic and forceful new strategy throughout Indochina.

Westmoreland recalled later that the troop request was designed to address a spectrum of contingencies from the worst to the best. If the Communists did well and the government did poorly, he would need additional troops as reinforcements. On the other hand, if all went well he could use the additional troops and air power for greater pressure on the Communists throughout South Vietnam, accelerated bombing in the North, ground operations to cut the Ho Chi Minh trail in Laos, raids on Communist border sanctuaries in Laos and Cambodia and/or amphibious and joint amphibious/air mobile operations into North Vietnam.

In its conclusions at the time, however, the Wheeler mission had much to say about existing perils as a justification for a larger force, and little to say about future opportunities. In buttressing the cause of a troop build-up, it produced one of the most somber assessments of the Vietnam situation ever to emerge from U. S. Command headquarters in Saigon.

The enemy had been hurt—so the story went—but he had taken over the countryside and was recruiting freely (something the U.S. military had steadfastly denied until then). His recovery was likely to be rapid. The enemy's Tet attacks had failed, as reported earlier, but it was a very near thing. In a dozen places, defeat was averted only by the quick action of U.S. troops. Enemy morale was down, but his indoctrination system could buoy it up. Enemy determination was unshaken.

On the government side, the Vietnamese armed forces were said to have fought well, but they were now hunkered down in the cities. Wheeler had personally appealed to Thieu and Ky to get the troops out of Saigon into the perimeter to pursue the Communists, but the Vietnamese leaders insisted that their government could not survive another major attack on Saigon. Nobody could tell how well the South Vietnamese Army would fight in the future. The Vietnamese government had not collapsed, but its effectiveness had suffered. As for the U. S. Command, it had been forced to deploy 50 per cent of all U.S. maneuver battalions to

I Corps, stripping the rest of the country of adequate reserves. If the Communists should attack in Khe Sanh, Hue and other points in northern I Corps, at the same time attack in the central highlands and also attack Saigon while keeping the pressure on the rest of the country—in other words, if it were Tet all over again and even bigger—the U. S. Command would be hard pressed to meet all the threats. Or so the story went.

The final problem of the Wheeler mission was the number of additional troops to request, and the answer was not entirely made in Saigon. Before Wheeler left Washington, the Pentagon's Joint Staff had produced estimates of the manpower which could be quickly dispatched to Vietnam, and that which could become available if the reserves were mobilized, draft calls were increased and terms of service were lengthened. Wheeler had some definite ideas about what Westmoreland might need. So did an unnamed "top military authority" in intimate contact with the Joint Chiefs who told *U. S. News & World Report* prior to Wheeler's departure: "What is required is another 200,000 American combat troops, immediately; which means mobilizing the National Guard and certain other reserve forces, both Army and Marines."

In Saigon Wheeler and Westmoreland and their staff aides compared notes, speaking mainly in terms of combat "packages" of infantry, ground support and air power. Wheeler had the Joint Chiefs of Staff studies; Westmoreland had the results of the studies he had ordered on February 7. The agreed request was for three divisions of ground troops with support elements (171,000 men); fifteen Air Force and Marine fighter squadrons (22,000 men) and additional Navy support (13,000 men). These forces were to be supplied in three increments—107,000 men almost immediately (by May 1), 43,000 more to be prepared for deployment by September 1, and the remaining 56,000 men to be prepared for deployment by the end of 1968. The actual total was 206,756 additional American troops.

General Wheeler and his party took off for Washington on February 25 in an Air Force KC-135 jet transport converted for executive travel. Wheeler and his counterinsurgency aide, General

DePuy, sat at a table in the aft section of the big jet writing and editing the report, feeding it by pages to an Army sergeant hunched over an electric typewriter. Wheeler stopped in Honolulu to consult Admiral U. S. Grant Sharp, the Commander in Chief Pacific, whose headquarters was theoretically in the chain of command between Saigon and Washington. While Wheeler continued his trip home, his report was cabled from Honolulu with copies to Secretary of Defense McNamara, Secretary of State Rusk, presidential assistant Rostow and CIA director Helms.

McNamara, with only three days remaining before turning the job over to Clark Clifford, received the action copy. Deeply opposed to the dispatch of additional U.S. troops, McNamara was nonetheless brisk and businesslike as usual in his handling of the troop request. He summoned the three civilian service secretaries and their uniformed chief of staff to consider Wheeler's report. McNamara expressed the opinion that the proposed troop increase would cost $10 billion the first year, but he did not otherwise indicate his own thinking. The trained executive and administrator was at work.

The Secretary of the Navy, Paul Ignatius, asked how it could be that the Communist forces had just suffered a great defeat and enormous losses, and yet Westmoreland needed another hundred thousand men within sixty days. General Harold K. Johnson, Army Chief of Staff, replied that the Viet Cong were actively recruiting in the countryside and might soon regain their strength. Unconvinced, Ignatius repeated that this urgent and massive troop request did not square with the reports of a great American victory at Tet. Townsend Hoopes, the Undersecretary of the Air Force (sitting in for Secretary Harold Brown, who was out of town), was shocked and dismayed. He had concluded long before that military victory in Vietnam was not feasible and that the United States should sharply limit its involvement. In the meeting on the troop request, Hoopes expressed the view that the additional fighter squadrons would jam the airfields in Vietnam and present a perfect target for Viet Cong gunners. He could not believe so many more planes could be needed.

At the end of the meeting, McNamara asked each service to

study the Wheeler-Westmoreland request in the light of three possibilities: full compliance, partial compliance and non-compliance with a decision to seek alternative military and political strategies in Vietnam. For the purpose of moving ahead, he requested that the studies concentrate initially on the possibility that the troop request be met in full.

The Fatal Leak

Considering the implications for the nation and the condition of American public opinion, the request for 206,000 additional troops was a state secret of immense sensitivity. If approved, it would have great impact on the lives and fortunes of many thousands of reservists, potential draftees and men already in service; it would affect American taxpayers, businessmen and financiers as well as the families of those involved in military service; and it would add a new scale and dimension to the American risks in the war. It was a sensation among those high in government who were critical of the war. Some of them considered it a scandalous grab for power by the military, and they were certain that any augmentation of American manpower would be matched by the North Vietnamese and, if necessary, the Chinese. There was no illusion that the ground war would remain within the boundaries of South Vietnam. If the troop request were granted, the Vietnam War seemed likely to widen into a broader conflict on the Asian mainland. In view of the consequences of the troop request and the opposition to it, the danger was great that the plan would leak. So it did, and at the moment of greatest impact on the American political process.

The way Lyndon Johnson told it later, "a trusted public servant—I think in the Pentagon—called in some reporters, or a newspaper reporter from a very well-known newspaper, and said, 'You want to do a little peeping here? Peep here. Johnson's going to order 206,000 men out there. He's going to ruin the country. He's going to do it in the guise of protecting our men but it's going to be just terrible for us, and us fellows set against the war, we really ought to stop this.' And so the headline is, 'Johnson Implementing Request of Westmoreland for 206,000'—and these men are going."

With his long experience with the art of the leak and the deliberate plant, and his Byzantine habits of mind, Johnson left no room in his version for luck, enterprise or journalistic diligence. In fact, the most resounding Washington scoop of many years began with a tip from an unhappy insider, but the tip was only a piece of the puzzle. The reporters had to work for the rest of it.

On Friday night, March 1, Edwin L. Dale, national economics reporter in the Washington bureau of the New York *Times*, attended a party at the home of Representative William Moorhead, a Pennsylvania Democrat who had been a classmate of Dale's at Yale University. Among the other guests was Townsend Hoopes, the Undersecretary of the Air Force who had attended the troop-request meeting called by McNamara earlier in the week. Hoopes had been a student at Yale at the same time as the congressman and the reporter and knew them both during college days.

Dale was well aware of the widespread rumors and hints of a major new United States commitment to the war and, as the *Times'* resident expert on the international monetary system, he was much concerned about the effect of such a move on the stability of the dollar. Doubts about the ability of the United States to solve its problems were causing overseas investors to trade their dollars for gold, and Dale was certain that a new troop commitment would bring on a far more serious run on gold stocks and endanger the international monetary system. "I know you guys in the Pentagon have other things than gold on your mind these days," said the *Times* reporter to the Undersecretary of the Air Force, "but you had better consider this in what you are doing. If you throw many more troops into the war, you're going to have something really grave on your hands in the gold markets."

Much to Dale's surprise, Hoopes agreed, and added that he and some others in the Pentagon were opposed to the dispatch of large numbers of additional troops to the war. Hoopes did not know the views of Clark Clifford, who had been sworn in that very day as Secretary of Defense, but he did know that a number of

Pentagon officials favored a reassessment of the entire war policy. Hoopes did not say how many additional troops were being requested by Wheeler and Westmoreland.

On Monday morning Dale reported his social conversation to the chiefs of the *Times'* Washington bureau and several of his bureau colleagues. Everyone felt it was highly significant that dissent was creeping into high reaches of the Pentagon and that some people—at least as high as Undersecretary of the Air Force—were balking at the military request for additional troops. Robert Phelps, the deputy bureau chief and managing editor of the Washington bureau, was particularly impressed. He convinced the editors in New York to detach Hedrick Smith from the State Department beat and Neil Sheehan from the Pentagon to work full time on the story.

Armed with their knowledge of Washington, the rumors of a large new troop request and Hoopes' tip about high-level dissent, the reporters began making their rounds. One of the first stops was Capitol Hill, which is the best source of highly sensitive news in Washington. The government sooner or later must tell lawmakers of its plans, for the people's representatives have the power to grant or withhold money and authority which are necessary to action. A few key legislators had already been informed of the troop request, and they were very unenthusiastic. On Tuesday, after a single day of inquiry, Smith heard the figure of 206,000 from a staff man at the Capitol and confirmed that an internal debate was taking place within the Johnson administration. The impression on the Hill was that the decision had been made to approve the request, but that the big troop hike would be announced piecemeal over many months. At this point, the *Times* reporters were certain this was a big story but felt they still lacked sufficient confirmation and detail.

Wednesday and Thursday Smith and Sheehan made it their business to see nearly everybody they knew or could think of who might have access to the details of the policy dispute in government. They saw officials in their offices for formal appointments, took contacts to lunch and telephoned others at their homes after working hours. They tried the old journalistic technique of seeming to know more than they really did, casually mentioning the 206,000 figure and the high-level disagreements and watching for squirming, a blink of the eye or other reaction on the part of the interviewee. By Thursday night the two reporters had confirmed the troop number in three places and obtained a better whiff of the dissension. Friday morning they began writing, making last-minute calls to check details. The *Times* editors decided to hold it out of the Saturday paper, waiting for the greater impact and readership of the Sunday edition.

Right up to the end, Smith and Sheehan and others in the Washington bureau felt the big news was the dissension at high levels over the war, but the editors in New York insisted that the big news was the figure of 206,000. The fact that this was not a rounded number—not 200,000 or even 205,000 but precisely 206,000 —added greatly to its authenticity and impact. The first paragraph, or lead, of the story was rewritten to conform to New York's wishes.

The Sunday paper of March 10, 1968, carried the story under a three-column headline at the top right-hand corner of page one, the traditional spot for the most important story of the day. It read:

WESTMORELAND REQUESTS
206,000 MORE MEN, STIRRING
DEBATE IN ADMINISTRATION

Force Now 510,000

Some in Defense and State
Departments Oppose Increase

The following dispatch was written by Hedrick
Smith and Neil Sheehan, assisted by Max
Frankel and Edwin L. Dale, Jr.

Special to the New York Times

WASHINGTON, March 9—Gen. William C. Westmoreland has asked for 206,000 more American troops for Vietnam, and the request has touched off a divisive internal debate within high levels of the Johnson Administration.

A number of sub-Cabinet civilian officials in the Defense Department, supported by some senior officials in the State Department, have argued against General Westmoreland's plea for a 40 per cent increase in his forces "to regain the initiative" from the enemy.

There are now about 510,000 American troops in Vietnam, and the President has authorized a level of 525,000 by next fall. Many of the civilian officials are arguing that there should be no increase beyond the movement of troops now under way. . . .

The first edition of the Sunday *Times* rolled off the presses on West Forty-third Street in New York City in mid-evening Saturday, and following routine practice the Associated Press photographed page one and transmitted it via wirephoto circuits to other newspapers throughout the country. Many of them consider *Times* treatment of national and international news to be a definitive judgment on what is important. When a situation hits page one of the *Times*, it is a certified national event; when a story leads that paper on Sunday morning, it is an event of major magnitude.

Editors, publishers and Washington bureau chiefs of the nation's leading newspapers, Vice-President Humphrey, members of the Cabinet, the Joint Chiefs of Staff, congressional leaders, leading state governors and key foreign ambassadors had gathered that Saturday night at the Statler-Hilton in Washington for the annual dinner of the Gridiron Club, the nearest thing to a general meeting of the American journalistic and governmental establishment. During the course of the dinner Benjamin Bradlee, executive editor of the Washington *Post*, received from his office a copy of the wirephoto of the Sunday *Times'* first page. Bradlee summoned Chalmers Roberts, the *Post's* senior national affairs reporter, and the two men buttonholed high officials in the ballroom, demanding confirmation or comment. The evasive and non-committal answers indicated to Bradlee and Roberts that the story was right. By now, word of the *Times* account had swept the room. Editors began ducking out to instruct their papers around the country to reprint the news from the New York Times News Service, which circulated major stories of the day to 183 client papers in the United

States, or from the Associated Press account of the *Times* article. The Washington *Post,* which was fast becoming the *Times'* major competitor for national impact, quickly put together a catch-up story by foreign affairs reporter Murrey Marder. It led the late editions of the Sunday *Post* under the headline "206,000 GI Call Hinted."

"This is one of the great ones," said an editor to Hedrick Smith a few hours after the story broke. Smith felt he had done a good week's work. For once, the press had let the public know about the government's plans while there was still time for the political system to react effectively. That had not happened often in this war.

For those already shaken by events in Asia, the request for 206,000 additional troops was the final confirmation that the Tet Offensive had been a tremendous Communist victory, that the war was a stalemate or worse and that the government had been lying about conditions in the field. If so many Communists were killed and their army routed, why were 206,000 more Americans required? If this 206,000 were dispatched to the war, what assurance was there that another 206,000 would not be needed then, and another group after that? Was there no alternative to the bottomless pit of an endless war on the mainland of Asia?

Because the *Times* account was precise and accurate, the government was in a poor position to deny it. Too many high officials knew it was true. The White House did not confirm the story, nor did it seek to explain it. Presidential Press Secretary George Christian said "no specific request" had reached the desk of the President, a weak and legalistic response which satisfied nobody. Under President Johnson, no proposal was an official request until he deemed it to be an official request—that is, until and unless he decided it would be approved.

Over the same weekend that the *Times* disclosed the proposal for 206,000 more troops, two more influential media voices were in the process of speaking out strongly on the nation's course and prospects in Vietnam. Both NBC News and *Newsweek* magazine were appalled at the idea of sending large numbers of additional men to the war.

Ever since Walter Cronkite had expressed his views on CBS in late February, NBC staff members were yearning to follow suit. Chet Huntley and David Brinkley were divided, Huntley tending to be a hawk and Brinkley a dove, which made it awkward for the NBC evening news anchor men to follow Cronkite's example. In early March NBC News correspondent Frank McGee proposed to review the Tet Offensive and render judgment on the war, and the network scheduled an hour-long special edition of the *Frank Mc-Gee Sunday Report* for that purpose on March 10.

McGee had been among the first television news "stars" to express serious doubts about the war. More than two years before, as anchor man for the NBC News special *Vietnam: December 1965*, McGee strongly criticized the Johnson administration's lack of candor. Moreover, he declared that if no compelling reason could be given why Vietnam was vital to the United States, "then this country should be mindful that our older partners, France and Britain, have found it possible to retire with honor from untenable positions."[2] McGee refined and deepened his conclusions about the war in 1967 during a month-long stay with an infantry platoon in Vietnam for an NBC documentary, *Same Mud, Same Blood.*

Now McGee and his staff had compiled nearly an hour of the dramatic highlights of Tet, beginning with flashbacks of rosy assurances by Johnson, McNamara and Westmoreland, and followed by battles and commentaries on battles at the American

[2] *Vietnam: December 1965* was also memorable for its broadcast introduction, a classic of its type. The show opened with McGee standing in front of the Main Station Recruiting Center in Chicago speaking of the young men who reported for duty there, and then shifted to GIs in the Ia Drang Valley, while McGee's voice told of the men who had died there. Then the titles of the program were shown and a network announcer's voice said:

"In another special report, NBC News presents *Vietnam: December 1965,* a definitive report of the war in Vietnam and the reactions in the United States, brought to you by Dial, the most effective deodorant soap you can buy. Aren't you glad you use Dial? Don't you wish everybody did? And by new Magic Spray Sizing, made to help you iron the shortcut way, new Magic Spray Sizing; and by Armour Star canned meats, the good meat meals that come in a can. Now, here is NBC News correspondent Frank McGee."

Embassy, the Presidential Palace, Tan Son Nhut Air Base, the Saigon suburbs, the An Quang Pagoda [General Loan shot the Viet Cong suspect on-camera again], Cholon, Ban Me Thuot, My Tho, Hue, Con Thien [September 1967], Dak to [November 1967] and Khe Sanh, with time out for a station break and commercials by Scope mouthwash, Duncan Hines cake mix, L&M Golden 100s, Wilkinson Sword razor blades and "Trimline" Bell telephones.

McGee began the special report with the news of the *Times* report that 206,000 additional troops had been requested, and he returned to the troop request in the final summation. "It is a new war in Vietnam," he began. "The enemy now has the initiative; he has dramatically enlarged the area of combat; he has newer, more sophisticated weapons; he has improved communications; he has changed his tactics; and he is fighting under a centralized command." Furthermore, the Vietnamese government and countryside had been dealt serious blows. "The grand objective—the building of a free nation—is not nearer, but further from realization. In short, the war, as the Administration has defined it, is being lost," McGee declared.

"Today, if published reports are correct, the President has before him a request for another two hundred thousand men to help restore the situation to what it was. This has brought warnings the enemy will match any new force we put into the field. All that would be changed would be the capacity for destruction. . . . Laying aside all other arguments, the time is at hand when we must decide whether it is futile to destroy Vietnam in the effort to save it," McGee concluded.

Newsweek's presses were rolling that weekend with an unusual editorial statement, complete with a battle action cover ("The Agony of Khe Sanh"); eight pages of color photographs from Khe Sanh by free-lance photographer Robert Ellison, who was killed in a plane crash at the combat base; and eight pages of gloomy text. "In recent weeks, the Communist Tet Offensive has created a crisis of decision in Vietnam—and produced something of a consensus at *Newsweek*," the editors said in a "Top of the Week" foreword. "The time had come for a searching reappraisal of the U.S. role. *Newsweek*'s editors recognize they do not have all the answers, but they believe that a responsible journal must at least explore alternatives to the Vietnam cul de sac."

The search for answers began with Everett Martin, who had been the magazine's bureau chief in Saigon for two years until he was hounded, threatened and finally ousted by the Thieu regime just before Tet. His offense had been to write a signed article in *Newsweek* belittling South Vietnam's theoretical "sovereignty" and suggesting that the way to win the war was to force the South Vietnamese to really fight. Back in the U.S.A., Martin met with the *Newsweek* brass about March 1. He expressed the view that the editors had been "taken in" by some of the Washington optimism prior to Tet, and recommended that the magazine now speak out. *Time* and *Life* had been edging toward opposition to the war policies of the Johnson administration; *The Wall Street Journal* and Walter Cronkite had taken stands. One of the editors expressed the fear that *Newsweek* would be the last to speak instead of being the pacesetter it aspired to be.

Martin turned out a fifteen-page memorandum of his views, and the editors sent requests for reassessment to the bureaus in Saigon and Washington. The *Newsweek* writers in Saigon, pessimistic about the war, sent strong replies. Members of the Washington bureau, affected by the steady-on-course utterances of the President, felt the editors in New York had become hysterical about the war and attempted to tone down the editorial statement.

As published on March 11, the *Newsweek* reappraisal declared that the Tet Offensive had exposed "the utter inadequacy" of the Johnson administration's war policies and underlined "one grim truth"—that "the war cannot be won by military means without tearing apart the whole fabric of [United States] national life and international relations." The magazine referred to the reports that 206,000 additional American troops were being sought for the war, but declared that the Communists had been able to match additional U.S. forces before, and probably would be able to do so in the future. "Accordingly, unless it is prepared to indulge in the ultimate, horrifying escalation—the use of nuclear weapons—it now appears that the U.S. must accept the fact that it will never be able to achieve decisive military superiority in Vietnam," it said.

Newsweek recommended that the United States should stop its large-scale search-and-destroy operations, withdraw its major forces from the sparsely populated borders of South Vietnam, particularly from the area just below the demilitarized zone, and seek to strike "a balance between its military forces and those of the enemy." At the same time, the United States should work for a political settlement of the war, including a withdrawal of American troops over a period of years. The magazine recognized that its recommendations were risky and cheerless. It declared, however, that "a strategy of more of the same is no longer tolerable."

New Hampshire

On March 12, amid national uproar over the request for 206,000 additional troops and a general depression over the situation in Vietnam, the citizens of New Hampshire went to their polling places in their cities, villages and hamlets. There were in the United States at that time roughly 120,000,000 citizens of voting age, of whom 82,000,000 were registered to vote. On Election Day in November some 73,000,000 would turn out. But in New Hampshire, in the changeable clime between winter and spring, less than 56,000 citizens voting in the Democratic presidential primary had a mighty effect on the politics and policy of the nation in 1968.

The New Hampshire primary is traditionally the first in each presidential election year, and while the state is far from typical of the country, this test of voter sentiment is keenly watched by politicians, press and the politically minded segment of the American electorate. In 1952, in the midst of the Korean War, Senator Estes Kefauver of Tennessee won the New Hampshire Democratic presidential primary over President Harry S. Truman on March 11. Eighteen days later, on March 29, Truman withdrew from the race.

In 1968 President Lyndon Johnson had not formally announced his candidacy for reelection and thus his name was not on the ballot, but his political managers and Democratic regulars in

New Hampshire and Washington had organized a write-in campaign on his behalf. The challenger was Senator Eugene McCarthy of Minnesota, who began with a chilly reception from the voters amid the snows of January. After Tet, the McCarthy campaign began to gather rapid momentum.

In January private polls taken for the Johnson-controlled Democratic National Committee estimated McCarthy's strength at 8 to 11 per cent of the Democratic primary vote; a month later, after the Tet Offensive, McCarthy had climbed to 18 per cent in the same polls. By early March Governor John King, a leader in the President's campaign, predicted privately that McCarthy might win as much as 25 to 28 per cent of the vote.

The newspaper ads on behalf of the President declared that "the Communists in Vietnam are watching the New Hampshire primary" and urged the voters to spurn "weakness and indecision" by voting for Johnson. The radio announcements said: "Support the loyal men who do serve this country by writing in the name of President Johnson on your ballot."

McCarthy's radio ads blared back: "Think now how you would feel to wake up Wednesday morning to find out that Gene McCarthy had won the New Hampshire primary—to find that New Hampshire had changed the course of American politics."

On election day, March 12, 23,280 New Hampshire citizens marked their Democratic ballots for Eugene McCarthy, winning him 42.2 per cent of the Democratic vote. He also received a substantial write-in in the Republican primary. When the two votes were added together, McCarthy's total vote in New Hampshire was only 330 short of the total vote of the incumbent President.

There was considerable controversy over the causes of the McCarthy surge in New Hampshire. Many analysts at the time interpreted McCarthy's strength as a "peace vote," a sign that the public was repelled by the war and seeking a way out. Others pointed to the fact that in New Hampshire, McCarthy campaigned more against Lyndon Johnson than against the war, arguing that the vote was anti-Johnson more than anti-war. Scholars at the University of Michigan asserted later on the basis of polls that the McCarthy vote was more "hawk" than "dove"—that "the only common denominator seems to have been a deep dissatisfaction with the Johnson administration."

Whatever the causes of the vote, there is little dispute about the impact. Just as the Tet Offensive was a mighty blow to the prestige of Lyndon Johnson's Vietnam policies, so the New Hampshire primary was a mighty blow to his political prestige. Neither his Vietnam policy nor his political power would ever recover.

CHAPTER VIII

Turnaround

"There must be no weakening of the will that would encourage the enemy or would prolong the bloody conflict. Peace will come of that response, of our unshakable and our untiring resolve, and only of that. The peace of Asia and the peace of America will turn on it. I do not believe that we will ever buckle.

"I believe that every American will answer now for his future and the future of his children. I believe he will say, 'I did not retreat when the going got rough. I did not fall back when the enemy advanced and things got tough, when the terrorists attacked, when the cities were stormed, the villages assaulted and the people massacred.'"

—Lyndon B. Johnson
February 27, 1968

"We are prepared to move immediately toward peace through negotiations. So tonight, in the hope that this action will lead to early talks, I am taking the first step to de-escalate the conflict. We are reducing—substantially reducing—the present level of hostilities, and we are doing so unilaterally and at once."

—Lyndon B. Johnson
March 31, 1968

WHEN March began, the United States Government was considering the augmentation of its 510,000-man expeditionary force in Vietnam by 206,000 more men; the removal of existing geographic limits on the war, spreading the ground battle into Laos and Cambodia and perhaps North Vietnam; and the lifting of remaining restraints on the aerial bombardment of Hanoi, Haiphong and other strategic targets. When March ended, all these proposals had been rejected, General William Westmoreland had been reassigned to the Pentagon, President Lyndon Johnson had announced his retirement from politics and the United States had halted the bombing of most of North Vietnam, the first step toward deescalation and ultimate disengagement from the war.

The policy turnabout of March 1968 has already become one of the most controversial episodes in modern American history, having been described from different vantage points, with different heroes and villains, different moments of conflict and resolution. In spite of, and to some extent because of, the efforts of various participants to describe and justify their roles, many questions are likely to be contested for a long time. It is impossible to provide a definitive judgment on the mental processes of the President or the relative influence of his various counselors, and, in any case, concentration on such matters might well obscure other realities of great importance. For the fundamental decision of February and March was made outside the government. Large segments of the American public and particularly the non-governmental elite of businessmen, lawyers, bankers, editors and publishers and the like, the influential leaders of "private opinion" in the United States, had lost confidence in the war. These people had approved and then tolerated the ever growing commitment of American troops and re- sources to South Vietnam, but time and events had strained their patience to the breaking point. After Tet, the promise of success had faded, the sense of futility and frustration had grown. The country would not go deeper into the quagmire without a clear and believable vision of success.

In a parliamentary system such as that of Great Britain, the government would have fallen and a new group of leaders, com- mitted to new policies, would have come to power. The American presidential system, with its fixed terms of office, works in other ways. In this case, the process seems to have been a form of po- litical osmosis by which public imperative penetrated the inner membrane of the decision-making cell of the American govern- ment. The President and his circle were confronted with some- thing akin to a national veto on the indefinite continuation or further enlargement of the United States involvement in the war in Vietnam. With all due respect to Lyndon Johnson, Clark Clifford, Dean Rusk and the others who took part in the governmental decision-making of March 1968, the number of sustainable courses of action was very limited.

At daybreak on February 28 General Earle Wheeler flew into Andrews Air Force Base on the last leg of his trip from Vietnam and came directly to the White House through the rain. The President and his senior counselors joined him at breakfast, in a mood to match the gray of the day. Wheeler's report had been received by cable two days before, and the day before, the counselors had met over lunch at the State Department for a deeply gloomy review, a "crepe-hanging session," one of them called it. That lunch had been dominated by the parting anguish of Secretary of Defense McNamara, who had spoken against the bombing policy in emo- tional terms and had urged his colleagues to make the most hard- headed possible examination of the new troop request, which he did not favor.

Now, at the White House breakfast on the twenty-eighth, Wheeler presented the gist of his report, and Johnson said it would have to be thoroughly studied. Where would the additional men come from? Would Congress lengthen the terms of service for men now in uniform? If the reserves were called up, would they go to Vietnam or fill spaces at home with little or nothing to do? How much would the additional force cost? Where would the money come from? Johnson set in motion a task force of his senior officials to study the Wheeler report. Clark Clifford, who was to be sworn in as Secretary of Defense on March 1, was designated as its chairman.

Clifford had been a member of the Johnson kitchen cabinet for many months and thus no newcomer to the Vietnam policy counsels, but his metamorphosis from an unofficial outside adviser to an official inside policy maker wrought changes in his perspective, his thinking and his influence. Living as a private lawyer in political Washington, Clifford had maintained a surer sense of the world beyond the White House gate than most of those who had been struggling to make the Vietnam policy work. He had a better grasp of what the public and the American system would accept, and he was more conscious of the domestic realities confronting Lyndon Johnson and his administration in 1968. He had no doubt that Johnson was a candidate for a second full term in the presidency. Perhaps most important of all, Clifford was not personally responsible for the formulation or execution of the previous policies —he had been an outsider, not an official—and thus could judge them coldly and realistically without judging himself. And he did.

At the time of his appointment as Secretary of Defense, nearly everybody was certain he was firmly committed to the war and would stiffen the case for stronger military action. Nearly everybody should have known better. In the Truman days, when Clifford won fame as a White House aide, the journalists thought he was a conservative, the insiders thought him a liberal and the President—who knew him best—saw him as a very smooth, incredibly bright and completely practical young man from Missouri. As he grew older and much richer as a Washington lawyer, he gained a reputation as one of the great power brokers of the city— but then the capital was like that. Those who focused on politics, power and money, who lived by the rise and fall of political leaders, ideas and coalitions as other men lived by the stock market, learned to ride the tides.

In July of 1945 Harry Truman, three months in office as President, prepared to go to Potsdam in the Soviet zone of Germany to meet Churchill and Stalin. Truman decided to take James K. (Jake) Vardaman, his friend and political supporter from Missouri whom he had named Presidential Naval Aide. Vardaman, a reservist who distrusted the career military, was casting around for someone he could trust to mind his office at the White House while he was gone, and he thought of the young Naval Reserve lieutenant named Clark Clifford, who had been the lawyer for his shoe manufacturing company back in St. Louis. Lieutenant Clifford was serving on the West Coast as special assistant to the commanding officer of the Western Sea Frontier, and it was arranged for him to come to the White House on temporary duty.

While Vardaman was gone at Potsdam, Clifford made himself useful doing legal chores for Samuel Rosenman, the overworked White House counsel. After the Potsdam conference, Rosenman requested that the young man remain, and he was reassigned to the White House as Assistant Naval Aide. After Vardaman went on to the Federal Reserve Board, Clifford became Naval Aide, and after the war was over he left the Navy and became Special Counsel to the President. Clifford was at once the youngest, strongest and most politically astute member of the White House inner circle, and he had deep rapport with Truman. One of his least imposing but most sensitive tasks was to line up poker friends for Truman's regular game. Once in a while the list included Lyndon B. Johnson, a young lawmaker who was rising swiftly in Washington under the tutelage of two powerful mentors, Speaker Sam Rayburn and Senator Richard Russell.

Clifford left the White House in 1950 and hung out his law shingle, and his contacts, knowledge and reputation quickly attracted a lucrative practice. He continued to prosper during the Eisenhower years, and in 1960 he was selected by John F. Kennedy as his chief consultant on the presidential transition. After Inauguration Day, Clifford continued in private practice, and additional clients flocked to his door. He was friendly with Lyndon Johnson in a casual way, but not a close friend or political ally.

A day or two after Kennedy was assassinated, the new chief executive summoned Clifford for a long talk about White House and executive branch organization. Having been a legislator nearly all of his political career, Johnson was a neophyte in the practice of executive power. He sensed his deficiencies, knew that Clifford was an old practitioner and trusted him enough to call him. The two men got on well, and the consultation continued. The telephone would ring in Clifford's law office, in sight of the White House, and within a few minutes he'd be in conference with the President about economic policy, difficulties with the steel barons, foreign policy, the choice for Vice-President in 1964 or whatever else happened to be on Johnson's mind. The President offered him the job of Attorney General, but Clifford preferred to maintain his independence and his law practice. He was older than Johnson and had been senior to him in their first relationship in the Truman days. Johnson had not made him, did not own him or control him— and yet he was close. Johnson and Clifford dealt almost as equals, which was unusual, perhaps unique, at the court of LBJ. After leaving office, Johnson said Clifford, along with Abe Fortas, had been consulted on every major decision of his presidency.

The two men spoke often about Vietnam, and Clifford supported the policy and the war. He had been one of the architects of the Truman policy of containing Communism, and the Vietnam effort seemed its logical extension. Clifford had privately opposed the thirty-seven-day bombing halt in late 1965 and early 1966 on the grounds that it would be taken by North Vietnam as "a sign of weakness" and would not work; his accurate prediction seemed to enhance his stature with the President as an adviser on the war. In November of 1967 he strongly advised Johnson against accepting Robert McNamara's secret proposals to halt the bombing, put a lid on American troop strength and prepare the South Vietnamese to take over the war.

As chairman of the President's Foreign Intelligence Advisory Board, Clifford had been briefed on Vietnam matters, and in the late summer of 1967 he and General Maxwell Taylor had been dispatched to Asia to check on the situation in Vietnam and to raise troops from other Asian nations. Clifford said later he was disturbed by the lack of commitment to the war among the Asian allies (though he gave no public hint of this at the time, saying on *Face the Nation* that he returned with "a feeling of enthusiasm . . . renewed dedication . . . encouragement"). For all his acquaintanceship with the war policy, Clifford had not delved deeply into the justifications or the details as a private citizen. He had been up to his hips in the problems, but never completely immersed until he was chosen to succeed McNamara as Secretary of Defense. For the first two weeks after Tet, Clifford was at the White House every day except Sundays to meet with the President and others about the dangerous situation in Asia.

The Clifford task force, formed to study the troop request, met for its introductory session at the Pentagon on the afternoon of February 28, and the group settled down to intensive discussions on March 2, the day after Clifford was sworn in as Secretary of Defense. The new man was an elegant figure with his well-tailored double-breasted suit, his wavy hair, his tie, his French cuffs just so, and his methods were as correct as his appearance. He was the outsider coming in, and he desired explanations of matters everyone else accepted. Many of the explanations were not logical or clear, because the situation had not developed that way, and Clifford persistently asked for an explanation of the explanation. Each question opened the door to other questions, and before long the task force had arrived by the Socratic method at an examination of the principles of the war.

Reflecting the post-Tet White House discussions, the President's apparent apprehensions and the stark assessment in the troop request itself, Clifford's initial question was whether the 206,000 additional men were necessary to prevent a military debacle in the war zone. It quickly became apparent this was not the case. Westmoreland had repeatedly told Washington verbally and in writing that he did not fear defeat.

Why then were the troops required? Wheeler, Rostow and Maxwell Taylor argued that the Tet Offensive provided the great opportunity to smash the enemy in Vietnam, rebuild the Strategic Reserve and mobilize the American people. From the military point of view the time to strike back hard was when the enemy was extended and in the open. But would 206,000 more troops, in addition to the 525,000 men already authorized, be enough to finish the job? There was argument about it; no one could be sure. How could the job be finished? And what was the job in the first place?

The military objectives in Vietnam, which had been spelled out many months earlier and never changed, were extremely ambitious. They were: to extend government domination, direction and control over South Vietnam; to defeat the Viet Cong and North Vietnamese troops inside South Vietnam; to force North Vietnam to withdraw its troops and cease its direction of the war; to deter the Chinese Communists from intervening in the western Pacific and to be prepared to defeat them if they should intervene. While the U. S. Government's political objective of "a free and independent South Vietnam" left room for interpretation and compromise, the military mission called for the utter defeat of the North Vietnamese and Viet Cong forces and the complete victory of the Saigon regime throughout South Vietnam. Given the history of Vietnam, the nature of the conflict, the jungle terrain and the geographic restrictions on the war, it was doubtful that 206,000 more troops or any other number could achieve such a sweeping victory. Deputy Secretary of Defense Paul Nitze, who feared the war was seriously distorting America's worldwide priorities, proposed that the United States should reduce its ends in Vietnam rather than increase its means. Nitze argued that a new strategic guidance should be sent to Westmoreland, limiting his objectives to protection of populated areas and such other missions as could be accomplished without an increase in American military power.

Assistant Secretary of Defense Paul Warnke (in charge of International Security Affairs) and Assistant Secretary Phil Goulding (in charge of Public Affairs) were also opposed to the troop request, and they gave Clifford their views in task force meetings and in private. Warnke argued that both the Tet Offensive and the war had been a stalemate, that neither side could win and that the United States should strive to reduce its casualties and costs and search for a "long haul" strategy which the American people would support. Goulding felt the war had become too lengthy and too costly to be supported by the public. He had two sons nearing military age—one seventeen, the other fifteen—and he was appalled at the thought of sending them and others off to fight in an endless war of attrition.

There was discussion of the public impact of another big troop request. Having just come from private life, Clifford was aware of growing dismay about the war among his friends and acquaintances as well as the public at large, and a "public affairs annex" prepared by Gouding confirmed his apprehensions. A Washington correspondent for the Cleveland *Plain Dealer* prior to joining the government, Goulding pointed out there had been no public preparation for large-scale mobilization and no national emergency to justify it. On the contrary, the government had asserted that the enemy was being beaten and that "we are winning" both the war and the Tet Offensive—and suddenly more than 250,000 reservists would be called to active duty and draft calls would be sharply increased. All those who had clamored for a reserve call-up before and had been told that they were wrong would now be heard from. Johnson and McNamara would be "proved" disastrously wrong in their earlier inaction. The draft calls would bring more massive demonstrations, on and off campuses. The doves would say the President was destroying the country by pouring men and resources into a bottomless pit; the hawks would insist the Administration had no moral right to send more Americans to die unless the bombing were stepped up and the geographical limits on the war removed. Even if the Administration should seek to keep the full extent of its plan secret, announcing its troop deployments in increments, the press and public would not be fooled—and the government would be hard put to deny today what would become obvious tomorrow.

Clifford was increasingly troubled by what he heard. Thinking back on the task force sessions, he recalled, "I could not find out when the war was going to end; I could not find out the manner in which it was going to end; I could not find out whether the new requests for men and equipment were going to be enough, or whether it would take more and, if more, when and how much; I could not find out how soon the South Vietnamese forces would be ready to take over. All I had was the statement, given with too little self-assurance to be comforting, that if we persisted for an indeterminate length of time, the enemy would choose not to go on."

Word of the tenor of the Pentagon deliberations quickly spread to senior U.S. commanders in Asia, who made eleventh-hour bids to buttress the case for a change in strategy. Early in the year West-moreland had authorized planning of Operation El Paso, a drive to cut the Ho Chi Minh trail with several divisions moving west through Khe Sanh into Laos, and on March 2 he urged anew that U.S. action in Laos be undertaken as soon as the necessary forces were available. The next day, he reported that Communist action in Laos was reaching a critical point. One plan under discussion in Saigon called for U.S. forces to intervene through Thailand under the sponsorship of the Southeast Asia Treaty Organization; Westmoreland asked its serious consideration in Washington. At CINCPAC headquarters in Honolulu, Admiral Sharp resurrected Operation Durango, a combined amphibious-air mobile campaign in the southern part of North Vietnam. Though the plan had been recently rejected by the Joint Chiefs, Sharp urged on March 4 that this decision be reversed.

Under existing conditions, any of these invasion plans would have required large numbers of additional troops. They would also have required a political decision to wage a wider war at a time when very many Americans—including some in the secret Pentagon meetings—believed the war was much too big already.

The formal report of the Clifford task force did not reflect the growing doubts by many of its members about the troop re-quest and the war policy. Perhaps because they were too weary to carry the implication of their thinking to its logical conclusion, perhaps because they wished to avoid a head-on clash among themselves which would be extremely unpleasant and doubtless unpalatable to the President, the members of the task force drafted a report giving very tentative approval to the principles of the troop request. It left the President with the flexibility to do nearly anything he might choose to do. Submitted to the White House on March 4, it recommended the immediate dispatch of 22,000 additional men to Vietnam, and a reserve call-up of more than 250,000 men and increased draft calls to fill the gap in the Strategic Reserve. Some 30,000 more men would be sent to South Korea if needed, and naval forces augmented in Korean waters. Total U.S. military strength would be increased by as many as 500,000 men over a period of time. If implemented, the recommendations would send only a few more men to Vietnam right away, but would send many more men later if desired.

The task force report recommended that in selling the public on this reserve call-up, emphasis should be placed on the uncertain picture worldwide and the need to increase and improve the Strategic Reserve. Whether Westmoreland's request for 206,000 men would be met would depend on a week-to-week reexamination of the developing situation in Vietnam, including the performance of the South Vietnamese government, and on a proposed study-in-depth of possible new political and strategic guidelines for the conduct of U.S. military operations in Vietnam. The task force report suggested that United States policy in Vietnam should be studied in the light of the nation's worldwide politico-military strategy—a muffled hint that some of its members thought the war was out of hand.

At the President's request, Clifford and Wheeler secretly sounded out the senior men in Congress, whose backing would be necessary, about national mobilization and a large increase in the American troop commitment in Vietnam. The reaction was strong —and negative. Remembering the bright promises of November, the lawmakers were increasingly critical of Westmoreland's generalship and increasingly disgusted with U.S. strategy in the war. In a series of meetings on Capitol Hill, the leaders of Congress told Clifford and Wheeler that more of the same would not do. Senator Richard Russell of Georgia could not see how the addition of more American troops would solve the Vietnam problem, but he could see that a reserve call-up under existing circumstances would exacerbate the problems at home. Senator John Stennis of Mississippi asked General Wheeler whether the 206,000 additional troops were being sought to pursue the old policy in Vietnam, or new policies in Vietnam. Wheeler replied that no change in policy had been authorized. Stennis said that under those conditions he was "absolutely opposed" to sending large numbers of additional troops. Senator Henry M. Jackson of Washington said a long war of attrition was unacceptable to the American people. He expressed the fear that Vietnam had become a "bottomless pit" for American lives under the war policies being followed. Other senior lawmakers felt the same way.

The attempt to persuade a reluctant Congress to send more troops was complicated by brightening news from Saigon, including well-publicized statements by a "senior military spokesman" that "I don't believe the enemy has any great capacity to assume any general offensive in the near future. He has been hurt and hurt badly. He is tired." The spokesman was in fact Westmoreland himself, speaking "for background" to Saigon newsmen. After some high-level dismay about his ill-timed optimism, the Pentagon on March 8 instructed Westmoreland to be conservative in his public assessments of the situation and to express the view that there would be tough fighting ahead against an enemy whose full resources had not yet been committed. Predictions of victory were forbidden. The Pentagon guidance pointed out that a reserve call-up would be much harder to sell in Congress unless there were a sober and conservative attitude toward the military situation in South Vietnam. Such a conservative public stance would enhance the public image of the government and support Administration policies aimed at pursuing the war to a successful conclusion. In Saigon Westmoreland replied that he would do his best to comply, consistent with intellectual honesty. He gave no more backgrounders during March.

The Clifford task force submitted a split report on the bombing of North Vietnam. Wheeler and the Joint Chiefs urged more intensive bombing of Hanoi and the closing of Haiphong harbor; others recommended a "seasonal step-up" of bombing through the spring within roughly the existing target limits. Little attention had been devoted by the task force to the reduction or cessation of the bombing; this did not seem consistent with the possibility of sending many more American troops. While not foreclosing later changes, the task force report proposed no new initiatives for peace.

Secretary of State Dean Rusk, who attended only the first task force meeting but was kept informed throughout by other State Department officials, doubted that Lyndon Johnson would decide to send large numbers of additional troops. Rusk had a hunch that Johnson would turn down this proposal, and he saw part of his role to be preparation of a military-diplomatic alternative for the President's consideration. In early March Rusk sent the President a proposal for an American bombing halt and diplomatic initiative; the proposal had come from British Foreign Secretary George Brown, a hitherto loyal supporter of U.S. policy in Vietnam. Rusk suggested that the Brown proposal be given consideration.

About the time the Clifford report came to the White House, Rusk renewed the discussion of bombing limitations as an alternative plan, and Johnson asked for a specific proposal. The Secretary of State returned with a letter in writing suggesting that the United States halt the bombing of North Vietnam in the area north of Vinh, but continue and perhaps intensify the bombing south of Vinh in the area which could be considered an integral part of the South Vietnamese battlefield. Rusk argued that the weather was unfavorable for bombing in the Hanoi-Haiphong area at the time, and would continue to be unfavorable for another month or two. Militarily, very little would be lost by a cessation in the far North during this period, and all wraps would be off in the DMZ area where the weather was more tolerable. Rusk said the United States should not set forth any formal conditions for continuation of the limited cessation, since North Vietnam had consistently rejected conditional bombing halts as military blackmail. The trick was to make the cessation conditional on North Vietnam's response without actually saying so, to preserve the fact of conditions without the semantics of conditions. Rusk's proposal made it clear that the United States would retain

the right to resume large-scale bombing throughout North Vietnam at any time, and would certainly do so in the event of
a massive assault against Khe Sanh or renewed major Communist
attacks against the cities.

A potential pitfall in this plan was the psychological impact
on the Saigon regime. Ambassador Bunker, who was urging extension of the war to Cambodia and Laos and stepped-up bombing of the North, reported on March 1 that the South Vietnamese
had been shaken by the United States' failure to respond militarily
to the challenge of the Tet Offensive. President Thieu could not
understand why the bombing of North Vietnam had not already
been increased. The U. S. Mission in Saigon was also concerned
about the possibility that Hanoi might change its political line, accept the San Antonio formula and move to peace talks with the
United States. The Mission Council had told Assistant Secretary of
State Philip Habib—who accompanied General Wheeler to Saigon
in late February—that such a shift by the Hanoi regime could cause
a major crisis in South Vietnam.

On March 6 Rusk prepared to send his plan to Saigon for
consideration by Ambassador Bunker, but Johnson decided to hold
it back. He would keep the proposal in his pocket for a while.
Rusk had been called to testify before the Senate Foreign Relations
Committee in open session March 11, and Johnson suggested later
that he wanted to protect the Secretary of State from having to
discuss his plan under questioning by the senators. This might be
more difficult if it had gone out to Saigon. It is also possible
that Lyndon Johnson feared a leak, which would complicate the
problems of his forces in the March 12 New Hampshire primary.

The President at Bay

Columnist Max Lerner had a private visit with the President
at the White House on March 5, and came away troubled.
Johnson cited statistics and intelligence reports to prove that the
Tet Offensive was a massive Communist failure and a giant op-
portunity for the United States, but the columnist wasn't buying.
The President reminded him, he wrote later, of "a last-ditch fighter

in a Western movie of the bad old days, surrounded by the savages, with his horse shot out from under him, embattled, unyielding, waiting for reinforcements to carry the day." Lerner sensed that Johnson was certain the reinforcements would arrive in time, but in the meantime he seemed to be a terribly lonely, stubborn man. "Above all, one must be impressed by the naked will power of the man, as if he were exerting sheer will to hold everything together at once—the war, the nation and his own inner universe," Lerner wrote.

The reinforcements did not arrive. Instead, the savages in the outside world broke through the defenses, and in mid-March Lyndon Johnson was beleaguered as never before. Everyone seemed to be deserting his surrounded camp. Everything seemed to be coming apart.

On the tenth the New York *Times* published its scoop about the 206,000-man troop request, setting off a wave of controversy and galvanizing leaders throughout the country to cry out against the war policies before all was destroyed. Johnson hated leaks of any kind, and this was the most dangerous and damaging of his presidency. NBC-Television presented Frank McGee's hour-long blast against the war. Lady Bird noticed that sties were popping out on her husband's eyes, red and swollen, and she thought that his life was more and more like the tribulations of Job. She sensed he was deeply worried about the war and about his own capability to unite the country in the years ahead.

On the eleventh Theodore Sorensen informed the President, in a previously arranged appointment, that Robert Kennedy was seriously thinking of entering the Democratic presidential race. Johnson was not surprised. From 10 A.M. to 6 P.M. Dean Rusk appeared in televised hearings before the hostile questioners of the Senate Foreign Relations Committee. Many of the questions dealt with the 206,000 story and possible American escalation. *Newsweek*'s "Agony of Khe Sanh" issue, with its strong stand against the war, was published.

On the twelfth New Hampshire voted, with results that were damaging to the President's prestige and ominous for his political future. The commentators and political reporters, and even

Sam Houston Johnson, his own brother, who was living in the White House, called the results a defeat for the President.

On the thirteenth Robert Kennedy all but announced his candidacy for President in an interview with Walter Cronkite on the *CBS Evening News*. That evening, the Kennedy camp began making calls to politicians throughout the country to take soundings on support.

On the fourteenth Robert Kennedy and Sorensen went to the Pentagon to see Clark Clifford about the idea of a presidential commission to study the war, repudiate the current strategy and turn the nation to a new course. The plain but unspoken idea was that if Johnson would agree to switch the war policy, Kennedy would agree not to run for President. Johnson rejected the plan immediately. Kennedy announced his candidacy two days later.

Dean Acheson, the former Secretary of State and elder statesman, came to lunch with the President on the fifteenth to talk about Vietnam. Like most of the other major figures of the private Establishment, Acheson had loyally supported the government's policy at the beginning. He had been a prominent signer of a November 1965 public statement that "we declare our support of the American commitment in Vietnam and resolve that whatever national resources are required shall be devoted to its fulfillment." More recently, Acheson, like many others, was having his doubts.

Late in February, in the wake of the Tet Offensive, Johnson had asked for his opinion about the United States' course in Vietnam, but the former secretary had declined to give a view without a full investigation of the facts. He had received occasional government briefings in the past and, after Tet, felt he had been misled about the true situation in the war. At his request, Johnson granted him authority to interview officials of his own choosing in State, Defense and the CIA, and gave ininstructions that the government men should speak frankly. Acheson had spent two weeks at the job of his private inquiry, speaking to Rusk, McNamara, Clifford and Helms, but concentrating on the second- and third-echelon men, including his son-in-law, William Bundy. The more Acheson looked into the Vietnam policy, the more he became convinced that it was hopeless.

At lunch alone with the President in the family dining room on the ides of March, Acheson reported his findings in typically unvarnished fashion. As he saw it, there was no correlation between the military objectives and the time and resources available to the United States to accomplish them. The Tet Offensive proved that the force of 500,000 Americans was woefully insufficient to drive out the North Vietnamese and subdue the Viet Cong, and the American people were not prepared to continue the present level of effort over the period of time required—perhaps five years. Certainly the public was not prepared to increase the level of effort. Acheson's conclusion was that the ground effort had to be reappraised and changed, the bombing stopped or greatly reduced and the war liquidated with the least possible damage to the United States.

Lyndon Johnson listened very soberly. He seemed to Acheson to be startled by the burden of the report, but he did not argue. There was no time, in any case. The President had to leave his luncheon guest for an urgent meeting of his financial counselors. The news that the United States was considering the dispatch of 206,000 more troops had set off a rush to trade dollars in for gold in the markets throughout the world. The London and Zurich gold markets had closed to halt the panic temporarily; the central bankers of the world were assembling in Washington to hear what steps the United States would take to put its financial house in order and reform the gold system. The President apologized to Dean Acheson and hurried away to the meeting with his worried bankers.

In New York Arthur Goldberg sat down to draft a personal "eyes only" memorandum to the President asking him to stop all the bombing of North Vietnam and change the direction of the war. He said good sense required it and public opinion demanded it.

At Johnson's behest, Goldberg had left his lifetime job as Associate Justice of the U. S. Supreme Court in 1965 to become Ambassador to the United Nations with special responsibility for seeking a settlement to the Vietnam War. The war kept growing and the peace hopes diminished. Despite some victories on negotiating language at the UN, Goldberg's influence on national policy turned out to be minimal. Beginning late in 1967, he had been trying to resign without an open break with the President.

In mid-March the United Nations Ambassador read in the paper that 206,000 more men might be sent to fight, and he was appalled. It was clear to him that since the Tet Offensive there had been a dramatic shift in American public opinion, and he felt Johnson must take it into account. In Goldberg's view it was a profound fact that the country simply would not continue on the present course. If the bombing of North Vietnam were halted, Goldberg believed, the Soviets would agree to cut back on their material support of the North Vietnamese and Viet Cong; it would also eliminate the bulk of the foreign criticism of the United States and help quiet the domestic dissent. Goldberg sent off his proposal and waited for the explosion.

Johnson's immediate reaction was just about what Goldberg had anticipated. He waved the United Nations Ambassador's memo in the air, denounced it in unmistakable language and declared that a total bomb stoppage was exactly what he was not going to do. At the same time, the proposal had its uses for the President. At his direction, the Goldberg total bombing halt plan and the Rusk partial bombing halt plan were dispatched by cable to Ambassador Ellsworth Bunker on March 16 without identifying the source of either one. The Goldberg plan would be the stalking-horse with Saigon, and under those circumstances a partial bombing halt might be easier to swallow. Bunker was told that Washington did not expect Hanoi to accept a limited bombing halt, but that the maneuver might help considerably to shore up support for the war among the American public.

Everything was going sour, nothing was working right. Five hundred and nine Americans were killed in Vietnam the week before, the generals wanted more men and a bigger war, Acheson and some of the others were advocating just the opposite and the bankers were raising hell about gold. The time for decision was coming, and Lyndon Johnson wanted to get off someplace where he could think. He flew to his Texas ranch and spent Sunday the seventeenth there with his family.

He went to church in the morning with his daughter Lynda and her husband, Chuck Robb, who would soon be leaving for Vietnam. His other daughter, Luci, and her husband, Pat Nugent, came for dinner; Pat had just received orders to join his old reserve unit in Washington, and he expected to be reassigned overseas before long. The President and Lady Bird watched Hubert Humphrey defending the Administration on a television panel show, and Lady Bird observed that Hubert and Rusk were the only people speaking out for the Administration. She felt like Prometheus bound, tied to a rock, exposed to the vultures and unable to fight back.

Johnson could not believe that the country would turn its back on its President and its fighting men in time of war. Maybe the country needed some bucking up. He decided to try.

The National Farmers Union was meeting in Minneapolis, Minnesota, a thousand miles from the LBJ Ranch, and the President decided at the last minute he would go. Flying north aboard Air Force One on Monday morning, he called in the press for a long, frank, private talk, to let them know the way he felt and perhaps to reach into their editorial board rooms at the other end of the communications wires.

He didn't want to talk politics but the reporters did, and he couldn't help himself. No, he wasn't surprised at the New Hampshire result, and certainly he wasn't surprised that Bobby wanted to run against him. He had to deal with primaries and a convention and possibly an election, but he believed in first things first. The very first was the war, and he thought the press would agree. Which is not to say the Administration would be defenseless. James Rowe, his old friend, was setting up a campaign to organize for the President, just as Lyndon Johnson had worked for President Franklin D. Roosevelt in another time of troubles, 1940. If you read the history of 1940, he advised the reporters, you could find a general comparison with what was being done in 1968. (On another occasion, Johnson told a group of newsmen that 1940 would be the "pattern" for 1968 and added, "Of course, Roosevelt was running for a third term while I am running only for a second term.")

Somebody asked if public support for the war had increased or decreased since the Tet Offensive. There were a lot of people in this country working full time around the clock to lose this war for us in this country, the President replied, a good many people who were powerful and influential who would like to see us pull out and quit. He believed they had this feeling all along, but now it was coming out and they were becoming vociferous.

You saw very few stories on Ho Chi Minh breaking the Tet truce, he observed. He'd been notified January 24 that Hanoi would break the truce, he said, and every American had been alerted. Some of the good Christian newspapers back home don't mention it, but here was a case where you were asked to put down your pistol, undress, and put on your pajamas and as you were crawling into bed they shot you. That was what happened at Tet, but Americans hadn't got the picture. It seemed significant that nobody was stressing it.

There always seemed to be some effort to discredit the policy and the effort, he went on, a pattern of attacks on it with a different topic every week—corruption, General Thieu, fire Westmoreland and so on—and some of this came from the Communist camp. The question now was whether to junk the policy of Eisenhower, Kennedy and Johnson, and he didn't believe the American people—when they knew all the facts—would vote to do it. The honorable thing was to keep the nation's commitments. He believed that was what the people wanted to do.

At the Leamington Hotel in Minneapolis, he told the Farmers Union that "your President has come to ask you people, and all the other people of this nation, to join us in a total national effort to win the war, to win the peace and to complete the job that must be done here at home." The President spoke of the triumphs and tragedies of war in other times—the sinking of the *Lusitania*, the attack on Pearl Harbor, the men in Korea fighting to hold the Pusan perimeter, the pilots in Berlin flying in zero visibility to break the blockade. Now the battle was joined anew. "We don't plan to surrender or let people divide our nation in time of national peril. . . . The time has come when we ought to stand up and be counted, when we ought to support our leaders, our government, our men, and our allies until aggression is stopped, wherever it has occurred," he declared.

The Farmers Union applauded long and loud, but its own union president, Tony Dechant, informed newsmen that Johnson's speech had not changed his mind about the war. Dechant called the war "a controversial and expensive military effort in a faraway place," and told the union that it meant tighter money and higher interest rates and production costs without the offsetting income gains experienced in other wartime periods.

The leaders of Lyndon Johnson's campaign for reelection met the following day, March 19, for their regular weekly luncheon with presidential assistant Marvin Watson. New Hampshire had been a shocker, and now the second big primary, Wisconsin, seemed likely to be even worse. Polls and private soundings by the Johnson organization there indicated that the President would be badly beaten by Senator Eugene McCarthy—and this time both men were on the ballot.

Johnson had never said explicitly that he was a candidate for reelection, and he had given clear indication to some of those closest to him that he might not run. Lady Bird was very much opposed to another term, and discussed it with him often. John Connally thought he should run only if he wanted another four years in the job, not out of any sense of obligation or inertial force, and suggested that he step out of the race in the fall of 1967 or in January 1968. In August of 1967 Johnson confided to Dean Rusk that he might not run again and Rusk became convinced that he would not. About the same time, the President said the same thing to Clark Clifford, but Clifford did not take it seriously, and the President's other actions convinced him that Johnson would be in the race. In November he had asked General Westmoreland what the impact on the troops would be if he should decide not to run; the general replied that the troops were fighting for their country, not their President, and would not be seriously affected. In early January Johnson prepared a surprise

ending to the State of the Union address announcing that he was
stepping down at the end of his term, but did not deliver it.

At the same time, he permitted and, in some instances, participated in the efforts to organize a reelection campaign. He
held a series of small private meetings in the living quarters
of the White House with James Rowe, Clark Clifford, Marvin
Watson and a few others to discuss the campaign; Rowe agreed
to be cochairman of Citizens for Johnson in 1968, the same
operation he headed in 1964. Postmaster General Lawrence O'Brien
and Henry Hall Wilson, a former Kennedy-Johnson White House
aide now president of the Chicago Board of Trade, helped line
up former Governor Terry Sanford of North Carolina to be the
formal campaign manager. The President personally asked Sanford
to take the job in mid-March, asking Sanford's advice about Wisconsin and discussing the political dissension over the war; Johnson did not say, "I'm running," but it never occurred to Sanford
that he might not be. The President brought Charles Murphy,
an experienced Roosevelt-Truman political operative, into the
White House from private law practice. In March Johnson summoned George Reedy, his long-time press secretary and aide,
who quit the best job he ever had in private life (president of
Struthers Research and Development Corporation) to rejoin the
White House staff. Reedy immediately went to work on political
chores, surveying the wreckage of the Democratic National Committee and reporting to the President it was in a mess. Reedy
and others close to Lyndon Johnson had heard him say periodically
for decades that he was quitting politics; most of them didn't
believe he really meant it before, and they didn't believe the
grumbles and rumbles in 1968. Reedy, for one, was certain Johnson was running for reelection.

The March 19 weekly campaign meeting convened in a funk.
The "win the war" line from the President's Farmers Union speech
in Minneapolis the day before had made the headlines and the
newscasts, and the politicians on the firing line were saying it was a
disaster. Hardly anybody seemed interested in a "win the war"
campaign in March of 1968. The LBJ political commercials in
Wisconsin, devised by men in touch with the public mood, were
saying, "Help the President win peace with honor."

The Johnson campaign leaders, including James Rowe, Law-rence O'Brien, Clifton Carter, Richard Maguire, William Connell, Robert Burkhardt, Martin Friedman and others, discussed the Minneapolis speech and the Wisconsin problem and sent two suggestions to the man in the Oval Office. First, the President must do something dramatic *before* the April 2 Wisconsin primary to recapture the peace issue. One of the politicians suggested sending Rusk to Geneva on a certain date to wait for a specified number of days for the North Vietnamese to show up and negotiate. Somebody else suggested a bombing pause of perhaps ten days, with international teams to monitor the increase in North Vietnamese traffic south during the letup. Second, it was essential that the President stop the "hard line" talk. The polls still showed that there were more self-described hawks than doves (Gallup's findings that this was no longer true were not out yet) but none of the politicians who met at Democratic headquarters could find more than one or two isolated hawks. Everyone had turned into a dove.

Gallup's latest poll showed only 32 per cent of the public approved the President's handling of the war—before the month was out, that would be down to 26 per cent, and the rating on Johnson's over-all performance as President down to 36 per cent approval (52 per cent disapproved and the rest were undecided). Gallup's rule of thumb was that any time a President's over-all job rating dipped below 50 per cent he was in trouble politically.

Why the disaffection? How did Americans come to feel this way about the President and the war? One of LBJ's political pros undertook to analyze the problem, and concluded that the immediate cause was the Tet Offensive. In his view, that was the reason for the popularity of McCarthy and the entry of Robert Kennedy. The great middle group of Americans on whom elections depend had been shocked by Tet, and they wanted out. Ho Chi Minh and General Giap had their offensive, and it worked. Now Lyndon Johnson must have his. The working politicians, who were in touch with the American people, said Johnson's must be a peace offensive.

The following morning, March 20, the President telephoned Clifford. Johnson had been thinking about war and peace, and decided that he would be "the peace candidate"—for a Churchill peace, not a Chamberlain peace. The President had decided he must have a new approach to signal a new direction. "I've got to get me a peace proposal," he said.

Movement in Hanoi

In the North Vietnamese capital the leaders of the Lao Dong Party were dealing with their own morning after. The mass meetings to hear the news of victory had come and gone, the red headlines in the Hanoi newspapers had faded back to black, the public and the troops had been told in subtle but unmistakable ways to go back to the long war. In case anyone should have any untoward ideas, the regime made public the decree on counterrevolutionary crimes, setting forth death sentences and prison terms for a long list of "plots" against the state and its policies, and started a press campaign to publicize and praise the new decree.

In the middle of March the Lao Dong leaders decided to make another public move toward the opening of negotiations with the United States, and they determined that this time it would be heard loud and clear in the U.S.A. About March 20 Hanoi authorities invited CBS correspondent Walter Cronkite to pay a visit to North Vietnam as soon as he could get there. At the same time, Harry Ashmore, executive vice-president of the Center for the Study of Democratic Institutions, and William C. Baggs, editor of the Miami *News* and a board member of the Center, received permission to make their second visit to Hanoi on a quasi-diplomatic private mission.

Cronkite was boating in the Caribbean, resting after his strenuous trip to South Vietnam and its editorial aftermath, when he received the news of the Hanoi invitation. Cronkite had tried for a North Vietnamese visa about a year before and after some encouraging preliminary soundings, nothing happened. When the welcome sign flashed on unexpectedly in March 1968, Cronkite had strong misgivings. After his criticism of the war in late February, it might seem to the American public that he was being rewarded by the Communist regime for his opinions. Cronkite would strive to be objective and hard-hitting in his Hanoi reporting, but suppose he discovered the North Vietnamese were not so evil after all—what would he say then? He was sick about missing a big story—perhaps the biggest one of all—but he told CBS he did not think he should go.

CBS' next choice was Charles Collingwood, who had been to South Vietnam fourteen times since 1960, spoke excellent French and had applied several times to enter North Vietnam. Collingwood was in Puerto Vallarta in Mexico, spending a year's sabbatical from his post as CBS News chief European correspondent. After the call from New York, he chartered a plane to Mexico City, flew to Paris and on to Phnom Penh, Cambodia, to see the North Vietnamese diplomats there and wait for the ancient International Control Commission airplane, the only way for American journalists to enter Hanoi. Collingwood was promised that CBS would be granted "important interviews" in the North Vietnamese capital.

Collingwood, Ashmore and Baggs arrived at Gia Lam Airport in Hanoi on March 29. Ashmore and Baggs began preliminary talks on a semiofficial level the following day with Hoang Tung, editor of the Party newspaper, *Nhan Dan*. Collingwood's official guides upbraided him for not arriving sooner, but informed him that the "important interview" with Foreign Minister Nguyen Duy Trinh was scheduled for him on April 2. They would not tell him what would be said, but he got the distinct impression that the North Vietnamese expected it to make news throughout the world.

Pullback in the South

In South Vietnam the military phase of the Tet Offensive was drawing to a close. Gradually it was becoming obvious that the major Communist units had pulled back from forward positions and were resting, retraining and regrouping in their jungle redoubts. The principal allied military problems were the deeply defensive psychology of the South Vietnamese Army, still holed up in or near the cities, and the continuing shelling and harassment by Communist small units which kept South Vietnam jittery.

Action around Khe Sanh, still the focus of many television

and press reports, was slowly diminishing. The last major ground assault against the base occurred the night of February 29–March 1. While Communist shelling and harassment continued in March, the ground probes against the perimeter were much weaker than before. Clear skies over Khe Sanh all but five days in March made United States air operations easier and more effective. Incredible tonnages of bombs rained down. By mid-March the U. S. Marine Command began to hear of major North Vietnamese units leaving the area, and Bru tribesmen reported that most of the Communist artillery had moved back across the Laotian border.

On March 15 Westmoreland reported to Washington that he was planning to mount offensive operations in the Khe Sanh area, including a drive to reopen Route 9—the road to the beleaguered base. The 9th Regiment of the 304th North Vietnamese Division, which had been slowly tunneling underground toward Khe Sanh from a coffee plantation nearby, was relieved of its mission on the twentieth, and moved back into the mountains. By the twenty-fifth, aerial photographs confirmed that the 325-C North Vietnamese Division had withdrawn, and the 304th Division—the heroes of Dien Bien Phu—was thinning out. After two months of suspense, the pressure was easing.

Elsewhere in South Vietnam the greatest worry centered on conditions in the countryside. Official American assessments estimated a "severe setback" (three to six months) in the pacification program in nineteen of South Vietnam's forty-five provinces. Some 280,000 people were believed to have fallen under Viet Cong control during the first month of the Tet Offensive, and another one million people formerly listed as "secure" had dropped into the "contested" category. Heavy pressure was being exerted on American units, South Vietnamese battalions and government pacification teams to return to the countryside. When they finally did so, the losses in the rural areas turned out to be less severe than most officials had been reporting. The Viet Cong had depleted their local force guerrilla units in the countryside to build the attack against the cities at Tet; now the rural areas were being tapped for men again in preparation for renewed attacks on the cities in the spring and later in the fall.

One of the most important changes in South Vietnam was in the minds of the Saigon generals, who sensed more than ever before that their survival might depend on their own resolve. The regime had been jarred by the Tet attacks, and further upset by the failure of the United States to respond. By mid-March news reports and official gleanings from Washington cast growing doubt on any large new troop commitment or national mobilization in the United States. In this situation, there was growing talk among the Saigon leaders of a massive troop commitment and national mobilization of their own.

Back in 1966 Ambassador Henry Cabot Lodge proposed general mobilization of South Vietnam's manpower to fight the war, but Prime Minister Ky had equivocated and the plan had died. When Ellsworth Bunker succeeded Lodge in 1967, he proposed such measures to Ky again—but again, Ky did not approve. Prior to Tet, the Saigon regime under U.S. pressure had agreed to augment its 670,000-man armed force by 65,000 more men during the 1968 calendar year. Now, in March, it decided to do much more. After discussions with Bunker and Westmoreland, President Thieu announced March 21 that 135,000 more men would be added to the government army during 1968. This would require extension of the draft and a large measure of mobilization among the Vietnamese people.

Mulling and Maneuvering

Lyndon Johnson's way of making tough decisions was, like the man himself, peculiar and unique. One day he would ridicule a proposal as "the most stupid-ass idea I ever heard" and berate the "jerks" who thought of suggesting it to him, and a day or two later he'd be discussing it or something like it as if the thought were all his own. One day he'd praise a proposal as fitting to the situation and his thoughts, the next day be suspicious and critical and the day after that denounce the idea as stupid and impossible. He was, by the testimony of close associates, hell to be around when he was mulling a big one, particularly in the foreign policy field, where he was least sure of his ground and of himself.

In the third week of March 1968, after his unsuccessful attempt to rally the country behind the war, he began moving warily toward a decision on the Vietnam problem and—unknown to most of his advisers—toward a decision on his own political future. The public was confused and unhappy, the political pot was boiling and there were suggestions from several quarters that the President should chart a new course. Johnson decided to speak on nationwide television prior to the April 2 Wisconsin primary.

On March 22 the President and his inner circle met in the family dining room to discuss the Vietnam address, which had been under preparation in draft form for many weeks. In the absence of a new policy decision by the President, the draft was a "more of the same" speech: an account of the Tet Offensive, with a report of Communist treachery and losses and United States and South Vietnamese government gains; an announcement of stepped-up aid to the South Vietnamese Army and a new drive against corruption in Saigon; a plea for the income tax surcharge to support the men at war; a declaration of the vital importance of Vietnam and Asia and of United States hopes for peace; and a "we shall prevail" sort of ending expressing the firm determination of the American government and people.

At this point, it seemed clear that the country wouldn't buy it. The newspapers and commentators would laugh it out of court, and it would be the perfect target for Kennedy and McCarthy. Clifford argued for a partial bombing halt as a bid for peace and a means of extending the lease on public support for the war. The difficulty was that a partial bombing halt was believed to be unacceptable in Hanoi, and a total bombing halt was unacceptable in Saigon. There was also the risk that failure of a partial halt would set back the chances for a full cessation later. No decision was made at the meeting, but Johnson was mulling—and maneuvering.

Later the same day the President called reporters to the Oval Office and announced military personnel decisions which would allow him great flexibility in his decision-making. General Wheeler, a team player, would remain for an additional year as Chairman of the Joint Chiefs. Admiral Sharp, a hard-line advocate of more troops and more bombing, would retire from his post as the Pacific commander, and his successor would be chosen later from nominations to be submitted by all three military services. This would permit the President to select a man to fit the policy he wanted.

The big news was that Westmoreland had been reassigned to Washington as Army Chief of Staff, and would leave the Vietnam post in midsummer. Though his successor was assumed to be Creighton Abrams, the President did not name him to the job at this point; first he would summon Abrams to Washington and hear the general's views on future strategy.

The diminishing action in South Vietnam had robbed the Wheeler-Westmoreland troop request of its justification, the reaction on Capitol Hill had left grave doubts that it could be supported and the public uproar after the publication of the New York *Times* story on March 10 had shown it to be politically explosive. By March 12, the day of the New Hampshire primary, the proposal for a large U.S. troop increase and reserve call-up was virtually dead, and by the fifteenth the nails were in the coffin. On March 23 Johnson dispatched Wheeler in secret to Clark Field in the Philippines to meet Westmoreland, tell him what happened to the 206,000 proposal and obtain agreement on a small number of additional troops to meet his needs.

Wheeler arrived at Clark Field about 9 P.M. after a flight of nearly twenty-four hours from Washington, and after a few social preliminaries, the two generals talked alone into the night in the office of the base commander. It must have been an uncomfortable meeting, even for two professional soldiers accustomed to the quirks of higher authority. Wheeler's messages from Washington and his trip to Saigon, all undertaken with the blessing of Lyndon Johnson, had opened up the prospect of many more troops and a big-war strategy. Westmoreland had gone along, and then the whole thing had blown up in his face. He was identified at home as the general who claimed victory and then asked for 200,000 reinforcements, and now the plan was being junked, he was being moved to Washington, and Wheeler, reappointed to another year of service as Chairman of the Joint Chiefs of Staff, was in the Pacific to explain it all.

Before leaving Washington, Wheeler and the Joint Staff had made a study of the troops which could be supplied without a reserve call-up or other mobilization measures. Johnson had approved the rough limits of the plan, and now the two generals worked out the details. Westmoreland settled for 13,500 more American support troops in addition to the supplementary force he had received on a temporary basis after Tet, plus authority to hire 13,000 additional civilians in Vietnam to meet supply and support needs. As it turned out, the troop request worked out in the base commander's office in the Philippines was to be the final increment of American men for the Vietnam War. From then on, it was to be all downhill—though that wasn't entirely clear at the time.

There now occurred in Washington, on March 25 and 26, a remarkable event, perhaps unique in American history, which demonstrated in unmistakable fashion the bankruptcy of the war policy on the home front. At the invitation of the President, another gathering of "Wise Old Men" was convened to hear briefings on the war and express their views. These were former Cabinet secretaries, ambassadors and generals, some of whom had helped design the nation's policies toward Vietnam and nearly all of whom were conservative and cautious men with personal ties to their successors in the high posts of the government. The November meeting of Wise Old Men, attended by roughly the same group with only a few changes, had ended in a nearly unanimous endorsement of the government's policy. This time, by a margin of two to one, the senior outside advisers told the President they no longer believed in the war as it was being waged. Several of them expressed the view that the American people would not long support it. It would have to be changed.

At the White House meeting earlier in March, Clark Clifford had suggested to the President that the senior advisers from November, plus additional men as appropriate, be reconvened to take a new look at the Vietnam problem. Clifford had an idea that Johnson would be surprised at the shift in opinion. The President, perhaps influenced by the strong support he received in November, welcomed the suggestion for a new meeting and suggested to several callers—among them Arthur Goldberg, who came to discuss his bombing halt plan—that they should try their ideas on the senior advisers.

The Wise Old Men assembled at the office of the Secretary of State at 7:30 P.M. on Monday, March 25. The outside advisers present were Dean Acheson, George Ball, Omar Bradley, McGeorge Bundy, Arthur Dean, Douglas Dillon, Abe Fortas, Robert Murphy, Matthew Ridgway and Cyrus Vance. Henry Cabot Lodge and General Maxwell Taylor both former Ambassadors to Vietnam, held positions in the State Department and White House, respectively, but were also considered senior advisers. Those present as senior officials of the government were Dean Rusk, Clark Clifford, Richard Helms, Walt Rostow, Nicholas Katzenbach, Paul Nitze, Averell Harriman, Arthur Goldberg, William Bundy and General John McConnell of the Air Force, representing the Joint Chiefs.

The meeting was secret, but Lyndon Johnson, who was in the State Department building that evening to address a Conference on Farm Policy and Rural Life, almost gave it away. "Secretary Rusk is having a meeting with some wise men in the next room," said the President in his opening remarks, but none of the White House reporters got the reference. The November meeting had not been publicized, and few members of the press had ever heard of the "Wise Old Men." After his speech to the farmers, Johnson slipped away to the room where the senior advisers and government officials were dining, and shook hands all around.

In a meeting after dinner and another the following morning at the State Department, they discussed the problems in Vietnam and the choices facing the United States. Three middle-rank government officials briefed the assembled group: Deputy Assistant Secretary of State Philip Habib on the political situation in Vietnam; Major General William DePuy on the military situation; and George Carver of the Central Intelligence Agency on pacification and the state of the enemy. The briefers presented factual, carefully balanced accounts with little indication of their personal

views. Even so, some of the senior advisers were struck with the
change in tone and substance from the highly optimistic briefings
of November. Douglas Dillon, the New York investment banker
who had served President Eisenhower as Undersecretary of State
and President Kennedy as Secretary of the Treasury, got the strong
impression from the November briefings that the war would be
pretty well cleaned up in a year. Now he asked how long it would
take to expel the North Vietnamese and pacify the country. "Maybe
five years, maybe ten years," was the answer. Dillon was stunned,
and instantly came to the opinion that the American people would
never stand for such a thing.

Clark Clifford described the choices open to the United States
as he saw them: (1) expansion of the war—a major increase in
ground troops, national mobilization, extension of ground action in
Laos, Cambodia and perhaps the southern part of North Vietnam,
stepped-up bombing in the North; (2) muddle along—perhaps a
few thousand more troops for Vietnam but no change in national
strategy; and (3) a "reduced strategy"—reduction in the bombing,
abandonment of isolated positions such as Khe Sanh, and the use
of American troops as a shield around populated areas while the
Vietnamese government and its troops were given time to assume
the burden of the war.

Former Secretary of State Acheson, the senior man present in
terms of prior governmental responsibility, said he had changed
his views since November. He had reached the conclusion that it
was not possible to achieve the nation's objectives in Vietnam by
military means. Therefore, he opposed the dispatch of more American troops and noted there were always more troops in North Vietnam as well. Arthur Goldberg made his plea for total cessation of
the bombing of North Vietnam. Averell Harriman spoke earnestly
about the dangers of military escalation. Acheson's turnabout appeared to have considerable impact on the group, as did the
change in Clifford's views since he had been one of the outsider
advisers at the November meeting.

At midday Tuesday most of the senior advisers, accompanied
by a few of the senior government officials, went to the White
House to submit their views. They were joined in the family dining

room by the President, Vice-President Humphrey, General Wheeler (who had just returned from Clark Field) and General Creighton Abrams, who flew back with Wheeler. After lunch, Abrams briefed the group on the progress of the South Vietnamese Army. Then the President dismissed Rusk, Clifford and most of the other government officials, and adjourned to the Cabinet Room to hear the views of the senior advisers. Those present were Johnson, Humphrey, Wheeler, Taylor and Lodge, and nine outsiders: Acheson, Ball, Bradley, McGeorge Bundy, Dillon, Fortas, Murphy, Ridgway and Vance.

McGeorge Bundy, president of The Ford Foundation and former While House foreign policy assistant to Presidents Kennedy and Johnson, summarized the views of the advisers. The predominant view was that of Dean Acheson—that American objectives could not be achieved within the limits of time and resources available, and therefore the policies would have to be changed. Bradley, Fortas and Murphy, it was noted, dissented from the general view.

The President was quite visibly taken aback. He went around the table, calling on each man to state his opinion.

The bombing of North Vietnam had been undertaken in February 1965 at the specific recommendation of McGeorge Bundy, who helped sell it to Johnson then as a lost-cost way to stave off defeat in South Vietnam and raise the potential price of insurgencies around the world. Later Bundy saw the bombing of the North essentially as a negotiating chip at some future bargaining table, and twice in the fall of 1967 he let the President know that he did not favor giving it up. Now he reversed himself, on the grounds that the bombing was more damaging to support for the war at home then it was militarily beneficial abroad. He recommended that the bombing should be stopped completely, not partially, and opposed sending additional American troops to Vietnam.

Henry Cabot Lodge, twice U. S. Ambassador to South Vietnam and the Republican political cover on Vietnam for both Kennedy and Johnson, read a statement he had written in longhand the night before. Lodge urged urgent consideration to a shift from "search and destroy" and "war of attrition," which he said pointed to an unobtainable goal of military victory, to a new strategy of using American military power as a shield behind which South Vietnam would be organized. "Less stress on search and destroy would mean fewer casualties, less destruction, fewer refugees, less ill will and more public support at home," Lodge said. More stress on the organization of Vietnamese society would "put the egg in the cake before putting on the frosting." He conceded that his strategy would take a long time, and concluded that "U.S. forces therefore should be in numbers sufficient only to enable us to keep faith with our troops in exposed positions such as Khe Sanh, and not to continue the past emphasis on search and destroy."

Douglas Dillon, another prominent Republican, said the United States should send no additional troops, it should stop the bombing completely and try to move toward a negotiated settlement. The President asked Dillon how he came to change his mind about the war. The financier said the briefing of the night before had an impact on his views, that it was quite clear to him the United States did not have five or ten years to conclude this war. Johnson seemed surprised, and said he wanted to hear the briefings.

Dean Acheson, sitting on the President's right at the Cabinet table, went over his position in detail. As summarized by one of the participants later that day, Acheson declared that the "belligerency" in Vietnam could not be brought to the point where the South Vietnamese government could handle it by the use of any permissible means within the time allowed this or any other President by the American people. "This fact, together with our broader interests in Southeast Asia, Europe and in connection with the dollar crisis, requires a decision now to disengage within a limited time," Acheson said. No actions should be taken inconsistent with this goal, and there should be some evidence of a new policy by midsummer, he urged. The fundamental problem in South Vietnam, in his view, was the missing element of popular support, which the United States could not supply. And the fundamental problem in the United States was lack of popular American support for the war. Acheson did not think the public would permit the government to continue its efforts in Vietnam for more than a year or so, and probably the time available would be shorter in the absence of a clear turn toward peace by midsummer. "One thing seems sure—the old slogan that success is just around the corner won't work."

George Ball, the former Undersecretary of State who had been the most articulate "devil's advocate" against the war within high Administration councils, recommended an immediate cessation of all bombing of North Vietnam. At one point Ball began to speak of the political problems in the United States, but the President cut him off. "That's the last thing that would affect me," he said.

General Matthew Ridgway, the field commander of U.S. troops in Korea after the dismissal of MacArthur and later Army Chief of Staff, recommended that the Vietnamese government be given arms and equipment and two years' time to prepare its armed forces to take over the fighting. The Vietnamese would be told that after two years the United States would begin withdrawing its troops. Ridgway did not know if this would work, but it would be worth trying; he himself had opposed the Vietnam intervention from the very start.

Cyrus Vance had been Deputy Secretary of Defense during the period of the Vietnam build-up, and a solid defender of the policy until a severe back ailment forced him to retire to private life in mid-1967. Had Vance remained in government, he would probably have become Secretary of Defense in early 1968, and he might well have continued to support the military effort—for it was his return to private life which shattered his earlier views. Back in New York in the law firm he had left a decade previously, Vance was stunned by the depth of feeling against the war on the part of nearly everyone he met: his law partners, their wives, the junior associates, the people at dinner parties, the clients of his law firm. For the first time, Vance understood how insulated he had been in government, hearing the briefings and reading the reports, making speeches calling for patience and never understanding that the people were not behind the war.

As a young lawyer, Vance had come to Washington in 1957 to be special counsel to Senator Lyndon Johnson's Preparedness Investigating Subcommittee, and he had always been considered Lyndon Johnson's man. When there was trouble in the Panama Canal zone in 1964, the new President sent Vance as his personal emissary; when the Dominican crisis erupted, he did the same; when the Detroit ghettos burst into flames, when Greece and Turkey were locked in dangerous conflict over Cyprus, when South Korea was in crisis after the Blue House raid, Johnson's answer was the same—send Cy Vance. Now Vance sat in the Cabinet Room and told the President that the war was dividing the country and it was time to change the policy. The government must find a way to move to negotiations, he said.

Justice Fortas, Johnson's old friend and still a solid supporter of the war, objected that this was not a favorable time for negotiations. Moreover, Fortas thought there had been too much emphasis among the senior advisers on the words "search and destroy." That did not mean big offensives, but was merely a synonym for fighting the enemy, he said.

General Wheeler agreed on both points. He had told Westmoreland at Clark Field that "search and destroy" was in bad repute—he had better find another term. (The U. S. Command subsequently banned the term from its lexicon and began referring to its offensive mobile operations as "combat sweeps," "reconnaissance in force," "spoiling attacks" or simply "raids.")

An objection was raised to Acheson's assertion that existing United States policy was bent on a military solution in Vietnam. "What in the name of God have we got 500,000 troops out there for—chasing girls? You know damned well this is what we're trying to do—to force the enemy to sue for peace," the blunt-spoken Acheson declared. "It won't happen—at least not in any time the American people will permit."

Retired General Omar Bradley, the World War II commander and former Chairman of the Joint Chiefs, had been to Vietnam on a semiofficial inspection tour in 1967 and returned publicly backing the policy. He continued his support of the basic policy now, but indicated it might be necessary to lower the sights of the nation's objectives.

Former Ambassador Robert Murphy continued to back the war in strong terms.

The President looked increasingly glum as one man after another spoke. His grandson, nine-month-old Lyn Nugent, had been brought in during the meeting, and the chief executive held the baby on his lap while the Wise Men gave their judgments on the war. "As I understand it, with the exception of Murphy, Bradley, Taylor, Fortas and General Wheeler, all of you favor disengagement in Vietnam," the President summed up. Lodge spoke up that he did not favor disengagement, but wanted to use American power in different fashion. Bundy quarreled with the word. (He decided later the word he preferred was "deescalation.") The others were silent. Johnson thanked them all and said goodbye.

The following day the President summoned the men who had briefed the senior advisers and ordered them to repeat their briefings. DePuy and Carver did so (Habib was out of town) and Johnson asked questions. Finally he decided that the briefings could not have been the cause of the disaffection.

Dean Rusk, Clark Clifford, Walt Rostow, William Bundy and speech writer Harry McPherson met on March 28 at the State Department to "polish the speech" which the President was to deliver three days later. McPherson's original drafts had undergone many changes since the last speech-writing meeting six days previously, but it was still a "more of the same" address. At this stage, it reflected the decision to send only a small number of additional troops to the war but said nothing about a halt or reduction in the bombing.

On March 23 the State Department had submitted twenty pages of proposed speech language, including a section announcing a bombing halt at the 20th parallel of North Vietnam, but the President would not allow this or any other suggestion of a bombing limitation to be circulated. Always secretive about his decisions, he was doubly so about this initiative. A leak would complicate his negotiations with the Saigon government and the Joint Chiefs of Staff and rob the proposal of the surprise and drama that he loved. He was holding even more closely to his chest another, more explosive secret—his own resolve to announce at the end of the Vietnam speech that he would not be a candidate for reelection.

The night before the March 28 "polishing" session Clifford read the latest draft of the Vietnam speech, and he thought it a disaster.

The President was going to the country to speak of the war in the same old terms the country was rejecting, to ask again for sacrifice, perseverance, patience and fortitude. Over lunch in Secretary Rusk's office at the State Department, Clifford told his colleagues that the country would not buy it. This was a speech for more war, and the President needed a speech about peace. Clifford marshaled the conclusions he had reached in the months since Wheeler's return—the problems and difficulties of the war, the futility of more of the same, the state of mind of the American public, the loss of confidence by private leaders. A democratic nation could not carry forward a war without broad support among the public. "Boys, it's not there," Clifford said emphatically. He argued that the President should reduce the bombing in a move toward peace, and give a peace speech.

Rusk did not argue. At the end of the meeting, it was agreed that McPherson would draft a whole new speech for the President. McPherson had come to hate the war and its effect on the President and the country. He left for the White House in high spirits.

After a nod from Rusk, William Bundy drafted a cable to Saigon instructing Bunker to clear the 20th parallel bombing halt with President Thieu. It was to be made clear that if Hanoi did not respond, the bombing limitation would be temporary. At 6:30 P.M. Rusk went to the White House for a private discussion with the President, and a little later there was a telephone call to the State Department. The cable was on its way, in code, by 8 P.M.

The Joint Chiefs considered the 20th parallel bombing halt in formal deliberations, and approved the plan after considerable debate with certain specific provisos. The United States would resume bombing throughout North Vietnam if the Hanoi regime failed to respond to the peace initiative by the time the weather cleared in a month or two, and it would resume the bombing if the Communists made a big military push in the South. The Joint Chiefs did not expect the limited cessation of bombing to be permanent, but there were serious misgivings. Some of the military men feared that once the bombing of the northern part of North Vietnam was stopped, it would be politically impossible to resume it.

March 31

On Sunday, March 31, the leaders of Lyndon Johnson's campaign for reelection met in Marvin Watson's office in the west wing of the White House to discuss the bleak prospects in the April 2 Wisconsin primary and plan strategy for the tough campaign ahead. Watson, Lawrence O'Brien and James Rowe were joined for the first time by Terry Sanford, who had agreed to be the campaign manager in a telephone conversation with the President at the beginning of that very week. Johnson greeted Sanford briefly, but did not participate in the strategy session. The political pros were told that the President would announce a limited bombing halt in the speech that night. Nothing was said about his political decision.

In the family quarters of the White House, the President was working with Horace Busby, a trusted former aide and sometime speech writer, on the surprise peroration announcing that he would not run again. Except for the final ending, the full speech had been discussed and approved line by line by the President and his advisers in a long session the previous day. When they came to the end of the prepared text, Johnson had told the group he might have an ending of his own.

Never having had sons of his own, Lyndon Johnson felt an almost paternal affection for several of the young men on the White House staff, among them Harry McPherson. McPherson was a fellow Texan and had been working for Johnson off and on since he came to Washington as a Senate aide in 1956. McPherson was working in his office in the west wing of the White House late in the afternoon when the President telephoned.

"Do you think it is a good speech?" the President asked his aide. McPherson thought it was.

"Do you think it will help?" McPherson thought it would, particularly at home.

"Do you think Hanoi will talk?" The aide was much less certain—the chances seemed to him to be less than 50-50.

"I'm going to have a little ending of my own to add to yours," the President told his aide and friend. McPherson had heard that it was in the works, and he caught a hint the day before of what Johnson might do.

"Do you know what I'm going to say?" Johnson asked. There was a pause. Yes, he thought so.

"What do you think?"

"I'm very sorry," said McPherson softly.

"Okay," responded the President with a Texas lilt in his voice —"so long, pardner."

McPherson put away the papers on his desk and left the White House. He went to a neighbor's house and proceeded to drink most of a fifth of bourbon.

Richard Nixon had scheduled a nationwide radio address for 6:30 P.M. on March 31 to begin to define his position on future strategy in the war. In the New Hampshire primary campaign, Nixon had "pledged" to end the war, but he gave no clue of how he would go about it. Political opponents and the press ridiculed him for implying he had a plan without explaining what it was, and there was a growing demand that he state a clear position. Nixon preferred to keep his views ambiguous for maximum political appeal and maneuverability, but in late March he reluctantly decided that the political cost of remaining silent was even higher than the cost of speaking up.

The radio address he had planned for March 31 was characteristically cautious, but it represented a significant departure from his original hawkish stand. "The answer to failure is not simply more of the same," he planned to say, making the point that Vietnam was basically a political war, which could be resolved only on a political basis. He planned to urge great diplomatic efforts to obtain a settlement, especially efforts to enlist the Soviet Union's support for an early end to the war, perhaps as part of a far-reaching agreement. He planned to say that a more effective military strategy might involve fewer American troops—not more troops. The working draft of the radio speech was a first step toward a Nixon commitment to liquidate the war, and implicit in it was the abandonment of the idea of military "victory."

The day before his address Nixon received word that Lyndon Johnson had requested television time for the same night. With relief mixed with curiosity, Nixon immediately canceled his own talk "in deference to the President." After he heard the speech, Nixon announced the first of a long series of self-imposed moratoriums on Vietnam comment, on the grounds that he should not "even inadvertently" say anything that might cause difficulty for U.S. negotiators. As his campaign for the presidency developed, he was never forced to state a clear position on the war.

Dean Rusk was aboard an Air Force jet flying over the Pacific to a previously scheduled meeting of the Vietnam War allies at Wellington, New Zealand, when he received a radiotelephone call from a White House aide. "There's going to be a final paragraph on the President's address," the aide said cryptically over the insecure radio channel. Rusk knew immediately what the message meant.

The President called Soviet Ambassador Dobrynin to the White House at 6 P.M. to explain the partial bombing cessation and give personal emphasis to the bid for peace. High-ranking American officials in Washington and around the world began similar briefings for other foreign leaders.

About 8 P.M. Clark Clifford and his wife, Marny, and Walt Rostow and his wife, Elspeth, arrived for drinks in the family quarters of the White House. After a few minutes the President called Clifford and Rostow into his bedroom and handed them a copy of his secret peroration. Clifford was very surprised, and asked Johnson if he had thought it through from every aspect. The President had; it was final. Rostow said little. Mrs. Rostow was on the verge of tears after her husband told her the news.

A few minutes before the scheduled air time of 9 P.M., the President, a few aides and guests walked over to the west wing. Johnson told Marvin Watson to begin calling members of the Cabinet and others who should know of his political decision, and then he stepped before the cameras in the Oval Office. Lady Bird looked radiant and happy, but Lynda and Luci, who cried when they heard the news, did not. Lynda had returned from California only that morning after seeing her husband off to combat duty in Vietnam. She desperately wanted the war to end, and felt her father was the man to do it. She was afraid she would never see her husband again.

The President sat down behind his desk. The still photographers came in and took their pictures. The producer checked the sound and lighting. The red light went on.

"Good evening, my fellow Americans:

"Tonight I want to speak to you of peace in Vietnam and Southeast Asia. No other question so preoccupies our people. No other dream so absorbs the 250 million human beings who live in that part of the world. No other goal motivates American policy in Southeast Asia.

"For years, representatives of our Government and others have traveled the world—seeking to find a basis for peace talks. Since last September, they have carried the offer that I made public at San Antonio. . . . Hanoi denounced this offer, both privately and publicly. Even while the search for peace was going on, North Vietnam rushed their preparations for a savage assault on the people, the government and the allies of South Vietnam.

"Their attack—during the Tet holiday—failed to achieve its principal objectives. It did not collapse the elected government of South Vietnam or shatter its army —as the Communists had hoped. It did not produce a 'general uprising' among the people of the cities as they predicted. The Communists were unable to maintain control of any of the more than thirty cities that they attacked. And they took very heavy casualties.

"But they did compel the South Vietnamese and their allies to move certain forces from the countryside into the cities. They caused widespread disruption and suffering. Their attacks, and the battles that followed, made refugees of half a million human beings.

"The Communists may renew their attack any day. They are, it appears, trying to make 1968 the year of decision in South Vietnam—the year that brings, if not final victory or defeat, at least a turning point in the struggle.

"This much is clear: If they do mount another round of heavy attacks, they will not succeed in destroying the fighting power of South Vietnam and its allies. But tragically, this is also clear: Many men—on both sides of the struggle—will be lost. A nation that has already suffered twenty years of warfare will suffer once again. Armies on both sides will take new casualties. And the war will go on.

"There is no need for this to be so. There is no need to delay talks that could bring an end to this long and this bloody war.

"Tonight, I renew the offer I made last August—to stop the bombardment of North Vietnam. We ask that talks begin promptly, that they be serious talks on the substance of peace. We assume that during those talks Hanoi will not take advantage of our restraint.

"We are prepared to move immediately toward peace through negotiations. So tonight, in the hope that this action will lead to early talks, I am taking the first step to de-escalate the conflict. We are reducing—substantially reducing—the present level of hostilities. And we are doing so unilaterally, and at once.

"Tonight, I have ordered our aircraft and our naval vessels to make no attacks on North Vietnam, except in the area north of the demilitarized zone where the continuing enemy buildup directly threatens allied forward positions and where the movements of their troops and supplies are closely related to that threat. . . ."

In Saigon, the hour of the President's address coincided with a scheduled meeting of the U. S. Mission Council. The high officials —including Ambassador Bunker, General Westmoreland, Robert Komer, Barry Zorthian, the CIA chief and Colonel George Jacobson, the Mission coordinator—had gathered in the third-floor conference room of the Chancery building. Most of the physical damage done by the Viet Cong commando team had been repaired, temporary gun nests had been built and the Embassy compound was a bristling fortress.

Several of the officials had been briefed in detail on the President's address, and a text of his prepared remarks had been transmitted from Washington several hours earlier. The Saigon Embassy officials listened without enthusiasm—there was much feeling that this was a step in the wrong direction—as Lyndon Johnson's voice floated into the room via Armed Forces Radio. As the President reached the end of the text, one of the officials stood up to turn off the radio—but, unaccountably, the President continued talking:

> "Finally, my fellow Americans, let me say this: Of those to whom much is given, much is asked. I cannot say, and no man could say, that no more will be asked of us. Yet, I believe that now, no less than when the decade began, this generation of Americans is willing to 'pay any price, bear any burden, meet any hardship, support any friend, oppose any foe to assure the survival and the success of liberty.' Since those words were spoken by John F. Kennedy, the people of America have kept that compact with mankind's noblest cause. And we shall continue to keep it.

> "Yet, I believe that we must always be mindful of this one thing, whatever the trials and the tests ahead. The ultimate strength of our country and our cause will lie not in powerful weapons or infinite resources or boundless wealth, but will lie in the unity of our people. . . . What we won when all of our people united just must not now be lost in suspicion, distrust, selfishness and politics among any of our people.

> "Believing this as I do, I have concluded that I should not permit the Presidency to become involved in the partisan divisions that are developing in this political year.

> "With America's sons in the fields far away, with America's future under challenge right here at home, with

our hopes and the world's hopes for peace in the balance every day, I do not believe that I should devote an hour or a day of my time to any personal partisan causes or to any duties other than the awesome duties of this office —the Presidency of your country.

"Accordingly, I shall not seek, and I will not accept, the nomination of my party for another term as your President. . . ."

When Lyndon Johnson had finally finished, there was a self-conscious silence in the Embassy conference room. The men sat there looking at one another, measuring each other's surprise and wondering about the future of the war the President had led and the future of those whose careers had been tied to his. Westmoreland remembered the half-forgotten conversation with Johnson in November, but no one else in the room had had the slightest warning. For the second time in eight weeks, the wheel of life was turning with a velocity and in a direction that no one had quite foreseen.

North Vietnam reacted quickly to the American President's initiative, which fit neatly into the diplomatic program its leaders had planned. Less than three days after Johnson's speech, the Hanoi regime broadcast an official government statement declaring its readiness to begin preliminary contacts with the United States looking toward a total bombing cessation and substantive negotiations. The statement also said that "the General Offensive and Uprising of the South Vietnam Armed Forces and people early this year have inflicted on the U.S. aggressors and their lackeys a fatal blow. . . . The Vietnamese people's fight for independence and freedom has entered a new period. The U.S. defeat is already evident."

Charles Collingwood's interview with Foreign Minister Nguyen Duy Trinh, originally scheduled for April 2, was postponed until three days later. Trinh reiterated North Vietnam's willingness to send a representative to meet the Americans. The following month "preliminary discussions" began in Paris and eight months later, after the United States halted the bombing of all of North Vietnam, official talks began in Paris involving the United States, North Vietnam, the National Liberation Front and the South Vietnamese government.

In the streets of Saigon the news of President Johnson's speech was quickly passed by word of mouth. Within a few hours knots of Vietnamese could be seen and heard speaking excitedly of "Johnson" and "Kennedy." The immediate consensus was that Johnson's partial bombing cessation and his withdrawal from the presidential race were tricks to ensure his reelection. A minority view, which grew steadily in the days ahead, was that the announcement was real, that the speedy withdrawal of American troops was now assured and that the mandate of heaven had passed from Lyndon Johnson to Robert Kennedy, the only other active American politician most Vietnamese had heard of.

President Nguyen Van Thieu's State of the Union message, which was written prior to Johnson's speech, was read that day to the deputies in the National Assembly building, the former French opera house situated between the Caravelle and the Continental Palace, the luxury hotels of the foreigners. Thieu's message declared that "the struggle against Communist aggression in South Vietnam is now in a decisive phase. The time has arrived for us to mobilize all our resources to win. We should not hesitate." The recently adopted 135,000-man increase in the government armed forces might be superseded by an even larger increase in the second half of the year, Thieu announced. General mobilization—conscription of men between seventeen and forty-five, and possibly conscription of women as well—would be necessary if the war continued.

This year 1968 was a "year of decision" for Vietnam, Thieu said in the message, and he predicted that Communist forces would attempt to launch a new attack before the year was up. For the present, the battle for the cities was over and all the invading forces had been wiped out. Thieu told the deputies and the people that "the Communist Tet Offensive can be considered as having completely failed."

Dr. Marjorie Nelson of the Quaker Rehabilitation Project and Sandra Johnson, an International Voluntary Services teacher, walked down mountain paths and across the plains to arrive in the middle of the night at the house of a peasant family on the outskirts of Hue. Viet Cong forces had taken the two American women prisoner in the city on the sixth day of the Lunar New Year, and marched them to a temporary camp in the nearby mountains. After a few days twenty-five American men who also had been captured—including two young IVS volunteers—were taken away in a different direction. They have not been seen since.

The Quaker doctor from Indiana volunteered repeatedly to work in Hanoi or in a liberated area in South Vietnam, but the answer was "The life is too hard for you here" or "We have enough Vietnamese doctors and nurses—we don't need your help, thank you." Both women spoke Vietnamese, and they had long talks with their guards about the war and about life in America. Late in March the People's Revolutionary Committee of Hue announced on Liberation Radio that the two women would be released, due to "the traditional humanitarianism of the Vietnamese people and the lenient policy of the revolutionary power and considering the attitude of the American women concerned." Their captors made souvenir combs for them from the aluminum of American napalm canisters, led them to the house of the Vietnamese family near the city and said goodbye. In the morning they were given breakfast and started down the path to the main highway north of Hue. They caught a civilian bus into town.

Marjorie Nelson was wearing gray Liberation Army trousers, a black shirt, South Vietnamese Army boots and carrying her purse and a Chinese Communist canteen. Sandra Johnson wore black Vietnamese women's trousers and a maroon blouse, and carried her belongings in an empty American sandbag. They walked up to two astonished GIs at a sentry post and identified themselves, and officers were immediately summoned to take them to headquarters. "Did you hear Johnson's speech?" a young lieutenant asked as they were riding through the streets of Hue toward the U.S. military advisory compound. Marjorie laughed and said they did not listen to the Armed Forces Radio network where they had been. "Johnson decided not to run and said he's going to stop the bombing," the lieutenant said. Marjorie wished for a moment she were back at the camp to see and hear the reaction of the forces in the mountains.

At the rear service base at "R," the Liberation Army Command headquarters across the Cambodian border, an official of the Central Office for South Vietnam informed the troops of the Johnson speech. He said Johnson's decisions were directly attributable to the sacrifices and exertions of the Lunar New Year attacks and were a great victory for the Liberation Army. The soldiers were very happy to hear this news, and wondered when the war would be over.

Four hours before the Johnson speech, the final military action of the Tet campaign was launched from a clearing called Landing Zone Stud, a few miles east of the Khe Sanh Combat Base near the Vietnam-Laos border. The objectives of Operation Pegasus, which involved the U.S. 1st Air Cavalry Division and 1st Marine Regiment and South Vietnamese airborne forces, were the relief of Khe Sanh, the reopening of Route 9 toward Laos and the eradication of any North Vietnamese forces still in the area. Five days later the first elements of Operation Pegasus reached Khe Sanh; they reported finding the bodies of hundreds of North Vietnamese troops strewn over the devastated hills and in the jungle surrounding the base. Three months later the U. S. Command announced that the base was being abandoned.

The Tet Offensive, which had begun amid the firecrackers in the cities, ended in the drive to relieve the remote Marine base in the bomb-cratered mountains near Laos. A U. S. Army staff officer, taking note of the cycle of events, closed his book on this phase of the war and recommended to his superiors that those who participated be commended. In due time, the Department of the Army issued General Order No. 54 to carry out this purpose. All officers and men who served in the "territorial limits of Vietnam and adjacent waters" during this period would be entitled to wear a Tet campaign star on their green, orange and red Vietnam Service Ribbon. According to the General Order, the "Tet Counteroffensive Campaign" began on January 30 and ended April 1, 1968.

Afterword
A PERSONAL VIEW

Because the war is still not over and the outcome is still obscure, the full significance of the Tet Offensive is beyond our grasp. One thing seems clear: history will not ignore it. For all sorts of people and in all sorts of ways, this was a pivotal event, one of the great turning points of our day.

The first question invariably asked of a chronicler of the Tet Offensive is, Who won? As of today, the answer is, Nobody. Everybody lost. The North Vietnamese and Viet Cong lost a battle. The United States Government lost something even more important—the confidence of its people at home.

From the vantage point of three years later, it is clear that the attack forces—and particularly the indigenous Viet Cong, who did most of the fighting and dying—suffered a grievous military setback. Tens of thousands of their most dedicated and experienced fighters emerged from the jungles and forests of the countryside only to meet a deadly rain of fire and steel within the cities. The Viet Cong lost the best of a generation of resistance fighters, and after Tet increasing numbers of North Vietnamese had to be sent south to fill the ranks. The war became increasingly a conventional battle and less an insurgency. Because the people of the cities did not rise up against the foreigners and puppets at Tet—indeed, they gave little support to the attack force—the Communist claim to moral and political authority in South Vietnam suffered a serious blow.

Under the stress of the Tet Offensive, the South Vietnamese government faltered but did not fold, and after the battle it became more of a working institution than it had ever been before. After Tet, the Saigon regime nearly doubled its military strength, from 670,000 men to roughly 1,100,000 men. This process of general mobilization, though supported by massive American economic and military aid, required more political will than the South Vietnamese had ever been able to muster before. Whether they will be able to sustain this military strength and psychological determination with declining American support is open to question—but before Tet there seemed not even a chance.

No one in the West can be sure what the leaders of the Lao Dong Party expected to accomplish by the Tet Offensive, or what price they were prepared to pay. Certainly they hoped for the glorious victory which was dangled as an inspiration before their troops, but it seems unlikely that the sophisticated men at the top actually counted on such complete success. One of the explicit, and lesser, objectives of the General Offensive and General Uprising was a "decisive victory"—like the Dien Bien Phu victory of 1954—one whose political consequences would be decisive even though its military significance might be limited. The irony of the Tet Offensive is that the North Vietnamese and Viet Cong suffered a battlefield setback in the war zone, but still won the political victory in the United States.

We have examined in detail the circumstances and events which contributed to this result: the erosion of support for the war among the American people, particularly in 1967; the dangerous gap between official rhetoric and the reality in Vietnam; the American government's foolhardy Success Offensive, which set the stage for a later collapse of confidence; the power of modern electronics, which transmits experiences and emotions instantaneously and transmits perspective poorly; the workings of American politics in a presidential election year; the ill-advised and ill-timed effort by the American military to obtain large additional resources in the aftermath of Tet. For good reasons and bad, the American people and most of their leaders reached the conclusion that the Vietnam War would require far greater efforts over a far longer time than it was worth.

The United States and Vietnam are nearly as far removed, from one another geographically as any two nations on earth, and the differences in national character, ways of life and ways of thought are also great—but the United States failed abysmally to understand the setting into which it was intruding. The Tet Offensive was an intelligence failure not so much for lack of information as for lack of understanding and belief. Had the traditions and theories of the Vietnamese Communists been taken seriously—to say nothing of their psychology and strategy—the Tet Offensive would have been no surprise. The United States never understood its foe.

As for "our" side, most American advisers had no idea of how or why their Vietnamese counterparts rose to their positions of authority, and no way to find out. Most American advisers and commanders had little comprehension of the roots of the conflict in their area of military operation and they knew little of the beliefs and workings of the people. They did not know where they were, with what they were dealing or even with whom they were dealing. The United States was in Vietnam fourteen years between the Geneva Conference and the Tet Offensive; but under the system of rotation that was adopted, it was closer to reality to say that the United States was in Vietnam one year, fourteen times. We were strangers in a land of strangers, in too much of a hurry to explore the country or the thinking of its people. "They all look alike," one of our generals said.

For the American press, the combination of high drama and low national understanding created a monumental challenge in Vietnam—and the press, like the government, was ill-equipped to meet it. Newsmen sensed that something in the official Vietnam picture was terribly wrong but were unable to put a finger on just what. Without a broad mosaic of knowledge, individual actions and attitudes often seemed to make little sense. Convinced that officials had been lying about conditions and prospects in the war zone, unable to trust the information gathered by the government or the judgments dispensed by it, unrestrained by censorship and goaded by competition, much of the press leaped to stark conclusions when sudden events in the previously untouched cities seemed to prove its theories right. The electronics revolution, which took the battlefield into the American living room via satellite, increased the power and velocity of fragments of experience, with no increase in the power or velocity of reasoned judgment. Instant analysis was often faulty analysis. This was particularly so in the case of editors and commentators at home, many of whom were in touch with the political situation in the United States more than with the military situation in the war zone.

The civilian and military leaders of the American government, accustomed to patriotic cheerleading from the press in time of war, were appalled by the refusal of the newsmen to get "on the team" in the Vietnam conflict. It was a far cry from World War II, when Edward R. Murrow flew with the bombers over Berlin and exulted in the "massive blow of retribution" falling from the skies, and George Hicks, broadcasting off the coast of France on D day, shouted aloud to the ack-ack gunners to "Give it to her, boys," and everyone cheered when the Nazi plane went down.

Fifteen American military men won the Medal of Honor during the nine weeks of the Tet Offensive, but little of this valor was celebrated. It says something about this war that the great picture of the Tet Offensive was Eddie Adams' photograph of a South Vietnamese general shooting a man with his arms tied behind his back, that the most memorable quotation was Peter Arnett's damning epigram from Ben Tre, "It became necessary to destroy the town to save it" and that the only Pulitzer Prize awarded specifically for reporting an event of the Tet Offensive was given two years later to Seymour M. Hersh, who never set foot in Vietnam, for exposing the U. S. Army massacre of more than a hundred Vietnamese civilians at My Lai 4.

One reason the press was not "on the team" was because

the country was not "on the team." To a substantial degree, the newsmen represented and reflected American society, and like the rest, they had no deep commitment to or enthusiasm for the war. As reporters learned more about Vietnam, they became more pessimistic, with inevitable impact on the public. The view of the public, in turn, influenced the mood of the press.

Battlefield surprises and tactical setbacks have brought trying times at home in other wars, but without nearly the impact of Tet. There was a battle setback for the United States in World War II more serious militarily than the Tet Offensive and equally unexpected, but the nation's confidence did not crumble when four thousand officers and men were killed, seventeen thousand were missing and twenty thousand were wounded in a little more than two weeks of the Battle of the Bulge. In the midst of that battle, General Dwight D. Eisenhower issued an Order of the Day which declared:

> By rushing out from his fixed defenses, the enemy may give us the choice to turn his great gamble into his worst defeat. So I call upon every man, of all the Allies, to rise now to new heights of courage, of resolution and of effort. Let everyone hold before him a single thought— to destroy the enemy on the ground, in the air, every-where—destroy him! United in this determination and with unshakable faith in the cause for which we fight, we will with God's help, go forward to our greatest victory.

Twenty-three years later, General William C. Westmoreland issued an Order of the Day in the midst of the Tet Offensive in Vietnam. In a tone as restrained as that of a corporate report, it declared that "your alertness, aggressiveness, professionalism and courage—individually, by team and by unit—add new luster to your outstanding reputation." There was no exhortation to "destroy the enemy" in this limited war, and nothing was said about the "unshakable faith in the cause for which we fight." There was no such faith. The nation did not have its heart in this war and, even in time of crisis, its leaders could not create a sense of dedication. As in the Korean conflict, the leaders did not attempt to inflame public passions and create a martial spirit. If successful, such an effort would have shored up public patience with the limited war only to destroy the patience with its limits.

For all the verbal fealty to the independence of South Vietnam, it is obvious that the United States did not undertake this long and costly effort because of sympathy for a people with whom it had no historical association and virtually nothing in common. Vietnamese Communism, obnoxious though it might seem, presented no clear threat to American national security. Had Vietnam been in Africa or west Asia rather than on the border of China, a Communist take-over from the colonial French or from a local anti-Communist regime would have occasioned only passing concern. The central purpose of the war was the containment of Chinese Communism, a seemingly logical extension of the postwar American role of "guardian at the gate" on the Communist frontiers. As the Cultural Revolution took its toll within China and ideological dissension broke out between the giants of Communism, the justification for the war diminished. It became increasingly clear that the Vietnamese Communist movement was hardier than had been supposed, and that the political and social fabric of the United States was more vulnerable than had been realized. By then, the political leadership of the United States was heavily committed, thousands of Americans had been killed in battle and it was difficult for those in power to reverse the nation's course.

The Tet Offensive was a dramatic and important event which clearly required a reconsideration of the strategy being followed. It caused the participants on all sides of the war to take a second look at their positions. In the United States Tet provided a rationale for turning around rather than going ever deeper into a war the nation was unwilling to pay for and many of its young men were unwilling to die for. In bewildering and awkward fashion, the people and private leadership of the United States made up their minds about the war at Tet, and they communicated their views forcefully to those in high public office. A democratic corrective was applied to a policy gone wrong—but only after terrible wounds had been inflicted which are likely to scar the nation for a generation.

It has been said that war is a series of mistakes, and in this perspective it is fitting that the mistakes of the United States should take their toll in the United States. What has been done to Vietnam and the Vietnamese is another question. No matter which Vietnamese ultimately "win" this proxy war of the great powers, they will have lost more than they have gained. Whoever wins must set about in his own way to bind up the wounds of a ravaged and divided nation, to salvage what is left of a way of life, to restore the old villages, the old pagodas and the old ways and to deal with the new cities and a new generation. The rice fields and fruit orchards are fertile and the people are resilient. They will find a way to deal with the past and the future, with or without our help. In the end it will be a Vietnamese solution, and we will probably never understand how it was reached. By then our nation, long since sick of the war, will have lost all interest in the outcome and will wonder why so many of our young men died so far away for a cause so few could name.

After this dark age of Vietnamese history, those who survive could justly repeat to us, with reproach, the message presented by their forefathers to the first group of French sailors who ventured up the Saigon River a century ago, during the earliest stage of the European conquest. "Your country belongs to the western seas, ours to the eastern," the proclamation said. "As the horse and the buffalo differ, so do we—in language, literature, customs. If you persist in putting the torch to us, disorder will be long. But we shall act according to the laws of heaven, and our cause will triumph in the end."

CHRONOLOGY
OF THE TET OFFENSIVE

1967

JULY 7—Funeral in Hanoi for General Nguyen Chi Thanh, followed by Lao Dong (Communist) Party decision to launch the General Offensive and General Uprising in South Vietnam.

JULY 7–11—Secretary of Defense Robert McNamara, accompanied by General Earle Wheeler and Undersecretary of State Nicholas Katzenbach, in South Vietnam on McNamara's ninth on-the-spot review of the war. U. S. Command informally agrees to accept 55,000 additional American men as the next troop increase, though initially it had asked for more.

JULY 9—Presidential assistant Walt W. Rostow, in *Meet the Press* interview, states that North Vietnam's strategy has "shifted from a posture of trying to win the war to keeping the war going."

JULY 13—President Johnson declares in news conference, "we are very sure we are on the right track" militarily in Vietnam but more troops will be needed. With Westmoreland by his side, President says, "The troops that General Westmoreland needs and requests, as we feel it necessary, will be supplied."

JULY 19—North Vietnamese delegation led by Deputy Premier Le Thanh Nghi leaves Hanoi for Peking on first leg of trip to secure additional weapons and other aid from Communist countries.

—Secretary of State Dean Rusk tells news conference enemy is "hurting very badly" but sees "still tough, long job ahead."

LATE JULY—Military commanders of South Vietnam People's Liberation Armed Forces (Viet Cong) meet at headquarters in Cambodia to begin planning of General Offensive and General Uprising.

All dates and times are local time, expect as noted. For publications, the issue date is the date given.

AUGUST 3—President Johnson announces he has raised troop ceiling of U.S. personnel in South Vietnam to 525,000; calls for 10 per cent surtax on individual and corporate income.

—Viet Cong internal document describes "new situation and mission" which will lead to climax of war. Says time is ripe for violent political and military moves to "split the sky and shake the earth."

AUGUST 5—China signs new aid pact with North Vietnam in ceremony in Peking.

—Civilian adviser Clark Clifford and retired General Maxwell Taylor return from troop-seeking trip to capitals of Asian allies. Clifford reports unanimous agreement among allies that bombing of North Vietnam should be continued at present or even higher level. He says all allies agree this is time for "a maximum effort" in Vietnam.

AUGUST 7—General Harold K. Johnson, Army Chief of Staff, reports "smell of success" in every major area of the war.

AUGUST 8—House Republican Leader Gerald Ford attacks Johnson administration for "pulling punches" in bombing of North Vietnam while sending more Americans to die in ground war.

AUGUST 11—North Korea signs military aid pact with North Vietnam in ceremony in Pyongyang.

AUGUST 15—Detroit *News* article by Robert Pisor reports concern in Saigon about "a massive, countrywide military strike" by enemy to improve position prior to peace talks.

MID-AUGUST—Extraordinary Congress of National Liberation Front of South Vietnam adopts new NLF (National Liberation Front) political program.

AUGUST 20—Associated Press survey reports U. S. Senate support for Johnson administration war policy has eroded sharply; of senators replying to survey, 44 generally support war policies, 40 disapprove.

AUGUST 22—Richard M. Nixon, in interview with *Christian Science Monitor*, calls for "massive pressure" short of nuclear weapons to shorten war.

AUGUST 25—Secretary of Defense McNamara tells Senate Preparedness Subcommittee the war cannot be won by bombing; gives pessimistic report on effects of bombing to date. Several senators reply that United States may as well "get out" if McNamara is correct.

SEPTEMBER 1—President Johnson, at news conference, says there is no "deep division" in Administration leadership concerning bombing of North Vietnam.

SEPTEMBER 3—Voters in South Vietnam elect General Nguyen Van Thieu as President and General Nguyen Cao Ky as Vice-President with 27 per cent of total vote. Peace candidate Troung Dinh Dzu wins second highest presidential vote.

SEPTEMBER 4—Governor George Romney, in Detroit television interview, says "brainwashing" in Saigon by U.S. generals and diplomats brought about his previous support of the war.

SEPTEMBER 14–16—Defense Minister Vo Nguyen Giap of North Vietnam, in lengthy analysis broadcast by Hanoi Radio, endorses strategy of protracted war but declares "our fight will be more violent in the days ahead."

—September 21—U. S. Ambassador to the United Nations Arthur Goldberg asks in major speech what Hanoi regime "would" do if bombing stopped.

SEPTEMBER 23—Soviet Union signs new aid agreement with North Vietnam in Moscow ceremony.

SEPTEMBER 26—*Christian Science Monitor* reports Johnson consensus on Vietnam policy eroding in U. S. House of Representatives. Of 205 House members responding, 43 said they recently shifted positions from support of Administration to more emphasis on finding a way out.

SEPTEMBER 28—Viet Cong Military Region 4 directive secretly orders intensification of political and military action in Saigon area.

SEPTEMBER 29—New United States Embassy chancery dedicated in Saigon ceremony. Architect Frank J. Martin says "security is our primary concern" and declares, "We'll be able to with-stand just about any type of minor attack."

—President Johnson declares in San Antonio speech that the United States will stop the bombing of North Vietnam "when this will lead promptly to productive discussions." Johnson adds that "we would assume that while discussions proceed, North Vietnam would not take advantage of the bombing cessation or limitation."

LATE SEPTEMBER—Hue City Committee of Viet Cong orders development of grass roots organization and plans for occupation of city.

IN SEPTEMBER—Sau Ha, self-described undercover political agent of Viet Cong, seeks direct contact with United States Embassy. While carrying out his mission, he is arrested by South Vietnamese National Police.

—Second Congress of Heroes, Emulation Combatants and Valiant Men of the South Vietnam People's Liberation Armed Forces meets in "Liberated Area" to present awards and build morale for coming offensive.

—Arrests of more than 200 officials and leading cadres begins in Hanoi. Among those arrested is Hoang Minh Chinh, director of the Lao Dong Party's school of theoretical studies.

OCTOBER 8—New York *Times* survey reports U.S. political and congressional support for Vietnam War is waning.

OCTOBER 12—Secretary of State Rusk calls Vietnam War testing ground for Asia's ability to withstand the threat of "a billion Chinese . . . armed with nuclear weapons."

OCTOBER 20—*Life* magazine, in editorial shift, calls for pause in the bombing of North Vietnam and declares that "home front support for the war is eroding."

OCTOBER 22—35,000 protesters march on the Pentagon in opposition to the continuation of war in Vietnam.

OCTOBER 29—273rd Viet Cong Regiment attempts to take and hold South Vietnamese district capital of Loc Ninh.

OCTOBER 30—National Assembly standing committee of Democratic Republic of Vietnam (North Vietnam) approves decree on punishment for counterrevolutionary crimes.

OCTOBER 31—Nguyen Van Thieu inaugurated as President of Republic of Vietnam (South Vietnam).

NOVEMBER 1—Defense Secretary McNamara secretly recommends termination of United States bombing and limitation of ground involvement in Vietnam.

NOVEMBER 2—Senior unofficial advisers—"Wise Old Men"—give broad approval of Johnson administration war policies in Washington meeting.

NOVEMBER 3—North Vietnamese regiments massing on Dak To engaged by U.S. forces in beginning of 22-day battle.

NOVEMBER 6—Document captured by U.S. forces near Dak To says battle aims to divert U.S. forces to mountainous areas, improve techniques of concentrated and coordinated attacks.

NOVEMBER 10—President Ho Chi Minh signs decree on counterrevolutionary crimes.

NOVEMBER 11—President Johnson begins Veterans Day tour of eight military installations to shore up support for the war.

NOVEMBER 13—Ambassador Ellsworth Bunker, on trip to Washington, reports "steady progress" in war zone.

NOVEMBER 16—General Westmoreland tells House Armed Services Committee in Washington meeting that United States military phaseout from Vietnam can begin within two years if trends continue.

NOVEMBER 17—National Liberation Front proclaims 3-day cease-fires for Christmas and New Year's, and 7-day cease-fire for Tet.

NOVEMBER 19—U.S. forces in Quang Tin Province capture Communist Party document ordering General Offensive and General Uprising, massive lowlands attacks and take-over of Saigon.

NOVEMBER 21—Westmoreland in major address tells National Press Club in Washington that war entering final phase "when the end begins to come into view."

NOVEMBER 24—MACV (U. S. Command) officially reduces estimate of Communist strength in South Vietnam to 223,000–248,000 men.

NOVEMBER 26—Senator Robert F. Kennedy says President Johnson has shifted war aims set out by President John Kennedy, and and seriously undermined the moral position of the United States.

NOVEMBER 29—President Johnson announces Robert McNamara will step down as Secretary of Defense to become president of World Bank.

NOVEMBER 30—Senator Eugene McCarthy announces he will enter primaries as a Democratic presidential candidate.

DECEMBER 4—General Westmoreland, General Cao Van Vien (chief of Republic of Vietnam Joint General Staff) begin discussion of Christmas, New Year's and Tet cease-fires.

DECEMBER 6—Republican leaders Senator Everett Dirksen and Representative Gerald Ford say Administration has not done all it could to negotiate settlement of the war.

DECEMBER 15—U. S. Command turns over full responsibility for defense of Saigon to South Vietnamese armed forces.

DECEMBER 18—President Johnson rejects McNamara plan to halt North Vietnam bombing and limit U.S. participation in war.
—General Wheeler tells Detroit Economic Club "we are winning the war" but it is entirely possible Communists may try last desperate effort similar to World War II Battle of the Bulge.

DECEMBER 19—In television interview, Johnson says talks between Saigon government and members of National Liberation Front "could bring good results."

DECEMBER 20—Westmoreland cables Washington that Communists have decided on intensified countrywide effort to win the war.

DECEMBER 21—President Johnson, in Canberra for Prime Minister Holt's funeral, tells Australian Cabinet "kamikaze" attacks are coming in Vietnam.

DECEMBER 23—Ho Chi Minh addresses national rally in Hanoi, calls for greater feats of battle in both North and South Vietnam to win the war.
—President Johnson meets Pope Paul in Rome, agrees to 12-hour extension of New Year's cease-fire in Vietnam.

DECEMBER 25—Viet Cong commanders reconnoiter assigned targets in Saigon during Christmas cease-fire.

DECEMBER 30—Ho Chi Minh's Tet poem delivered by messengers to officials and diplomats in Hanoi.
—Foreign Minister Nguyen Duy Trinh announces North Vietnam "would" begin talks with United States if bombing and acts of war against the North are stopped.

1968

JANUARY 1—President Johnson imposes mandatory curbs on most direct U.S. investments abroad, asks for restrictions on overseas travel of U.S. citizens and other moves to cut sharply growing balance of payments deficit and gold drain.

JANUARY 3—Senator McCarthy expands challenge to President Johnson by entering New Hampshire primary.

JANUARY 5—U.S. press release in Saigon reports Communist order that troops should flood lowlands, attack Saigon and launch the General Offensive and General Uprising.

—Dr. Benjamin Spock, three others, indicted for counseling draft resistance.

JANUARY 9—Brigadier General William R. Desobry, retiring as senior U.S. adviser in Mekong delta, says Viet Cong in region are "poorly motivated and poorly trained" and that "ARVN [Army of the Republic of Vietnam] now has the upper hand completely."

JANUARY 10—Westmoreland, after conference with Lieutenant General Frederick Weyand, orders redeployment of U.S. forces from border areas to positions closer to Saigon.

MID-JANUARY—Romanian Deputy Foreign Minister Georghe Macovescu flies to Hanoi to sound out North Vietnam about Trinh offer to begin talks; United States restricts bombing of Hanoi and Haiphong in show of good faith.

JANUARY 15—Westmoreland at U. S. Mission Council in Saigon predicts attacks before or after Tet.

JANUARY 15–17—National Liberation Front presidium meets, hears reports on impending military action.

JANUARY 18—Singer Eartha Kitt at White House luncheon blames crime and riots on Vietnam War.

JANUARY 19—Johnson names Clark Clifford to replace McNamara as Secretary of Defense effective March 1.

JANUARY 21—North Korean infiltrators unsuccessfully attempt raid on South Korean presidential mansion at Seoul in most dramatic action since Korean War.

JANUARY 23—U.S. intelligence ship *Pueblo* seized by North Koreans in waters off Korea.

JANUARY 24—Bunker and Westmoreland cable Washington that Communists may break Tet truce; urge cancellation of truce in I Corps Tactical Zone.

JANUARY 25—President Johnson orders 14,787 reservists to active duty in Korean crisis, sends nuclear carrier *Enterprise* toward Korea.

—Westmoreland reports situation at Khe Sanh is critical, may represent turning point of Vietnam War.

—National Liberation Front appeals publicly for scrupulous observance of Tet cease-fire.

JANUARY 26—Viet Cong units move to villages on outskirts of Can Tho and Vinh Long in Mekong delta.

—Offensive and uprising plan for Right Bank of Hue signed by Hue City Committee.

JANUARY 27—Communist 7-day cease-fire for Tet begins; troops restricted to their posts and all leaves canceled under last-minute orders.

JANUARY 29—Lunar New Year's Day celebrated in North Vietnam.

—Tet cease-fire of allies canceled for I Corps Tactical Zone; cease-fire takes effect in rest of South Vietnam at 1800.

—Evening cocktail party on lawn of U. S. Embassy, Saigon.

JANUARY 30—(Vietnam time) Lunar New Year's Day celebrated in South Vietnam.

—12:35 A.M. Communists launch surprise attack on Nha Trang, followed by attacks on two cities in I Corps and five cities in II Corps.

—9:45 A.M. Allies cancel Tet cease-fire throughout all of South Vietnam.

—11:25 A.M. MACV orders all U.S. units on "maximum alert."

JANUARY 30—(U.S. time) Robert Kennedy says he will not oppose Johnson for the presidency under "any foreseeable circumstances."

—U. S. Senate confirms Clark Clifford to be Secretary of Defense.

JANUARY 31—(Vietnam time) 3 A.M. Simultaneous attacks on major cities, towns, military bases throughout South Vietnam. Major battles of Tet Offensive begin.

—2:47 A.M.–9:15 A.M. Battle of U. S. Embassy.

—President Thieu declares martial law.

—(P.M.) COSVN (Central Office for South Vietnam) Current Affairs Committee and Military Affairs Committee meet to assess Tet attacks.

—(Night) Children and old people of Hanoi evacuated to countryside in preparation for anticipated U.S. bombing attacks.

JANUARY 31—(U.S. time) American news media dominated by accounts of heaviest fighting of Vietnam War. CBS and NBC present 30-minute special reports on Tet Offensive.

—President Johnson briefs leaders of Congress at White House meeting.

FEBRUARY 1—(U.S. time) President Johnson confers with retired General Matthew Ridgway, Vice-President Humphrey, Joint Chiefs of Staff.

—Richard Nixon formally announces candidacy for presidency.

FEBRUARY 2—Johnson in White House news conference says Tet

Offensive was "complete failure" militarily.

—Thieu calls for increased bombing of North Vietnam in retaliation for attacks; says Viet Cong "totally defeated."

—Heavy fighting continues in South Vietnam, though number and intensity of new attacks begin to ebb.

—Peking *People's Daily*, organ of Chinese Communist Party, hails Tet attacks as "brilliant victories" and declares, "The East Wind has brought us happy tidings."

—MACV report lists 12,704 Communist troops killed in action since Tet began; U.S. battle deaths listed as 318 and those of South Vietnamese forces as 661 in same period.

FEBRUARY 3—Major fighting continues in Hue, Kontum, Pleiku, Dalat, Phan Thiet and suburbs of many cities.

—Central Committee of National Liberation Front calls for Liberation Army and people to strike "even harder, deeper and on a wider front."

—Senator Eugene McCarthy accuses Johnson administration of deceiving itself and American people about progress of war.

FEBRUARY 4—Administration officials appear on television interview programs to defend war policy: Secretary of State Rusk and Secretary of Defense McNamara on NBC-Television's *Meet the Press;* Undersecretary of State Nicholas Katzenbach on CBS-Television's *Face the Nation;* and presidential assistant Walt

W. Rostow on ABC-Television's *Issues and Answers.*

—Fighting continues in Hue and around several major cities. MACV lists enemy losses at 15,595 killed in action; 415 U.S. and 905 ARVN listed killed.

—Brigadier General Philip Davidson, MACV J-2, says Communists retain capability of another round of heavy city fighting.

FEBRUARY 5—*Nhan Dan,* official organ of Lao Dong Party in Hanoi, declares, "The once-in-a-thousand-year opportunity has come. The bugle has sounded victory."

—President Thieu creates Central Recovery Committee headed by Vice-President Ky.

FEBRUARY 6—U.S. spokesman in Saigon says 21,330 enemy troops killed since Tet began. "We cannot relax for a moment," Westmoreland tells troops in congratulatory message. "We must continue to stand ready for the enemy's possible second-wave offensive."

—MACV reports fighting has diminished throughout South Vietnam; 900 Viet Cong reported still in Saigon-Cholon.

—Ho Chi Minh in congratulatory message to President Nguyen Huu Tho of National Liberation Front declares "very favorable situation has been created" but adds that "the closer the victory, the more difficult the problem."

—Communist Party Current Affairs Committee in Can Tho Province, Mekong delta, declares General Offensive is long-term project which may last three or four months, not just a few days.

—Richard Nixon in Wisconsin campaign stop calls on Johnson administration to "tell the truth" about Viet Cong strength.

—2000 persons headed by the Reverend Martin Luther King, Jr., march through Arlington National Cemetery to protest "cruel and senseless" war.

FEBRUARY 7—Russian-built tanks and North Vietnamese troops overrun Lang Vei Special Forces Camp near Khe Sanh. First use of tanks by Communist forces in Vietnam War.

—Viet Cong blow up bridges over Perfume River in Hue; battle there continues.

—Westmoreland flies to Da Nang; orders military redeployments and study of troop needs beyond 525,000-man ceiling.

—Third anniversary of beginning of U.S. bombing of North Vietnam.

FEBRUARY 8—Joint Chiefs Chairman Wheeler offers Westmoreland additional men from 82nd Airborne Division and a U. S. Marine division; Westmoreland asks plans be made for redeployment of the units to Vietnam.

—Senator Robert F. Kennedy, speaking in Chicago, says Tet Offensive has shattered official illusions about Vietnam; continuation of military drive can lead

to military disaster on Asian mainland.

—Hanoi Radio quotes Foreign Minister Trinh as saying negotiations will begin as soon as United States proves it has stopped unconditionally bombing and other acts of war against Democratic Republic of Vietnam.

FEBRUARY 9—Helicopters land U. S. 199th Light Infantry Brigade at Saigon race track to speed clearing of Communist forces from city area.

—Westmoreland tells Wheeler he welcomes reinforcements any time they can be made available.

—Viet Cong Command in Hau Nghia Province, near Saigon, says in secret report that "to a large extent, our successes were limited" in Tet Offensive.

—Secretary of State Rusk, in background briefing, demands of newsmen, "Whose side are you on?"

—President Thieu announces plans for partial mobilization of South Vietnam.

FEBRUARY 10—Rusk in Atlantic City speech declares Vietnam War enters climactic period.

—Communist Party committee in Bien Hoa Province near Saigon says in secret report that "the people's spirit for uprising is still very weak."

—U.S. planes raid Haiphong area for first time in a month.

FEBRUARY 11—Saigon government announces call-up of 65,000 more men to armed forces.

—Communist Command in South Vietnam orders second-wave attacks on cities and towns.

FEBRUARY 12—White House officials discuss changes in Communist, U.S. strategy; decide Westmoreland has not yet expressed a firm demand for additional troops. In response, Westmoreland cables firm "requirement" for extra troops. Dispatch of 10,500 additional men from 82nd Airborne Division and 27th Marine Regimental Landing Team approved.

—President Johnson tells college students "nearly every option open to us is worse than what we are doing."

—Louis Harris poll reports U.S. public support for war increases in wake of Tet attacks.

—South Vietnam begins bombing Citadel at Hue; U. S. Marines move north of Perfume River in battle to regain control of city.

—Congressional debate on Westmoreland breaks out in U. S. House of Representatives.

FEBRUARY 13—Pentagon announces 10,500 additional men being airlifted to South Vietnam in response to Westmoreland request.

—Gallup poll reports 50 per cent of public opinion sample disapproves President Johnson's handling of war; 35 per cent approve; rest undecided.

—President Thieu states more U.S. troops are needed if the war is to be ended soon.

—National Liberation Front declares in communiqué that "we have made a really good start" but continuing and unremitting efforts are required for victory.

FEBRUARY 14—Senator Stuart Symington reports cost of Vietnam War for fiscal year 1969 was $32 billion.

FEBRUARY 15—U. S. Air Force F-4 Phantom becomes 800th U.S. aircraft lost in three-year air war over North Vietnam.

—*Wall Street Journal* calls for rigorous reexamination of the nature, scope and consequences of U.S. commitment to Vietnam.

FEBRUARY 16—Johnson in surprise press conference backs Westmoreland, says rumors that he may be relieved originated abroad. President says troops will be added in Vietnam as needed.

—Three U.S. pilots released by North Vietnam as a gesture of good will.

—Selective Service system rules out draft deferments for all graduate students except medical specialists cited by law.

FEBRUARY 17—Johnson flies to Fort Bragg, N.C., and Camp Pendleton, Calif., to visit reinforcements departing for Vietnam, and then flies to USS *Constellation* at sea in the Pacific.

—All-time weekly high of U.S. casualties is set during 7 days ending February 17: 543 killed in action, 2547 wounded in action.

FEBRUARY 18—Communist gunners attack 45 cities and major installations including Tan Son

Nhut Air Base. 122-mm. rockets used against Saigon for first time. Ground attacks launched against four cities.

—Johnson briefs former President Dwight Eisenhower in California stopover; presidential assistant Rostow tells newsmen South Vietnam government and Army may have been strengthened by Tet Offensive.

—Wheeler notifies Westmoreland he will visit Saigon for comprehensive review of war.

FEBRUARY 20—Senate Foreign Relations Committee begins hearings to determine whether U.S. deliberately provoked 1964 Gulf of Tonkin incidents.

—Chairman Mendel Rivers of House Armed Services Committee calls for military step-up to achieve victory in Vietnam.

FEBRUARY 21—Fresh U. S. Marine reinforcements sent to continuing battle at Hue.

—Standing Committee and Military Affairs Committee of COSVN order Communist forces to continue scaled-down offensive actions; say additional large-scale attacks not advisable in immediate future.

—General Earle Wheeler leaves for meeting with Westmoreland in Saigon.

—South Vietnamese National Police arrest Buddhist leader Venerable Tri Quang, presidential candidates Truong Dinh Dzu and Au Truong Thanh.

—Hanoi radio station, 3.5 miles southwest of city center,

bombed for first time by U.S. aircraft.

FEBRUARY 22—House of Representatives passes bill to eliminate remaining 25 per cent gold cover of U.S. currency as measure to free reserves to meet international demand for gold.

FEBRUARY 23—Department of Defense announces Selective Service call for 48,000 men—second highest number of Vietnam War.

—*Wall Street Journal* says American people should be getting ready to accept prospect that whole Vietnam effort may be doomed.

—1307 rounds of artillery, rocket and mortar fire bombard Khe Sanh Combat Base.

—Wheeler arrives in Saigon for inspection and policy review.

—Rostow sends word to Saigon that two fresh North Vietnamese divisions may be headed south as part of major new enemy effort.

—Communist forces in Hue receive permission to withdraw from city.

FEBRUARY 24—South Vietnamese troops storm former Imperial Palace in Citadel of Hue; National Liberation Front flag torn down from Citadel flagpole and Republic of Vietnam flag run up.

FEBRUARY 25—Wheeler leaves Saigon after mapping out Westmoreland request for 206,000 additional U.S. troops.

—Westmoreland tells Associated Press additional U.S. forces will probably be needed in war zone.

—Defense Secretary McNamara convenes service secretaries and Joint Chiefs of Staff to consider cabled version of Wheeler troop request.

—Last enemy forces cleared from city of Hue.

FEBRUARY 27—McNamara makes emotional statement against bombing and troop increase at State Department luncheon.

—CBS commentator Walter Cronkite, in special report, says war is a stalemate and negotiation is only way out.

—South Vietnamese Joint General Staff announces Major General Nguyen Van Manh relieved by Major General Nguyen Duc Thang as commander of IV Corps Tactical Zone (Mekong delta); Lieutenant General Vinh Loc relieved as II Corps commander by Major General Lu Lan.

FEBRUARY 28—Wheeler makes verbal report in White House meetings; Johnson names Clifford task force to study troop request; task force convenes at Department of Defense.

—Farewell reception for retiring Secretary of Defense McNamara at White House.

—President Thieu announces "permanent" closing of Saigon nightclubs and dance halls.

FEBRUARY 29—Pentagon military farewell review for McNamara.

MARCH 1—Clark Clifford sworn in as Secretary of Defense.

—Three trawlers containing ammunition and supplies for Communist forces sunk off South Vietnam.

—Frontal assault on Khe Sanh by 1500 North Vietnamese troops is driven back. OPEN?

—Ambassador Bunker recommends U.S. military action against Communist forces in Laos and Cambodia and stepped-up bombing of North Vietnam.

—Republic of Vietnam begins drafting nineteen-year-olds.

MARCH 2—Clifford task force begins intensive meetings.

MARCH 4—Secretary of State Rusk sends to President proposal for bombing halt originating with British Foreign Secretary George Brown.

—Clifford task force recommends immediate dispatch of 22,000 more U.S. troops to Vietnam; reserve call-up of 250,000 men; increased draft calls; further study of developing situation to determine if larger number of additional troops should be dispatched.

MARCH 5—Rusk recommends limited bombing cessation in area north of Vinh in North Vietnam.

MARCH 6—Westmoreland in Saigon background briefing likens Tet Offensive to Nazi Battle of the Bulge attack in 1944; says South Vietnam returning to normal.

—Washington *Post* editorial expresses grave misgivings about rumored dispatch of additional U.S. troops to Vietnam.

MARCH 7—Chairman J. W. Fulbright of Foreign Relations Committee and other senators publicly ask Administration to consult Congress before any new troop build-up in Vietnam. Fulbright cites rumors that more than 200,000 additional troops have been requested by Westmoreland.

MARCH 9—Gallup poll reports new wave of pessimism about the war in U.S.A.

MARCH 10—New York *Times* reports Westmoreland has asked for 206,000 additional men, says request has stirred controversy within Administration ranks.

—NBC commentator Frank McGee, in special report, says United States is losing Vietnam War by Administration's definition of its objectives.

MARCH 11—Rusk tells Senate Foreign Relations Committee U.S. is reexamining Vietnam policy "from A to Z."

—U. S. Command Operation Quyet Thang billed as largest allied offensive operation of war.

MARCH 12—Senator Eugene McCarthy wins 42 per cent of Democratic Party vote in New Hampshire presidential primary; Johnson receives 49 per cent.

MARCH 13—Fourteenth anniversary of Viet Minh assault on Dien Bien Phu.

MARCH 14—Senator Robert Kennedy and Theodore Sorensen meet Secretary of Defense Clifford to discuss possible U.S.

commission to reverse government's Vietnam policy; Johnson rejects plan.

—Gold buying soars in all European banks; Great Britain closes London gold market at U.S. request after record day; Federal Reserve Board raises U.S. discount rate to 5 per cent to strengthen the dollar and curb inflation.

MARCH 15—Former Secretary of State Dean Acheson, in private report to Johnson, says U.S. victory in Vietnam is not feasible within the limits of public tolerance; Acheson recommends liquidation of war.

—U. N. Ambassador Arthur Goldberg says Tet Offensive has shocked U.S. public; recommends total cessation of bombing of North Vietnam.

MARCH 16—Senator Robert Kennedy announces candidacy for Democratic presidential nomination.

—State Department cables Ambassador Bunker asking practicability of total or partial cessation of bombing of North Vietnam.

—Company C, 1st Battalion, 20th Infantry, American Division invades My Lai 4 hamlet, Quang Ngai Province, and kills more than a hundred unarmed Vietnamese men, women and children.

—Total U.S. combat deaths since January 1961 reaches 20,096.

—Heads of six European central banks confer in Washington on gold crisis; U.S. and European bankers to limit gold sales to private market; anti-war groups picket gold crisis conference at Federal Reserve Bank.

MARCH 18—President Johnson tells reporters to look at Franklin D. Roosevelt's 1940 reelection campaign as guide to 1968 campaign.

—In address to National Farmers Union in Minneapolis, Johnson calls for "total national effort to win the war."

—139 members of U. S. House of Representatives call for immediate review of war policy; debate on war takes place on House floor.

MARCH 19—President's political advisers and operatives foresee disaster for Johnson in April 2 Wisconsin primary, recommend dramatic presidential peace move to restore public confidence shattered by Tet Offensive.

—North Vietnam authorities cable Walter Cronkite, Harry Ashmore and William Baggs permission for Hanoi visit as soon as possible.

MARCH 20—Johnson tells Clifford that presidential peace proposal is imperative; President meets Goldberg on bombing halt plan.

—304th North Vietnamese Division relieved of tunneling mission near Khe Sanh base; ordered to withdraw to east; Bru tribesmen report Communist artillery has withdrawn into Laos.

MARCH 16–20—Gallup poll interviewers find more doves than hawks among population sample

for first time, in sharp reversal of hawkish first reaction to Tet Offensive.

MARCH 21—Decree on counter-revolutionary crimes published in Hanoi.

—Thieu announces South Vietnamese armed forces to be increased by 135,000 men.

MARCH 22—Johnson announces Westmoreland will step down as U.S. commander in Vietnam to become Army Chief of Staff.

—Presidential inner circle meets in White House to begin planning for speech to the nation announcing new moves in Vietnam.

—More than 1100 rounds of rocket and mortar fire bombard Khe Sanh Combat Base.

MARCH 24—Wheeler flies secretly to meet Westmoreland at Clark Field in the Philippines, tells Westmoreland that large number of additional U.S. troops will not be sent to Vietnam; Westmoreland agrees to submit minimal troop request.

MARCH 25—Wheeler returns to Washington accompanied by General Creighton Abrams, deputy U.S. commander in Vietnam.

—Harris poll reports 60 per cent of public opinion sample believes Tet Offensive was a standoff or defeat for U.S. cause in Vietnam.

—"Wise Men" group of senior unofficial advisers convene for briefings at State Department.

MARCH 26—In White House meeting, Wise Men say public has

lost confidence in war and U.S. disengagement is necessary.

MARCH 27—Johnson summons government briefers to determine what Wise Men advisers were told.

MARCH 28—Luncheon of high officials at State Department to polish Vietnam speech; Clifford objects to "war speech," says "peace speech" and presidential peace maneuver are essential.

—In meeting with Rusk, Johnson approves idea of 20th parallel bombing halt. Cable dispatched to Bunker to seek South Vietnamese approval of plan.

MARCH 29—CBS correspondent Charles Collingwood and unofficial emissaries Ashmore and Baggs arrive in Hanoi aboard International Control Commission plane; Collingwood is told he will be granted "important interview" by North Vietnamese authorities on April 2.

MARCH 30—Marine Major Charles Robb, son-in-law of President, departs U.S.A. for Vietnam combat duty.

—President and high officials review final draft of Vietnam address to nation; President says he will prepare personal peroration.

—Gallup poll reports all-time low in public approval of Johnson's performance: 52 per cent disapprove, 36 per cent approve his over-all handling of his job as President; 63 per cent disapprove, 26 per cent approve his handling of Vietnam War.

MARCH 31—Johnson political advisers meet in White House session to plan 1968 Johnson campaign.

—Johnson announces partial cessation in bombing of North Vietnam in bid for peace, dispatch of 13,500 additional U.S. troops. In surprise peroration, the President announces he will not run for reelection.

APRIL 1—(March 31, U.S. time) Operation Pegasus, ground relief of Khe Sanh Combat Base, launched against light opposition.

—Tet Counteroffensive campaign ends, according to U. S. Army special order.

—President Thieu declares Tet Offensive has "completely failed."

CHAPTER NOTES

Acknowledgments and Sources

Chapter I   "THEY'RE COMING IN!"

I am grateful for the assistance of Peter Arnett, Gary Lee Bel, Peter Braestrup, William Bundy, Ambassador Ellsworth Bunker, John Carroll, Leo Crampsey, Colonel Marvin D. Fuller, Robert J. Furey, Philip Geyelin, Ronald Harper, George Jacobson, Robert L. Josephson, Robert Komer, Ralph Laurello, Lee Lescaze, Henry Cabot Lodge, Murrey Marder, Benjamin Read, Eugene Risher, Chalmers Roberts, Dean Rusk, Charles W. Sampson, John B. Thompson, E. Allen Wendt, General William C. Westmoreland, General Frederick C. Weyand and Barry Zorthian.

By far the most comprehensive account of the Embassy action previously published is "The Viet Cong Attack That Failed," by Joseph L. Dees, in the *Department of State News Letter,* May 1968, pp. 22–30. This painstaking account by a U. S. Information Agency writer was based on interviews in Saigon with many of the U.S. defenders shortly after the attack. Another useful account is "That Long Night at the U. S. Embassy," by Peter R. Kann in the *Wall Street Journal,* February 19, 1969, based in part on a chronological record kept by political officers of the Embassy.

PAGE

2   Colonel Jacobson was interviewed at his Embassy compound villa in Saigon in November 1969. A two-page document headed "Observations," written by him on February 12, 1968, provided further details.

4   The Republic of Vietnam Armed Forces history, *The Viet Cong "Tet" Offensive,* pp. 24–28, provides a useful social commentary on the perspective of the Saigonese as the Year of the Monkey was ushered in.

4 There are varying figures on the number of Communist troops committed nationwide. I have taken the MACV (U. S. Command) estimate of the time, 67,000.

6 Nguyen Van Sau and Ngo Van Giang, two of the Viet Cong sappers, were captured in the Embassy attack. They provided details of the planning and preliminary movements during their initial period of captivity.

7 For the ordeal of the American defenders, see Joseph L. Dees, "The Viet Cong Attack That Failed," *Department of State News Letter*, May 1968.

8 U.S., ARVN (Army of the Republic of Vietnam) and Korean strength totals are MACV figures for January 31, 1968. For the text of the "maximum alert" order, see Chapter IV.

9 Details of the conduct of the Vietnamese policemen were gathered by U. S. Embassy security officers during their post-attack investigation.

11 Crampsey, Wendt, Harper, Jacobson, Josephson, Furey, Bunker, Komer, Bel, Braestrup and Zorthian were interviewed by me.

18 The Washington *Post* staff members were Philip Geyelin, Chalmers Roberts, Murrey Marder and Ward Just.

19 I interviewed Thompson, Read, Wendt and others. The Thurmond speech can be found in the Congressional Record for January 30, 1968.

21 "Battle in the Dark" is based in part on interviews with Westmoreland, Weyand, Fuller and a chronology kept by Embassy political officers.

23 The quotation beginning "The VC are inside the compound" was taken from a remarkable tape recording of the MP radio net during the early hours of the attack. The recording was made by Rear Admiral K. L. Veth, Commander of U. S. Naval Forces, Vietnam, and distributed to some of his friends.

 Details of the situation on the Viet Cong side were provided to U.S. officers by the captured sappers Sau and Giang. On the U.S. side, I relied on interviews with Jacobson, Wendt, Harper, Sampson and Weyand.

27 Arnett was interviewed by Hannah Kaiser in Saigon, April 1970.

28 The estimate of fourteen million Americans watching ten million sets was obtained from NBC News and is based on National Nielsen ratings.

31 To pinpoint editors' changes in the UPI copy, I compared the file as it left Saigon with the UPI dispatches distributed to clients in the United States.

31 The Jacobson interview and his written "Observations" dated February 12, 1968, were a prime source.

33 The description is based on Sampson, Lescaze, Carroll, Zorthian interviews. Westmoreland's remarks were reported in the Washington *Post* of January 31, and broadcast January 31 on CBS' special report, *Saigon Under Fire.*

34 Furey, Crampsey and Laurello furnished information about the Embassy drivers. The data on compensation was furnished by the U. S. Embassy, Saigon, to Hannah Kaiser in May 1970.

37 The quotations are from transcripts in the possession of the author. "Bunker's Bunker"—the *Vietnam Courier* account was published in the issue of June 10, 1968, pp. 7–8. The paper is published in English in Hanoi.

39 General Do's reaction was reported by Colonel Tran Van Dac of the Viet Cong, who later defected. He was interviewed by me in Saigon in December 1969.

The epilogue is based on visits to the Embassy and interviews with Harper and Jacobson. The awards to the civilians were presented on December 5, 1968, at the 16th Annual Honor Awards Ceremony at the Department of State, Washington, D.C.

Chapter II   DECISION IN THE NORTH

To report the decisions and military preparations on the other side while a war continues is a formidable task, and the closed nature of the Vietnamese Communist system is an added difficulty. On the other hand, this war has been unique in the amount of open contact with the opposing camp. American citizens have been visiting Hanoi, Vietnamese Communist pamphlets in English are available in bookstores and libraries and reports of third-country journalists as well as Americans have been published in the United States under the Hanoi dateline. The United States Government added greatly to the raw material by translating and compiling the daily record of broadcasts from Hanoi Radio and the NLF's (National Liberation Front's) Liberation Radio, by translating the Hanoi press and making it available through the Department of Commerce Joint Publications Research Service (referred to in these notes as JPRS) and by translating a massive volume of captured Communist documents. The documents cited by me, all of which have been declassified, were translated by the U. S.-Vietnamese Combined Document Exploitation Center (CDEC) near Saigon, and are identified by their CDEC Log numbers. Another source—perhaps the most useful of all in this research—is the memory of several high-ranking Viet Cong officials who were later captured or defected, and whom I interviewed in Saigon.

My thanks to David Elliott of Cornell University, Bernard-Joseph Cabanes of Agence France-Presse, Donald Rochlen of the U. S. Information Agency, William Bundy, Wilfred Burchett, Sven Kramer, Douglas Pike, Frank Sieverts, and to the two former Viet Cong officers, Colonel Tran Van Dac and Ba Tra.

The headnote in Chapter II is taken from a poem written by Ho Chi Minh while he was imprisoned in China in 1942–43, and published in Ho Chi Minh, *Prison Diary* (Hanoi: Foreign Languages Publishing House, 1966). The poem from which this stanza comes is entitled "Learning to Play Chess." The Vietnamese version of chess is close to a national pastime.

PAGE

42   The official announcement of the death of General Nguyen Chi Thanh and accounts of his funeral were broadcast by Hanoi Radio on July 8, 1967. The full text of Le Doc Tho's funeral oration was published in the periodical *Tuyen Huan* (Propaganda and Training), No. 7, Hanoi, July 1967, and was translated in JPRS: 42,595, September 13, 1967, pp. 4–7.

Thanh's injury in South Vietnam and his journey to Hanoi were reported by Hedrick Smith, "U.S. Believes Raid Killed Foe's Chief," New York *Times,* December 3, 1967, p. 3.

44   The quotation from *Hoc Tap* can be found in Patrick J. McGarvey's helpful book, *Visions of Victory* (Stanford: Hoover Institution, 1969), p. 68. Nguyen Chi Thanh's speech to the conference of officials is printed as Speech by Anh Sau (Nguyen Chi Thanh) in "Viet Cong Documents on War Tactics," U. S. Mission Press Release, Saigon, March 30, 1967.

45   The Giap interview, by Oriana Fallaci, was published in the Washington *Post* of April 6, 1969. My statement that the Tet Offensive was ordered in the North in July of 1967 is based on strong circumstantial evidence, plus the document from the Binh Dinh Provincial Committee quoted later in this chapter.

The details of the North Vietnamese diplomatic movements were supplied by American officials in early 1970. The London *Times* and Reuters dispatches were published on July 13, 1967. Cabanes reported the reaction of the official sources in an AFP (Agence France-Presse) dispatch from Hanoi, July 16.

46   For the revolts against Chinese rule see Joseph Buttinger, *The Smaller Dragon* (N.Y.: Praeger, 1958), pp. 177–78. This volume and Buttinger's two-volume *Vietnam: A Dragon Embattled* (N.Y.: Praeger, 1967) list many of the anti-French revolts.

46   The most extensive non-Communist account of the August revolution is in Buttinger's *Vietnam: A Dragon Embattled,* pp. 292–300.

49 Giap's 1951 campaigns are described in Edgar O'Ballance, *The Indo-China War 1945–1954* (London: Faber & Faber, 1964), pp. 120–39; and in Bernard B. Fall, *Street Without Joy* (Harrisburg, Pa.: The Stackpole Company, 1964).

For a discussion of "decisive victory," see Melvin Gurtov, *Hanoi on War and Peace* (Santa Monica: Rand Corporation Memorandum P-3696, December 1967), pp. 15–17. This is all the more interesting for having been published before the Tet Offensive.

50 The dates of the Viet Minh moves on the war front and peace front in late 1953 were taken from pp. 45–46 of Philippe Devillers and Jean Lacouture's *End of a War* (N.Y.: Praeger, 1969), a French account of the final period of the First Indochina War.

50 The oft-quoted and prophetic statement by Pham Van Dong to Bernard Fall can be found in Fall's *Vietnam Witness* (N.Y.: Praeger, 1966).

51 The resolution and a discussion of the 12th Plenum of the Lao Dong Party was published as "Resolution of the Central Office for South Vietnam of March 1966," U. S. Mission Press Release, Saigon, August 18, 1967. The quotation on decisive victory is from p. 17. The quotation on fighting and negotiating is from p. 16.

General Vinh's talk is printed in "Viet Cong Documents on War Tactics," U. S. Mission Press Release, Saigon, March 30, 1967, p. 3.

54 The Binh Dinh document, a resolution of the province committee dated December 20, 1967, was captured on July 31, 1968, by the U. S. 173rd Airborne Brigade. It was translated and published as CDEC Document Log No. 08–1298–68.

The description of the military preparations relies extensively on a day-long interview with Tran Van Dac in Saigon on December 12, 1969. Dac, who defected on April 19, 1968, is a forthright and convincing witness on the events he knows from personal experience during twenty-three years in the Resistance.

58 The Conference of Heroes was reported in detail in *Hoc Tap* (Studies), Hanoi, No. 12, December 1967, pp. 72–75. This was translated in JPRS: 44,391, February 15, 1968, pp. 59–63.

The U. S. ammunition data cited in the footnote were taken from Secretary McNamara's budget statement to Congress of January 1968, p. 107. It was published by the Department of Defense. The PX statistics were published in the Washington *Star*, August 2, 1967.

Chinh Huan and several other principles discussed in this chapter are explained in an unpublished paper by David Elliott, "Vietnamese Communist Perceptions of 'Victory.'"

59   "'The New Situation and Mission': A Viet Cong Training Document," was published as Document No. 20, March 1968, in the Vietnam Documents and Research Notes series of the American Embassy, Saigon. The "split the sky" quotation is from pp. 8–9.

60   The political program of the NLF was broadcast by Hanoi Radio on September 1, 1968, and published by the U. S. Mission, Saigon, in October 1967 in booklet form.

61   I interviewed Ba Tra in Saigon in January 1968. There is no doubt of his authenticity or knowledge. He is a most impressive man.

62   The Buttercup affair was reported to me by officials and former officials of the U. S. Government. What little was known publicly at the time can be found in the New York *Times* of December 2, 1967, the Washington *Post* of December 10, 1967, and the *Wall Street Journal* of December 12, 1967.

65   The Communist version of the death of Le Thi Rieng can be found in the *Vietnam Courier,* the English-language publication from Hanoi, April 1, 1968, p. 8.

65   The Hoang Minh Chinh affair was reported in the Saigon newspaper *Tu Do* in articles beginning December 6, 1968. Similar accounts were given by Captain Vuong Quang Xuan, a defector from the North Vietnamese Army, at a press conference in Saigon, April 17, 1969, and in an interview with Hannah Kaiser in Saigon, March 13, 1970. The decree on counterrevolutionary crimes was broadcast by Hanoi Radio on March 21, 1968.

66   Ho's appearance and speech were reported by Bernard-Joseph Cabanes in an AFP dispatch dated December 25, 1967. Cabanes added further details in an interview in Paris, December 17, 1969.

     The quotation from *Nhan Dan* was reported by Cabanes in an AFP dispatch, December 26, 1967. The *Quan Doi Nhan Dan* quotation can be found in JPRS: 44,809, March 26, 1968, p. 3. The *Ban Tan Viet Hoa* quotation is found in JPRS: 44,670, March 13, 1968, p. 18.

67   The text of Ho's poem is taken from the Hanoi Radio broadcast.
     "A Call for Negotiations"—Cabanes described the scene in an interview in Paris, December 17, 1969. New York *Times* accounts were published December 31, 1968, and January 3, 1968.

69   "Just almost any step" is a quotation from President Johnson's press conference of February 2, 1967.

69   The Romanian's mission was discussed by Averell Harriman in his book *America and Russia in a Changing World* (Garden City, N.Y.: Doubleday, 1971), pp. 124–25.

70   The National Liberation Front announcement was broadcast by

Liberation Radio on November 17, 1967. The 1965 pamphlet from which the Tet quotation is taken is "Command Information Topic Number 5–65, Vietnamese Tet," Headquarters MACV, 7 December 1965.

Giap's 1944 attack on French posts is reported in Buttinger, *Vietnam: A Dragon Embattled*, p. 277. The 1960 Tet attack is reported in Dennis J. Duncanson's book *Government and Revolution in Vietnam* (London: Oxford University Press, 1968), p. 266.

71 My account of the Quang Trung affair was translated from the Vietnamese book *Quang Trung: People's Hero*, by Hoa Bang (Saigon: Educational Institute, 1950).

The Hanoi circular was reported in *Quan Doi Nhan Dan* and is translated in JPRS: 44,523, February 23, 1968, pp. 3–4.

The description of Hanoi at Tet is taken from Cabanes's dispatches of January 24 and 29, 1967; and JPRS: 44,491, February 26, 1968 ("Trade Branch Serves Tet"); and JPRS: 44,974, April 8, 1968 ("Food Supply Increased During the Tet Season").

73 The *Nhan Dan* editorial is translated in JPRS: 44,491, February 26, 1968, p. 30.

74 The final preparations, details and quotations are taken from U. S. Mission Press Release 20–68, "Documents Show Viet Cong Plans for 1967–1968 Winter-Spring Campaign," February 13, 1968.

75 The Liberation Army Order of the Day was published in Douglas Pike's paper, "The 1968 Viet Cong Lunar New Year Offensive in South Vietnam," distributed by the U. S. Mission, Saigon, February 14, 1968. It bears a striking similarity to the Dien Bien Phu Order of the Day which is quoted in Jules Roy, *The Battle of Dienbienphu* (N.Y.: Harper & Row, 1965), pp. 156–57.

Chapter III   AMERICA ON THE EVE

Much of the thinking and documentation in this chapter began with my survey of congressional and public opinion toward the war in late 1967 for the New York *Times Magazine*, published December 17, 1967, under the title "The 'Wobble' on the War on Capitol Hill."

The headnote quotation is from a speech by Major-General Tran Do delivered in August 1966 to a conference of representatives of the North Vietnamese 7th Division operating in South Vietnam. A tape recording was captured by U.S. forces during Operation Cedar Falls in January 1967, and a translation was released by the State Department in May 1967.

PAGE

79 Troop requests and authorizations were a matter of much speculation, essentially because President Johnson took the public position he would meet all of General Westmoreland's "needs." The
key question was the definition of what was needed.

The actual record for Vietnam, from authoritative sources, is
this:

1. In June 1965 Westmoreland requested that forces in Vietnam
be increased from 70,000 men to 210,000 by the end of 1965.
Secretary McNamara recommended approval of the 210,000.
On July 28 Johnson announced a build-up to 125,000 men and
said that "additional forces will be needed later, and they will
be sent as requested."

2. In February 1966 Westmoreland requested the force level be
raised to 459,000 men. The Joint Chiefs of Staff, directed by
McNamara to provide a deployment schedule that would not
require a call-up of reserves, recommended a ceiling of 437,000
men. McNamara approved this on April 11, 1966.

3. In mid-1966 Westmoreland requested the Vietnam ceiling be
raised to 556,000 by the end of calendar year 1967. McNamara
approved 469,000 on November 11, 1966.

4. In March 1967 Westmoreland recommended an increase in the
total troop strength to 565,000 men by June 30, 1968. He set
forth a "minimum essential force" of 80,576 more men and an
"optimum" augmentation of 199,017, figured on a slightly different base. In July Westmoreland and McNamara agreed on
a 525,000-man ceiling, plus additional forces from Asian allies.

81 The draft data are from Selective Service headquarters, Washington. The figures on the probability of being assigned to Vietnam
or killed in Vietnam were taken from an article on the subject
by Philip Meyer in the Charlotte *Observer* of February 13, 1969,
p. 1. Data on causes of death among the general population can
be found in the World Almanac, 1969, p. 759.

81 The economic data were supplied by Assistant Secretary of the
Treasury Murray Weidenbaum, who conducted studies of the
war costs before joining the government.

The Gallup poll on what the war was about was released June
17, 1967. The question was, "Do you feel that you have a clear
idea of what the Vietnam War is all about—that is, what we are
fighting for?" The result: 48 per cent, yes; 48 per cent, no; 4
per cent, no opinion.

The incident in the House Appropriations Committee can be
found in the hearings on the Department of Defense Appropriations for Fiscal Year 1969, Part 1, p. 546–47.

83 The Survey Research Center study was published as "'Silent

Majorities' and the Vietnam War," by Philip E. Converse and Howard Schuman, *Scientific American*, June 1970, pp. 17–26. It is one of the best surveys of opinion toward the war that I have seen.

83 The Gallup returns were reported in the Washington *Post*, October 25, 1967, p. A-14, and in a Gallup release dated October 8, 1967. The Harris survey was reported in the Washington *Post*, August 28, 1967, p. 1. See also the Harris poll of October 2, 1967.

83 *The Christian Science Monitor* survey, by Godfrey Sperling, was published September 26, 1967. The New York *Times* survey was published October 8, 1967.

The Morton interview was with me, and was the lead of my December 17 New York *Times Magazine* article.

86 The newspaper shifts and positions were reported by Min S. Yee in the Boston *Sunday Globe* survey, February 18, 1968, p. A-2.

The Time-Life section is derived from an April 24, 1970, interview with Hedley Donovan, whose help is gratefully acknowledged, from interviews with staff members of the Luce publications and a study of the Vietnam editorials of *Life*. The February 1965 *Life* editorial was published in the issue of February 19. The August editorial was in the issue of August 6, 1965.

92 The bombing statistics are from an article by George Wilson in the Washington *Post*, December 3, 1967. The Andrews quotations are from a floor debate about the war in the House of Representatives, June 13, 1967. See Congressional Record, p. H7084.

93 The Stennis air war hearings were published by the Preparedness Subcommittee. For an inside account of McNamara's preparations, see Chapter 6 of Phil Goulding's book *Confirm or Deny* (N.Y.: Harper & Row, 1969).

98 The November meeting of the Wise Old Men was reported to me by participants in the meeting.

99 The Johnson quotes are reported by Professor Henry F. Graff in his fascinating book *The Tuesday Cabinet* (Englewood Cliffs, N.J.: Prentice-Hall, 1970), pp. 148–50. The LBJ quotation comparing his own "assassination" to Kennedy's was from a talk with White House newsmen on May 5, 1968.

99 The Rostow quotations are from persons who sat in the Psychological Strategy Group. The *Business Week* charts were published in the issue of August 6, 1967. *The Christian Science Monitor* article was published September 14, 1967. The Los Angeles *Times* article was published December 13, 1967.

101 The New England congressman was Representative Louis C. Wyman of New Hampshire. The letter was published in the Congressional Record, p. H12323.

101 The Washington *Star* article was November 7, 1967, p. 1.

103 The story of Westmoreland's selection is told in Ernest B. Furgurson's valuable book *Westmoreland: The Inevitable General* (Boston: Little, Brown & Co., 1968).

105 The Dak To document was read to the newsmen by Westmoreland at his Pentagon briefing on November 22, 1967, and was later released in full by the Department of State.

For the shoring up of support after the Success Offensive, see the Harris survey published in the Washington *Post* on December 4, 1967, p. 1, and the Gallup polls for December 1967 as published in the Gallup Opinion Index, March 1968.

108 My thanks to "Foreign Service," who told me the story in an interview October 16, 1969.

The story of the patrol at Khe Sanh is documented in the useful Marine history *The Battle for Khe Sanh*, Historical Branch, G-3 Division, Headquarters, U. S. Marine Corps, pp. 29–30.

112 Tom O'Connor's thoughts on the death of his son were reprinted in the Congressional Record for January 29, 1968, extension of remarks of Representative L. Mendel Rivers, "The Time Has Come."

The Jesup Veterans of Foreign Wars resolution was printed in the Congressional Record of February 5, 1968, extension of remarks of Representative Williamson S. Stuckey, "Vietnam Resolution."

113 The Kennedy breakfast has been reported in several of the political histories of 1968, including Theodore H. White's *The Making of the President, 1968* (N.Y.: Atheneum, 1969) and Jules Witcover's *85 Days* (N.Y.: Putnam's, 1969). Some of the quotations are from notes kept by one of the reporters present.

Chapter IV   ATTACK!

The two official histories which contain basic information on the Tet attacks are General Westmoreland's *Report on the War in Vietnam* (Washington: U. S. Government Printing Office, 1968) and the Republic of Vietnam Armed Forces volume, *The Viet Cong "Tet" Offensive* (Saigon, 1969), a 490-page history I have referred to in these chapter notes as *ARVN History*. In addition, I have relied on data made available in Saigon in late 1969 by the Military History section of the Military Assistance Command, Vietnam, under Colonel Robert J. Parr, and in Washington by Colonel Reamer W. Argo, Jr., who was the MACV historian during the Tet Offensive. A number of corps-level reports, prepared by military historians or operations officers just after Tet, were also helpful.

Any history of the attack which relied on the official papers alone would be both dull and misleading. Some of the most valuable sources for my account were individuals who played a role in this military drama and who shared their recollections. I gratefully acknowledge the assistance of John Balaban, Major General Philip B. Davidson, Colonel Marvin D. Fuller, Brigadier General Daniel Graham, Colonel John F. P. Hill, Richard Kreigel, Major General Edward G. Lansdale, Dr. Charles B. MacDonald, Robert Matteson, Lieutenant Commander Robert Mueller, Lieutenant General William R. Peers, Robin Pell, Robert Pisor, Edward J. Slack, Charles Sweet, General Cao Van Vien and General Frederick C. Weyand.

PAGE

116   There are several different counts and lists of the Tet attacks. Mine is taken from a memorandum by Brigadier General Hal C. Pattison, Chief of Military History of the U. S. Army, dated March 30, 1970. The 67,000 estimate for the attack force is the one used at the time by the U. S. Command, and is preferable to the 84,000 estimate of *Report on the War*, apparently based on the staff work connected with the Wheeler mission (see Chapter VII). Communist troop strength of 240,000 was constructed from the official MACV estimate of 223,000 to 248,000 for January 1968. The strengths on the U.S. and government side are official MACV figures.

117   Aircraft estimates from *Newsweek*, January 1, 1968, p. 20. Helicopter estimate from *Report on the War*, p. 131. The armored vehicle estimate was from Pentagon sources.

The earliest and most remarkable published report I have seen which foreshadowed the Tet Offensive was Robert Pisor's front-page story in the Detroit *News* of August 15, 1967, only a month after the Communist planning began. Under the headline "Do Reds Plan Quick Attacks, Then Talks?" Pisor reported concern over the possibility of a "massive, countrywide military strike" before the end of 1967. The objective would be temporary victories at Saigon, Da Nang, Hue, Kontum, Pleiku, Bien Hoa airfield, possibly several cities in the Mekong delta, Marine base camps at Dong Ha and Phu Bai and possibly an attack on the U. S. Seventh Fleet. The goal would be "a call for negotiations, broadcast to the world from an undeniable position of strength." The source of Pisor's report, a well-informed or prescient intelligence officer from a free-world country, was transferred out of Vietnam for being "too pessimistic."

122   For the Nha Trang attack details, see *ARVN History*, pp. 359ff.

122   In late March 1968 I interviewed American officials, police and

several of the Viet Cong sappers in Nha Trang and wrote a lengthy report, published April 21, 1968, in the Miami *Herald*, p. 1, and in several other newspapers.

124 Most of the times are from the *ARVN History*, p. 29.

125 For the Lam story, see "Major's 'Dream' Fulfilled," *The MACV Observer* (Saigon), February 21, 1968, p. 1.

126 "Urgent Combat Order Number One," also known as the Gia Lai plan, was translated as CDEC Log No. 01–1999–68.

127 The capture of the Qui Nhon tape is described in *ARVN History*, p. 383. The text was issued as a U. S. Mission Press Release, February 15, 1968.

128 For the Pleiku incidents and other details for II Corps, see Richard Kreigel's "Tet Offensive: Victory or Defeat?" *Marine Corps Gazette*, December 1968, pp. 25–28.

129 The story of the missionaries is told in James C. Hefley, *By Life or By Death* (Grand Rapids: Zondervan Publishing House, 1969), Chapter XII.

130 Three American sources, all with firsthand knowledge, told me the story of the Loc incidents.

131 An account of the Westmoreland negotiations can be found in *Report on the War,* p. 158.

137 The figures on the Saigon circle and other useful data on the Saigon attacks can be found in "Tet Offensive in III Corps," a briefing for the U.S. press in Saigon in March 1968 by Lieutenant Colonel David Hughes of the G-3 section of II Field Force, Vietnam.

137 I was one of the newsmen at the Weyand interview. My account was published on p. 1 of the Miami *Herald,* January 12, 1968.

139 The arrival and departure date in the footnote is from "Tan Son Nhut Airport . . . The Gateway to Saigon," by the USIA's (U. S. Information Agency) Vietnam Feature Service, March 1969.

139 From an interview with Fuller, October 19, 1969.

141 From an interview with Weyand, July 6, 1970, and the briefing, "Tet Offensive in III Corps."

142 The best account of the Independence Palace action is by John Randolph in the Los Angeles *Times* of February 1, 1968. The network news presentations were clocked by me from kinescope recordings. Satellite cost data was obtained from NBC News, June 1970. The cost estimate for the Viet Cong weaponry was by Harold Johnson of the Department of Defense Foreign Service and Technology Center. The weapons list, obtained by American authorities from Viet Cong survivors, was: 8 kilograms of TNT, 7 kilogram charges of TNT, 4 hand grenades per man, 14 AK-47 rifles and 120 rounds per man, 3 B-40 rocket launchers and 30

rounds, 2 pistols and 24 rounds, and 2 gasoline tins of explosives.

143 The MP log is printed in Robert Pisor's excellent article in *Army Magazine*, "Saigon's Fighting MPs," April 1968.

144 The radio station data was obtained from Edward J. Slack and the *ARVN History*, pp. 133–34. Slack was awarded the Department of State Award for Heroism for his action during Tet.

146 Miss Do's account was recorded by her brother-in-law, a U.S. official in Saigon. The facts are real, but I have changed her name.

147 Sources for the Tan Son Nhut-headquarters area battles include the *ARVN History*, the "Tet Offensive in III Corps" briefing and interview with General Cao Van Vien in Saigon, December 7, 1969.

148 The radio transmissions are from the tape of the MP tactical net made that night by Rear Admiral R. L. Veth, Commander of U. S. Naval Forces, Vietnam.

149 From the Vien interview and the other sources cited above.

150 The assassination plans and results were reported by the Security Section of the Saigon-Gia Dinh Viet Cong Region. A copy was translated as CDEC Log No. 03–2497–68.

151 By far the best thing written on the Tet Offensive in the Mekong delta is Harvey Meyerson's valuable book *Vinh Long* (Boston: Houghton-Mifflin, 1970). Pale by comparison but a source of some data is the official "Historical Summary of the VC Tet Offensive IV CTZ," compiled by the U. S. Army Advisory Group, IV Corps, 8 April 1968. I have relied on my own notes of the time and on the personal experiences of officers who were present in the delta at Tet.

152 The Desobry quotes are from the New York *Times* of February 6, 1968.

153 The Manh story is a firsthand account from U.S. sources.

153 The Lippincott story is told in *Vinh Long*, pp. 131–32.

Chapter V   THE SHOCK WAVE

Television played a large role in the reaction to the Tet Offensive and the Vietnam War, and its workings and impact deserve far more study. The Loan execution story, one of the most powerful ever shown by television news, was examined in detail by George A. Bailey, a graduate student and instructor at the University of Wisconsin, who generously made available a copy of his Master's thesis on the subject. Bailey and Dr. Lawrence Lichty, Associate Professor of Communication Arts at the University of Wisconsin, have carried forward the research in a scholarly paper, "The NBC TV Film Story of the General Loan Execution: A Case

Study in Gatekeeping from the Vietnam War." I am grateful to them both for their assistance, as well as to Wallace Westfeld and John Chancellor of NBC News and Eddie Adams of the Associated Press.

On the Washington political background, I am indebted to my colleagues in the press corps, particularly to Charles W. Bailey II, Washington bureau chief of the Minneapolis *Tribune*.

I am also grateful for the assistance of Peter Braestrup, Lieutenant General John Chaisson, Walter Cronkite, Richard Holbrooke, Robert Komer, Jason McManus, Colonel Robert Montague, General Matthew Ridgway, Major General Winant Sidle, General Earle Wheeler, Barry Zorthian and others already mentioned in these notes.

PAGE

158   The Cronkite and McManus reactions are from interviews.

158   For pollsters' reports of the initial hawkishness after Tet, see Louis Harris, "War Support Spurs After Tet Attacks," in the Washington *Post*, February 12, 1968, and the Gallup release of February 14, 1968.

159   The Nielsen ratings for the Tet period were obtained from the networks.

160   The Steinman quote is from a report prepared by the NBC News bureau, Saigon.

"The Flight of a Single Bullet" is based on George Bailey's study and interviews with Eddie Adams and John Chancellor about the Loan story. The activities of President Johnson were recorded in notes kept by White House newsmen at the time.

170   This is the text of Secretary Rusk's blowup at the press in the State Department backgrounder, February 9, 1968:

Q. (John Scali, ABC) Are you saying, Mr. Secretary, you are satisfied there was enough intelligence?

A. No. One is never satisfied. But the point is, I don't see quite why you have to start from dissatisfaction. There gets to be a point when the question is whose side are you on? Now, I'm Secretary of State of the United States, and I'm on our side!

Q. You're not implying—

A. Now during World War II there was never a time when you couldn't find a reason to bitch at your allies or at intelligence or the commander of the adjoining unit or the quartermaster who wasn't giving you your portable toilet seat at the right time. There wasn't a time when you couldn't find something to bitch about.

Q. That isn't what I'm trying to ask—

A. I know. But on my 59th birthday forgive me if I express myself on these matters because none of your papers or your broadcasting apparatuses are worth a damn unless the United States succeeds. They are trivial compared to that question. So I don't know why, to win a Pulitzer Prize, people have to go probing for the things that one can bitch about when there are 2,000 stories on the same day about things that are more constructive in character. . . . This is my speech for the day.

172 The incident of the President, Lynda and the cables, and the "nearly every option" quote are from a presidential talk to White House fellows and college students from "Choice 1968" at the White House, February 12, 1968.

172 The Ridgway quotation is from an interview, April 20, 1970.

174 McCarthy's statement was reported in the New York *Times* of February 4, 1968. Romney's reaction is from the Washington *Post* of February 6, 1968. The first Tet reaction of Richard Nixon is quoted in Theodore H. White's *The Making of the President, 1968*, p. 6. The Nixon pullback was much publicized at the time, and was amplified for me by one of his then advisers. The "glowing reports" quote is from the Washington *Post* of February 6.

176 Robert Kennedy's history on the war is well covered in Chapter 12 of William Vanden Heuvel and Milton Gwirtzman, *On His Own: Robert F. Kennedy 1964–68* (Garden City, N.Y.: Doubleday, 1970), from which the February 1962 quotation is taken. The Kennedy speech in Chicago is printed in the Congressional Record of February 8, 1968.

177 The author was among the correspondents on the incoming flight. I had gone to Laos on the eve of Tet, certain as most other people that nothing would happen in the midst of the holiday itself. Keyes Beech, one of the real pros of the Vietnam press corps, recorded our return to Saigon in a dispatch which was printed on the editorial page of the Washington *Post*, February 6, 1968.

179 The 125,000 Saigonese homeless was the estimate of an American municipal adviser, and was reported by me in the Miami *Herald* of February 7, 1968. The countrywide totals for the Tet Offensive are taken from news release 81–68 of the U. S. Mission in Vietnam, May 3, 1968.

180 Many journalists reported the widespread rumors of U.S. "collusion," including Flora Lewis in the Washington *Post*, February 16, 1968. Of 405 Vietnamese interviewed by the Rand Corporation in the Saigon area shortly after Tet, 137 said they had heard the rumor. Some of the most sophisticated Vietnamese I knew told me they believed the rumor.

182 Operation Shock was reported by American officials involved.
     The press accreditation figures were obtained from the Office of Information, MACV.

184 The Viet Cong orders on respecting the lives and property of the people are taken from the "Guidelines for indoctrination of troops in the liberation of towns and cities," dated January 27, 1968, and captured in the Mekong delta, February 11, 1968, by the U. S. 9th Infantry Division. It was translated as CDEC Log No. 03–1765–68.

187 Details of the Lang Vei attack are taken from an excellent study by Major John A. Cash, "Battle of Lang Vei, 7 February 1968," published in *Seven Firefights in Vietnam*, Office of the Chief of Military History, U. S. Army, Government Printing Office, 1970.

189 The Westmoreland quotations are from notes kept by Chaisson.

192 Sources for the Johnson trip include an extensive account in *U.S. News & World Report*, March 4, 1968; articles in the Washington *Post* and New York *Times* of February 18 and 19, 1968; the Rostow briefing, which was printed in the Congressional Record of February 21, 1968; the National Archives and Records Service's Weekly Compilation of Presidential Documents, Vol. 4, number 8 (February 26, 1968); and the recollections of LBJ staff aides. The story of Ed White and the "Saigon appeared relatively quiet" dispatch was told by the Associated Press in its house organ, the *AP Log*.

Chapter VI   *DEATH IN HUE*

The foundation for this chapter was a visit to Hue of several days' duration in mid-February 1968, during the battle; another visit in late February, just after the battle was over; and a return visit in December 1969 to reconstruct experiences of the Hue people. I was accompanied on the last trip by Paul Vogle, who had been my companion on trips to the city during the 1966 Buddhist crisis. His knowledge of the city and its people and his fluency in its dialect made it possible for me to learn the story of what happened at Tet from the Hue people themselves. I am grateful to him and to all those citizens of the city who allowed us to intrude upon their memories despite the pain and potential risk involved. The names of everyone who is still living in Hue and some street locations have been changed by me, and in some cases circumstances have been slightly altered to make those involved unrecognizable.

The recollections of several Americans were of great value. My thanks to Christopher Jenkins, who made available a copy of the diary of his experiences during Tet; Jeff Fiedler, one of the many Americans who succumbed to the fascination of the city; Bill Biggs, who lost many friends there; Len Ackland, James R. Bullington, Thomas Jefferson, Sergeant Major Harry C. Manion and Mr. and Mrs. H. E. Rigg, the son-in-law and daughter of Dr. and Mrs. Horst Gunther Krainick.

Brigadier General Ngo Quang Truong of the 1st ARVN Division and Captain Pham Van Phuoc, the district chief of Gia Hoi, helped me understand the battle and its aftermath. Son Lam, the captured Viet Cong leader, told me his side of the story in a lengthy interview. Trinh Cong Son, South Vietnam's celebrated composer and writer, generously gave permission to reprint his "Ballad to the Dead," which serves as the headnote, and the poem at the end of the chapter. The translations are by Paul Vogle.

Stephen T. Hosmer's Rand Corporation study, *Viet Cong Repression and Its Implications for the Future,* was helpful in identifying Viet Cong target lists and other documents, and Donald Rochlen was invaluable, as ever, in obtaining and declassifying them. Douglas Pike's monograph, *The Viet Cong Strategy of Terror,* privately published in Saigon in February 1970, contained important data on the Hue killings. Historical Study 2–68, *Operation Hue City,* prepared by Major Miles D. Waldron and Specialist 5 Richard W. Beavers of the 31st Military History Detachment, Headquarters Provisional Corps Vietnam, August 1968, was a valuable source on the military aspects.

PAGE

198 The description of sights and sounds is from Chris Jenkins' diary. Identification of the North Vietnamese units is from *Operation Hue City,* p. 7.

The activities of the armed security unit were described in a tape recording by Hoang Thi Su, one of its members, made for a Viet Cong training school. The tape was captured by U.S. forces in the Ashau Valley.

The description of the reaction at the U.S. advisory compound and the Jesuit compound are from eyewitness accounts.

200 Mr. Tran, Mr. Bui and Mr. Pham (not their real names) were interviewed by me.

201 The 2800 figure is calculated from data in Pike, *The Viet Cong Strategy of Terror,* p. 51.

202 For the ancient history of Hue, see Buttinger, *The Smaller Dragon,* especially pp. 197 and 267.

203 For the modern history of Hue, see Buttinger, *Vietnam: A Dragon Embattled,* especially pp. 605–6 and 1253.

205 Son Lam, also known as Ho Ty, was arrested by government police in September 1969 and interviewed by me at the house of the province chief in Hue in December 1969.

205 "Plans for the Offensive and Uprising of Mui A," the Right Bank

attack plan for Hue, was captured in late 1968 and translated as
CDEC Log No. 09–1371–68.

207 The target list quotation is from a Viet Cong document, "Location
of a Number of Objectives in Hue City," captured in June 1968 by
the U. S. 1st Air Cavalry Division and translated as CDEC Log
No. 06–1909–68. Names have been altered by me. Another detailed target list, containing the shift schedule at the Hue hospital
and other Viet Cong intelligence, was translated as CDEC Log No.
06–2851–68.

209 The flag-raising is described in *ARVN History,* p. 248.

210 I interviewed Colonel Khoa in Hue in late February 1968. Details on the death of Stephen Miller are from interviews with James
Bullington and Bill Biggs.

211 Bullington's story is told in his article "And here, see Hue!" in the
Foreign Service Journal, November 1968.

        The story of Courtney Niles is from an interview with Bill
Biggs.

212 The story of Father Elizalde was told in a letter to friends in
spring 1968 by one of the Jesuits who was in Hue at Tet.

213 Background information on the Krainicks was provided by their
son-in-law and daughter, Mr. and Mrs. H. E. Rigg of Washington,
D.C. Details on their capture by the Viet Cong were provided by
an American who had taken refuge in the attic of their apartment.

214 For an account and photographs of the story of Father Urbain
and Father Guy, see *Communist Carnage in Hue,* 10th Polwar
Battalion, I Corps Tactical Zone, pp. 21 and 28–29.

        The Phu Cam story was told by residents of the area. An
account is published in Pike's *The Viet Cong Strategy of Terror,*
pp. 49–50.

215 The story of Father Buu Dong and a copy of his three letters was
obtained from his nephew, a Hue seminarian, in an interview in
December 1969.

216 For the early U.S. and ARVN military action, see *Operation Hue
City.*

        The misinformation data in the footnote is from news releases
from the commands cited with two exceptions. The Wheeler statements are from the Military Procurement authorization hearings of
the Senate Armed Services Committee, pp. 9 and 74. The Chaisson statements are from a transcript of his briefing at the Five
O'Clock Follies.

219 The two reporters were the author and Anthony Day of the
Philadelphia *Bulletin,* who shared many of my experiences of the
Tet period and made them bearable.

220 Among the reporters the author found at the Citadel was Al

Webb of UPI, whose account of life with the Marines inside the Citadel, originally intended as a note to his Saigon bureau chief, Gene Risher, was one of the great news dispatches of the Vietnam War. The story was distributed by UPI on February 17, 1968. A few days later Webb and David Greenway of *Time*, another Hue battle veteran, were wounded while going to the aid of a dying Marine. Charles Mohr of the New York *Times*, who shared in their mission of mercy, narrowly escaped injury.

220 Right Bank information is from the Son Lam interview. The withdrawal request by the Communist commander in the Citadel was picked up by radio intercept and is reported in *Operation Hue City*, p. 40.

221 The story of the "Vinh" family was written from detailed notes made available to me by a visitor in their home.

225 The organizer's first moves in Gia Hoi were reported in an interview with "Mr. Pham," December 1969. The description of the meeting at the school is from an unpublished manuscript by Len Ackland.

226 "Nguyen Thanh" was interviewed by me in Hue in late February 1968. According to the National Police records of January 1970, Thanh was found guilty of collaborating with the Viet Cong by the Security Council and was still serving time at Con Son Island prison. According to members of his family in Hue, Thanh was released by the government after several months in custody and was drafted into the Army.

227 From an interview with "Mr. Tran," December 1969.

228 In each case, these are based on accounts of eyewitnesses.

230 The meeting in the mountains was described by Son Lam, who was present. The report on "the victory of our armed forces in Hue" was captured by the U. S. 1st Air Cavalry Division on April 25, 1968, and translated as CDEC Log No. 05–1131–68.

231 The Presidential Unit Citation was awarded by President Nixon, June 13, 1969, to the 1st Marines "for extraordinary heroism in action against hostile forces during Operation Hue City." Casualty figures cited are from Headquarters, U. S. Marine Corps. The *Leatherneck* magazine article, entitled "House to House," was published in the issue of May 1968.

232 The story of the Viet Cong prisoners was reported to me by an eyewitness to the incident.

233 The *Christian Century* article, by D. Gareth Porter and Len E. Ackland, was published November 5, 1969. It was cited by Tom Wicker in the New York *Times*, May 12, 1970. The rebuttal was placed in the Congressional Record of May 21, 1970, by Senator Gordon Allott of Colorado.

Chapter VII   AMERICA THE VINCIBLE

Information on the domestic scene came from Benjamin Bradlee, Walter Cronkite, Joseph B. Cumming, Edwin L. Dale, Joseph Evans, Townsend Hoopes, Everett Martin, Frank McGee, Hedrick Smith; and George Gallup, George Gallup, Jr., and John Davies of the American Institute of Public Opinion.

In connection with the Wheeler mission and the Westmoreland troop request, I am grateful to General Earle Wheeler, General William Westmoreland, Major Paul Miles, Colonel Reamer Argo and Paul Ignatius. A valuable firsthand account of the initial Pentagon meeting on the troop request was published by Townsend Hoopes in his book *The Limits of Intervention* (N.Y.: David McKay, 1969).

PAGE

240   The Nielsen ratings were obtained from the networks. Data on the size of the Saigon television news bureaus was published in "The 21-inch View of Vietnam," by Leonard Zeidenberg, *Television Magazine*, January 1968. *Broadcasting Magazine* reported on network use of the Pacific satellite in its February 12, 1968, issue. The intensity of Khe Sanh coverage was estimated by Peter Braestrup.

241   For poll data in late February and March, see the Gallup release of March 9, 1968, "New Wave of Pessimism on Vietnam Conflict Found Throughout Nation," and the Gallup release of May 1, 1968, "Sharp Increase Found in Number of 'Doves.'"

242   The quotation from Tran Ngoc Chau is from his book *Forty-five Days in the Capitals of USA, France, England and Italy*, published in Vietnamese in Saigon, 1968. The translation is by Mrs. Ngo Dinh Tu.

        Joseph Cumming's notes were in a report to *Newsweek*, and are reprinted with his permission.

244   Galbraith's remarks were in the Washington *Star* of February 15, 1968. Bunker's reaction was reported by Geoffrey Drummond in an interview with Jan Wentworth.

244   Joseph Evans was interviewed by me, June 1970.

245   The Salina *Journal* editorial can be found in the appendix of the Congressional Record of February 20, 1970, in the extension of remarks of Robert Dole.

246   The Gallup data cited are from the release of March 10, 1968. "The Passage of Walter Cronkite" is based in part on an interview with Cronkite in New York, March 6, 1970.

        For the role which the Cronkite interview played in the fall of Diem, see Roger Hilsman, *To Move A Nation* (Garden City, N.Y.: Doubleday, 1967), pp. 497–98.

The Kraft poll results and Bailey's comments are from Bailey's speech to the Western States Democratic Conference as reprinted in the Congressional Record of August 31, 1967.

The Christian quote is from p. 123 of *To Kill a Messenger* (N.Y.: Hastings House, 1970), a useful book by William Small, the CBS News bureau chief in Washington.

248 The 1965 quotation is from Cronkite's introduction to *Vietnam Perspective* (N.Y.: Pocket Books, 1965).

251 The atmosphere in the Communist camp was reported by a former staff member of COSVN (Central Office for South Vietnam), interviewed by me in Saigon, December 5, 1969. Ho's seven "musts" are quoted from Document No. 38, Vietnam Documents and Research Notes, July 1968, "The Sixth Resolution, Central Office of South Vietnam," p. 8.

252 Colonel Dac's actions were reported in an interview with me in Saigon.

253 The February 1 COSVN circular based on the January 31 assessment was captured by the U. S. 9th Infantry Division near Saigon on February 23, 1968, and issued as Press Release 56–68 on March 29, 1968, by the U. S. Mission in Vietnam, "Viet Cong Headquarters Assess Tet Offensive."

255 The February 6 resolution from Can Tho was captured February 28, 1968, and was translated as CDEC Log No. 03–1956–68.

The "erroneous conception" quote is from COSVN Resolution 9 of July 1969, issued in translation by the U. S. Mission in December 1969, p. 9.

256 The first directive is the February 1 COSVN circular, quoted from U. S. Mission Press Release 57–68.

The February 21 COSVN order was captured by the U. S. 1st Infantry Division and issued as U. S. Mission Press Release 120–68 on June 26, 1968, "COSVN Report Outlines Viet Cong 'Second Offensive' Tactics."

260 The quotation from the Senate Armed Services Committee member was taken from Jim G. Lucas' article "Manpower Worries Congress," February 21, 1968, in the Washington *News.*

264 The *U.S. News & World Report* article, "A Showdown in Vietnam?" was the lead story in the issue dated February 19, 1968. The quotation is from p. 36.

265 For a description of the Wheeler message and the Pentagon meeting, see Hoopes, *The Limits of Intervention*, pp. 159–65.

266 The Johnson quotation is from his CBS News special, *LBJ: The Decision to Stop the Bombing*, February 6, 1970.

272 Frank McGee was interviewed in New York, June 11, 1970. The commercial listing and quotations are from a transcript of the *Frank McGee Sunday Report* of March 10, 1968.

273 The *Newsweek* quotations are from the issue dated March 18, 1968, published on March 11, 1968.

276 The January LBJ poll and Governor King's March estimate of McCarthy's strength are from Theodore H. White's *The Making of the President, 1968,* pp. 8 and 84.

For the appeal of the LBJ forces in New Hampshire, see the New York *Times* of March 7, 1968, "McCarthy Accuses President's Backers of Applying 'McCarthyist' Tactics Against Him." The text of the McCarthy ad was taken from Jack Newfield, *Robert Kennedy: A Memoir* (N.Y.: Dutton, 1969), p. 215. The final vote totals are from the *Congressional Quarterly* of March 22, 1968.

276 The University of Michigan study, "Continuity and Change in American Politics: Parties and Issues in the 1968 Election," by Philip E. Converse, Warren E. Miller, Jerold G. Rusk and Arthur G. Wolf, was prepared for delivery at the American Political Science Association Annual Meeting, New York, 1969.

Chapter VIII   TURNAROUND

What happened in the United States Government in March of 1968 is a subject of controversy three years later, and it seems likely that some aspects will be controversial for years to come. My account of what took place is based on extensive interviews with all those who were available to me, plus a study of previously published materials. I regret that former President Johnson declined to see me on this project, though I did have the benefit of his television interview with Walter Cronkite and an informal presentation of his views on a later occasion. I wish to acknowledge the contribution of Dean Acheson, George Ball, McGeorge Bundy, William Bundy, George Carver, Clark Clifford, Douglas Dillon, Arthur Goldberg, Phil Goulding, Philip Habib, Robert Komer, Henry Cabot Lodge, Harry McPherson, George Reedy, General Matthew Ridgway, James Rowe, Dean Rusk, Terry Sanford, General Maxwell Taylor, Cyrus Vance, Paul Warnke, General William Westmoreland, General Earle Wheeler and Richard Whelan. The chapter is my formulation, not theirs—but it could not have been written without them.

Because of the ground rules of interviews and the continuing sensitivity of the subject, it is not possible to give detailed attribution for most of what is in this chapter.

The headnote quotation from President Johnson on February 27, 1968, was from his address to the National Rural Electric Cooperative Association Convention in Dallas, Texas. The March 31 quotation was from his televised address to the nation.

PAGE

292 Max Lerner's column, which resulted from his March 5 visit to the White House, was published in the New York *Post* of March 18, 1968.

302 The account of the North Vietnamese overtures to Walter Cronkite and the trip of Charles Collingwood is based on interviews with them. The facts of the Ashmore-Baggs mission is based on their book *Mission to Hanoi* (N.Y.: Berkley Medallion Books, 1968).

325 The section on Marjorie Nelson and Sandra Johnson is based on an interview with Dr. Nelson, who has since become Mrs. Robert Perisho. The statement of the People's Revolutionary Committee of Hue was printed in *The Vietnam Courier,* the English-language newspaper from Hanoi, April 8, 1968.

326 The scene at the rear service base of "R" was reported by a former COSVN staff member who was there.

326 General Order No. 54, awarding Vietnam Campaign Participation Credit to those who took part in the "Tet Counteroffensive Campaign," was issued by the Department of the Army on August 8, 1969. The order was signed by the Army Chief of Staff, General William C. Westmoreland.

AFTERWORD

The Order of the Day during the Battle of the Bulge was quoted in General Eisenhower's book *Crusade in Europe* (Garden City, N.Y.: Doubleday, 1952), pp. 354–55.

The Westmoreland Order of the Day was issued by the U. S. Command on February 6, 1968.

The final quotation, "Your country belongs to the western seas," is from Buttinger, *Vietnam: A Dragon Embattled,* p. 495, citing Pierre Dabezies, *Forces politiques au Viet-Nam.*

INDEX

Smith, Sen. Margaret Chase, 162
Son Lam, 205–9, 220–21
Sorensen, Theodore, 293
Soto, Sgt. Rudy A., Jr., 12, 24, 26
South Vietnamese people, reaction to Tet Offensive. *See* Tet Offensive of 1968, South Vietnamese people, reaction to
Spock, Dr. Benjamin, 111
Steinman, Ron, 160
Stennis, Sen. John, 93, 289–90
Stone, Maj. Gen. Charles P., 126
Symington, Sen. Stuart, 97

Tan Son Nhut Air Base, attack on, 147–48
Taylor, Gen. Maxwell, 284–86, 309, 315
Television, impact of, 28, 36–37, 98, 142–43, 159–60, 163, 169–71, 239–43, 246–51, 272–73
Tet. *See* Lunar New Year
Tet Offensive of 1968, North Vietnamese and Viet Cong military preparations for, 6–7, 55–60, 74, 106–7, 109–10, 116, 205–9; North Vietnamese and Viet Cong political preparations for, 61–65, 67–69; North Vietnamese and Viet Cong reaction to, 39, 251–56, 302, 323, 326; South Vietnamese people, reaction to, 146, 154, 179–80, 187, 292, 323, 325; U.S. domestic political reaction to, 20, 173–77, 275, 293, 299, 318; U. S. Government reaction to, 18–20, 29, 158–59, 161–62, 167, 171, 182, 186, 243, 257, 281; U.S. press reporting of, 16–17, 26–30, 33, 35, 158, 163, 166, 183–85, 192–93, 220, 245, 266–71, 273–74, 294, 298, 331–32; U.S. public reaction to, 20, 158–59, 238, 242, 246–47, 257,

276, 280, 287, 301, 308, 315, 334–35; warnings and alerts prior to, 9, 10, 109–10, 117–21, 126, 131–34, 137–38, 152, 169, 209, 331
Tet truce. *See* Lunar New Year
Thang, Gen. Nguyen Duc. *See* Nguyen Duc Thang, Gen.
Thanh, Gen. Nguyen Chi. *See* Nguyen Chi Thanh, Gen.
Thieu, Nguyen Van. *See* Nguyen Van Thieu, President
Tho, Lt. Col. Pham Minh. *See* Pham Minh Tho, Lt. Col.
Thomas, Sgt. Jonnie B., 8
Thompson, John B., 19
Thompson, Maj. Robert, 220
Thompson, Ruth and Ed, 130
Thurmond, Sen. Strom, 21, 96
Time, 87–92, 158
Times of London, 45–46
Tra, Lt. Gen. Tran Van. *See* Tran Van Tra, Lt. Gen.
Tran Do, Maj. Gen., 39, 77
Tran Ngoc Chau, 242
Tran Van Dac, Col., 55–58, 59–60, 252–53
Tran Van Tra, Lt. Gen., 56, 59
Trinh, Nguyen Duy. *See* Nguyen Duy Trinh
Trinh Cong Son, 197, 235
Troops, requests for, 79–81, 190–91, 259–60, 261–66, 285–92, 307; strength, 116, 262
Truman, Harry S., 275, 283–84
Truong Chinh, 47–49
Truong, Brig. Gen. Ngo Quang. *See* Ngo Quang Truong, Brig. Gen.
Tuckman, Robert, 16
Tuckner, Howard, 167–68
Tuong, Col. Le Trung. *See* Le Trung Tuong, Col.

PHOTO CREDITS

THE AUTHOR

DON OBERDORFER, a native of Atlanta and a graduate of the School of Public and International Affairs at Princeton University, is a veteran Washington journalist. He has reported many of the critical engagements of the Vietnam War both on the home front and on the battle front. His third extended visit to Indochina, in early 1968, coincided with the Tet Offensive. A former contributing editor of *The Saturday Evening Post* and Washington correspondent of the Knight newspapers, he is now a reporter and columnist for the Washington *Post*. Mr. Oberdorfer lives in Washington with his wife and two children.

Other Da Capo titles of interest

Available at your bookstore